INTERNATIONAL HUMAN RESOURCE MANAGEMENT

INTERNATIONAL HUMAN RESOURCE MANAGEMENT

AN INTEGRATED APPROACH

edited by

Anne-Wil Harzing and Joris Van Ruysseveldt

OU *in association with the*
Open University of the Netherlands

SAGE Publications
London • Thousand Oaks • New Delhi

© Open Universiteit, Heerlen, 1995

First published 1995

SAGE Publications Ltd
6 Bonhill Street
London EC2A 4PU

SAGE Publications Inc
2455 Teller Road
Thousand Oaks, California 91320

SAGE Publications India Pvt Ltd
32, M-Block Market
Greater Kailash – I
New Delhi 110 048

British Library Cataloguing in Publication data

A catalogue record for this book is available from the British Library.

ISBN 0 8039 7950 9
ISBN 0 8039 7951 7 pbk

Library of Congress catalog card number 94–69057

Typeset by Photoprint, Torquay, S. Devon
Printed in Great Britain by The Cromwell Press Ltd,
Broughton Gifford, Melksham, Wiltshire

Contents

Foreword   *Arndt Sorge*   vii

Introduction   ix

Acknowledgements   xii

Notes on the contributors   xiii

PART 1   INTERNATIONALIZATION: CONTEXT,
STRATEGY, STRUCTURE AND PROCESS
  1   Internationalization and the international division of labour
     Anne-Wil Harzing   1
  2   Strategic planning in multinational corporations
     Anne-Wil Harzing   25

  3   Organizational structure of multinational corporations:
     theories and models
     Jaap Paauwe and Philip Dewe   51

  4   Human resource management in multinational corporations:
     theories and models
     Jaap Paauwe and Philip Dewe   75

PART 2   PERSONNEL AND ORGANIZATION FROM A
COMPARATIVE PERSPECTIVE
  5   Cross-national differences in personnel and organization
     Arndt Sorge   99

  6   The 'culture' factor in personnel and organization policies
     René Olie   124

  7   Compensation and appraisal in an international perspective
     Ed Logger, Rob Vinke and Frits Kluytmans   144

  8   Human resource development and staff flow policy in
     Europe
     Marcel van der Klink and Martin Mulder   156

PART 3   MANAGING AN INTERNATIONAL STAFF
  9   Composing an international staff
     Malcolm Borg and Anne-Wil Harzing   179

  10   Training and development of international staff
     Kerstin Baumgarten   205

  11   Women's role in (international) management
     Hilary Harris   229

12 Compensation and appraisal of international staff
Ed Logger and Rob Vinke 252

PART 4 INTERNATIONAL BUSINESS, INDUSTRIAL
RELATIONS AND INDUSTRIAL DEMOCRACY
13 International human resource management and industrial
relations: a framework for analysis
Willem de Nijs 271

14 National variations in worker participation
Hans Slomp 291

15 Multinational corporations and industrial relations: policy
and practice
Ulke Veersma 318

16 European social policy and European industrial relations
Ad Nagelkerke 337

References 363

Index 378

Foreword

Arndt Sorge

There are many textbooks on international management and organization, international human resources, international industrial relations and the international enterprise; but events and developments in these various fields cannot be seen as separated from each other. The merit of this book is that it offers an integrated treatment of many organizational, management, human resource and industrial relations matters affected by internationalization, and by the challenge of international comparisons, although in many of the contributions the focus narrows to internationalization and international comparisons within Europe. The editors and contributors think that such a regional focus allows the larger integrated theme to be addressed at the required level of detail and specificity. Internationalization may happen in different ways, depending on which region of the world you are looking at. Internationalization and comparisons in Europe – and for our present purposes this is still very much focused on Western Europe – represents a challenge of its own.

The present book is based on an integrated concept. In other words, the editors have tried to produce a book on the basis of a coherent idea about what the final product should be. This is different from a mere assembly of autonomous papers. Sub-themes were planned, and appropriate authors selected. This central control is good to have, particularly when the field to be covered is a large one.

Many of the contributors are Dutch, which goes against the trend favouring authors from the Anglo-Saxon countries. The great advantage of Dutch scholars, however, is that they are frequently better informed about approaches from different disciplines and more culturally versatile in their outlook. To that extent, the 'Dutchness' of this volume does not mean that its outlook is less international. On the contrary, it is more tolerant of different approaches to the phenomena covered. Four years of teaching at a Dutch university taught me that the Dutch, in addition to their pervasive sobriety and solidity, have an eminent strength in synethizing contributions from different cultural backgrounds. This strength has been turned into an asset of the present book.

It is unusual for a contributor to a book to write the foreword as well. In this case, I am particularly pleased to do so, however, because of the great pleasure that this venture has given me. Through my contacts with the Dutch Open University, I have become convinced that they produce textbooks and courses which are usually better than much of what is available in more widely understood languages. After helping to compile a splendid course on international industrial relations in Dutch, I became extremely frustrated that the best book on that subject was written in a language which reaches 30 million people in the world at most. I therefore put pressure on my colleagues to produce the next book in English and enter the top world league. Here it is.

Introduction

The process of internationalization consists of much more than simply seeing a production process in one country and reproducing it in another. Multinational corporations (MNCs) can be seen as global networks which straddle not only national borders but sectoral divisions too. Production processes are often subdivided into smaller components, each located wherever the necessary production conditions are most favourable. The integration of such geographically distributed components requires a sound organizational structure which allows company management to respond flexibly to complex situations and unexpected developments. At the same time, such organizational structures should also further the specific strategic objectives of the relevant MNC.

Given the current economic climate, many companies see transfrontier operations as a logical, even unavoidable step in developing their own competitive potential. Managing the complexity associated with such a move should not, however, be at the expense of the organization's flexibility and manoeuvrability. Cross-border operations require not only a sound strategy, but also the people and the organization that can implement it. The purpose of this book is to help readers understand the consequences of the internationalization process in trade and industry for company organizational and personnel policy (or human resource management). Our intention is two-fold: to point out various personnel problems and show how a more systematic analysis of such problems can lead to better and more practical insights into strategic and organizational development; and to inspire readers to formulate their own strategic solutions.

As stated above, internationalization increases the complexity of a company. International companies must learn to deal with unstructured, often paradoxical circumstances and events. The present book does not try to avoid such paradoxes, nor does it attempt to reduce the complexity of real life to simpler, more manageable elements. In many cases there are no indisputable best solutions for personnel problems. This book is by no means a volume of recipes listing the most appropriate ingredients and techniques for solving personnel problems within MNCs.

A recurring paradox in this respect is that the gradual increase in cross-border business activities has led to a growing interest in cultural and institutional specificities and idiosyncrasies. The closer we get to creating cross-border policy, the more sharply drawn are the features of personnel policy in national subsidiaries. That is particularly the case when national practices and customs are deeply entrenched and obstinately resist any interference from the MNC's headquarters. In this book, *both* the international *and* the national perspectives will play a role in the analysis.

A guide to this book

The present book consists of four clearly delineated parts. Each part can be studied as an independent unit, so that readers may choose to study the parts most interesting to them, if-they so desire. Taken together, however, the four parts present a consistent picture of the way in which international HRM can be approached as a discipline.

In Part 1 we place international HRM in a wider context. These chapters have a relatively theoretical and normative character. Our discussion focuses on the principles and problems of internationalization and the consequences of this process for the personnel and organizational policies of internationally operating companies. In this and subsequent parts we concentrate on the 'Triad' – the United States, Japan and Europe – which together account for more than three-quarters of the world's international activities. Chapter 1 describes the international context. We touch on recent developments in the field of internationalization and offer various theoretical models which attempt to explain the existence of international trade and multinational corporations. We also look at the social consequences of the increasing internationalization of the global economy. Chapter 2 describes the strategic decision-making process within multinationals. We establish a link between the international context described previously, general company strategies and strategies related to personnel and organization. The final two chapters of this part present a detailed discussion of various theories and models of organizational structure and HRM policy in multinational corporations.

Part 2 focuses on describing and explaining differences between countries in the area of personnel and organizational policy. The first two chapters introduce two important theoretical models which attempt to explain national differences in human resource management: the societal effect approach and culturalism. The rest of this part describes differences related to specific HRM aspects, such as staff-flow policy, training and development, and compensation and appraisal. It is naturally highly important for multinational corporations to understand the differences described in this part of the book. After all, they will be confronted with such differences whenever they establish and operate subsidiaries in other countries/cultures. The emphasis here, however, will be on acquiring a certain outlook when dealing with cross-national differences. Any factual description of such differences would soon be out of date and would, moreover, take up more space than we have available to us here. Chapters 7 and 8 should therefore be viewed as the thematic application of a way of thinking, rather than as an exhaustive description.

In Part 3 we return once again to the perspective of the internationally operating company, specifically to the problems which a personnel administrator might encounter in such an organization. This part has a relatively practical, hands-on character, covering such topics as how to assemble an international staff (Chapter 9), how to prepare expatriates for their assignment abroad (Chapter 10) and how to assess and reward international managers (Chapter 12). Chapter 11 is devoted to the role of women in management, in particular within international organizations. In this part we concentrate primarily on expatriate management, i.e. the problems that arise when staff from the *parent* company are posted abroad. Such staff are known as parent-country nationals (PCNs). Focusing on them by no means implies that the selection, training, development and compensation of third-country nationals (TCNs) and host-country nationals (HCNs) is of lesser importance. What we demonstrate in several chapters of this book, however, is that both companies and researchers tend to be relatively ethnocentric in outlook. The majority of international managers are PCNs and most of the research conducted in this field concentrates on expatriate management. In addition, this research is highly segmented. Like most national studies on personnel management, the topic of selection is the province of psychologists, training is explored by educationalists and also compensation has its own specialists. The lack of horizontal and vertical integration (the first being integration between the various personnel instruments, the second meaning integration between personnel and company strategy) is also a prominent feature in international HRM, both in actual practice and in research.

The fourth and final part of this book focuses specifically on the issue of industrial democracy and industrial relations in an international context. Both exercise an important influence on the way in which companies design their personnel policy. For example, in designing the employment relationship, it is not only the employer and employee who are involved, but also numerous other interest organizations, such as employee participation bodies and trade unions. On the other hand, companies, whether national, international or multinational, actively intervene in both industrial democracy and industrial relations. The fact that multinational corporations operate in various different countries means that both the MNC and the interest organizations face specific problems, not the least of which are the sharp differences between countries in this area. A good example is social dumping, the transfer of the production process or parts thereof to countries with more 'favourable' terms of employment, working conditions and labour relations. Part 4 begins with a chapter in which we discuss the relationship between personnel policy and industrial relations in detail and analyse it from an international perspective. Chapter 14 subsequently describes institutional diversity in the area of industrial democracy, while in Chapter 15 we look at the strategies used by MNCs in the field of industrial relations and discuss the phenomenon of social dumping. The fourth and final chapter of this part, Chapter 16, sketches the difficult path toward a European system of industrial relations and the possible future socio-economic and political development of the European Union.

Acknowledgements

A book such as the present one, which covers so many different perspectives, could only be the product of teamwork. We would like to begin by thanking the various authors for their persistence and patience in the face of our repeated requests to revise their texts. We particularly want to mention Arndt Sorge and Frits Kluytmans, who offered useful comments on the various chapter drafts and assisted us in both a pleasant and instructive fashion in editing the texts. We would also like to thank those students who gave the first draft of the manuscript a trial reading for their critical and useful comments.

We would further like to express our thanks and admiration to Cecilia Willems, who translated the chapters written in Dutch and tried to introduce some consistency in the German, Dutch, Swedish and New Zealand notions of the English language. Brigitte De Craene provided educational support in compiling the textbook. Annette Bouwels, Angelique Verhoeff, John Schobre, Jet Quadekker and Albert Kampermann contributed to preparation, layout and word processing of the script, and provided logistical support.

We have been most impressed by the punctuality, alertness and conscientiousness with which our script was turned into a book by Sage. This, in addition to the friendliness and helpfulness of our contacts made the cooperation with Sage a very pleasant one. We would especially like to thank Stephen Barr, Nicola Harris and the freelance copyeditor, Elaine Leek.

Although we both take full responsibility for the finished product, Parts 1 and 3 of the book were coordinated by Anne-Wil Harzing and Parts 2 and 4 by Joris Van Ruysseveldt.

Anne-Wil Harzing
Joris Van Ruysseveldt

Notes on the contributors

Kerstin Baumgarten was born in Germany and grew up in Brazil and Canada. She studied business administration in England and applied educational science in the Netherlands, where she has lived for the past eight years. She presently owns a consultancy business (Baumgarten & Scholten), specializing in training and education in profit and non-profit organizations. In her work she advises and supports organizations on a wide range of educational issues, for example by analysing training needs, designing training material, evaluating training activities, and planning and determining macro-level corporate training policy.

Malcolm Borg entered the field of international management with his MBA thesis 'Repatriation of Executives', which was presented at the 1982 EIBA conference at INSEAD. After two years working in the food retail trade in France, he started to write his dissertation: 'International Transfer of Managers in Multinational Corporations', published in 1988. He was assistant professor at Uppsala University and a senior management consultant at PA Consulting Group. He now runs his own business in Stockholm (Borg Consulting Network) and develops projects for various corporations in the field of international business.

Philip Dewe serves as professor and head of the Department of Human Resource Management at Massey University, Palmerston North, New Zealand. He was educated at Victoria University in Wellington and at the London School of Economics. His principal fields of research have been industrial relations, and stress and coping. He was a senior research officer with the Work Research Unit based in the Department of Employment in London. He has published widely in a number of international journals and is on the Editorial Board of the journals *Work and Stress* and *International Journal of Selection and Assessment*.

Hilary Harris is a lecturer in human resource management at the University of Buckingham, responsible for human resource management and organizational behaviour courses for an international student body. Her main research interest is in the area of women's careers in the international environment, which forms the topic of the dissertation she is preparing. She has a professional background in human resource management with a variety of companies, followed by consultancy experience in the field of computerized HR information systems with specialist expertise in equal opportunity monitoring.

Anne-Wil Harzing is assistant professor at both the Department of Human Resource Science at Tilburg University and at the Open University of the

Netherlands. She studied economics, business administration and international management at the University of Limburg in Maastricht. She has published on international human resource management, expatriate management and the labour market position of migrant women in Europe. She is currently preparing her dissertation, which focuses on international transfers as a coordination strategy in multinational companies.

Marcel van der Klink is a member of the Faculty of Educational Science and Technology of the University of Twente in the Netherlands. He studied adult education and organizational development at the University of Nijmegen, specializing in work-specific learning. He has published articles on on-site learning and on the renewal of vocational training in agriculture. He is presently studying the effectiveness of training in the workplace.

Frits Kluytmans studied sociology at Tilburg University and is presently associate professor at the Open University of the Netherlands. He is responsible for developing course material for distance education in the field of personnel and organization. Among his publications are *Human Resource Management: verzakelijking of vernieuwing* (1989), *Leerboek Personeelsmanagement* (1990) and *Management van human resources: stromen, stimuleren, structureren* (1992).

Ed Logger was employed by DAF Trucks in 1980, after completing his studies in business administration at the Technical University of Eindhoven in the Netherlands. In 1986 he joined Hay Management Consultants as a senior consultant, focusing on compensation practices and policy, the evaluation of employment terms and the impact of policy changes on costs. He publishes regularly on the topic of compensation, for example on executive compensation, total remuneration, primary and secondary terms of employment and international compensation.

Martin Mulder is currently with the Faculty of Educational Science and Technology of the University of Twente in the Netherlands. He studied educational science at the University of Utrecht. His dissertation focused on the evaluation of the curriculum conference as a tool for curriculum content determination and justification in vocational education. His main publications include *Basic Skills for Vocational Education*, *Strategic Human Resource Development*, and *Studies in Vocational and Industrial Training*. His present research interests include the effectiveness of human resource development programmes and computer-assisted curriculum development.

Ad Nagelkerke works in the Industrial Relations Unit of the Faculty of Economics at Tilburg University in the Netherlands. His main topics of research have been the development of industrial relations systems, the labour market in theory and practice and institutional economics. He is the co-author of four textbooks on industrial relations. His dissertation was entitled 'Institutions and economic action: an inquiry into the scientific nature of institutional economics'. He is presently involved in research projects focusing on the development of European industrial relations and institutional economics.

Willem de Nijs is associate professor of human resource management and industrial relations at the University of Nijmegen in the Netherlands. He studied sociology at Tilburg University. His dissertation (1987) focused on 'Alain Touraine: the sociological conscience of the programmed society'. Other important publications are *Regels rond Arbeid* (with A. Nagelkerke) (1991), *Macht in banen: arbeidsverhoudingen in theorie en beleid* (with W. van Voorden and A. Nagelkerke) (1993) and *Integraal Management* (with J. Doorewaard, eds.) (1992). His main research interests are the organizational and human resource aspects of team-based work.

René Olie studied social psychology at the Free University in Amsterdam. He currently serves as assistant professor for the Faculty of Economics and Business Administration at the University of Limburg in Maastricht. His research interests are mergers, cross-border cooperation and comparative management. His publications include articles in *Organization Studies* and the *European Management Journal*, and chapters in books on European business systems as well as textbooks on organizations. His dissertation on integration difficulties in international mergers, particularly Dutch–German mergers, was published in 1994.

Jaap Paauwe studied business economics at the Erasmus University, Rotterdam. From 1980 to 1983 he worked for SHV/GTI-holdings in the field of personnel management, training and development, and in 1983 joined the Dutch Federation of Christian Trade Unions (CNV) as head of the Research Department. He has been a member of the Faculty of Economics at Erasmus University since 1988, and was appointed Professor of the Department of Business and Organization in 1992. His main research interests are (international) human resource management, strategic management, industrial relations and organizational change.

Hans Slomp is associate professor at the University of Nijmegen. He acquired his doctorate in 1977 with a study on economic policy in communist countries. Since then he has published widely on European labour relations, including *Arbeidsverhoudingen in België* (with Tjeu van Mierlo) (1984), *Labour Relations in Europe: a History of Issues and Development* (1990) and articles on Dutch and Belgian labour relations.

Arndt Sorge specializes in the organization and management of industrial enterprises, vocational education and training, and personnel policy and industrial relations. He studied economics and sociology at the universities of Freiburg and Cologne, Germany. Since 1972 he has held academic posts in Germany, England, France and the Netherlands. His books include *Informationstechnik und Arbeit im sozialen Prozess* (1985) and *Comparative Factory Organization* (with Malcolm Warner) (1986). Since the end of 1992 he has served as Professor of Industrial and Organization Sociology at Humboldt University, Berlin.

Joris Van Ruysseveldt is assistant professor at the Open University of the Netherlands. He studied labour and organizational sociology at the Catholic University of Louvain in Belgium and is preparing his dissertation on recent developments in industrial relations and personnel policy in Belgium. He has served as editor for *Kwaliteit van de arbeid* (1989) and *Oosteuropese arbeidsverhoudingen* (1993). He is presently preparing two books on industrial relations in Europe.

Ulke Veersma is assistant professor at Tilburg University. He studied labour and organizational sociology at the University of Amsterdam and graduated from the Technical University of Eindhoven in 1992 in the field of technology and labour. His publications include articles on working conditions and the Labour Inspectorate. His present interests are European industrial relations, in particular the development of European industrial democracy in multinationals.

Rob Vinke is a senior consultant and a Research for Management practice leader at Hay Management Consultants in Utrecht. After completing his technical training, he spent over ten years working in the field of electrical engineering at the Dutch steel giant Hoogovens. He studied labour and organizational psychology at the University of Amsterdam and worked for five years as a researcher, lecturer and study coordinator within the same faculty. He is preparing his dissertation, which explores the tension between intrinsic and extrinsic motivation and the role of compensation.

PART 1
INTERNATIONALIZATION: CONTEXT, STRATEGY, STRUCTURE AND PROCESS

1 Internationalization and the international division of labour

Anne-Wil Harzing

1	Introduction	2
2	Statistics on internationalization trends	2
	International trade	2
	Foreign direct investment	2
3	Determinants of international trade	4
	Absolute and relative comparative cost advantages	4
	The Heckscher–Ohlin theorem	5
	Economies of scale	6
4	The reason for multinational enterprises	7
	Product life cycle	8
	Dunning's eclectic theory	9
5	The comparative and competitive advantage of nations	11
	Criteria for a theory of national comparative and competitive advantage	11
	The four determinants of national comparative and competitive advantage	12
	Factor conditions	12
	Demand conditions	13
	Related and supporting industries	14
	Firm strategy, structure and rivalry	14
	Japan as an example of Porter's analysis	14
6	Trends in the international division of labour	16
	Reich's new world order	17
	Professional categories in the new world order	18
	Scenarios for the future	20
	Consequences for the Western world	21
7	The competitive advantage of multinational companies	22
	Differences in input and output markets	22
	Economies of scale	23
	Economies of scope	23
8	Summary and conclusions	24

1   Introduction

This chapter aims to answer a number of questions concerning internationalization. Section 2 offers some statistical data which demonstrate the importance not only of international trade but also of foreign direct investment (FDI), while Sections 3 and 4 discuss a number of theories to explain these phenomena. Section 5 explores why one country produces a certain product while another country produces a different one, using Porter's analysis to explain the competitive advantage of nations. In Section 6 we will go on to the global level and look at the (new) international division of labour and the economic and social consequences thereof. Finally, we will discuss the sources of competitive advantage for multinationals.

2   Statistics on internationalization trends

International trade

Figure 1.1 shows that international trade has become more important in the past 40 years. While the world's Gross National Product in 1990 was nearly five times as high as in 1950, international trade was nearly 13 times as high. In Section 3 we will discuss a number of theories which try to explain the existence of international trade.

Foreign direct investment

Foreign investments of multinational corporations are even more important than international trade for the growth of the world economy. About

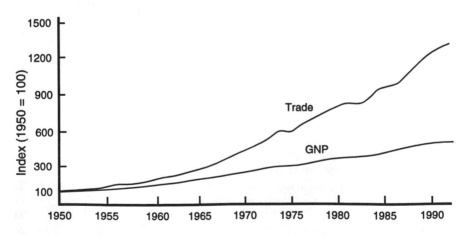

Figure 1.1 *Growth of world production and world trade, indexed at 1950 = 100 (Eurostat)*

Table 1.1   *Stock of foreign direct investment, by country and region, 1987–1992 (billions of dollars)*

Region/country	1987	1988	1989	1990	1991	1992[1]
A Outward						
France	41	56	75	110	134	151
Germany (Federal Republic)	91	104	122	140	169	186
Japan	78	112	156	204	235	251
United Kingdom	135	172	208	226	244	259
United States	339	353	379	408	438	474
World	1,000	1,169	1,382	1,616	1,799	1,949
B Inward						
Developed countries	787	920	1,088	1,260	1,369	—
Western Europe	357	419	507	616	702	—
North America	342	405	476	528	544	—
Other developed countries	88	96	105	116	123	—
Developing economies	212	241	270	300	338	—
Africa	22	25	30	32	35	—
Latin America and the Caribbean	84	95	104	114	129	—
East, South and South-East Asia	106	121	136	154	174	—
Central and Eastern Europe	—	—	—	—	—	—
World	999	1,161	1,357	1,560	1,709	—

The levels of world-wide inward and outward FDI stocks should balance, in principle; however, in practice, they do not. Several reasons have been cited as the cause for the discrepancy, including differences in the treatment of unremitted branch profits between inward and outward direct investment; treatment of unrealized capital gains and losses; the recording of transactions of 'offshore' enterprises; differences in the recording of reinvested earnings between inward and outward direct investment; differences in the method of collection, valuation and reporting of FDI between countries; differences in the treatment of real estate and construction investment; and differences in the threshold definition between inward and outward direct investment (which, however, has not been found to be a significant source of the discrepancy).

[1] Estimated.

Source: UNCTAD, 1993

one-third of the world's private sector productive assets are owned by multinational companies (UNCTAD, 1993). The influence of multi-national companies is reflected in the increase in the stock of foreign direct investment (FDI) and the growth in the number of multinationals and their foreign affiliates. As shown in Table 1.1, the total stock of foreign investment has reached almost $2,000 billion. The more than 170,000 foreign affiliates of about 37,000 parent corporations contributed approximately $5,500 billion to world sales in 1990 (UNCTAD, 1993). In Section 4 a number of theories will be discussed in order to explain the existence of foreign direct investment.

3   Determinants of international trade

We will now briefly consider a number of theories which attempt to explain why *countries* trade with one another. The emphasis therefore will be on the country level. In the following section we will then shift our discussion to theories focusing on the multinational organization. With these theories we will try to explain why *multinationals* exist.

First we will consider two 'classic' theories of trade which are based on the idea that country-specific factors (also known as location-specific factors) are decisive for international trade. Such country-specific factors may offer absolute or relative comparative cost advantages. A third and final theory explains why international trade may arise even in the absence of such cost advantages. The key term here is 'economies of scale'. Later, in Section 5, we will explore Porter's analysis, the latest in a long line of international trade theories reaching back more than two centuries.

Absolute and relative comparative cost advantages

This theory takes us back to the founding father of modern economics: Adam Smith. In his book *An Inquiry into the Nature and Causes of the Wealth of Nations* (1776), Smith explains that the division of labour can lead to increased productivity because each person does what he or she is best at or can produce more efficiently than others. This applies at every level – for example, within families or within a country as a whole. We can speak of an efficient division of labour *between* countries whenever location-specific advantages, such as the presence of certain natural resources, make it possible for one country to produce a certain product more cheaply than another.

> It is the maxim of every prudent master of a family, never to attempt to make at home what it will cost him more to make than to buy. The tailor does not attempt to make his own shoes, but buys them from the shoemaker . . . What is prudence in the conduct of every private family, can scarce be folly in that of a great kingdom. If a foreign country can supply us with a commodity cheaper than we ourselves can make it, better buy it of them with some part of the produce of our own industry, employed in a way in which we have some advantage. (Adam Smith, 1776: 424–425)

There is one problem with this theory, however. What if a country has no location-specific advantages and therefore no cost advantages? Will it still be in a position to trade with other countries? And even if it is, wouldn't it end up importing far more than it exports, so that an ever increasing amount of money will leave the country?

David Ricardo (1772–1823) showed that even if a country has no absolute cost advantages, it will still be able to grow wealthier through international trade. We can demonstrate this by using a simple model involving two countries (A and B) and two commodities (x and y). Country A produces both Commodity x and Commodity y against the lowest possible costs.

	Country A	Country B
Commodity x costs	5	12.5
Commodity y costs	20	25

The difference between Country A and Country B is larger for Commodity x, however, than it is for Commodity y. If we consider the terms of exchange (the number of units of Commodity x exchanged for one unit of Commodity y and vice versa), we can construct the following table.

Country A	Country B
1x=¼y	1x=½y
1y=4x	1y=2x

The inhabitants of Country A can profit by buying Commodity y in Country B. In Country B they only have to pay 2x, while in their own Country they have to pay 4x. Inhabitants of Country B will be better off buying their commodity x in Country A. In doing so they only have to pay ¼y, while in their own Country it would cost them ½y. We can say that Country A has a relative comparative cost advantage in producing Commodity x, while Country B has a relative comparative cost advantage in producing Commodity y. Inhabitants of Country A will therefore try to exchange their Commodity x for the Commodity y of Country B. The inhabitants of Country B will be eager to do so because the exchange is to their benefit as well. This is how international trade is born. To comply with the extra foreign demand, Country A would have to specialize in producing Commodity x and Country B in producing Commodity y.

According to Smith and Ricardo, then, international trade arose because of the existence of comparative cost advantages, whether absolute or relative.

The Heckscher–Ohlin theorem

The above brings us to the question: where do such cost differences come from? One answer, known as the Heckscher–Ohlin theorem, was introduced by the Swedish economists Eli Heckscher and Bertil Ohlin. Comparative cost differences are the result of differences in factor endowments (labour, land and capital). Some countries, for example, have a relatively large quantity of capital and a relatively small labour force (e.g. Western nations). Other countries have relatively little capital and a large labour force (most of the developing nations). Note that it is the relative position of these production factors with respect to one another that is important. We cannot say, for example, that Zaire has more labour than the United States (which is not true) or that it has more labour than capital (how would one go about measuring that?). We can, however, say that Zaïre has more labour available per quantity of capital than the United States does.

Production factors available in relatively large quantities are inexpensive, and vice versa. (For the time being we will not consider the demand conditions. A country may, for example, have absolutely no demand for a domestic good produced with scarce production factors, resulting in a low price.) In a country that possesses a relatively large amount of capital and very little labour, capital-intensive products will be cheap and labour-intensive products expensive. The reverse will be true for a country with a relatively small amount of capital and a large labour force. The same arguments can be offered for the production factor 'land'. The impact on international trade is that

> commodities requiring for their production much of [abundant factors of production] and little of [scarce factors] are exported in exchange for goods that call for factors in the opposite proportions. Thus indirectly, factors in abundant supply are exported and factors in scanty supply are imported. (Ohlin, 1933: 92, cited in Lindert, 1986: 31)

In global terms, we can explain international trade flows rather well using this theorem. Japan, a country with a relatively limited amount of land, imports many of its prime products. Third World countries with a relatively large body of (unskilled) labour export labour-intensive products such as textiles and shoes.

There are, however, two postwar trends that have presented a considerable challenge to the H–O theorem. First, there is the fact that a large and increasing share of international trade takes place between countries with similar large incomes. Secondly, a large and increasing share of international trade consists of two-way trade, involving similarly manufactured products (known as intra-industry trade). As a result, new theories of trade have been introduced which reject country-specific factors to a certain extent and which turn instead to sector- or company-specific factors that might lead to a strong competitive position. The key term in these new theories is 'economies of scale'.

Economies of scale

We have not yet mentioned an important assumption underlying the classic trade theories: yield remains constant regardless of the scale of production. In other words, the average cost per product will remain the same. In actual practice, however, we see economies of scale in many branches of industry – as the scale of production increases, the average cost per product decreases. These economies of scale might appear in production, in R&D, in purchasing, in marketing or in distribution. A very simple example of economies of scale are the discounts offered on quantity purchases (which are in turn based on the supplier's economies of scale). Economies of scale in production may be the result of a division of labour and specialization or of cost-cutting measures (for example, the use of robots in automobile manufacturing), which only become profitable at a certain minimum production level. After all, it would hardly pay to set up a robot assembly line if you were only going to produce three cars.

In addition to these economies of scale, which are known as internal economies of scale (in other words, within one company), there are also external economies of scale. These are closely related to the size of an industry and not to the size of the individual company. A concentration of companies in a particular region, for example semiconductor manufacturers in Silicon Valley in California, may give rise to a good infrastructure, a specialist labour force and a network of suppliers. This means that individual companies within this industry can achieve economies of scale despite the fact that large companies do not produce more efficiently in the sector than small companies do.

How do such economies of scale affect international trade? We noted previously that international trade depends on absolute or relative comparative cost advantages, which are the result of differences in factor endowments. According to the classic theories of trade, countries with comparable factor proportions will not trade with one another, because they will not be able to gain absolute or relative comparative cost advantages. However, when economies of scale are applied, a system in which one country produces one product and a second country produces another product can nevertheless offer advantages. As production can take place on a larger scale, the average costs of both products will decrease. Both countries can therefore gain through specialization and international trade.

How can we predict which country will produce which product if neither country can gain a cost advantage? The answer is: we cannot. It is frequently a combination of serendipitous factors which leads to a certain industry setting up first in a certain country. Through internal and/or external economies of scale, this country will be able to create such an advantage that it becomes very difficult for anyone else to catch up.

4   The reason for multinational enterprises

The theories discussed in the previous section attempt to explain how international trade – the conveying of goods across borders – arises and what it consists of. A second assumption – the first being constant returns to scale, discussed in Section 3 above – of the classic theories is that the production factors present in a particular country will move about within the country itself, but will not cross the national borders. According to the H–O theorem, international trade will gradually eliminate differences between production factor rewards in various countries. In this way, exporting labour-intensive goods to a country with a relatively small labour force may have the same effect as actually relocating labour as a production factor to this country.

In reality, however, production factors do move across borders. Cash capital and to a lesser extent labour become increasingly mobile. A large proportion of the international cash flow is motivated by a desire simply to invest money to get a return on investment, just as one would do by putting money in a savings account. British investors, for example, may purchase shares on the stock market in a Japanese company in order to gain an income from their investment (dividends and/or gains made by stock fluctuations), either in the short term or in the long term. However, a portion of this cash flow consists of Foreign Direct Investment (FDI). These are investments made in foreign countries *with the explicit goal of maintaining control over the investment*. By making use of FDI a company may, for example, be able to set up production facilities in a foreign country, thereby joining the ranks of multinational concerns.

The question, however, is why a company would choose direct investment when it can simply export the goods produced in its own country and import the raw materials or semi-manufactures required, or even license the relevant know-how. Initially the answer to this question consisted of incomplete explanations. First, companies in highly protectionist countries made use of direct investment to get around import restrictions and tariff walls. Secondly, direct investment enabled companies whose production relied heavily on certain raw materials to secure the supply of such materials. A third explanation was that the high costs of transport made exporting more expensive than establishing foreign production facilities. Sometimes foreign direct investment can also be viewed as a strategic market tactic. American companies may invest, for example, in the Japanese market for the sole purpose of making life so difficult for Japanese corporations that they will no longer have the resources left to enter the American market. None of the above-mentioned arguments, however, have offered a systematic explanation for the rise of multi-nationals in general. In the following sections we will discuss two theories that do offer such an explanation: Vernon's product life cycle theory and Dunning's eclectic theory of direct investment.

Product life cycle

Vernon's product life cycle (PLC) theory takes its name from the product life cycle familiar to students of marketing theory. In the first phase, the introductory or start-up phase, the new product is introduced. It is innovative, it has not yet been standardized and it is relatively expensive. Because the product will evolve throughout this phase, the producer and the consumer must be in direct contact. Production and sales can only take place in the country where the product is developed, for example in the United States (in principle the PLC theory concerns high-tech products which, at the time this theory was introduced, came largely from the US). In the expansion phase the product becomes more standardized and the price decreases slightly. Turnover increases sharply and production costs begin to drop. To extend this phase, a company will attempt to export its product. As the price is still rather high, export will largely go to countries that have a similar income level, for example, Europe.

At the end of the expansion phase and the beginning of the maturity phase, the company will start manufacturing the product in Europe.

Turnover there will have increased to such an extent that it pays to set up foreign production, particularly in view of import tariffs and transport costs. By this time, however, the product has become standardized in such a way that European companies will be eager to produce their own. By setting up its own subsidiaries in Europe, then, the American company is applying a defensive strategy designed to protect its market position.

In the end the production process will be completely standardized, making economies of scale and mass production possible. The quality (level of skill) of the workforce in the production process becomes less important than the costs. Production will therefore increasingly take place in labour-abundant countries. This harkens back to elements of the classic theories of trade.

The product life cycle model made an important contribution to explaining the enormous scope of direct investment by American companies in the 1950s and 1960s (see Chapter 2). The model fails to answer two important questions, however. First, why does one company in a specific country become a multinational, while another does not? Secondly, why would a company choose to maintain control of the production process by setting up subsidiaries? It would be much simpler to license the know-how required to manufacture the product to a foreign company. Both of these questions can be answered by Dunning's eclectic theory, which also incorporates the location-specific advantages proposed in the classic theories of trade.

Dunning's eclectic theory

Dunning's eclectic theory, also known as the transaction cost theory of international production, explains why corporations produce abroad, how they are able to compete successfully with domestic corporations and where they are going to produce. The theory selectively combines elements of various other theories (hence the name 'eclectic'). According to Dunning, a company that wishes to set up production in a foreign country and wants to operate as a multinational must simultaneously meet three conditions: it must have ownership advantages, location advantages and internalization advantages.

Ownership advantages, also known as corporation-specific advantages, are advantages in the production of a good or service which are unique to a particular company. The range of advantages (both tangible and intangible) can be very wide. According to Rugman (1987) they can be summarized as follows:

- proprietary technology due to research and development activities;
- managerial, marketing, or other skills specific to the organizational function of the corporation;
- product differentiation, trademarks, or brand names;
- large size, reflecting scale economies;

- large capital requirements for plants of the minimum efficient size.

The presence of ownership advantages, however, in no way fully explains the existence of the multinational company. For example, if a company gains an ownership advantage over other companies for a certain foreign market, it could simply export its products to that market. For this reason, the second condition must also be met: location advantages.

Location advantages include all of the factors discussed earlier with respect to the classic theories of trade and which will be discussed further in Section 5, with respect to Porter's analysis, ranging from an abundance of fertile land and cheap labour to a liberal capital market and a sound infrastructure. To that we can also add the favourable investment conditions offered by some countries in order to attract foreign investors. These may be in the form of subsidies, tax exemptions or cheap housing. At any rate, the benefits for the corporation must proceed from the combination of ownership advantages and location advantages. Even if this is the case, however, it will not necessarily lead to foreign direct investment and, therefore, to the establishment of a multinational concern. After all, the company can also sell its ownership advantages or license them out to another company in the foreign market. That is why finally the third condition must be met as well: the internalization advantages.

A company possesses internalization advantages if it is more profitable for this company to exploit its ownership advantages in another country itself than to sell or license them. In actual practice, there are countless arguments in favour of internalization. To a large extent these arguments have their origin in Coase's (1937) and Williamson's (1975) transaction cost approach. In the first place, if the ownership advantage is actually a combination of highly specific company factors, it might be difficult to sell or license it. And even if it were possible, the advantages and the contract for these advantages would be so complex that setting up and exploiting them would be highly expensive. This applies to a lesser degree if the advantage being sold is a specific, easily isolated invention. The problem in this situation, however, is that it would be difficult for the buyer/licensee to get a good idea of what he is purchasing or acquiring a licence for. After all, if the licensor releases too much information before concluding the contract, he will have very little left to sell or license. Finally, the company may be afraid that by licensing certain company-specific knowledge, this knowledge will either leak out, making further licences difficult, or be used in such a way that it damages the name of the licensor. In each case there are such internalization advantages that the company will decide to carry out the relevant activity in the foreign country itself.

Like rival theories, Dunning's approach is not seen as the be-all and end-all explanation for the existence of multinationals. It does, however, succeed in bringing together, in an elegant manner, what until then were a number of relatively separate schools. We will, therefore, end our discussion of the explanations offered for the existence of international trade and multinationals with this theory.

By now, we have discussed a number of reasons for international trade and foreign direct investment. However, we cannot as yet concretely explain why a particular nation is able to achieve international success in a *particular* industry. In other words: why are certain products successful in one country while other products are produced in another country?

As we mentioned earlier, the theory of absolute and relative comparative cost advantages (Section 3) offers a reasonable explanation for general trends in international trade flows. Usually, however, these advantages cannot explain why a certain country imports or exports specific industrial goods. As we will discover in Section 7, economies of scale (Section 3 above) are an important source of competitive advantages in many sectors of industry. Yet we have seen that this theory does not really answer the question as to which country will produce which product. The product life cycle theory (Section 4) has certainly made an important contribution to explaining the distribution of some high-tech products, but it raises almost as many questions as it answers. Why is it that one particular country is the leader in a new industry? Why are some industries seemingly immune to the loss of competitive advantage suggested by Vernon? And why is it that in many sectors of industry, innovation is now seen as an on-going process and not a one-off event, after which an invention quickly becomes standardized and production is taken over by low-wage countries? Finally, Dunning's eclectic theory (Section 4) provides us with a very interesting and more or less comprehensive explanation of the existence of multi-national enterprises. It does not, however, explain why some countries gain particular ownership advantages while others do not.

5   The comparative and competitive advantage of nations

Criteria for a theory of national comparative and competitive advantage

In this section we will discuss Porter's analysis. Porter attempts to provide an explicit answer to the questions listed above. According to him, a theory of national comparative and competitive advantage must meet the following criteria:

- Firms can and do choose strategies that differ. A new theory must explain why firms from particular nations choose better strategies than those from others for competing in particular industries. . . .
- Successful international competitors often compete with global strategies in which trade and foreign investments are integrated. Most previous theories have set out to explain either trade or foreign investment. A new theory must explain instead why a nation is the *home base* for successful global competitors in a particular industry that engage in both. . . .
- A new theory must move beyond the comparative advantage to the competitive advantage of a nation. It must explain why a nation's firms gain

competitive advantage in all its forms, not only the limited types of factor-based advantage contemplated in the theory of comparative advantage. . . .

- A new theory must start from the premise that competition is dynamic and evolving. Much traditional thinking has embodied an essentially static view focusing on cost efficiency due to factor or scale advantages. Technological change is treated as though it is exogenous, or outside the purview of the theory. . . .
- A new theory must make improvement and innovation in methods and technology a central element. We must explain the role of the nation in the innovation process. Since innovation requires sustained investment in research, physical capital and human resources, we must also explain why the rate of such investments [is] more vigorous in some nations and not in others. . . .
- Since corporations play a central role in the process of creating competitive advantage, the behaviour of corporations must become integral to a theory of national advantage. . . . From a manager's perspective much of trade theory is too general to be of much relevance. A new theory must give firms insight into how to set strategy to become more effective international competitors. (Porter, 1990: 19–21)

Porter naturally attempts to satisfy these conditions in his own analysis. After conducting a four-year study involving ten countries (Denmark, Germany, Italy, Japan, Korea, Singapore, Sweden, Switzerland, the United Kingdom and the United States), he was convinced that national competitive advantage depends on four determinants, represented as a diamond (Porter's diamond). (The complete model also includes the factors 'government' and 'chance', which make their influence felt through the four determinants.)

The four determinants of national comparative and competitive advantage

We will discuss the four determinants below, paying particular attention to 'factor conditions' and 'firm strategy and structure', which have the greatest bearing on this book.

Factor conditions

The first determinant, *factor conditions*, shows traces of the classic international trade theories proposed by Smith, Ricardo and Heckscher/Ohlin. However, whereas these theories concentrated on the traditional production factors such as land and, specifically, labour and capital, Porter goes much further. He agrees with the factors labour (which he calls 'human resources'), land ('physical resources') and capital ('capital resources'), but in his view these categories are much broader than the classic theories suggest. For example, while Ricardo principally saw labour as a large, undefined mass of cheap workers, Porter emphasizes quality as well as quantity and divides human resources into 'a myriad of categories, such as toolmakers, electrical engineers with PhDs, applications programmers, and so on'. Physical resources also cover the location of a country

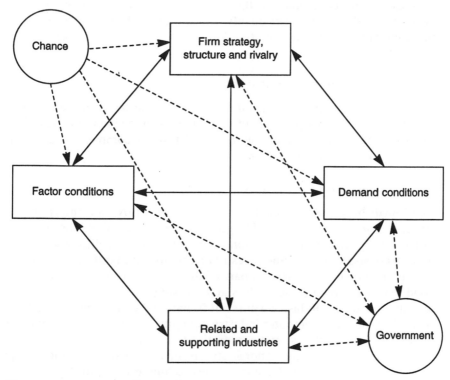

Figure 1.2   *Porter's diamond (Porter, 1990)*

with respect to its customers and suppliers, while capital resources can be divided into 'unsecured debt, secured debt, "junk" bonds, equity and venture capital'. In addition to these 'traditional' production factors, Porter also identifies knowledge resources and infrastructure as factors which can be decisive for the competitive advantage of a country. He considers knowledge resources as 'the nation's stock of scientific, technical and market knowledge bearing on goods and services', while infrastructure includes transport and communications systems, the housing stock and cultural institutions. The differences described in Parts 2 and 4 of this book with respect to education, training, skills, industrial relations and motivation can all be seen as factor conditions which influence a country's competitive advantages.

Demand conditions

The second determinant is *demand conditions*. Traditional trade theories tended to neglect the demand side. According to Porter, demand in the home market can be of great importance to a country's national competitive advantage. In addition to the size of the demand (which can lead to economies of scale), the quality of the demand is equally significant. If consumers in a company's own country, for example, are the most progressive and demanding in the world, this country will have to do its very best to deliver product quality, innovation and service. In this way, the company and/or the country gains a competitive advantage on the world market.

Related and supporting industries

The third determinant, *related and supporting industries*, exercises a similar type of influence. The presence of related and supporting industries which can compete at an international level will force a company to meet the same high international standards.

Firm strategy, structure and rivalry

The fourth broad determinant of national competitive advantage is *firm strategy, structure and rivalry*. The goals and strategies of corporations can differ sharply from nation to nation. There are also huge differences in the way corporations in the same industry are organized in different countries, as will be shown in the second part of this book. According to Porter, a good match between these choices and the sources of competitive advantage in a particular industry will result in national competitive advantage. If, for instance, the computer industry demands flexible, non-bureaucratic organizational structures, and corporations in a particular country tend to favour this kind of organizational structure, they will – all other things being equal – have a good chance of succeeding in this industry.

The important question thus is: why do corporations in particular countries favour particular strategies and structures? The answer is that there are many national characteristics that influence the ways in which corporations are organized and managed. According to Porter, some of the most important aspects are attitudes towards authority, norms of interpersonal interaction, labour–management relationships, social norms of individual or group behaviour and professional standards. Porter places special emphasis on labour–management relationships because he believes they are central to the ability of corporations to improve and innovate. All these aspects in turn find their basis in a nation's educational system, its social and religious history, its family structures, and many other often intangible but unique national characteristics (see the box opposite and Chapters 5 and 6).

Finally, domestic rivalry is a very important factor, in that companies force one another to lower their prices, improve quality and introduce a constant stream of innovations, all of which also benefits the international competitive position of the country in which they operate.

Japan as an example of Porter's analysis

Porter uses his analysis to explain why certain countries are successful in certain industries. For example, Japan's prominent position in consumer electronics, electronic components and computing equipment, office

Societal effect

Many of the factors identified by Porter can be seen in social science research as well. In the first place, a number of these factors, such as attitudes towards authority, are considered part of a country's national culture. (This topic will be discussed in Chapter 6.) In addition, authors such as Streeck, Maurice, Sorge, Warner and Lane have pointed out national differences in the area of organizational structuring, differentiation and integration mechanisms, qualifications and industrial relations. Such factors influence one another, and although this reciprocal effect can be found in every society, it is highly specific to the society in which it is taking place. This approach, which is known as the societal effect theory, will be discussed in Part 2 of this book. For now, however, bear in mind that the authors mentioned above suggest that through a particular constellation of factors, certain countries will be successful in certain industrial sectors. An example from Lane can be used by way of illustration:

> The strengths of German manufacturing enterprises are widely seen to emanate from two core institutional complexes – the system of vocational education and training and the system of industrial relations. The first not only creates high levels of technical skill throughout the industrial enterprise but also engenders a homogeneity of skills at all levels of the hierarchy, as well as fostering certain orientations to the work task and the work community. These characteristics, in turn, structure organizational relations, influence communication and cooperation along both horizontal and vertical lines and encourage labour deployment in accordance with the principle of responsible autonomy. The craft ethos permeates the whole of the organization and creates a common focus and identity for management and production workers, although not necessarily a community of interest. The cooperative works culture, fostered by the training system, is further reinforced by the system of industrial relations, particularly by the work council. The autonomy and responsibility encouraged by the organization of work is parallelled and enhanced by the participative industrial relations style, flowing from the system of co-determination. (Lane, 1989: 298)

machines, motorcycles, ships and sewing machines can in the first place be attributed to the country's rapid and continual upgrading of human resources, in which in-company training dominates. Research focuses on applications and process optimization rather than basic technological innovation, resulting in high-quality products which are nevertheless competitively priced. Secondly, demand conditions have also favoured competitive advantage in these industries. In the 1950s and 1960s, while Japan's home market was growing rapidly in sectors such as sewing machines, ships and motorcycles, these markets had begun to level off in other countries. As a result, Japanese corporations invested aggressively in large, efficient facilities with the latest technology. US and European competitors, on the other hand, simply added on to existing, less efficient older plants. The result was higher productivity for Japanese corporations. The rapid growth of Japan's industrial economy also aided supporting industries such as robotics, copiers and semiconductors. Even more important than the size of the home demand is the pressure from demanding and sophisticated buyers. Japanese consumers insist on quality and superior service and will readily switch brands if a quality difference is noticeable. Needless to say, this forces corporations continually to upgrade their products. As to the third determinant, Japan has a strong position in semiconductors, machine tools and robotics, which are essential supporting industries to many other sectors. Regarding the fourth determinant – firm strategy, structure and domestic rivalry – the strategy of Japanese corporations is geared largely towards standardization and mass production combined with high quality. This approach has made it the leader in industries such as consumer electronics and office machines. The commitment to their corporation of both workers and managers, and the corporation's investment in upgrading skills and norms of cooperation have led to an unusual rate of success in industries in which a cumulative learning effect is essential (consumer electronics, semiconductors, office machines). Finally, in almost every industry in which Japan is internationally competitive, there are several and often a dozen or more competitors; in semiconductors and shipbuilding there are as many as 34 and 33 respectively (Porter, 1990: 384–421).

Now that we have provided a tool for answering why certain products are produced in some nations and not in others, we will extend our analysis further. In the next section we will take a look at the international division of labour. Our analysis will not be carried out at the level of the individual country but rather within the broad division of First World, (ex-)Second World and Third World countries.

6   Trends in the international division of labour

The logical consequence of the theories discussed above is that a country must concentrate on the production of those goods and services in which it has a competitive advantage, so that it can export these goods and import goods and services to those industries where it is less productive. In this way, international competition helps to upgrade productivity over time. The process implies, however, that market positions in some segments and industries must necessarily be put aside if a national economy is to progress. This is certainly true in a macro-economic sense, but on a micro-level this may mean the loss of thousands of jobs in less productive industries, causing serious personal anxiety and social problems. No wonder that many governments have tried to maintain such industries by means of subsidies, protective tariffs or other forms of intervention. In these days of trade liberalization, globalization of the world economy and economic integration in many regions of the world, however, such policies are increasingly difficult to sustain. The world is moving towards a new international division of labour, a process in which multinational companies are playing a leading role. In this section we will look at the economic and social consequences of this development.

Reich's new world order

In his book *The Work of Nations: Preparing Ourselves for 21st-Century Capitalism*, Reich (1991) prophesies a new world order. The most important objectives for companies, including multinationals, are to satisfy the market demand and to make profits. If these companies can save money by moving production processes elsewhere, they will do it. This may not be so important to the companies themselves, but it does have an impact on the social structure and prosperity of the individual countries involved. The countries that have nothing to offer in international competition are doomed to lose out badly. First World countries that do not have a supply of cheap labour will have to concentrate on the production of other, more specialized products with a high knowledge and capital content. This will result in an increasing demand for highly educated and creative people. A problematic social consequence is that Western nations will be confronted with a large surplus of unskilled production workers who cannot compete against low-cost labour in (ex-) Second and Third World countries. A proper education for all citizens (and not only the top 25 percent) is therefore an absolute prerequisite for future prosperity. The only problem is: who is going to supply this education? Governments very often do not have the necessary resources to do this. Businesses do, but fail to see why they should apply their resources in this fashion. Furthermore, the global economy makes it possible to have special services performed anywhere in the world, so that in-house training becomes unnecessary.

The text given below, taken from a Dutch daily newpsaper, *NRC Handelsblad*, indicates that this is already common practice. It is interesting to note that it is by no means only unskilled labour which is being affected.

'These people have been well trained and if you give them the right tools and encourage and motivate them, they work hard.' Percy Barnevik, president of Asea Brown Boveri, was almost jubilant as he discussed his 25,000 new employees in Eastern Europe last March at ABB headquarters in Zurich . . . 'Nowadays they are doing the work that used to be done in Western Europe . . .' Percy Barnevik's ABB is not the only Western concern to shift operations to Eastern Europe, but for political/social reasons most of them prefer to keep it quiet. Philips, for example, wants to move its consumer electronics production to low-wage countries like Hungary, Poland, China, Malaysia, Indonesia and Mexico. Besides relocating complete production processes, companies are also contracting out sub-activities and purchasing components elsewhere – a trend known as 'outsourcing'. Swissair, for example, has a major share of its accounting done by Indian registered accountants in Bombay, while KLM will soon be contracting out labour-intensive programming to Malaysia or Thailand . . . If you want to have texts or numbers typed into a computer, 'typing factories' in the Philippines can offer you a rate of 90 [Dutch] cents per ten thousand characters, although lately they have been under pressure from China, where the going rate is 40 cents. In Jamaica, thousands of people working in 'office parks', which are connected to the US by satellite dish, process all kinds of ticket reservations and credit card requests submitted by Americans or handle toll-free information hotlines. They do this for a quarter of the usual wage paid in the US for this type of work . . . Bangalore, a city in southern India with four million inhabitants, has seen more than 30 Western computer and electronics factories spring up since the early 1980s. 'We came here because of the tremendous amount of talent available,' says Richard Gell, local manager for Texas Instruments. 'We weren't able to find enough software designers in Europe, and India produces more than it can use. Bangalore is one of dozens of cities in southern and particularly in eastern Asia where hundreds of Western and Japanese companies have set up operations in order to profit from a hard-working, increasingly skilled, and very cheap labour supply.' (*NRC Handelsblad*, 19 June 1993)

Professional categories in the new world order

Companies and their owners can look forward to a bright future, but can the same be said of their employees? Reich distinguishes three professional categories which in global terms cover three-quarters of the labour force (the remaining part mainly consists of employees working in agriculture and in the public sector).

1   *Routine production services*. The traditional example in this category is the employee who works on the assembly line performing short-cycle, repetitive tasks. However, according to Reich this category also includes the 'routine supervisory jobs performed by low- and mid-level managers – foremen, line managers, clerical supervisors and section chiefs – involving repetitive checks on subordinates' work and the enforcement of standard operating procedures'. It has often been said that in the present and future information age, this type of work will become less and less important. Cynics, however, remind us that many information-processing jobs fit perfectly into this category. The raw material of the industrial era has simply been replaced by the raw data of the information age. Entering and processing such data is essentially just as routine and monotonous a task as working on an assembly line in an automobile plant. These routine production services are not associated with a particular country; they can be performed anywhere and everywhere. Wage costs are therefore the only criterion for deciding where to locate them.

2   *In-person services*. Like the previous category, this one also covers basically simple and repetitive tasks requiring relatively little training. Examples of jobs in this category are: salespeople, hair stylists, waiters and

waitresses, cleaning staff and receptionists. The major difference between this category and routine production work is that in-person servers provide their services directly to the consumer and that their work must therefore be performed at the location where the consumer is present. Consequently, they have nothing to fear from lower wage costs in other countries (except, of course, from immigrants, whether legal or illegal, who may work for lower wages). They are, however, under greater threat from the increasing computerization of the many jobs they perform. Consider, for example, the cash dispensers which have become an indispensable part of life for so many people. And as many of these jobs require no special training, in-person servers are finding themselves competing more and more with unemployed routine production workers. Finally, this category of employee depends very heavily on the affluence of its customers. If a country is unable to attract enough economic activity, it will not have the financial resources to cover in-person services.

3 *Symbolic-analytic services.* The most important feature of the jobs in this category is that they require skills in problem-solving and problem-identification. Some examples are research scientists, engineers, consultants and managers, but also architects, musicians, film producers and journalists. These occupations are highly specialized; by definition they entail a proper education. Most of the jobs in this group require at least a university degree or higher vocational training. This group of employees will benefit the most from prosperity, simply because they bring added value to the production process. Like the work performed by a routine production worker, the activities of symbolic analysts are not bound to a particular location. By using the available communication and information technology, companies can avail themselves of their services anywhere in the world. And since the definitive criterion here is not wages but special skills, these activities are not automatically carried out in low-wage countries.

The number of people who can actually benefit from the new opportunities is therefore quite limited. The future seems particularly bleak for unskilled labourers in Western countries, simply because they will be unable to make a clear-cut contribution – either in the form of specific skills or in the form of low wages – to the global production process. They simply cannot compete against the wage levels of employees in poor countries who perform exactly the same type of work. Even dismantling the social security system – which in Europe is regarded as the main culprit behind the high cost of labour – offers no real alternative. After all, wages and terms and conditions of employment will never be cut so drastically that they can compete with low-wage countries. Because a large section of the population in the West remains underqualified (there are by the way huge differences between different countries: the United Kingdom, for example, is much worse off in this respect than Germany), we will ultimately be dealing with increasingly greater differences in income and, possibly, the rise of a social underclass.

Scenarios for the future

In this connection, Reich has sketched three scenarios for the future. He calls the first *zero-sum nationalism*. The assumption is that there are only two outcomes possible in economic warfare: either we win or they win, so we had better make sure that we win. Countries therefore close their eyes to globalization and try to protect and improve their own position. Government subsidies for deteriorating industries and a renewed interest in protectionism are the hallmarks of this scenario. Obviously it will be the routine production workers and in-person service workers and their representatives (for example, trade unions) who will be particularly keen on this option. This course of action will, however, be of very little benefit to companies and investors, meaning that in the long term this scenario will simply not be sustainable.

The second scenario is *cosmopolitanism*, in which the ideal of free trade is championed. This is not a zero-sum game: the world as a whole can improve through free trade. By making products where they can be made most cheaply, we all benefit in the end. The major advocates of this scenario will often be symbolic analysts. After all, they have nothing to lose in such a world order; in fact, they will be the big winners. According to Reich, this is the attitude that will most likely determine the future.

Neither of the scenarios described above is ideal, but according to Reich there is yet another option: *positive economic nationalism*. The crux of this idea is that 'each nation's citizens take prime responsibility for enhancing the capacities of their countrymen for full and productive lives, but also work with other nationals to ensure that these improvements do not come at others' expense'. Nationalism as seen by the zero-sum nationalists and individualism as advocated by the cosmopolitans are traded in for globalism. This scenario combines a pious belief in the benefits of free trade with arguments for some form of government intervention. Governments should invest in education and infrastructure, and they should even subsidize companies that offer high value-added production in their own country, regardless of the nationality of the company owners. To prevent a situation in which countries bid against each other to attract certain companies, they should instead negotiate with one another on the appropriate subsidy levels and targets. The result, according to Reich, would be a sort of GATT for foreign direct investment establishing guidelines for the way in which countries are allowed to grant such subsidies. Countries with a large unskilled labour force, for example, would be allowed to offer bigger subsidies than countries which already possess high-tech facilities and expertise. Ultimately, more people would be able to share the prosperity.

A second group of subsidies might go to basic research. This would involve projects of which the results could not be contained strictly within a country's borders. A pertinent example is the exploration of space. Since the entire world benefits from such exploration, national governments will not be inclined to subsidize space research. Such subsidies should therefore be determined at supranational level. Decisions like these are already being taken at regional level within the European Union, although not always efficiently. The EU subsidizes countless studies carried out both at universities and in companies. In any event it is clear that this scenario calls for a new global/supranational institutional order. It is less clear whether the scenario itself has a real future. According to Reich: 'Those who are threatened by global competition feel that they have much to lose and little to gain from an approach that seeks to enhance world wealth, while those who are benefiting the most from the blurring of national borders sense that they have much to lose and little to gain from government intervention to spread such benefits.'

Consequences for the Western world

We should mention that the impact of the developments described above on the West does not worry everyone to the same degree. The article quoted previously from *NRC Handelsblad* pointed out that the cheap labour force of today will be the consumers of tomorrow. In 15–20 years, for example, the more than 300 million East Europeans will consume considerably more articles from Western Europe than they do nowadays. As an example the article cites the relationship between the United States and Mexico. After ten years of trade liberalization between these two countries, Mexico now spends annually $10 billion more in the US than it did in 1982. According to the American economist Dornbush, this figure is good for 350,000 jobs in the US, which exceeds the number of jobs lost to Mexico because of cheaper labour. In the short term, Europe has no reason to panic, according to the Dutch labour market expert Stiphout. European (and Japanese) companies generally maintain a longer term perspective than US companies; they invest more in personnel and are less likely to relocate. In addition, because of protectionism world markets are still less global than many people realize, while labour costs have become less significant in certain sectors of industry. Finally, it can sometimes be important for producers to stay close to their product market so that they can register and process any changes in time. The final three comments were also made by the Japanese author Ohmae in his book *Triad Power: The Coming Shape of Global Competition* (1985).

This does not mean that we can rest on our laurels, however. By switching to new high-tech growth sectors such as computers, semiconductors and biotechnology, Western countries can escape having to compete with poorer countries on labour costs. As the examples given above show, however, cheaper labour is not the only issue. The West may specifically lack those people who have the right training and who can be found elsewhere, certainly a problem in many countries when it comes to technical qualifications. An additional factor is that, compared with the US and certainly with Japan, Europe requires far more employees to maintain the same level of production. In order to survive in the face of competition, the West must invest in continual training, increased productivity and transport and telecommunication infrastructures.

7   The competitive advantage of multinational companies

After having surveyed the scene from an increasingly elevated perspective in the previous section, we will now return to company level. What can we say about the competitive advantage of multinationals? According to Ghoshal (1987), there are three fundamental ways of building global competitive advantage: to exploit differences in input and output markets in different countries; to exploit economies of scale; and to exploit economies of scope.

Differences in input and output markets

Porter's analysis, discussed in Section 5, is highly relevant when considering the first source of competitive advantage, that is, differences in input market. Multinational companies have a unique advantage in that they can transfer activities from one country to another. A multinational company must have a clear home base for each product line, and that home base should be located in the country with the most favourable diamond.

> Nestlé has shifted the world headquarters for its confectionery business to Britain. That is because Nestlé believes that in this business the British home base is a more dynamic one because of the advertising agencies, marketing environment, and a very high per capita consumption of confectionery products in the UK. In pasta Nestlé has made its Italian company, Buitoni, the world centre of their pasta operations. (Porter, 1990)

According to Porter, companies will make increasing use of this mode of operation. It is almost impossible to coordinate facilities for production, R&D, marketing and product development when they are distributed among equivalent subsidiaries in different countries. A company with a clear home base in a dynamic location will be able to innovate faster than a company which is trying to coordinate its dispersed activities. To use a popular term, companies are creating 'centres of excellence' for each activity. It is important to realize that this concept upsets the traditional notion of having one headquarters and many dependent subsidiaries. The company becomes a kind of network with different centres for different activities. We will see in later chapters that this approach is particularly compatible with what is called the transnational company.

But national differences do not exist in input markets alone; they are important in output markets as well. For one thing, consumer tastes and preferences may differ from one country to the next. Each country is likely to have a unique distribution system, unique technical requirements and unique government regulations. And even a simple difference such as climate can influence the sort of product a company will be able to sell. For example, certain materials might be sensitive to large temperature swings. A corporation can turn these differences into a competitive advantage by tailoring its products to fit the unique requirements of different national markets. This is known as a strategy of national differentiation, and multidomestic companies (see later chapters) know how to apply this strategy to their advantage.

Economies of scale

A second source of competitive advantage is economies of scale (see Section 3). A corporation can achieve scale economies by doing nothing more than expand the volume of its output. In scale-sensitive industries, a corporation may even be forced to do this to retain its competitive viability. Otherwise, competitors will undercut its market prices by building up their own cost advantages. The nice thing about scale economies is that they can also lead to what is called the experience or learning effect. By producing the same product a large number of times, the producer will probably invent ways to make the production process more efficient. As the scale of production increases, progressive cost reductions will result. While the concept of scale economies is not unique to multinational companies, the sheer size of such concerns often makes it easier to exploit them.

Economies of scope

The last source of competitive advantage is economies of scope, also called synergy effects. The basic notion here is that it can be less expensive to produce two (or more) products within the same corporation than to produce them separately. Ghoshal distinguishes three important sources of scope economies.

- The first is that the corporation must be diversified, that is, produce several different products, and share not only production equipment but also cash or brand names across different companies and markets. Flexible manufacturing systems using robots to produce different items are an example of the first; cross-subsidization of markets and exploitation of a global brand name are examples of the second and third.
- A second important source of scope economies is shared external relations. This applies to customers, suppliers, distributors, governments and other institutions. It is often easier to sell new products through existing distribution channels to existing customers.
- Finally, shared knowledge is the third important component of scope economics. The fact that NEC can share R&D in computers and communications makes it possible for the company to create new products which give it a competitive advantage over competitors who are technologically strong in only one of these areas.

Again, the concept of scope economies is not unique to multinational concerns, but they are more likely to have a diversified portfolio of companies, thereby increasing the opportunity to apply scope economies.

Summary and conclusions

In the first section of this chapter, we used statistical material to demonstrate that both international trade and foreign direct investment have increased sharply in the past few decades. In the subsequent sections we discussed a number of theories which might help to explain why international trade and foreign direct investment, or multinationals, exist. We then tried to answer why certain products are produced in certain countries and described current changes in the international division of labour. This led us to two important conclusions. First, the competitiveness of nations is determined by many more factors than simply (an over-abundance of) labour, land and capital. And secondly, increasing globalization has had a tremendous impact on the competitive position of various countries and may lead to far-reaching social changes in the West in particular. Finally, in the last section we dealt with the sources of competitive advantage for multinationals.

This chapter started its analysis at the level of the country, proceeded to the multinational level, returned to the country level, progressed yet another step to the global level and finally returned to the multinational. For the time being we will remain at this level; the next three chapters will discuss strategic planning, organizational structure and HRM in multinationals, in that order.

2 Strategic planning in multinational corporations

Anne-Wil Harzing

1	Introduction	26
2	Differences between domestic and multinational corporations	26
	Multiculturalism and geographic dispersion	26
	Complexity	27
	Potential benefits of multiculturalism and geographic dispersion	27
3	The strategic planning process of multinational corporations	28
4	External analysis	30
	Global (worldwide) level	30
	The multidomestic era	31
	The international and global era	31
	The transnational era	32
	Efficiency, quality, flexibility and innovativeness	32
	Industry level	33
	Multidomestic industries	33
	Global industries	33
	International industries	34
	Transnational industries	34
5	Internal analysis	34
	Core competence	35
	Organizational capability	35
	Administrative heritage	36
6	International competitive strategies	36
	Competitive strategies for multinational corporations	37
	Multidomestic strategy	37
	Global strategy	37
	International strategy	38
	Transnational strategy	38
	Competitive strategies compared	39
	Competitive strategies and ownership, location and internalization advantages	40
7	Functional strategies	43
	Human resource management	43
	Finance and accounting	44
	Marketing	45
	Production	45
8	The strategic planning process integrated	46
	Four configurations	46
	Integration of functional policies	48
9	Summary and conclusions	49

1   Introduction

The main subject of this book is international human resource management. We cannot, however, look at this subject in isolation. In the previous chapter we explained the reasons for internationalization and discussed the (future) international division of labour. We discussed various theories in this respect and showed that human resources also play their part in these theories. Although we did pay some attention to the multinational corporation, the most important level of analysis was the country or region. In this chapter we will focus on the strategic planning process of multinational corporations, as human resource management is both an input and an output factor in this process.

In Section 3 we will sketch most of the strategic issues multinational corporations have to cope with. In this chapter we will limit our discussion to four subjects: external analysis at a global and industry level, internal analysis, competitive strategy and functional strategies. These issues will be dealt with in Sections 4, 5, 6 and 7. In Section 8 we will present a framework that allows us to integrate the external environment, the competitive strategy and the organizational structure (which will be dealt with in the next chapter). We will also link the functional strategies with this framework. But first of all, in the next section we will distinguish what are considered to be the key differences between multinational and domestic corporations.

2   Differences between domestic and multinational corporations

Multiculturalism and geographic dispersion

What are the fundamental differences between domestic and multinational corporations? Adler (1983) tried to identify the major differences between domestic and multinational corporations by asking a selected group of experts in this field. Two factors were considered to be of prime importance in differentiating between domestic and multinational corporations: multiculturalism and geographic dispersion. Multiculturalism is defined as 'the presence of people from two or more cultural backgrounds within an organization'. Geographic dispersion is defined as 'the location of various subunits of the parent corporation in different countries'.

According to Adler the combination of *both* multiculturalism and geographic dispersion is of fundamental importance. So far, most international business studies have focused on the consequences of geographic dispersion and tended to give little attention to the consequences of multiculturalism. Most comparative management studies had the opposite preference. They tended to focus on cultural differences, while more or less neglecting the geographic dispersion aspect of multinational corporations. To get a complete picture of multinational corporations, both perspectives are equally important. As the subjects in this chapter are mainly in the field of international business, multiculturalism will play a modest role. Other chapters in this book, however, will afford this aspect more attention.

Complexity

For a multinational organization the main effect of multiculturalism and geographic dispersion was considered to be a greater complexity. When asked to describe this complexity more concretely by completing the statement: 'In comparison with domestic organizations, complexity is greater in multinational organizations because of . . .' the experts predominantly agreed with the following (the figure in parentheses represents the percentage of experts that agreed with the statement):

- the need for multinational corporations to be more sensitive to government, labour, and public opinion concerns (91.7 percent) and regulations (62.5 percent);
- home-country philosophies and practices that are inapplicable in foreign locales (83.3 percent);
- the impossibility of implementing uniform personnel practices (83.3 percent) and performance standards (70.8 percent) (Adler, 1983: 15).

These different factors will be dealt with extensively in this chapter and subsequent ones.

Potential benefits of multiculturalism and geographic dispersion

Multiculturalism and geographic dispersion can have advantages and disadvantages. Regarding multiculturalism, the panel of experts made a distinction between current and future benefits. According to the panel, the most important *future* benefits of multiculturalism are:

- increasing creativity and innovation (83.3 percent);
- demonstrating more sensitivity in dealing with foreign customers (75 percent);
- being able to get the best personnel from everywhere (that is, not being 'stuck' with just local talent) (66.7 percent);
- taking a global perspective (e.g. the MNC choosing the best opportunities globally) (62.5 percent);
- creating a 'superorganizational culture', using the best of all cultures (based on the need for a unifying, transcending culture) (62.4 percent);
- greater flexibility within the organization both to adapt to a wider range of environments and to change within those environments (62.5 percent) (Adler, 1983: 21).

When the future benefits were compared with the benefits that were currently realized, the only major decrease in importance was that financial risks could be spread over a wider range of economies (-41.6 percent) and that more successful product-development and marketing strategies could be created in terms of both locally tailored and worldwide products (-25 percent). A general conclusion might therefore be that current benefits are related more to the functional areas of marketing and finance, whereas potential future benefits are related more to human resource management. In the next chapters we will see that human resource management is of fundamental importance in realizing an efficient and effective multinational organization.

3   The strategic planning process of multinational corporations

Strategic planning, in its broadest sense, seeks to match markets with products and other corporate resources in order to strengthen a corporation's competitive position. In order to be able to perform this matching process a corporation must execute both an external and internal analysis, which would result in a product/market combination (or in a number of those combinations), also called strategic business units (SBUs). For each SBU, a multinational corporation should define its market entry/ participation strategy (the choice for export, licensing/franchising or a wholly- or partly-owned subsidiary) and its competitive strategy. In implementing these strategies, organizational structure, control and coordination strategies and functional strategies are of prime importance. A final important topic in this respect is the relationship with host and home country governments.

Figure 2.1 shows the main elements to be considered in the process of strategic planning in multinational corporations. It is based on the environment–strategy–structure paradigm, which suggests that superior performance is the result of a good fit between strategy and environmental demands, and between organizational structure and strategy. However, we also focus explicitly on the internal factors of the corporation, which can facilitate, constrain or form the basis of certain strategies. In the following sections we will deal with some of these strategic issues (those marked with a bullet) in more detail: external analysis at global and industry level, internal analysis (core competence, organizational capability and administrative heritage), competitive strategy and functional strategies. Organizational structuring and control and coordination mechanisms will be dealt with in the following two chapters. The remaining issues – market selection (including political risk analysis), entry and participation strategies and the relationship with host and home country governments – are slightly less relevant for this book. The reader is therefore referred to general textbooks on international management for more information on these subjects.

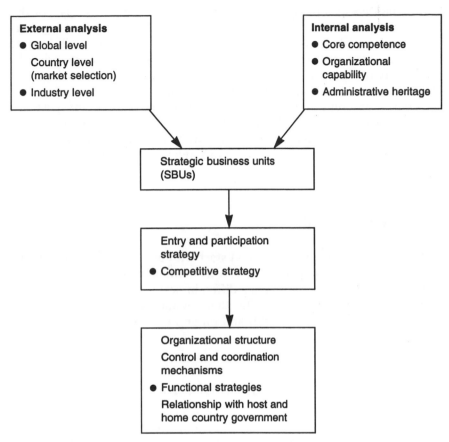

Figure 2.1 *Strategic planning in multinational firms*

Before addressing the different elements of the strategic planning
process, two important remarks must be made. First, in reality the process
will not be as linear as it is shown here. There are numerous feedbacks and
repetitions. Furthermore Figure 2.1 assumes a very systematic approach to
strategy formulation. Often strategy will be emergent (Mintzberg, 1988a),
incremental (Quinn, 1988) or take a muddling-through approach (Lindblom, 1987). The reader is referred to the extensive literature on the
subject. Secondly, one very important intervening variable in this strategic
planning process is the manager him/herself. Changes in the environment
will not influence strategy unless they are enacted (Weick, 1979) and
managers do have some choice of action (Child, 1972). An important
influential factor in this process is the societal/cultural effect. Society/
culture can on the one hand form a constraint on certain choices (for
example, democratic leadership will not work in countries where people
favour hierarchical decision processes) and on the other hand influence the
values of managers so that certain environmental changes are not enacted

and certain choice options are not considered. In the second part of this book we will see how society/culture can influence personnel and organization policies in different countries. Multinational companies will have to take these differences into account, but at the same time they do bring the nationality of their home countries into the game. In this and subsequent chapters we will see that multinationals from different countries have developed different strategies, structures and policies in the past and probably will continue to do so in the future, despite common developments in the environment. So in addition to national differences in management, there are also national differences in international management.

4   External analysis

A strategic planning process should start with an analysis of the environment. The strategic planning process in multinational corporations does not differ in this respect. It does differ in scale; the environment to be considered is much broader. In this section we will deal with the environment on a global (world) and on an industry level.

Confusion of terms

In this chapter and in the rest of this book we consistently use the terms multidomestic, international, global and transnational for environment, industries, strategies and structures. The terms polycentric, ethnocentric and geocentric are used for functional policies. In terms of strategy, there are a number of other terms in use: country-centred, simple global and complex global (Porter, 1986a,b) and nationally responsive, worldwide integration and multifocal (Prahalad and Doz, 1987). Although the emphases sometimes differ, generally speaking these terms can be compared to our terms multidomestic, global and transnational respectively. A final note: in some literature the term global is used to describe characteristics of what we would call a transnational environment, industry, strategy or structure. The wisest thing is to compare characteristics and not labels.

Global (worldwide) level

When analyzing the environment on a global (worldwide) scale, one of the most important trends for multinational companies is the increasing internationalization of the world economy. In this section we will briefly sketch the different eras that can be distinguished in the internationalization process. The description is based on Bartlett (1986) and Bartlett and Ghoshal (1989).

The multidomestic[1] era (1920–1950)

The period between the wars was characterized by a rise in nationalistic feeling. Countries became more and more protectionistic and erected high tariff barriers. There were large national differences in consumer preferences and communication and logistical barriers remained high. These circumstances favoured national companies. For *multi*national companies, the strategy of centralized production in order to capture economies of scale (see Chapter 1), combined with exports to various countries, was made impossible by high tariff and logistical barriers. In order to be able to compete with national companies, multinational corporations had to set up a larger number of foreign manufacturing subsidiaries. These subsidiaries were usually relatively small plants that produced for the national market only. Differences in consumer preferences and high communication barriers led to a decentralization of decision-making, so that the foreign subsidiaries were relatively independent of their headquarters. European companies dominated foreign investment in this era.

The international and global era (1950–1980)

The postwar years were characterized by a worldwide boom in demand. Consumers were catching up for the years of scarcity and soberness. The United States was in a predominant economic position during this period and led the way. Most European companies were preoccupied with the reconstruction of their domestic operations, while American companies were almost untouched by the war. US companies developed more and more new technologies and products. They were almost forced into the international market by spontaneous export orders and opportunities for licensing. Later they started making their products in manufacturing facilities in Western Europe and in developing countries. These companies followed the classic product life cycle pattern (Vernon, see Chapter 1). By 1960 the United States' share in foreign investment had risen to 59 percent (Bartlett and Ghoshal, 1989: 47).

In the 1960s and 1970s the successive reductions in tariff barriers began to have their full impact. They were accompanied by declining international transport costs and communication barriers. Furthermore, new electronic technologies increased the minimum efficient scale in many industries. Finally, consumer preferences became more homogeneous because of increased international travel and communication. All these developments made centralized and relatively standardized production with exports to various countries profitable again. Japanese companies, which internationalized during this period, were very successful with their large-scale intensive production facilities they were able to produce low-cost, high-quality products under tight central control.

---

[1] As we prefer to use the term multinational as a general term describing companies operating in more than one country, we have consistently substituted Bartlett and Ghoshal's term multinational by the comparable term multidomestic.

The transnational era (1980–?)

But the times, they were a-changing again. By the late 1970s there was a rising concern among host countries about the impact of MNCs on their balance of trade, national employment levels, and on the international competitiveness of their economies. As a consequence, they gradually started to exercise their sovereign powers. Trade barriers were erected again to limit exports and foreign direct investments were regulated by industrial policies. Other forces counteracted the previous globalization process as well. Flexible manufacturing, for instance, reduced the minimum efficient scale by employing robotics and CAD/CAM technologies. The use of software became very important in a growing number of industries (from telecommunications to computers and consumer electronics). This development facilitated conformity to consumers who were once again asking for products tailored to their local needs. The problem is, however, that we do not witness a complete reversal to the multi-domestic era again. The worldwide innovation of the international era and the global efficiency of the global era remain important competitive factors. Today, in more and more industries, companies struggle with three different and sometimes opposing demands: national responsiveness, global efficiency and worldwide innovation (transfer of knowledge).

Efficiency, quality, flexibility and innovativeness

In the previous section we described different eras with a focus on either national responsiveness, transfer of knowledge or global efficiency. The transnational era was characterized by the necessity to pay attention to all three of these market demands. In this section we will discuss a second study that distinguishes different phases in the business environment. Bolwijn and Kumpe (1990) distinguish four phases, each phase having different market demands and performance criteria and requiring a different ideal type of corporation (Table 2.1).

The 1960s were characterized by growing internationalization, partly as a result of trade liberalization. A side-effect of this growth of international trade was fierce price competition, because products could be produced in low-wage countries. Price was the ruling market demand and efficiency the

Table 2.1 *Market requirements, performance criteria and ideal types of firms in the period 1960–2000*

	Market requirements	Performance criteria	Firm (ideal type)
1960	Price	Efficiency	The efficient firm
1970	Price, quality	Efficiency + quality	The quality firm
1980	Price, quality, product line	Efficiency + quality + flexibility	The flexible firm
1990	Price, quality, product line, uniqueness	Efficiency + quality + flexibility + innovative ability	The innovative firm

Source: Bolwijn and Kumpe, 1990

overruling performance criterion. The 1970s brought a new competitive weapon: quality. Customers became more critical and demanded high-quality but affordable products. Companies thus had to comply with the market demands of both price and quality. Japanese companies were and are especially good at this. We only have to think of Japanese cars, which offer a higher quality for a lower price. In the 1980s, Japan once more took the lead in offering a large variety of products. Freaks of fashion abounded and demand became more whimsical. Apart from price and quality, a wide range of choices and short delivery times were important market demands which forced companies to be flexible. According to Bolwijn and Kumpe the market demand of the 1990s will be uniqueness. Companies will have to offer a product that is unique in one way or another. In order to be able to do this companies have to be innovative. Flexibility is a prerequisite for this: innovation requires change and change requires flexibility. However, an innovative corporation also has to conform with the market demands of price and quality. The actual practice in companies lags behind, however. According to Bolwijn and Kumpe the industrial world as a whole is only in the phase of transition to flexibility, while some companies are still struggling with quality.

The market demands and periods described above differ somewhat from those used by Bartlett and Ghoshal (we will offer a partial explanation for this in Section 6 below, see pp. 39–40). The main conclusion, however, is the same: we are now living in an era where companies have to conform with different strategic demands at the same time.

Industry level

In our analysis at the level of individual industries we encounter four familiar terms: multidomestic, international, global and transnational, again based on Bartlett and Ghoshal (1989, 1992b).

Multidomestic industries

In a multidomestic industry, international strategy in fact consists of a series of domestic strategies. Competition in one country is essentially independent of competition in other countries. Typical industry characteristics are determined by cultural, social and political differences between countries. A classic example of a multidomestic industry is the branded packaged products industry (such as food and laundry detergents).

Global industries

In a global industry standardized consumer needs and scale efficiencies make centralization and integration profitable. In this kind of industry a corporation's competitive position in one country is significantly influenced by its position in other countries. The global industry is not merely a collection of domestic industries, but a series of linked domestic industries in which the rivals compete against each other on a truly worldwide basis. A classic example of a global industry is consumer electronics.

International industries

The adjective international refers to the international product life cycle (see Chapter 1), which describes the internationalization process in this type of industry. The critical success factor in these industries is the ability to transfer knowledge (particularly technology) to units abroad. It is a process of sequential diffusion of innovations that were originally developed in the home market. A classic example of an international industry is telecommunications switching.

Transnational industries

Transnational industries are characterized by a complex set of environmental demands. Companies in these industries must respond simultaneously to the diverse and often conflicting strategic needs of global efficiency (as a characteristic of global industries), national responsiveness (as a characteristic of multidomestic industries) and transfer of knowledge (as a characteristic of international industries).

In the first section of this chapter above, we saw that the international environment has evolved towards the transnational era. However, the industry in which a company competes can be an important mediator in this respect. Some industries still have a distinctive multidomestic, international or global focus. And although more and more industries develop transnational characteristics, there will always be industries that continue to be more or less multidomestic, international or global. As we will see later on, this has important consequences for the strategy and structure of companies in the industries concerned. But first we will discuss internal analysis for multinational corporations.

5   Internal analysis

Often the internal side of the analysis is forgotten or played down. Adherents of the resource-based view of the corporation are refocusing their attention on internal resources that can be used to develop distinctive competitive advantages. According to them, corporation-specific resources and capabilities provide far stronger predictors of performance than industry characteristics. Due attention to the resources of the company, human resources being not the least important among these, implies a two-way or integrated relationship between business and HRM strategy (Golden and Ramanujam, 1985). On the one hand, characteristics, quality and limitations of the (human) resource pool influence, constrain or form the basis for strategic options, on the other hand they are influenced by strategic options themselves.

In this section we will discuss the approach advocated by Collis (1991). Collis identified three important elements of the resource-based view of the corporation – 'core competence', 'organizational capability' and 'administrative heritage'. We will discuss these three elements below.

Core competence

A corporation's core competence, a term that has become widely known through the writings of Prahalad and Hamel (1990), is the entire system of tangible and intangible resources in which a corporation has unique advantages. One can think of technological/marketing/production skills, a strong corporate culture, a well-trained workforce, a strong trade name etc. It is important to note that a core competence should be 'distinctive'. A corporation should evaluate its resources in the light of the resources possessed by its competitors. Only if the corporation's own combination of resources has something unique or is superior to the combination of their competitors can the corporation be said to have an economically valuable core competence.

The external environmental demands and opportunities are the same for each corporation that is operating in a particular industry. However, the necessary resources every corporation must acquire to comply with these demands and exploit the opportunities of a certain product market will differ, because the combination of resources each corporation possesses (its core competence) is different. Therefore, corporations will choose product market positions that make the best use of their core competence, even if this leads them to choose product market combinations that are 'objectively' seen to be second best. Furthermore, corporations will in the first place acquire resources from their domestic factor markets. They will therefore preferably build their core competence around factors that are abundantly available in their country (see also the related discussion in Chapter 1).

Organizational capability

We already referred to intangible resources as a source of core competence. Organizational capability consists of a very specific form of intangible resources. It comprises the managerial capability to improve and upgrade a corporation's efficiency, effectiveness, flexibility and innovativeness in a continuous way. In fact, organizational capability can be a source of sustainable competitive advantage in its own right. According to Collis, to achieve this organizational capability 'the corporation must create dynamic routines that facilitate innovation, foster collective learning, and transfer information and skills within the organization'. This cannot be achieved by any specific organizational structure. Flexibility is therefore an extremely important element of organizational capability. The corporation needs to be able to perform the constant adaptations necessary to adjust to both changing external circumstances and the administrative heritage of the corporation (see next section). Further on we will see that organizational capability is very important when transforming to a transnational organization.

Administrative heritage

According to Bartlett and Ghoshal (1992b), administrative heritage 'can be, at the same time, one of the company's greatest assets – the underlying source of its key competencies – and also a significant liability, since it resists change and thereby prevents realignment or broadening of strategic capabilities'. Both intangible (cultural) factors and tangible (physical) factors can form administrative heritage. Examples of the intangible factors are the charismatic leadership of the company's leader or the culture of the organization. The physical heritage can consist of plant locations, office facilities, communication systems. New investments are clearly influenced by the physical assets already in place. Because these assets are generally very durable, most investments are essentially incremental decisions. For instance, once a decision in favour of a certain plant location is taken, it will continue to influence the location of new facilities, even if the original decision proved to be wrong. These two aspects of administrative heritage, cultural and physical heritage, can act as a constraint on strategy. Therefore, we cannot refer only to external product and factor markets to predict the behaviour of a corporation. Furthermore, because most of these assets and resources are relatively difficult to change, corporations will only periodically try to optimize their strategies and structures.

In sum, internal resources are certainly not to be overlooked in describing a corporation's strategic behaviour. They can form both a constraint on and the basis for strategic choices. This is why both an external and internal analysis are necessary to justify choosing a number of product/market combinations, also called strategic business units (SBUs). In the next section we will discuss possible competitive strategies for these SBUs.

6   International competitive strategies

In the literature on competitive strategy there are a few recurring basic choices: a cost-efficiency or cost-leadership strategy, a differentiation strategy, a quality strategy (which can be considered as a form of differentiation) and an innovation strategy. In international management literature, the terms familiar from Bartlett and Ghoshal (1989 and 1992b) – multidomestic, global, international and transnational – are used to describe competitive strategy. Later in this section we will also discuss the aforementioned choices and try to relate them to the literature on multinational competitive strategies. Furthermore, we will go on to show that the competitive strategies as distinguished by Bartlett and Ghoshal can be related to the transaction cost theory of international production, described in Chapter 1 (see Dunning's eclectic theory, p. 9).

Competitive strategies for multinational corporations

In this section we will describe the competitive strategies that can be chosen by multinational corporations. Here our main focus is the strategic *objectives* of each type of strategy; in Section 7 of Chapter 1 we referred to the basic *sources* of competitive advantage for multinationals. The examples given illuminate not only these strategies, but also the industry characteristics and the historical developments described in Section 4 above.

Multidomestic strategy

Companies following a multidomestic strategy give prime importance to national responsiveness. Their products or services are differentiated to meet different local demands. Their policies are differentiated to conform to different governmental and market demands. The competitive advantage of multidomestic companies often lies in the downstream value chain activities (see Porter, 1986b for a discussion of the value chain concept) such as sales and marketing or service. These activities are more closely related to the buyer and are usually tied to the buyer's location. This is the strategy traditionally followed by European multinationals.

> Historically, branded packaged goods companies had to respond primarily to differing market needs. In laundry detergents, for example, there was little scope for standardizing products within Europe, let alone worldwide. As late as 1980, washing machine penetration ranged from less than 30 percent of households in the United Kingdom to over 85 percent in Germany. In northern European countries 'boil washing' had long been standard, whereas hand washing in cold water represented an important demand segment in Mediterranean countries. Differences in water hardness, perfume preferences, fabric mix, and phosphate legislation made product differentiation from country to country a strategic necessity. (Bartlett and Ghoshal, 1989: 20–21)

Global strategy

Companies following a global strategy give prime importance to efficiency. They integrate and rationalize their production to produce standardized products in a very cost-efficient manner. The competitive advantage of global companies often lies in upstream value chain activities such as procurement, inbound logistics (warehousing, inventory control, material handling etc.) and operations (machining, assembly, testing etc.). These activities are optimized on a worldwide scale. This is the strategy traditionally followed by Japanese multinationals.

> The development of the transistor by the Bell Laboratories in 1947 signaled a new era in consumer electronics. The replacement of vacuum tubes by transistors greatly expanded the efficient scale for production of key components, and the subsequent development of printed circuit boards made mass production feasible by reducing both the amount and skill level of labour required to assemble radios, TVs, tape recorders and the like. The introduction of

integrated circuits in the late 1960s further reduced the number and cost of components and increased optimum manufacturing scale. . . . Through the 1970s, the clear dominant trend in the consumer electronics industry was a progressive increase in the benefits of the world-scale economies, driven primarily by technical changes and reinforced by the homogenization of customer tastes and a significant decline in trade barriers. In our rather constrained use of the term, this was a classic global industry – one whose basic characteristics were defined by the need for global scale, relatively unimpeded by national differences. (Bartlett and Ghoshal, 1989: 22–23)

International strategy

Companies following an international strategy give prime importance to the development and diffusion of innovations world wide. Their competitive advantage often lies in research and development. New technologies are developed in the home country and transferred and adapted to foreign countries, following the product life cycle as discussed in Section 4 of Chapter 1. They do not strive for the efficiency of global companies or the complete national responsiveness of multidomestic companies, but do pay *some* attention to both of these goals. This is the strategy traditionally followed by US multinationals.

The telecommunications switching industry traditionally required a more multidimensional strategic capability than either consumer electronics or branded packaged goods. Monopoly purchasing in most countries by government-owned post, telegraph, and telephone authority (PTT) created a demand for responsiveness – a demand enhanced by the strategic importance almost all governments accorded to developing local manufacturers of telecom equipment. At the same time, global integration and coordination of activities were also required, because of significant scale economies in production and the need to arrange complex credit facilities for buyers through multinational lending agencies. However, the most critical task for switch manufacturers was the ability to develop and harness new technologies and to exploit them worldwide. This ability to learn and to appropriate the benefits of learning in multiple national markets differentiated the winners from the losers in this highly complex business. (Bartlett and Ghoshal, 1989: 24)

Transnational strategy

Companies following a transnational strategy recognize that they should pay attention to global efficiency, national responsiveness and worldwide learning at the same time. In order to do this their strategy must be very flexible. The strategy (literally) is to have no set strategy, but to let each strategic decision depend on specific developments. Strategy becomes unclear and it may become dissolved into a set of incremental decisions with a pattern which may only make sense after the fact. Issues get shaped, defined, attended to, and resolved one at a time in a 'muddling through' process. A transnational strategy would be a deliberately planned strategy to have an 'adaptive' (Mintzberg, 1988b), 'incremental' (Quinn, 1988), 'muddling through' (Lindblom, 1987) or 'emergent' (Mintzberg, 1988a) strategy.

Transition to transnational strategies

In the 1980s each of these industries described above underwent major changes. In laundry detergents producers faced a growing penetration of washing machines, a trend toward lower-temperature washing and an increasing use of synthetics in clothing. While these developments made a more standardized and cost-effective approach feasible, this approach was made necessary by the increasing oil prices in the mid-1970s. Product innovations made standard products with local variations possible. In consumer electronics political pressure for local manufacturing, increasing trade barriers and a renewed consumer preference for differentiated products made more local differentiation necessary. Rapidly changing technology and shortening product life cycles were the driving forces behind worldwide innovations. In telecommunications switching, a new generation of technology and deregulation of the telecommunications industry made global efficiency both necessary and feasible. However, national governments also became very sensitive to the strategic importance of telecommunications. The introduction of the computer in telecommunications placed the digital switch at the core of a country's information infrastructure. Telecommunications companies were thus forced to be sensitive to the needs of national governments (based on Bartlett and Ghoshal, 1989: 25–29). So we see that, in fact, companies in all three of these industries were forced to conduct more transnational strategies.

Competitive strategies compared

As said before, in the 'traditional' literature on competitive strategy there are a few recurring basic choices: a cost-efficiency or cost-leadership strategy, a differentiation strategy, a quality strategy (which can be considered as a form of differentiation) and an innovation strategy (see for instance Porter, 1980; Schuler and Jackson, 1987). How do these strategies relate to the strategies discussed in the previous section?

Superficially we can postulate a one-to-one linkage. A global strategy is based on efficiency, so this would basically be a cost-efficiency or cost-leadership strategy. An international strategy boils down to the worldwide diffusion of innovations from the home country, so this could easily be related to an innovation strategy. Companies following a multidomestic strategy can be said to differentiate their products according to local needs, so the differentiation strategy would be applicable. But what about the transnational strategy? We have seen that this is basically a very flexible strategy, so perhaps the transnational strategy can be equated with the strategy aimed at compliance with the market demand of flexibility (see Section 4 above).

On closer examination, however, this one-to-one relationship does not hold. Porter (1986b), for instance, describes how a corporation following a global strategy can choose between global cost leadership and global differentiation. Global differentiators such as IBM can use their scale and learning advantages to lower the cost of differentiating (for example, offering many models and frequent changes). A national responsiveness strategy, according to Porter, can focus on either differentiation or low cost in serving the particular needs of a national market. Also this one-to-one relationship does not conform with our picture of the transnational strategy, which should focus on global efficiency, national responsiveness and worldwide learning, all *at the same time*. Furthermore, in Section 4 above we saw that Japanese companies, which are assumed to follow global strategies, were masters in complying with the demands of both efficiency, quality and later flexibility. Finally, Schuler and Jackson (1987) acknowledge that companies might be pursuing different strategies at the same time and that even different parts of the company can follow different strategies. An R&D department will often follow an innovative strategy and a production department a cost-efficient strategy.

We may draw two conclusions from this discussion. First, the competitive strategies described at the beginning of Section 6 have a high level of generality. Within these strategies there is room for a choice between cost-efficiency, quality, differentiation, innovation or other strategies. Second, a choice *between* these strategies might not be necessary or even desirable. And here we come back to our discussion in Section 4: perhaps today's competitive environment requires a *simultaneous* focus on all competitive choices. This would apply for both the 'general' and the 'specific' competitive choices. In Section 7 we will see that even with regard to general strategies, companies can and should make different choices for different business units, functions and tasks.

Competitive strategies and ownership, location and internalization advantages

In a recent article Rugman and Verbeke (1992) make an effort to link the transaction cost theory of international production, as discussed in Chapter 1, to the configurations distinguished by Bartlett and Ghoshal. Their analysis is rather complex. However, it is probably the first analysis that managed to incorporate both the economic perspective on multinationals as discussed in Chapter 1 and the managerial perspective we take in the rest of this book.

Their analysis takes as a starting point that foreign direct investment has been chosen as a more efficient mode of entry than export, licensing or a joint venture. In terms of Dunning's eclectic theory, there are advantages to internalization.

Rugman and Verbeke then go on to distinguish two types of ownership-specific advantages – which they call firm-specific advantages (FSAs) –

namely location-bound firm-specific advantages and *non*-location-bound firm-specific advantages. The benefits of location-bound firm-specific advantages depend on their being used in one particular location (or a set of locations). They cannot easily be transferred and cannot be used in other locations without significant adaptation. An example would be a corporation's expertise in dealing with the idiosyncrasies of the Japanese distribution system. Transferring this specific expertise to other locations would be useless. Non-location-bound firm-specific advantages do not depend on their being used in one particular location. They can be used on a global scale, because transferring them to other locations can be done at low cost and without substantial adaptation. The best-known example in this respect is proprietary technology resulting from research and development activities, but specific marketing skills and managerial capabilities can also form non-location-bound firm-specific advantages.

With regard to location advantages – or country-specific advantages (CSAs) as Rugman and Verbeke call them – they distinguish two sources: home and host country, and two ways of using them: *static* and *leveraged*. Home country country-specific advantages, for example a highly skilled technical workforce, may be used in a *static* way, that is to support *current* firm-specific advantages. However, they can also be used in a *leveraged* way, that is to develop *new* firm-specific advantages, for instance a new type of technology. The same goes for host country country-specific advantages. For some examples of home and host country country-specific advantages, refer to Chapter 1.

In Figure 2.2 Rugman and Verbeke distinguish the two types of firm-specific advantages discussed above, location-bound and non-location-bound, and three different combinations of country-specific advantages:

- home country country-specific advantages, used in a leveraged way;
- host country country-specific advantages, used in a static way;
- a combination of home and host country country-specific advantages, used in either a static or a leveraged way.

The four types of companies distinguished by Bartlett and Ghoshal (1989) are situated in this figure.

The type of company that is captured best by the original theory on multinational corporations (Dunning's eclectic theory) is the inter national company. The original framework assumes that firm-specific advantages are non-location-bound, that is that they can be used anywhere in the world. The actual choice for the optimum location for subsidiaries in this type of company is based on static host country country-specific advantages (such as a cheap labour force). The product life cycle model described in Chapter 1 also describes the characteristics of this type of company.

In the case of multidomestic companies, differences between countries with regard to customer preferences, market conditions and government

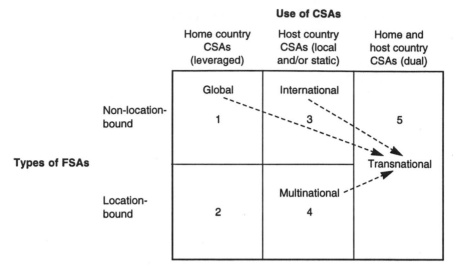

CSA   Country-specific advantage
FSA   Firm-specific advantage

Figure 2.2 *Sources of international competitive advantage – a*
transaction cost model (Rugman and Verbeke, 1992)

regulation force companies to develop location-bound firm-specific advantages. These location-bound firm-specific advantages will often complement the country-specific advantages of the countries involved, such as the local marketing infrastructure or protected government markets.

Global companies would obviously have non-location-bound firm-specific advantages that can be exploited on a global scale. Home country country-specific advantages are more important than host country country-specific advantages, because production operations are often concentrated in the home country.

The transnational company operates with a combination of location-bound and non-location-bound firm-specific advantages. Location-bound firm-specific advantages would be necessary in countries with a need for national responsiveness. Non-location-bound firm-specific advantages would permit global exploitation. With regard to country-specific advantages, the transnational company draws advantages from both home and host countries. And in contrast to the situation in international and multidomestic companies, host country country-specific advantages can also be used in a leveraged way. In Chapter 1 we referred to the fact that the transnational company would choose the country with the most favourable domestic diamond to locate its home base for each particular SBU. Porter's emphasis on innovation and the constant upgrading of competitive advantages is highly compatible with the leveraged use of country-specific advantages. In Chapter 4 we will see that transnationals can use another, even more sophisticated, form of using country and firm-specific advantages: globally linked innovation (p. 97).

7 Functional strategies

Strategy formulation is one thing; succeeding in implementing this strategy is a second and often far more difficult step. In the next chapter we will discuss organizational structure and control and coordination mechanisms. In this section we will go into the different functional strategies: human resource management, finance and accounting, marketing and production management. We will see that most of the activities can be characterized by the terms ethnocentric, polycentric or geocentric.

Human resource management

Perlmutter (1969) distinguished three states of mind or attitudes of international executives: ethnocentric (or home-country oriented), poly-centric (or host-country oriented) and geocentric (or world oriented). These attitudes should be regarded as ideal types. Every corporation will probably have *some* degree of ethnocentrism, polycentrism and geocen-trism, but usually one can distinguish a dominant state of mind. The ethnocentric attitude implies that management style, knowledge, evalu-ation criteria and managers from the home country are considered superior to those of the host country. A logical consequence is that only parent-country nationals are considered to be suitable for top management positions, both at headquarters and the subsidiaries. The polycentric attitude takes a completely different point of view. It explicitly recognizes differences between countries and believes that local nationals are in the best position to understand and deal with these country-specific factors. A local manager, however, will never be offered a position at headquarters, because parent-country nationals are considered more suitable for these positions. Geocentrism is world oriented. A geocentric company draws from a worldwide pool of managers. Managers can be appointed at headquarters or subsidiaries regardless of their nationality.

In later literature, Perlmutter's headquarters orientations became equated with strategies of international human resource management, which is not surprising if one looks at the subjects he discusses. Table 2.2 summarizes the implications of these three types of headquarters orien-tation.

Referring to our discussion in Section 6 these orientations also have a rather high level of generality. They do not guide an HRM practitioner in making specific choices about task design, training programmes, compen-sation packages etc. Until now there has only been a very limited amount of research done on the specific HRM strategies multinational corporations should follow in order to achieve their strategic goals. The fact that HRM has only very recently been acknowledged as a strategic issue might be a reason for this lack of research.

Table 2.2   *Three types of headquarters orientation toward subsidiaries in an international enterprise*

Organization design	Ethnocentric	Polycentric	Geocentric
Complexity of organization	Complex in home country, simple in subsidiaries	Varied and independent	Increasingly complex and interdependent
Authority; decision-making	High in headquarters	Relatively low in headquarters	Aim for a collaborative approach between headquarters and subsidiaries
Evaluation and control	Home standards applied for persons and performance	Determined locally	Find standards which are universal and local
Rewards and punishments; incentives	High in headquarters low in subsidiaries	Wide variation; can be high or low rewards for subsidiary performance	International and local executives rewarded for reaching local and worldwide objectives
Communication; information flow	High volume to subsidiaries (orders, commands, advice)	Little to and from headquarters; little between subsidiaries	Both ways and between subsidiaries; heads of subsidiaries part of management team
Identification	Nationality of owner	Nationality of host country	Truly international company but identifying with national interests
Perpetuation (recruiting, staffing, development)	Recruit and develop people of home country for key positions every-where in the world	Develop people of local nationality for key positions in their own country	Develop best men everywhere in the world for key positions everywhere in the world

Source: Perlmutter, 1969

Finance and accounting

International finance is often equated with the handling of foreign exchange rates, exchange controls and tax optimization. These activities are usually centralized at the treasurer's office at headquarters (ethnocentric approach), because only at this level is there a complete overview of all factors involved. However, activities such as financial planning and control can have ethnocentric, polycentric and geocentric solutions (Rugman, 1987). At the one extreme, the ethnocentric solution is to integrate all subsidiary operations completely into the planning and control system of the parent company. At the other extreme, in the polycentric solution financial management is essentially portfolio management. The performance of each subsidiary would be evaluated individually against the performance of comparable domestic or foreign companies. Decision-making on financial matters would be mostly decentralized. Only major new projects and financing subsidiaries would have to solicit permission from headquarters. The geocentric attitude promotes an 'it all depends' solution. Investment in developing countries is more likely to be centralized, because of the lack of local expertise and inadequately developed financial markets. In industrialized countries, the advantages of centralization are less evident, because the financial and economic systems of the various countries are already highly integrated. Furthermore, the quality of local management makes decentralization a more feasible option.

Closely associated with financial management are the numerous accounting problems that arise. Accounting practices are culture-bound, in that every country has its own accounting rules. Local accountants have to meet local requirements, so a polycentric solution would be most logical. Consolidated accounts, however, will have to conform to home country standards.

Marketing

In a strategic sense, the choice in marketing management is often between standardization and adaptation. Corporations that choose standardized marketing see customers the world over as essentially having the same needs and tastes (that is, the same as the home country). This is of course a rather ethnocentric view. However, for a fairly large number of products this approach can work very well. Think for instance of Coca-Cola, Levi jeans, raw materials or high-tech industrialized products. Corporations that choose adaptation see customers the world over as having different needs and tastes. They deliberately adapt their products to these differences. This is consistent with a polycentric view. In a geocentric view, products would be rather standardized but adapted to foreign markets by means of slight product changes, distribution and promotion. A corporation with a geocentric view would stress flexibility. Of course a choice in favour of standardization or adaptation (or a combination of both) is largely dependent on the product, the country and the customer group. All in all, however, the marketing function is often rather polycentric in attitude, since host-country knowledge of consumer tastes is important.

Production

Finally, in production management we can also distinguish ethnocentric, polycentric and geocentric solutions (Rugman, 1987). The ethnocentric solution would be *centralized sourcing*. Production takes place in one or a few plants that are tightly controlled centrally. The main function of the logistic manager would be to take care of exporting in the most cost- and time-efficient manner. The polycentric solution would be indigenous sourcing. Production takes place in each country the multinational is serving and each manufacturing facility produces only for the local market. Therefore, international logistics is often de-emphasized. The geocentric solution, finally, would be *distributed sourcing*. The same product could be manufactured in a number of countries, but some countries can also specialize in certain products depending on their distinctive advantages (high technology, low wages, see also our discussion in Chapter 1). Production can also be specialized into four different types of functions: low unit cost, seasonal, stockpile and flexible plants (Rugman, 1987). The low unit cost plant (located in low-wage countries) should always produce at full capacity. If the demand for a product is seasonal, but the variations can be forecast accurately, a seasonal plant could be the solution. Ideally such a plant should be located in an area with a stable seasonal workforce (for instance tourist resorts in the winter). A stockpile plant would produce buffers and should be located in countries that offer inventory tax deductions or subsidies for warehousing. Flexible plants, finally, are destined to shift production flexibly into new or existing products. The geocentric solution requires a separate logistics department which can coordinate all activities between the different input and output markets and manufacturing locations.

8   The strategic planning process integrated

Four configurations

In this section we will integrate what has been said so far about the environment, industry, the corporation's strategy and functional policies. We will also incorporate the organizational structures that will be dealt with extensively in the next chapter. It will probably not come as a surprise that corporations in a multidomestic industry should preferably follow a multidomestic strategy and have a multidomestic organizational structure (see next chapter). The same goes for international, global and transnational industries. We can capture these four configurations in the integration/responsiveness framework (see Prahalad and Doz (1987) for an extensive description) sketched below in Figure 2.3. The vertical axis represents the level of global integration, and hence of central coordination by headquarters; the horizontal axis represents the extent of national responsiveness or differentiation, and consequently of the desired influence of subsidiaries in strategic and operational decisions.

Although this framework is very convenient to summarize the different configurations, there are some additional points that should be stressed. First, a corporation can choose to follow a strategy and choose a structure that would not provide an optimal fit with the industry, but is more in accordance with its core competence, organizational capability and administrative heritage. If these internal resources point to a very different choice than the industry the corporation is competing in, the corporation would have three basic options. One, to find a small niche in this industry that fits its internal characteristics. Two, to try to modify the industry characteristics, which would often be very difficult, if not impossible. And three, to gradually move into other industries.

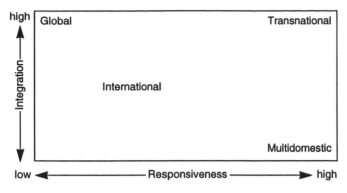

Figure 2.3   *The integration–responsiveness framework*

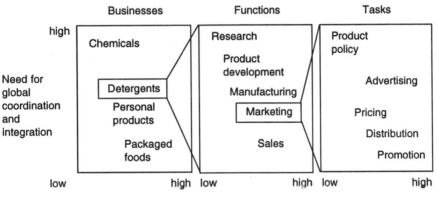

Figure 2.4   *Integration and differentiation needs at Unilever (Bartlett and Ghoshal, 1987b)*

Secondly, the place of the transnational in the upper right corner does not mean that it is always high on both integration and responsiveness. The transnational approach is to decide whether to stress integration or responsiveness for each particular situation. The accent can be different for each business, function, task or country. Figure 2.4 shows the varying needs for global integration and national responsiveness in Unilever's business strategies, functional strategies and tasks.

Thirdly, the aspect of worldwide learning and innovation, dominant for international companies and also important for transnational companies, is not adequately captured in this framework. This is not surprising, because the constructors of this framework did not distinguish international companies. It does make it difficult to position the international configuration in the framework. Some authors (Sundaram and Black, 1992) simply equate it with the transnational configuration, others (Ghoshal and

Nohria, 1993) place it in the lower left corner. As said above, an international strategy assumes *some* concern with both integration and responsiveness. We therefore suspect the actual position would be somewhere in between, leaning somewhat more to the lower left corner.

Integration of functional policies

So far, we have dealt with the international environment, industry, strategy and structure. But what about the functional policies? How do these fit in? Broadly speaking, we can say that ethnocentric policies would fit with global industries, strategies and structures, polycentric policies with multidomestic industries, strategies and structures, and geocentric policies with transnational industries, strategies and structures. But that is easy. How about the motivation? As the subject of this book is human resource management, we will try to give some evidence from the field.

To start with, Perlmutter (1969), in describing his management attitudes, mentions many characteristics that can easily be recognized in the multidomestic, global and transnational organizational models. The ethnocentric orientation stands for a complex organization at headquarters and a simple one in subsidiaries, and for a high one-way flow of orders, commands and advice from headquarters to subsidiaries, with the greatest authority at headquarters. This is consistent with the global concept of centralization of decision-making at headquarters and the treatment of subsidiaries as simple delivery pipelines. A polycentric corporation is defined by Perlmutter as 'a loosely connected group with quasi-independent subsidiaries as centres – more akin to a confederation'. There is little communication to and from headquarters and between subsidiaries with relatively low authority at headquarters. This is of course very consistent with the multidomestic organizational model with its decentralized federation structure and its decentralized decision-making. In a geocentric corporation, according to Perlmutter, 'the firm's subsidiaries are neither satellites nor independent city-states, but parts of a whole whose focus is on worldwide objectives as well as local objectives, each part making its unique contribution with its unique competence'. The organization is increasingly complex and interdependent. We have heard this before: in the description of the transnational organization model, with its complex interdependent network structure and its focus on both global and local demands. It is remarkable how well Perlmutter's headquarters orientations fit in with the organizational models sketched 20 years later by Bartlett and Ghoshal.

Research by Tung (1988) showed that Japanese corporations tend to use far more expatriates at all levels of the organization than American or European corporations, following an ethnocentric HRM policy. This is consistent with the fact that Japanese companies often have global strategies and structures which emphasize central control by headquarters. This can be most easily achieved by employing expatriates in subsidiaries, because they will propagate headquarters' attitudes.

Tung's research showed that European corporations do use fewer expatriates than Japanese corporations, which would be consistent with their dominant multidomestic strategy focusing on local demands. Local employees will be more likely to be familiar with these. However, in Latin America and the Far East the number of expatriates is very high (79 percent, 85 percent at senior management level). So it seems that in countries at a greater cultural distance, ethnocentric HRM policies are still in use.

Edström and Lorange (1984) found a fit between structure and the management of human resources. Global companies tended to use more expatriates (ethnocentric HRM policy) than country-based (multidomestic) companies. Then again, in one country-based company there were more expatriates as managing directors of subsidiaries than host-country nationals, and in another country-based company the difference was not that large. In management development and organization development all companies had a rather ethnocentric policy. HRM policies in multinationals still seem more likely to be ethnocentric than polycentric or geocentric, even if organizational strategy and structure would suggest otherwise.

International management research itself is also rather ethnocentric. International human resource management is often equated with expatriate management. There is a large and growing number of studies on the problems encountered in recruitment and selection, training, compensation, career development and repatriation of expatriates. However, studies that focus on host- and third-country nationals (HCNs and TCNs) do not abound. The dearth of studies on HCNs and TCNs is also reflected in this book. In Part 3, on managing an international staff, there is still a strong emphasis on expatriate management.

9 Summary and conclusions

In this chapter we have discussed the strategic planning process of multinational corporations. Its main conclusions are summarized below:

1   HRM and organizational structure should not be viewed in isolation. They depend on environment, industry and strategy and in turn influence the feasible strategy.
2   One can create configurations of industry characteristics, strategies, structures and functional strategies. Independent of environment and business strategies, however, some functional strategies will often be more centralized/integrated (e.g. finance) than others (e.g. marketing). Furthermore, internal resources also influence and constrain strategic choices.
3   Current environmental developments suggest that focusing on either efficiency/integration or differentiation/responsiveness will no longer be a very feasible choice. Multinational corporations will have to

comply with demands for efficiency and responsiveness simultaneously, while at the same time being internally flexible and innovative. Transnational companies will be best suited to comply with these demands.

4   In spite of environmental demands and even in spite of their formal strategy, most multinationals are still rather ethnocentric-oriented. Even international management researchers have a strong ethnocentric bias.

As both international organizational structures and international human resource management are of fundamental importance in multinational companies, we will discuss these subjects in more detail in the next two chapters.

3 Organizational structure of multinational corporations: theories and models

Jaap Paauwe and Philip Dewe

1	Introduction	51
2	Environmental factors and their implications for organizations	53
	Why are changes required?	53
	What sort of changes must be made?	53
	How will these changes be achieved?	54
3	Strategy–structure investigations: some findings	54
4	From strategy–structure to process: second-generation approaches	56
5	Beyond structural configurations: the transnational corporation	58
	From multidomestic, global and international to transnational	58
	Multidomestic organizational model	59
	International organizational model	59
	Global organizational model	60
	The transnational corporation: description of the ideal	61
6	Analyzing multinationals: the longitudinal structure/process framework	63
	Administrative heritage, history of internationalization and attitude of top management	65
	Administrative heritage	65
	History of internationalization	66
	Attitude of top management	66
	Process design criteria for second-generation models	67
	Design parameters for second-generation models	67
	Structural and formal coordination mechanisms	68
	Systems and tools	68
	Cultural transformation	68
	Performance	69
7	Management of the transition process from first- to second-generation models	70
	Structuring the organizational anatomy	71
	Building the organizational physiology	71
	Developing the organizational psychology	72
8	Summary and conclusions	73

1 Introduction

In his book *Managing for the Future*, Drucker, one of the most influential management gurus of the moment, argues that 'organizations will undergo more and more radical restructuring in the 1990s than at any time since the modern corporate organization first evolved in the 1920s' (1992: 16). Several questions come to mind when considering Drucker's statement. What sort of organizational structures will evolve and which environmental factors will influence these structures? And how will these new corporations be managed? Researchers and practitioners have, for some time, been trying to find answers to these questions and this chapter sets out to explore the different explanations that have emerged. Our main focus will be on multinational companies, although some developments might also be relevant for domestic companies.

Section 2 begins by identifying different environmental factors that have contributed to the 'turbulent times in the world of organizations' (Miles and Snow, 1986: 59). For (multinational) organizations, the increasingly turbulent environments call for different organizational structures. The nature and extent of those structural changes must, as Ghoshal and Nohria (1993) point out, match the organization's strategic aspirations, a concept referred to as 'structural fit'. In Section 3, then, we will look at the strategy–structure argument. This is the idea that multinational organizations typically adopt different structures at different stages of international expansion (Galbraith and Kazanjian, 1986) to achieve a fit between strategy and structure. We call this approach the first-generation model.

As strategies and structures become more complex, however, a basic problem begins to emerge. This problem can be summed up in the idea that as organizations sought structural fit they invariably only took into account what structure the organization should have and 'this single tool proved to be unequal to the task of capturing the complexity of the strategic task facing most organizations' (Bartlett and Ghoshal, 1992b: 516). Managers are now realizing that what is needed is strategic and structural flexibility. How does one achieve this? By focusing on managing people and processes. This is what we call a second-generation model[1] and such models are discussed in Sections 4 and 5 of this chapter.

But how does one get there? The critical strategic requirement, as Bartlett and Ghoshal point out, 'is not to devise the most ingenious and well-coordinated plan but to build the most viable and flexible strategic process; the key organizational task is not to design the most elegant structure but to capture individual capabilities and motivate the entire organization to respond cooperatively to a complicated and dynamic environment' (1990: 139–140). Thus the challenge lies in managing a process that is responsive to the strategic demands of the organization – a challenge

---

[1] Van Dijck (1991: 154ff.) uses a classification of three generations of models, in that he adds as a second generation those models that emphasize the values and qualities of top managers. Because of the importance of the values and attitudes of top management in every phase and every model we do not see a reason to classify the studies that emphasize these as a separate generation of models. We do recognize, however, the importance of the values and qualities of top managers as intervening variables in the process of designing the organization as a reaction to market developments and strategy, but this is also true of a domestic company.

somewhat different from the traditional approach of identifying and establishing the best structure. The variables in managing this process are manifold, as we will discover. In Section 6 of this chapter we will summarize these variables in a longitudinal structure–process framework for analyzing organizations, and describe the management of the transition process from first- to second-generation models. But first we will look at some factors that are at the root of the turbulent times in the world of organizations.

2   Environmental factors and their implications for organizations

A range of environmental factors can be identified that continually require organizations to (re)consider their structure, strategies and management. Many of these factors have come into play in the past decade, demanding almost instant change and signalling the need to better understand how organizations grow and develop. This new reality, almost a new order, has accelerated the search not only for new organizational forms but also for new creative management processes as to how such organizations should be run. This search can be summarized in three main questions:

- Why are changes required?
- What sort of changes must be made?
- How are these changes to be managed?

Why are changes required?

This question can be answered by looking at the environment organizations must operate in. The rate of technological change and the growth in knowledge-intensive products, product differentiation, more value on product design, more attention to fashion and a move away from mass production are just some of the demands faced by organizations. The internationalization of economies is another factor. Intense international economic competition brings with it the recognition that there are alternative ways of doing business, that management techniques can be changed and that markets will be increasingly transnational. Add to this the demands of free markets, changing industrial relations policies, increased consumer awareness and flexible manufacturing processes, and organizations must almost be mandated to redefine their strategies and reconfigure their structures (Bartlett and Ghoshal, 1987a; Drucker, 1992; Toffler, 1984). We referred to some of these developments in the previous chapter.

What sort of changes must be made?

Some general principles on restructuring organizations have been suggested by Van Dijck (1991). These include developing structures that are adaptive and flexible when responding to uncertainty and change; developing a culture of creativity and a strong performance orientation; restructuring and integrating functions such as marketing, research and development and production; and developing a strategic approach to human resource management. New ways of organizing will require a shift from inflexibilities of bureaucracies towards the dynamics of networks. Vertical hierarchies will give way to new forms of organizing such as matrix or transnational structures. The role of middle management will change as organizations reconsider the centralization of control versus the decentralization of operations. The way in which power, autonomy, accountability and responsibility are distributed throughout these new structures is another dimension that must also be added to the already long list of challenges facing organizational developers and structural analysts.

How will these changes be achieved?

New management approaches are continually being developed to facilitate change. These include, as Byrne (1992) suggests, becoming familiar with and using ideas such as 'learning organizations', 'business process re-engineering', 'sound organizational architecture', 'leveraging core competencies' and becoming a 'timebased competitor'. Each of these approaches and ideas represents a new language for management, a language that reflects the new organizational structures and how they should be managed. Managers will need to become facilitators; control-driven principles will give way to value-driven principles; organizational culture will assume a new importance and leadership will inspire by developing a supportive environment where individuals are empowered to achieve in a creative, open organization.

Further on in this chapter we will come back to these subjects in more detail. But first we will discuss first-generation models and how they explained the strategy–structure relationship.

3   Strategy–structure investigations: some findings

Most investigators would agree that the starting point when considering the strategy–structure relationship is the work of Chandler (1962). He distinguished four growth strategies: expansion of volume, geographic dispersion, vertical integration and product diversification. These strategies called for different administrative structures, hence his adage 'structure follows strategy'. Stopford and Wells (1972) were the first to investigate this relationship with regard to multinational companies. Their empirical investigation of 187 large US multinational companies identified two strategic variables as being strong predictors of organizational structure. These two strategic variables were product diversity and foreign sales.

Table 3.1 *Stopford and Wells: stages in internationalization*

Stage	Strategy	Structure
Early stage of internationalization	Low product diversity; low foreign sales	International division
Alternative path[1]	Increasing product diversity	Product division structure
Alternative path[1]	Increasing foreign sales	Area division structure
Final stage of internationalization	High product diversity; high foreign sales	Global or matrix structure

[1] Both of these are alternative paths of development that can eventually lead to a global or matrix structure.

Taking these two variables, Stopford and Wells were able to show stages in the internationalization of organizations. These findings are presented in Table 3.1.

Stopford and Wells' (1972) work has become the seminal research when discussing the link between strategy and structure for multinational organizations. However, the intervening years have raised a number of issues that need to be addressed when considering the Stopford and Wells model. These include whether other strategic variables influence structure, how best to classify multinationals, the strength of the relationships between structure and strategy and other alternative approaches. For example, Daniels, Pitts and Tretter (1984), building on the earlier work of Stopford and Wells, compared different organizational structures in terms of such variables as product diversity, dependency on foreign operations, strategic emphasis and ownership and control characteristics. Again, the results tended to support the idea that foreign sales and product diversity were the primary catalysts for structural changes in multinational organizations.

In a later study (Daniels et al., 1985), however, these authors found that although it was possible to identify different organizational structures, the relationships between these structures and strategic variables such as vertical integration, research and development intensity, level of foreign sales and method of diversifying was not so clear-cut. Finally, Egelhoff (1988) found that when the strategic variable 'relative size of foreign manufacturing' was introduced, a clearer distinction emerged between area division and product division structures. Multinationals with area division structures had higher levels of foreign manufacturing than multinationals with product division structures.

The studies mentioned above are not meant to represent a complete review of the field. Our aim is simply to provide examples of the type of empirical research that has been carried out since the Stopford and Wells work. Quite obviously the studies cited are only interested in strategy–structure linkages. Variables such as managerial values and attitudes and other process considerations have yet to be explored. These studies are in effect first-generation approaches. They provided valuable insights into the relationships between strategy and structure, but, as the authors themselves point out, this kind of research is not without its difficulties (see Daniels et al., 1984, 1985).

These difficulties, which are common to most empirical research, include getting a representative sample of organizations, a problem which is often compounded by a low response rate. A second problem is the fact that organizations are not always clearly identifiable as one type or another, yet for research purposes have to be classified into a particular category. Furthermore, there is the difficulty of determining whether the appropriate strategy variables are being included. The range of strategic variables that could potentially influence the structure of an organization is almost endless and this raises the question of whether important strategic concerns are being overlooked. Finally, there is the cross-sectional, not longitudinal, design of the studies. Perhaps the best way to study strategy–structure linkages is not by taking a survey reflecting one point in time but to follow an organization over a period of time to gauge structural changes. Nevertheless, these studies represent an important development in our understanding of strategy–structure relationships and an awareness of such difficulties provides us with the context critically to review such results and to seek new methodologies to advance our knowledge.

4   From strategy–structure to process: second-generation approaches

In the previous section, we referred to first-generation models. These studies focused on identifying and classifying organizational structures and then attempted to determine structural fit on the basis of strategic concerns. What has happened is that a second generation of models has been developed because the complexity and dynamic nature of environmental demands has made structural fit less relevant and harder to achieve (Bartlett and Ghoshal, 1992b). Coupled with this has been the growing realization that just focusing on one variable in the equation – organizational structure – may not be enough to implement complex strategic concerns successfully. Managers must now start thinking beyond first-generation ideas.

What has happened to bring about this change? At least three things seem to have influenced this shift away from seeing the principal task as identifying and initiating the ideal structure (Bartlett and Ghoshal, 1992b: 516). The first is the sheer complexity of the environment. Focusing on structure alone forces managerial thinking away from recognizing the multidimensional nature of the environment within which strategy has to be implemented. Secondly, merely thinking that structure is the only variable that needs considering infers that individual responsibilities and roles within the organization are basically static. In a dynamic environment this is just not so. The need is for organizations to adopt, develop and create new roles, responsibilities and reporting relationships that allow the dynamics of the environment and strategic concerns to be met creatively. Finally, simply making structural changes to meet strategic realignments often in practice failed to give the organization the flexibility needed to operate in such turbulent environments.

Second-generation models now stress organizational and strategic flexibility rather than structural fit. To build the most viable strategic process, second-generation models shift towards considering the management process that will make strategic decisions work. As Galbraith and Kazanjian (1986) point out, all structural forms are not equally effective in implementing a given strategy. The role of management must therefore be to create an internally consistent and balanced design. Having the right strategy is one thing, but, as Galbraith and Kazanjian argue, its successful implementation is a question of fit between the strategy and how the organization is managed. Second-generation models, then, are those that emphasize the management process as the intervening variable and the key to successful strategy implementation.

The 'soft side' of the organization

In this chapter we are concentrating on theories and developments related to multinational organizations. In general management literature, however, we also see a move away from the focus on structural variables and a tendency to bring 'the soft side of the organization' into the picture, combined with an emphasis on flexibility. Mintzberg, for instance, sees the adhocracy (one of his organizational configurations, the others being the simple structure, the divisionalized form, the machine bureaucracy and the professional bureaucracy) as the organization of the future (Mintzberg, 1983: 275). The adhocracy is a highly organic organization, flexible and decentralized to cope with dynamic and complex environments, with mutual adjustment as a rather informal coordination mechanism. Mintzberg himself states that diversified markets formerly led multinationals to use the divisionalized form, grouping their major divisions either by area or by product line. However, 'those multinational corporations with interdependencies among their different product lines, and facing increasing complexity as well as dynamism in their environment, will feel drawn toward the divisionalized adhocracy hybrid' (Mintzberg, 1983: 269). More than 30 years ago Burns and Stalker already identified the organic organization – with characteristics such as continual adjustment, lateral communication and commitment – as opposed to the mechanic organization. And finally, in Peters and Waterman's best-seller *In Search of Excellence* (1982) the 'soft' aspects of organizing – skills, shared values, style (of management) and staff – are at least as important as the formal aspects of structure, strategy and systems.

If second-generation models require us to take other variables into account, particularly the management process, then we need different ways to conceptualize organizations and their ability to implement strategy. An example of what represents second-generation thinking is Bartlett and Ghoshal's (1992b) description of the organization in terms of a physiological model. The idea behind this analogy is to emphasize the point that while structure is critical in defining the organization's *anatomy*, its role is not to be seen as dominant or the only variable to be taken into account. To be effective, Bartlett and Ghoshal argue, structural change must be accompanied by change and adaptation in two other parts of the organization. These include the organization's *physiology* (procedures, systems and decision processes) and the organization's *psychology* (culture and management values). Recognizing that change is required across all three aspects of the organization (anatomy, physiology and psychology) should provide not just structural fit but organizational flexibility and thus the tools for operating in a complex environment. In Section 6 we will come back to this typology when we discuss the transformation process from first-generation to second-generation models.

In the next part of this chapter we will focus on the topic 'beyond structural configurations' by emphasizing the shift from 'structure' to 'process'. We will develop a longitudinal structure–process framework. This framework will not only help us to summarize the essence of this chapter, but can also help to analyze the development of multinational companies. First, however, we will discuss the shift from first- to second-generation models in more detail.

5   Beyond structural configurations: the transnational corporation

From multidomestic, global and international to transnational

The preceding sections were intended to give a broad overview of the shift from first-generation to second-generation models. In this section we discuss this shift in a little more detail and associate it with different organizational structures. This discussion is based on the ideas of Bartlett and Ghoshal (1989). The key idea that we are trying to get across is that whereas first-generation models could concentrate on being either nationally responsive, innovative, or efficient, second-generation models, because they operate in more dynamic environments, have to be conscious of and develop structures and strategies that embrace all three. So multidomestic, international and global organizations reflect first-generation models, and transnational organizations, second-generation models.

According to Bartlett and Ghoshal (1989), the increasing degree of complexity forces companies that operate internationally to meet three

Table 3.2 *Outline of different strategic demands and their corresponding dominant organizational structure*

Main strategic demand	Dominant structure
National responsiveness	Multidomestic organizational model
Worldwide innovation (transfer of knowledge)	International organizational model
Global efficiency	Global organizational model

requirements simultaneously: responsiveness, learning and efficiency. In the past it was enough, given the characteristics of the relevant product–market combinations, to excel in only one of these areas, leading to the categories given in Table 3.2: The main characteristics of these models are discussed below (based on Bartlett and Ghoshal, 1989).

Multidomestic organizational model

Companies that expanded between the world wars often adopted the multidomestic organizational model. Responsiveness to differences between national markets made these companies decentralize both their assets and decision-making. The result was a configuration that can be described as a *decentralized federation*, and which is organized by area. This kind of structure – which is comparable to the area division structure of Stopford and Wells – was particularly compatible with the management norms of the mainly European companies that sought international presence in that particular era. Family ownership had been the dominant tradition and therefore organizational processes were built on personal relationships and informal contacts rather than formal structures and systems. Operational decisions were simply delegated to trusted parent company nationals who were assigned abroad. The main approach to controlling and coordinating foreign subsidiaries was a rather informal one: direct personal contact between headquarters and subsidiary managers. Some simple financial control systems often supplemented this informal coordination.

International organizational model

The early postwar decades saw the birth of a new dominant organizational model: the international organization. Transferring knowledge and expertise to countries that were less advanced either in technology or market development was the key task for these organizations. The United States were the masters in this game. Local subsidiaries still had some freedom to adopt new products or strategies, but coordination and control by headquarters became more important. Subsidiaries were dependent on the parent company for new products, processes or ideas. A *coordinated federation*, often structured according to function, is the name given to the structural configuration of this organizational model. As stated above, US-based companies were dominant in this period. The managerial culture of these companies provided a good fit with this structure. This culture was based on professional management, which implied a certain willingness to delegate responsibility. At the same time, however, these companies used sophisticated management systems and specialist corporate staffs to retain overall control.

Global organizational model

The global organization is in fact the earliest international organization model, used by pioneers in internationalization such as Henry Ford and John D. Rockefeller. Home-based global-scale facilities produced standard products that were exported world wide. Strategy was tightly and centrally controlled. The model re-emerged in Japanese companies and was the basis of their worldwide competition in the 1970s and early 1980s. In a global configuration, assets, resources and responsibilities are centralized. The role of subsidiaries is often limited to sales and service and their freedom of action is very limited compared with their counterparts in multidomestic or international organizations. The structural configuration of this organization is called a *centralized hub* – comparable to Stopford and Wells' product-division structure. This configuration was particularly compatible with the managerial norms and processes in Japanese companies. Centralized decision-making and control allowed these companies to retain their complex management system requiring intensive communication and personal commitment.

The main characteristics of these three organizational models are summarized in Figure 3.1.

As we described earlier, the increasing degree of complexity means that this one-dimensional approach is no longer enough. Companies that operate internationally are increasingly required to meet all of the following demands:

- global efficiency (utilizing economies of scale);
- local responsiveness;
- learning or transfer of knowledge across different boundaries (including cultural ones).

Organizations which are able to meet these multiple demands simultaneously are known as 'transnational organizations' (Bartlett and Ghoshal, 1987a,b).

What is a transnational organization? Does it imply a particular organizational structure (for example, a refined version of the matrix structure noted by Stopford and Wells)? The answer is no. The transnational organization cannot be described in terms of structure alone; instead, concepts such as 'process', 'capabilities' and 'systems' must be applied as well. This also means that we cannot view it as a subsequent

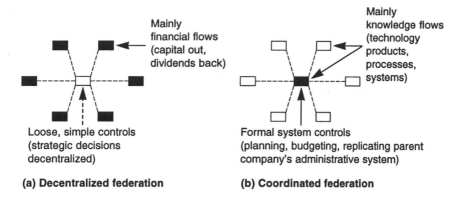

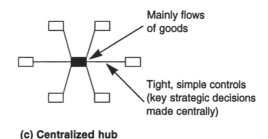

(c) Centralized hub

Figure 3.1 *Organizational configuration models (Bartlett and Ghoshal, 1992b)*

stage in Stopford and Wells' stages model, for example; rather, we must apply a framework that goes beyond structural configurations.

Before going on to discuss this new framework or paradigm, we will need a clearer description of the ideal transnational corporation.

The transnational corporation: description of the ideal

Bartlett used the term 'transnational' to describe companies which are required to meet the demands of both local responsiveness and global efficiency simultaneously. He then added a third characteristic, 'transfer of learning', in an article written in collaboration with Ghoshal (Bartlett and Ghoshal, 1987a). Hedlund (1986: 21ff.), who uses the term 'heterarchy' to describe the same sort of multinational organization, elaborates this concept by describing the most prominent features of the transnational organization.

1 *Many centres.* Competitive advantages are not inherent in one particular country, but can originate in many different countries simultaneously in the form of new products and ideas. Expertise is therefore spread throughout the entire network of the company, a network consisting of locations, relationships and countries. Each subsidiary or operating

company might therefore serve as a strategic centre for a particular area of attention (for example a certain product–market combination) and, at the same time, play a much smaller role as a production or distribution centre for the rest of the range. This and the following feature fit in well with Porter's approach, which emphasizes the importance of having different home bases for different SBUs. We pointed this out in Section 7 of Chapter 1.

2 *Subsidiary managers are also given a strategic role.* As a result of the previous feature, managers of subsidiaries can also play a strategic role, not only in their own operating companies, but also in the company as a whole.

3 *No overriding organizational dimension.* Companies organized in this fashion do not have an easily identifiable organizational structure, for example, organization by country or in divisions based on product groups. Depending on the relevant area of attention, the function or the product group, a structure will be chosen that makes the best use of any competitive advantage.

4 *Different degrees (high or low) of linkage between organizational units (flexibility in selecting different governing modes).* Depending on the circumstances, the various sections of the company will be governed either very strictly or very loosely. The degree of freedom that each organizational section is allowed in forging alliances with other sections or with third parties for contracting, etc., will also fluctuate in time and between different locations and topics. The task is to find the institutional arrangements that appear to offer the best results, given a particular goal. That is why there can be no single, dominant preference.

5 *Integration is achieved through normative control (culture).* Considering the great variety of markets, activities, products, countries and organizational forms (with widely varying degrees (strict–loose) of bureaucratic control), integration must primarily be achieved through the corporate culture and management style.

6 *Information about the whole is contained in each part.* Although it cannot be assumed that every organizational unit will be aware of every single interface with the organization as a whole, there is a great deal of emphasis on disseminating information throughout the company, sharing common goals and viewing short-term or local interests within the context of the entire company, now and in the future.

7 *Thinking is present in the whole organization.* Whereas one-dimensional organizations tend to separate 'thinking' and 'doing' (think of the 'corporate planning' department), the transnational organization brings these two activities together at every possible level, including the periphery of the organization.

8 *Coalitions with other companies and other actors.* In order to make optimal use of every opportunity to exploit synergetic effects and competitive advantages on a global scale, the transnational company forges multiple relationships with other companies and actors (including governments). These relationships take a wide range of different forms, leading to

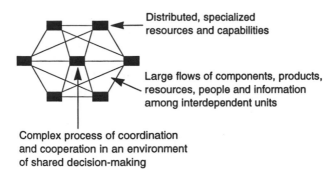

Figure 3.2   *Integrated network model (Bartlett and Ghoshal, 1992b)*

a multitude of governance forms and different degrees of internalization (Hedlund, 1986: 26).

9   *Radical problem-orientation.* Frequently, the existing competitive advantages will not serve as the governing strategic principle. Instead, there will be an ambitious concentration on problem-solving, in which context the company's global presence is seen as an important opportunity in that it provides an extensive network of available resources, people, systems etc.

In conclusion, the transnational is an organization with a network structure, which continuously makes selective choices when it comes to structuring the company. Figure 3.2 reviews the most important characteristics of the transnational organization.

6   Analyzing multinationals: the longitudinal structure/process framework

The description given above of the typical transnational organization (or the heterarchical MNC, as Hedlund calls it) illustrates that we are no longer discussing unambiguous structural characteristics. It is therefore no longer possible to see this organizational form as a subsequent stage within the Stopford and Wells model. Rather, it creates an entirely new frame of reference emphasizing concepts such as multidimensionality and heterogeneity (Doz and Prahalad, 1991: 146).

In this context, *multidimensionality* refers to the fact that companies that operate globally have multiple markets, multiple product lines and multiple functions. Such companies are therefore faced with the task of structuring and managing the entire range of interfaces between these multiple organizational dimensions (Doz and Prahalad, 1991: 146).

Heterogeneity 'results from the differences between the optimal trade-offs for different businesses, countries, functions and tasks as a function of a whole range of economic and political characteristics which differ between countries and affect individual businesses and tasks in quite varied ways' (Doz and Prahalad, 1991: 146) (see, for example, Figure 2.4 describing the varying needs for global integration and national responsiveness in Unilever's business strategies, functional strategies and tasks).

Time and again, decisions must be made as to the structural features when it comes to managing businesses/products, countries/areas and functions. Interpreting such situations in terms of structure alone is no longer enough, however. In fact, it is the processes, systems and capabilities which matter most when managing complex flows of goods, products, financial, technical and human resources and critical flows of information and knowledge.

Is it possible systematically to describe the pertinent variables related to structuring the transnational organization? Bartlett and Ghoshal themselves (1987b) provide an initial description, in which they link the need to meet the multiple demands of efficiency, local responsiveness and learning to three forms of management:

1 *Geographic management.* Geographic management is necessary in order to develop responsiveness. This form developed originally in the multidomestic organization and led to the important position of area divisions and the area managers who supervise them.
2 *Business management.* Business management has to achieve global efficiency and integration. It developed initially in the global organization, where the worldwide business of product managers assumes an important role.
3 *Functional management.* With genuine functional management an organization tries to realize organizational learning and the transfer of core competencies and capabilities. Originally it was a key factor in the international organization, in which functional managers (may) play a prominent role in developing, tracing and spreading knowledge and innovations.

We will discuss these three management forms (based on Bartlett and Ghoshal, 1992b, Chapter 7) and the relevant skills required in the following chapter within the framework of the importance of management development. In and of themselves, however, these categories do not make it possible for us to develop systematic insights into the variables which are important in structuring companies that operate on a global scale and in tracing development over time (longitudinal analysis). The framework given below does, and fits in well with the arguments which have been given thus far in this chapter. It also reflects a significant point about second-generation models: that it is the management process which is all important. Managing the process and recognizing the important variables in that process is what distinguishes second-generation from first-generation models.

In the following sections we will discuss each of the elements in this model in greater detail (see, however, Sections 3 and 5 above for first-generation models). First-generation models are characterized by an unambiguous fit between strategic demands and structural features. Examples are the stages model by Stopford and Wells, discussed previously, and follow-up studies based on this model.

Administrative heritage, history of internationalization and attitude of top management

Because the level of complexity is increasing, unambiguous strategic demands and organizational models based on such demands are no longer enough. This marks the transition to second-generation models, in which, in addition to structural features, process dimensions are highly decisive for the design and structure of the organization. The transition from first generation to second generation depends on three interrelated characteristics of the organization (based on Bartlett and Ghoshal, 1987a,b, 1989; Perlmutter, 1969):

- administrative heritage;
- history of internationalization;
- attitude of top management.

We have taken special care to include administrative heritage in Figure 3.3 because it is in fact the end result of the history of internationalization up till now. In addition to the circumstances and contingencies of the environment/market, the attitude of top management has also been highly influential in the way the organization has developed. Both in fact shape the administrative heritage of the organization.

Administrative heritage

According to Bartlett and Ghoshal (1987a: 14; 1989: 41), the essence of the administrative heritage of a company evolves from the following historically determined elements:

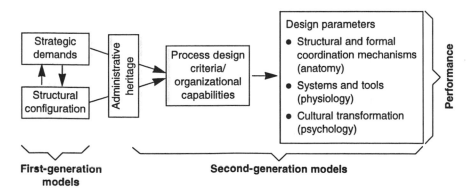

First-generation models

Second-generation models

Figure 3.3 *The longitudinal structure/process framework*

- configurations of both tangible and intangible assets and capabilities that have been built up over decades;
- existing patterns of managerial responsibilities and influence;
- dominant management styles;
- ingrained managerial values.

Administrative heritage is a key concept in understanding and becoming aware of a company's one-dimensional bias, which was created/formed (and very often has proved to be successful) in the past.

History of internationalization

Organizations go through a learning process as they move towards becoming international. This process might be very gradual or it might take place in stages, or development might be by leaps and bounds (see Hedlund, 1986: 15).

In the history of organizational internationalization it is also important to recognize two other factors: the period when international expansion took place, and the regions it took place in. For example, between the two world wars Europe saw the introduction of protectionist measures which forced a number of European companies to start up production in different countries. In contrast, in the 1970s all types of trade barriers were lifted, creating opportunities for large-scale production units which would be able to supply the world market in the most efficient way possible. Japanese companies in particular are a good example of this (for a more extended overview, see Chapter 2, Section 4).

Attitude of top management

Perlmutter (1969) distinguishes three different ways in which top management approach doing business around the world. Their orientation or attitude towards 'foreign people, ideas and resources, in headquarters and subsidiaries, and in host and home environments' (1969: 11) is one of the determining factors in shaping a company's administrative heritage. According to Perlmutter we can distinguish three different states of mind:

- ethnocentric: home-country oriented;
- polycentric: host-country oriented;
- geocentric: world oriented.

We referred to these three attitudes in Chapter 2, when discussing functional strategies. In Chapter 4, we will return to the subject of the influence of top management's attitudes, especially with regard to HRM policies.

On the one hand, administrative heritage is a barrier to the process of transformation into a transnational. At the same time, proper understanding of the administrative heritage of a company may be the key to initiating this transformation process (Bartlett and Ghoshal, 1987a: 16). We will discuss this further later in this section. That is why this concept has been given a prominent place in our framework when it comes to the transition from first-generation to second-generation models.

Process design criteria for second-generation models

Second-generation models place a great deal of emphasis on the importance of dealing effectively with:

- an increasing level of complexity;
- extensive, often ambiguous flows of information;
- a high level of uncertainty and the risks arising from this.

The above-mentioned characteristics imply a great deal of ambiguity in the process of both strategic and operational decision-making, which has to be organized in an effective manner. Design criteria for second-generation models therefore focus on emphasizing process dimensions in addition to strategy and structure. The point is to create organizations which will possess the following organizational capabilities:

- able to create interdependent networks;
- able to facilitate linkages between these networks;
- able to manage critical flows of information, knowledge, skills, goods and resources (financial, technical and human) on a global scale;
- able continuously to improve efficiency, effectiveness, quality and flexibility;
- able to develop and nurture a climate conducive to learning and innovation.

For a more detailed description, the reader is asked to review the description of the ideal transnational organization given above.[2]

Design parameters for second-generation models

Now that we have summarized the requirements within our framework, we can proceed to the next step: how can one design an organization such as this? We should begin by making the point that it is of course not the case that every company active at the international level must match the description we have given of the transnational. Ghoshal and Nohria (1989, 1993) correctly point out that the degree of complexity of the organizational structure must match the degree of complexity of the environment. After all, developing and maintaining a complex organizational structure is

[2] Interesting in this respect is the almost identical description of Doz and Prahalad (1991: 147), who develop a new paradigm for scientific research on DMNCs (diversified multinational corporations). On the basis of a characterization of the transnational in terms of multidimensionality and heterogeneity they arrive at the following seven characteristics or requirements: structural indeterminacy, internal differentiation, integrative optimization, information intensity, latent linkages, networked organization and fuzzy boundaries, learning and continuity.

an expensive affair and its necessity must be borne out by the complexity of the environment. In short, there should be a 'fit', and a simpler structure should be applied whenever this is adequate (for example, because competition is less fierce and the relevant technology is less dynamic).

To help us design a second-generation model, as well as to analyse the design process within existing DMNCs (diversified multinational corporations), we can make use of a large number of design parameters. We will discuss the following ones:

- structural and formal coordination mechanisms;
- systems and tools (administrative mechanisms);
- cultural transformation (socialization/normative integration).

Structural and formal coordination mechanisms

Examples are the design parameters familiar to us from the Aston studies (Pugh et al., 1968): centralization, formalization and specialization. *Centralization* (or decentralization) refers to whether the locus of decision-making authority lies at the upper or lower levels of the chain of command. *Formalization* (sometimes also called standardization) is the extent to which policies, rules, job descriptions etc. are written down in manuals and other documents, and procedures are established through standard routines. Finally, the degree of *specialization* indicates the number of specific tasks that are carried out through separate and distinct functions.

Systems and tools

Given the complexity of the hybrid network structures and the great variety of products, countries and markets, the coordination mechanisms mentioned above will need to be supported and supplemented by various systems and tools.

Doz and Prahalad (1981: 16; see also Doz, 1986: 222) highlight the following three categories of administrative mechanisms, which can be used by top management to deal with the complexity, multidimensionality and heterogeneity inherent in the transnational (or multifocal as they call it) organization.

- Data management mechanisms: information systems, measurement systems, resource allocation procedures, strategic planning, budgeting processes.
- Managers' management systems: choice of key managers, career paths, reward and punishment systems, compensation schemes, management development, patterns of socialization.
- Conflict resolution mechanisms: decision responsibility assignments, integrators, business teams, coordination committees, task forces, issue resolution processes.

Cultural transformation

Apart from these administrative systems and tools, the evolution from first-order to second-generation ways of organizing cannot succeed without the use of mechanisms for cultural change and transformation. Bartlett and Ghoshal refer to the necessity of creating a matrix in the mindset of managers in order to deal with all the diversity and complexity involved in managing a transnational organization effectively.

The question, naturally, is how to achieve this. The socialization of managers in key positions (at headquarters and subsidiaries) is crucial. It is important to ensure that values are internalized to such an extent that managers will come to make strategic choices and operational decisions that are in line with the mission and strategic goals of the company as a whole and with the relevant underlying points of departure and values. In this context we might mention the following possibilities:

- job rotation, regular transfer of people, management development;
- building up an informal network through management development programmes;
- international conferences and forums to facilitate international and inter-unit transfer of knowledge and learning;
- task forces;
- encouraging informal communication channels.

Performance

The final component of our model is the performance of the organization. Some indicators of performance are:

- financial-economic ratios and indicators such as cash flow, liquidity, solvability and return on investment and/or equity, revenue growth etc.;
- personnel indicators such as turnover, job satisfaction, absenteeism, etc.;
- other qualitative considerations such as those utilized by stock market analysts, investment experts, quality auditors etc. to supplement the above-mentioned quantitative criteria.

Ghoshal and Nohria (1989, 1993) conducted empirical research into the different forms of differentiation and integration (not to be confused with the terms discussed in Chapter 2, global integration and local responsiveness, used by Prahalad and Doz) of companies which operate internationally as compared with the performance of these companies. They focused on the relationship between headquarters and subsidiaries, using the contingency approach, in which the effectiveness of a company is determined by the 'fit' between the demands of the environment (including the market) and the organizational structure of the company. After collecting extensive data from 41 international companies and carrying out statistical analyses, they formulated the principle of requisite complexity: the complexity of a corporation's structure must match the complexity of its environment.

The degree of complexity of a corporation's structure can be charted using the following dimensions:

- centralization;
- formalization;
- normative integration or socialization.

We see that a number of the design parameters mentioned previously appear in this list. The complexity of the environment is related to the familiar dichotomy between global integration and local responsiveness (see Section 8 of Chapter 2) and leads to the categories of environment distinguished in the previous chapter: multidomestic, international, global and transnational.

Ghoshal and Nohria distinguish four patterns of differentiation and integration: structural uniformity, differentiated fit, integrated variety and ad hoc variation. Each has a different combination of the dimensions given above and each is best suited to a particular environment. It would be beyond the scope of this chapter to report all of the findings of the study. It is important in this context, however, to demonstrate that MNCs which have adapted their structure to their environment perform better than MNCs which have not done so.

In reality, Ghoshal and Nohria harken back to the environment–strategy–structure paradigm as introduced in Chapter 2, the strategy–structure link of which was discussed earlier in this chapter. By including elements of the management process approach, however – in the form of the integration/responsiveness framework (see Section 8 of Chapter 2), the transnational environment (see Section 4 of Chapter 2) and the importance of normative integration or socialization (see Section 5 of this chapter) – their study forms a bridge between both 'schools of research'. The remark made previously, that not every company should attempt to become a transnational, adds a critical note to the somewhat one-sided management-process approach.

In summary, the longitudinal structure/process framework described above not only shows that researchers have evolved in their way of thinking about the development of international companies, but also provides a platform for analyzing the specific development which an actual company undergoes within the internationalization process, with structure and process features being the primary concern. In the next section we will take a look at the management of the transition process from first- to second-generation models.

7   Management of the transition process from first- to second-generation models

There is no simple recipe available telling us how to manage the transition from first- to second-generation models of organizing internationally operating companies. A great deal depends on the specific organization and its structure, cultural characteristics, history, geographic background and the nature of the activities which it has developed in different markets. A general approach to the transition process from one-dimensional organizational forms to more complex multidimensional forms carries the risk of oversimplification. However, keeping this warning in mind we can use the analogy applied by Bartlett and Ghoshal (1992b: 525–531), which resembles or represents the same division of design parameters used in Section 6 above for the design and analysis of second-generation models (see pp. 67–69). They apply the metaphor of the human body in order to acquire a better insight into the meaning and interrelationships of the different design parameters involved. Based on this metaphor they make the following distinctions:

- *Organizational anatomy*: formal hierarchical structure and supporting or surrounding structure.
- *Organizational physiology*: both formal and informal systems for handling and processing flows of information.
- *Organizational psychology*: a set of explicit or implicit corporate values and shared beliefs.

(See also Figure 3.3, the longitudinal structure/process framework, where this distinction has already been made.)

Structuring the organizational anatomy

In view of the complexity of second-generation forms of organization such as the transnational, the concern here is not only to make the structure of the line organization manifest, but also to develop a surrounding structure which will ensure that all those involved – even those who do not have line responsibilities – can participate and influence the complex decision-making process.

Whereas task forces and special committees in first-order models are frequently ad hoc or temporary solutions, in 'transnational' structures they are a vital element. In the words of Bartlett and Ghoshal: 'If the formal structure is the organization's backbone, then the non-line structure is its ribcage, and these microstructural tools are the muscle and the cartilage that give the organizational skeleton its flexibility' (1992b: 527).

Building the organizational physiology

In second-generation models there is a high level of task complexity and a high degree of uncertainty. That is why decision-making requires the collection, exchange and processing of a great deal of information, information which is often contradictory or ambiguous. Formal structures alone are not enough to deal with the information-processing needs of 'transnational' structures. They need to be supplemented by numerous informal information channels and relationships and by a variety of systems and tools for data processing, analyzing and decision-making. Such systems and tools cover the whole range from formal and prescribed (planning, budgeting) to the more informal and subtle mechanisms (personal contacts during conferences and meetings).

Developing the organizational psychology

Shared values are especially important for a company that operates in different countries. After all, however sophisticated the different organizational structures, systems and tools may be, coordination will be much easier if everyone shares the same values and norms to some extent. Since the employees will often come from different countries, there will be a high level of cultural diversity, at least in terms of the influence of the national culture. A close-knit company culture will provide a good counterbalance. How can we achieve this? Bartlett and Ghoshal indicate the importance of the following three elements:

1   Formulate and disseminate the mission and strategic goals of the company in unmistakable terms, ensuring that these are known and recognized by all.
2   Exploit (in the positive sense) visible and public gestures by top management; exemplary behaviour by the top should serve as a symbol emphasizing the importance of the chosen mission and objectives.
3   Use personnel policies, practices and systems to select, educate and develop people who fit in with the relevant company; examples are: company-specific assessment centres, job rotation and management development.

In contrast with the sequence given above, and in contradiction to the way transformation processes are traditionally viewed (in particular in the United States), Bartlett and Ghoshal (1992b) refer to the European and Japanese approach towards facilitating far-reaching transformation processes. In this approach, a change in attitude and mentality is the first task; only when this has been achieved is the structure changed, or rather adapted to the new insights and relationships (see Figure 3.4).

This approach is usually cited as typical for Japanese companies. Structural organizational change is achieved only after lengthy discussions that give organizational members the chance to adjust their attitudes and

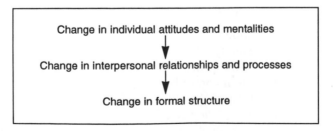

Figure 3.4   *The emerging change process (Bartlett and Ghoshal, 1992b: 531)*

opinions gradually. The actual structural change is less traumatic and therefore probably less problematic. However, in times of crisis a radical change in structure might serve as a rapid shock therapy, as individual change takes a long time to accomplish.

Of course the actual change process will never be as linear and simple as sketched above. The design parameters do not operate in isolation; all change processes involve substantial interaction between changes in anatomy, physiology and psychology. However, irrespective of their interrelatedness, the important fact to remember is this: any transition must take all three design aspects into account. Each is part of a whole and all three are necessary in developing flexibility and the competencies for operating in a complex environment.

8   Summary and conclusions

In this chapter we have discussed the different structures organizations adopt at different stages of international expansion to achieve a fit between strategy and structure. The main conclusions are summarized below.

First, organizations nowadays have to operate in dynamic, somewhat turbulent environments. These environments have made organizations face the fact that the strategies–structures that they adopted in the past may no longer be appropriate for the future. Not only are new organizational forms required, new creative management processes will also be needed to manage such structures. This raises the question of whether the theories and models we use to explain the strategy–structure links are adequate.

Secondly, theories and models about strategies–structures must now move from first-generation thinking to second-generation thinking. First-generation thinking focused simply on the relationship between strategy and structure. It identified and classified organizational structure and then attempted to determine structural fit on the basis of strategic concerns. Second-generation models now stress organizational and strategic flexibility rather than structural fit. To build the most viable strategic process, second-generation models are more concerned with the management process that will make strategic decisions work.

Thirdly, we question what are the variables that need to be considered when designing organizations to operate in a dynamic environment? The longitudinal structure–process framework presented identified some of the important ones and the transitional nature of the process. These include understanding the organization's administrative heritage, recognizing the design criteria necessary for creating structural flexibility and identifying the design tools needed to begin the transitional process. Finally, some performance analysis is needed to determine the success of the transition.

The aim of this chapter has been to provide an overview of the shift from first-generation to second-generation models. The different approaches, whether first- or second-generation, are in themselves examples of evolutionary thought and theory. Each in its way contributes to our understanding of organizational growth and development. Just as organizational structures evolve over time and in response to environmental demands, so too do our theories. This chapter illustrates the transition in thinking when we try to understand and explain strategy–structure relationships.

In the following chapter, on human resource management in multinational corporations, we will discuss in greater detail how HRM concepts and models have contributed to creating the necessary conditions for international companies and organizations.

4 Human resource management in multinational corporations: theories and models

Jaap Paauwe and Philip Dewe

1	Introduction	75
2	From personnel management to human resource management: domestic and international developments	77
3	An overview of HRM activities from an international perspective	79
	Staffing	80
	Training and development	81
	Assessment and compensation	82
4	Models for linking organizational configurations to HRM activity patterns	83
	Introduction	83
	Perlmutter's top management attitudes towards internationalization	84
	Adler and Ghadar's phases of internationalization	85
	The influence of culture	85
	Phases and areas of focus in HRM	86
	The two logics of Evans and Lorange	89
	Product–market logic	89
	Social–cultural logic	89
5	From universal to specific: a framework to account for the differences	90
	The two dimensions of HRM in both a domestic and an international context	91
	Increasing complexity	92
	Management attitudes, strategic choice and room for manoeuvre	93
	Organizational configurations	93
	Product/market/technology dimension	93
	Social/cultural/legal dimension	94
	International HRM and outcomes	94
6	The main challenge: developing capable transnational managers	95
	Global business management	96
	Worldwide functional management	96
	Geographic subsidiary management	97
	Top-level corporate management	97
7	Summary and conclusions	98

1 Introduction

In the previous chapter we looked at the different approaches that have been taken when attempting to explain the relationship between organizational strategy and structure. We identified a number of different approaches and concluded, after building on the works of others, that a distinction can be made between first- and second-generation models. First-generation models were those that distinguished between organizational structures primarily on the basis of strategic concerns. Second-generation models, while accepting the link between strategy and structure, are more concerned with the process of management. Rather than simply designing structures, second-generation models are more concerned with what Bartlett and Ghoshal describe as 'capturing individual capabilities and motivating the entire organization to respond to the demands of the environment' (1990: 140). Thus second-generation models are those that emphasize 'managing' as the intervening variable and the key to successful strategy implementation.

What this means, according to Bartlett and Ghoshal, is that many organizations are now structurally incapable of carrying out the sophisticated strategies they have developed. Why? Because they have overlooked that people are the key to managing complex strategies and organizations. The formal structures that have been devised to implement strategic objectives only go as far as establishing the organization's framework. The trap, as Bartlett and Ghoshal describe it, is that companies believed that by changing their structure they automatically changed the 'shared norms, values and beliefs that shape the way individual managers think and act' (1990: 140). Thus the focus and challenge facing organizations lie not in developing or thinking in strategy–structure terms alone but in developing an organizational culture that emphasizes corporate beliefs and values, that reshapes individual perceptions and attitudes and in this way changes the energy and synergy to carry through organizational strategies.

It seems that, no matter which book you pick up on organizational change and development, the authors place great emphasis on the fact that organizations, if they are to grow, develop and prosper, must develop a creative, consultative culture in which individuals can contribute to the organization. Naisbitt and Aburdene (1985), for example, argue that human capital rather than dollar capital will be the strategic resource of the future. Chalofsky and Reinhart (1988) develop a similar theme in their book and suggest that if managers are the key to implementing corporate strategies, their role must change from simply directing to facilitating, coaching and counselling. Organizations of the future must, according to Savage (1990), build into their very structure the capacity for individual learning and development.

What does all this mean? It means that management of human resources will become crucial. The emphasis on human resources is especially crucial for multinational organizations. Prasad and Shetty (1976) state that while multinational organizations may have considerable resources in terms of production and technology, these will be under-utilized if they lack the human resources to realize their potential. This chapter will therefore outline some of the issues associated with the management of human resources in multinational organizations. Section 2 begins by exploring the factors underlying the shift from personnel to human resource management. We will also argue that multinational organizations are even more prone to these factors than domestic organizations. From here we develop a profile of human resource practices and their role in multinational organizations. In Section 3 we discuss staffing, training and development and assessment and compensation. In Section 4 we present a number of models that try to link organizational configurations to specific HRM activities and policies. Subsequently, Section 5 provides a framework that incorporates the relevant variables for analyzing different HRM activities and policies. Finally, in Section 6, we will discuss the different types of managers that are needed in a transnational company and will outline their roles and responsibilities.

2   From personnel management to human resource management: domestic and international developments

Human resource management is more a philosophy than a specific management practice. For that reason it is difficult to give a precise definition of HRM. A better way to grasp the meaning of this concept is to look back at certain developments which took place at the end of the 1970s. These developments were mainly of an economic and technological nature. With respect to economic developments, there were three important trends: first, during this period there was a major shift in the international division of labour. Newly industrialized nations and blocs entered the international market and successfully contested the position held by traditional industrial sectors in America and Europe, forcing them to lower their prices and search for new ways to survive international competition. In addition to cost price, quality, flexibility and innovation became important competitive criteria. It is precisely these criteria which are largely determined by the quality and utilization of human resources.

Secondly, at the same time another shift took place with respect to the relative sizes of the various sectors. The service sector started to claim a growing share of the GNP in terms of value added. This shift between sectors also meant an increase in the need for intelligent (knowledge-based) labour and, given the nature of this type of work, also required a different management approach. Finally, the demand from the market changed as consumers wielded their purchasing power to insist on more tailor-made products. Companies responded to this demand by shifting their attention from products and production to the market.

A second source of change which is often associated with the transition to HRM was in the area of technology. The end of the 1970s and the start of the 1980s witnessed major advances in new technologies. This technical revolution had a tremendous impact on the nature and content of many tasks and therefore on traditional personnel and organization issues.

Because it became possible to integrate various production processes to a much higher degree and assign responsibility for production at much lower organizational levels, the importance of the human contribution increased. As early as the 1950s, Touraine (1955) identified the computerization paradox: a great deal of work is being computerized, but the remaining tasks are increasing in importance and cannot be subject to hierarchical control and supervision because the employees concerned are required to take initiative and to assume responsibility for their work. That is why creating the necessary conditions for optimal commitment is one of HRM's most important objectives.

The rise of human resource management as a more active and strategic approach to personnel and organization should be viewed in the light of these developments. The increased level and altered quality of competition, the greater emphasis on the market and the changing nature of work itself made it necessary to adopt a different management approach. The changeover became evident both in international and domestic enterprises, but international companies felt the need for change earlier and more intensely, because in general they are more complex, apply different strategies simultaneously and operate on what are often extremely turbulent, international and therefore complex markets. The change did not affect the traditional areas of concern within personnel management as much as it affected the way in which these areas are interpreted and linked to strategic options, paralleling the strategy–structure debate discussed in the previous chapter. The focus has shifted from structure and system-thinking to developing a specific management practice which stimulates a corporate culture, commitment among employees and the extensive use of employee resources. Although multinationals do not differ from domestic companies in their HRM activities as such, they do face some special issues. According to Acuff (1984), there are five basic points that distinguish the activities of an international human resource manager from those of his domestic counterpart.

1   *More functions*. There are functions to perform in international HRM that do not occur in domestic HRM. Acuff mentions international taxation, international relocation and orientation (including pre-departure training), administrative services for expatriates and host-government relations as the most important.
2   *More heterogeneous functions*. Even if the same functions have to be performed, they become more diverse and complex, because they have to be administered to different groups of employees, namely parent-country nationals, host-country nationals and third-country nationals.
3   *More involvement in employees' personal lives*. As the success of international transfers is crucial for a multinational company, the selection, training and management of expatriates often involves a greater degree of involvement in employees' personal lives. Company assistance to find housing and adequate schools for the children in the

host country and perhaps rental of the family's house in the home country are activities that generally do not arise in domestic settings.

4   *Different emphasis*. As foreign operations grow more established, the initial heavy reliance on expatriates is often replaced by a focus on host-country nationals. This development brings yet another broadening of traditional HRM functions such as staffing, compensation and training and development, as these functions are likely to be different in different cultures (see also Part 2 of this book).

5   *More external influences*. According to Acuff, the major external factors that influence international HRM are the type of government and the state of the economy. But one could also think of unions, consumer organizations and other interest groups. Of course these groups also exist in the home country, but there their influence is familiar, which is not the case in the foreign country. Furthermore, these groups often put more pressure on foreign than on local companies.

P.V. Morgan (1986) sees three factors that differentiate domestic and international HRM, of which only one, *risk exposure*, differs from the factors mentioned above. Doing business on an international scale brings more exposure to risk. Political risks, such as expropriation, and financial risks, such as volatile exchange rates, are well known. However, international HRM also involves risks that differ from those encountered in a domestic setting. For instance, the costs of expatriate failure are much higher than for failure in domestic assignments (see also Chapters 9 and 10). Furthermore, political risk in the form of riots and terrorism considerably increases the risks and costs of international assignments.

However interesting these distinctions are, it is perhaps more useful to look behind these differences to see what the fundamental factors are that distinguish international from domestic business. This brings us back to Adler's (1983) terms (see Chapter 2): multiculturalism and geographic dispersion. Multiculturalism is defined as 'the presence of people from two or more cultural backgrounds within an organization'. Geographic dispersion is defined as 'the location of various subunits of the parent corporation in different countries'. In fact all of the differences mentioned above can be ascribed to these two characteristics. Furthermore, in general we can say that geographic dispersion and multiculturalism lead to a business environment characterized by greater complexity, more operating risk and a larger amount of uncertainty. For international HRM this means that the difference from domestic HRM lies not so much in *what* is done but rather *how* it is done, given the difference in environmental factors.

3   An overview of HRM activities from an international perspective

In the preceding section we looked at differences between domestic and international HRM. One of our main conclusions was that it is not so much the concrete activities themselves which give rise to such differences. After all, some of the most important tasks in international HRM involve staffing, assessment and compensation, training and development, and industrial relations/employee participation, which are also considered to be the main activities in domestic HRM. It is rather the way in which these activities are to be performed that gives rise to such differences.

By way of illustration we will describe a number of HRM activities which are considered crucial to this field, and indicate to what degree and in what fashion operating in an international context influences these activities. The emphasis will be on possible problem areas and bottle-necks. For a more detailed discussion, we refer the reader to the relevant chapters in Part 3. The topics will be discussed in the following order: staffing; training and (management) development; assessment and compensation.

Staffing

In general, staffing issues in an international setting involve filling critical management positions. As almost all employees at the middle management and more operative levels are recruited locally, there is no difference between international and domestic human resource management in this respect. This is not the case, however, when candidates for upper management posts are being recruited. There are various options to choose from: parent-country nationals, host-country nationals and third-country nationals. The ultimate choice in the first place depends on the attitude of top management at the parent organization. According to Perlmutter (1969), such attitudes can be divided into the following three categories.

- *Ethnocentricity*: top management favours parent-country nationals: managers who are posted abroad for a certain period of time after undergoing some form of training in the parent country.
- *Polycentricity*: top management considers national subsidiaries as independent units and allows them to fill management posts themselves (with host-country nationals).
- *Geocentricity*: top management recruits managers from anywhere in the world who can be assigned to posts anywhere in the world, or sets up management development projects to train such managers.

In the second place, it is of course very important that a sufficient number of qualified managers are available for such posts. The issue of 'make or buy' becomes important in this respect. Should top management initiate an on-going executive search, or should it so organize its staffing policies and management development activities that it is able to nurture a continuous supply of potential candidates for international management positions?

With respect to quality, top management must continuously weigh professional managerial skills and technical competence against contextual or environmental adaptiveness. The ability to adapt to local cultures is a crucial factor, involving not only the management candidate himself but also his (or her) partner and family.

At first we might perhaps be inclined to ascribe a greater measure of professional and technical competence to parent-country nationals than to host-country nationals, who (naturally) score much higher when it comes to knowing the local customs and traditions, the relevant values and, last but not least, the language. However, as early as 1984, Pucik correctly remarked that the important question is 'how to develop corporate human resources possessing both of the critical skills' (Pucik, 1984: 409). Seen in this context, it is important that management trainees should be recruited not only by headquarters in the home country, but also by subsidiaries in the host countries. Once recruitment has taken place, management development activities will initiate a process leading to exchanges between headquarters and the subsidiaries. In this way, managers involved will acquire the professional and/or technical expertise as well as the environmental adaptiveness required.

Training and development

The emphasis of training and development activities within international HRM systems is shifting from the preparatory training needs of expatriates to a truly international training and development system which is available to any manager and which will improve his performance from a global perspective, regardless of his country of origin.

Various authors have stated that training and development are international HRM's most crucial activities. Companies such as Shell and Unilever have an international reputation in this field. Numerous other companies have quite a bit less to offer, as Tung (1981) showed in her study comparing US, European and Japanese corporations. American corporations, it seems, tend to underestimate the importance of training, whereas most European and Japanese corporations see this as a highly important area of attention (see also Chapter 10).

The areas for which training is required are wide-ranging: not only does the manager in question need to know the specific organization to which he will be assigned and the job and task skills required of him there, but he must also acquire an understanding of the local situation (social, cultural and legal) and develop the necessary personal skills to perform well in this situation. The importance of the latter two areas was pointed out in a survey conducted by Baumgarten (1992a,b, see also Chapter 10), which mentions cultural sensitivity, ability to handle responsibility and ability to develop subordinates as a general manager's three most important skills.

According to Pucik (1984), when training and development are reserved for the 'elite' from corporate headquarters (that is, parent-country nationals), the consequences will be negative. By permanently reserving a subsidiary's upper management positions for expatriate staff, top management may be discouraging potential local managers. A policy such as this impedes the integration of local managers into the company. Their insights remain limited to knowledge of the local market and they are barred from further growth which they might have achieved by making strategic contributions to the company as a whole. That is why it is important to train young management candidates who come not only from the parent company, but from all over the world. Only in this way can effective management teams be put together, made up of a variety of nationalities and cultural backgrounds. Adler and Bartholomew very cogently describe this shift in emphasis in the following manner:

> Foreign assignments in global firms are no longer used primarily to get a job done in a foreign country (expatriation) or to socialize foreign country nationals into the home country headquarters' culture ('inpatriation'). Using a 'trans-patriation' approach, Royal Dutch Shell, for example, strongly believes in the importance of multifunctional and international experience to gain corporate-wide, transnational skills. (Adler and Bartholomew, 1992: 191)

Assessment and compensation

The complex nature of assessing and compensating international managers is reflected in the criteria applied in such assessments. These criteria apply not only to professional expertise, but also to the manager's ability to adjust to local circumstances and culture, which may differ sharply from those in the home country (see also Section 4).

Basing their research on the criteria applied in the case of expatriates (that is, parent-country nationals), Hossain and Davis (1989: 131) have compiled the following list of criteria in their survey of the literature: technical ability, managerial skill, cultural empathy, adaptability and flexibility, diplomatic skill and language aptitude.

Adler and Bartholomew (1992: 182) are correct in pointing out that these criteria reflect a traditional approach to international managers, in the sense that they are still based on ethnocentric attitudes held by a top management which predominantly uses parent-country nationals to staff the company's foreign subsidiaries. Such subsidiaries are subordinate to headquarters, both organizationally and culturally.

In the case of actual international, or better still transnational (see Chapter 3) assignments, other criteria are at issue when it comes to assessment and compensation. The object then is to approach the business environment from a global perspective, and not to focus on one particular country, even temporarily, to the exclusion of all others. In conjunction with this, it is important to be familiar with an entire range of preferences, values and business approaches which are inherent to the task of dealing, simultaneously and on an almost daily basis, with people, colleagues and clients, from a series of different cultures, countries and regions.

All of this makes demands on the relevant assessment and compensation systems, first of all because they should be accessible, easy to understand, equitable and motivating for every manager, regardless of his nationality and/or cultural background, and secondly because they must be competitive on a world scale. There are a number of problem areas involved in designing such assessment and compensation systems.

First, in addition to the ability to adapt to local circumstances, the subsidiary's contribution (often expressed in terms of profits and sales figures) to the overall strategic objectives of the company must also be taken into account in assessing an international manager's performance. The financial results are not always a good yardstick for measuring the subsidiary's actual contribution, however. Internal transfer prices (instituted in part as a result of fiscal considerations and exchange risks) may, for example, camouflage actual performance. Or a low price level may be maintained in a certain region in order to thwart a global competitor. It is true that a tactic like this will whittle away the subsidiary's results, but its contribution has been highly significant in the context of the entire concern. It is therefore important to view the results achieved by the individual subsidiaries, whether financial or not, from the perspective of their actual contribution to the concern's overall objectives.

A second problem area is that complications arise when a 'long distance' assessment takes place. Even with access to management information systems, the staff involved at headquarters will have difficulty forming a precise image of the circumstances in which the various subsidiaries have had to operate to achieve their results.

The third and final problem area involves the design of the compensation systems, which, in addition to taking into account differences in purchasing power, competition in the local or regional labour market, fiscal regimes and extra compensation for expatriate 'hardships', must also include elements which will increase the employee's commitment to the overall/ global objectives of the company and to the company's organizational culture. After all, the more top management can achieve coordination with the objectives and norms and values of the company through a process of socialization, the less it will have to fall back on formal coordination and control mechanisms. This means that in addition to direct and delayed (shares, pensions) forms of material compensation, attention must be given to compensation which is more immaterial in nature. This might involve the manager's career prospects, for example, and opportunities presented to him or her to grow within the company or to participate in international exchanges of information which allow him or her to get involved in strategic policy planning.

4 Models for linking organizational configurations to HRM activity patterns

Introduction

In Chapter 3 we dealt with a number of organizational configurations reflecting different stages and forms of multinational companies (general term). Such organizational configurations included multidomestic, global, international and transnational companies. Is it now possible to indicate a specific configuration for the HRM activities which should take place in the various stages and forms that an internationally active company passes through in the course of its development? In the following sections we will discuss three different models:

1   Perlmutter's top management attitudes towards internationalization.
2   Adler and Ghadar's phases of internationalization.
3   The two logics of Evans and Lorange.

Perlmutter's top management attitudes towards internationalization

Perlmutter (1969) offered an important – and historic – description of 'the tortuous evolution of the multinational corporation'. In his view, the attitude of top management at headquarters is particularly important in the development of a multinational. As mentioned previously (Chapter 2, Section 7 and Table 2.2, and Section 3 of this chapter), Perlmutter distinguishes three attitudes, namely ethnocentric, polycentric and geocentric. These attitudes or orientations not only influence the organizational structure and the lines of communication and information, but also the approach to HRM activities in the following way.

1   *Ethnocentric*. Personnel management focuses to a great extent on recruiting and training parent-country nationals for key positions, regardless of location. Their approach, working methods and culture are decisive for the organization of the subsidiary. Lines of information and communication are often one-directional and can be described in terms of 'assignments' and 'advice' issued by corporate headquarters. Home-country attitudes dominate the concern's organizational culture, whereas the foreign subsidiary plays an operational rather than a strategic role.

2   *Polycentric*. Personnel management is based largely on the view that values, norms and customs differ from country to country and that local markets can therefore best be reached by local managers (host-country nationals). The subsidiaries are allowed a relatively large measure of autonomy, although financial controls ensure that headquarters can intervene immediately if anything goes wrong. Career prospects for host-country nationals are limited to top positions within the subsidiary. They will not be considered for a position at corporate headquarters.

3   *Geocentric*. A major theme in this approach is to utilize the best managers throughout the world, regardless of their nationality. The main concern is to implement a global approach, both at headquarters and at the various subsidiaries, in which the exchange between headquarters and subsidiaries of information, ideas, working methods and personnel is a seen as a key activity.

We can, of course, find combinations of these three approaches within existing companies, but often there is one dominant attitude, which is determined by the phase of internationalization in which the company finds itself and by its history. This particular dominance is in turn reflected in the specific configuration of the HRM activities. Table 2.2 serves as a good illustration of this process.

Adler and Ghadar's phases of internationalization

Adler and Ghadar's model (1990) is based on Vernon's life cycle theory (1966; see Chapter 1, Section 4). Vernon distinguishes three phases in the international product life cycle. The first phase ('high-tech') focuses on the product, research and development (R&D) playing an important role as a functional area. The second phase ('growth and internationalization') concentrates on developing and penetrating markets, not only at home but also abroad. The focus therefore shifts from R&D to marketing and management control. In the third and final phase ('maturity'), intense efforts are made to lower prices by implementing cost control measures.

According to Adler and Ghadar (1990: 239), the average length of the product life cycle shortly after the Second World War was 15–20 years. Nowadays this is 3–5 years; for some products it is as short as 5 months. An important implication is that the various areas of emphasis in Vernon's life cycle must increasingly be dealt with simultaneously. Adler and Ghadar saw this as sufficient reason to suggest a fourth phase (incidentally following in the footsteps of Hedlund, Bartlett and Ghoshal, and Prahalad and Doz, as described in Chapter 3), in which the company must achieve differentiation (as a way to develop and penetrate markets) and integration (as a way to achieve cost control).

Having introduced a fourth phase, the authors proceed to develop a model in which cultural aspects and human resource management form the main focus of attention. In short, they link Vernon's phases, which concentrate largely on strategic and structural issues, to culture and human resource management.

The influence of culture

According to Adler and Ghadar (1990), the impact of the cultural background of a country or region differs from one phase to the next. They identify these phases as:[1]

I   Domestic: focus on home market and export.
II   International: focus on local responsiveness and transfer of learning.
III Multinational: focus on global strategy, low cost and price competition.
IV   Global: focus on both local responsiveness and global integration.

The cultural component hardly plays a role in the first phase (*domestic*). Management operates from an ethnocentric perspective and can afford to ignore the influence of foreign cultures. The attitude towards foreign buyers – which is a somewhat arrogant one – is the following: 'We allow you to buy our product' (Adler and Ghadar, 1990: 242).

---

[1] NB: Adler and Ghadar use the same terms as Bartlett and Ghoshal but attach them to different phases, which could be confusing.

By contrast, in the second phase (*international*) the cultural differences of each foreign market are highly important when entering into external relations. From the polycentric perspective, product design, marketing and production will concentrate on finding a good match between the product and the preferences and style of the relevant foreign market segment. That is why production is often transferred to the relevant country and/or region.

During the third phase (*multinational*) the product must be globalized to such an extent that competition with other 'global players' emphasizes a lower cost price as a way of keeping up with price competition. This has less to do with emphasizing cultural sensitivity than with the exploitation of cost advantages arising from price differences between production factors in each country and/or region, and with the exploitation of economies of scale (see also Chapter 1, Section 3). It is, however, important that a certain internal sensitivity or awareness develops of the various cultural differences (cultural diversity) within the global concern.

Finally there is the fourth phase (*global*). In addition to cost advantages and low prices on the world markets, the products and services must at the same time meet standards of high quality. This quality is expressed in the adaptation of the product to the tastes, preferences and/or specifications of the individual markets and market niches. Adler and Ghadar (1990: 243) describe this as follows:

> Successful corporations understand their potential clients' needs, quickly translate them into products and services, produce those products and services on a least-possible-cost basis, and deliver them back to the client in a culturally appropriate and timely fashion.

Cultural sensitivity becomes crucial, not only internally but externally as well.

Figure 4.1 illustrates the relative importance of the cultural component and the direction of the interaction between organization and environment in the various phases.

Phases and areas of focus in HRM

Starting from the idea of a link between the phases of internationalization, the (market) environment and the influence of culture, Adler and Ghadar go on to sketch the appropriate HRM policies/instruments and the skills required of the managers involved for the various different phases. Table 4.1 illustrates their theory. For clarity's sake, we have added the terms used by Bartlett and Ghoshal to the table.

Phase I In this phase we can scarcely speak of international human resource management in any real sense. There may be incidental brief visits to foreign agents/sales offices or a short assignment on a project basis, in which product and technical competence of the manager in question are the most important factors.

Phase II International human resource management becomes manifest in this phase as managers are assigned to posts in foreign markets to

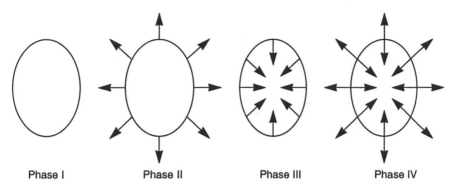

Phase I   Phase II   Phase III   Phase IV

Figure 4.1   *Location of cross-cultural interaction (Adler and Ghadar, 1990: 244)*

provide general management, technical expertise and financial control. The various markets require a differentiated approach and adaptation of the product and business methods to local circumstances. In addition to technical competence, then, selection criteria such as language skills, cross-cultural adaptability and sensitivity are also important. Since understanding of local circumstances is a requirement, host-country nationals are frequently recruited for management positions in the area of sales, marketing and personnel.

Phase III   As it is highly important that integration and cost advantages are exploited world wide, the selection in this phase focuses on recruiting the best managers for international positions, regardless of their country of origin. Developing a management corps in which all the members share the same organizational values and norms is one of human resource management's most important tasks. After all, this will contribute to achieving the goal of integration, regardless of the fact that the company is operating in different geographical markets and its managers come from different countries. Management development, careers counselling and periodic transfer to a different assignment (every 3–5 years) are the spearheads of phase III human resource management.

Phase IV   A major issue for international human resource management in this phase is how the company is to satisfy the requirements of global integration and national responsiveness. We can find traces of both phase II and phase III here. The large measure of cultural diversity becomes manifest both in the markets to be covered and in the organization itself. The real art is to view this cultural diversity as an opportunity rather than as a problem which has to be solved. One example is to increase creativity and flexibility by being able to maintain a variety of perspectives, an important approach for solving problems and encouraging innovation. International human resource management focuses on offering promising managers the opportunity to grow and gain experience so that an environment for continuous learning will be created throughout the entire organization. The degree to which such human resource management can

Table 4.1   *Globalization and human resource management*

	Phase I Domestic	Phase II Interrnational	Phase III Multinational	Phase IV Global
Primary orientation	Product/service	Market	Price	Strategy
Strategy	Domestic	Multidomestic	Multinational	Global
Worldwide strategy	Allow foreign clients to buy product/ service	Increase market internation- ally; transfer technology abroad	Source, produce and market internationally	Gain global, strategic, competitive advantage
Staffing				
Expatriates	None – (few)	Many	Some	Many
Why sent	Junket	To sell, control, or transfer technology	Control	Coordination and integration
Who sent	—	'OK' per- formers, sales people	Very good performers	High-potential managers and top executives
Purpose	Reward	Project 'To get job done'	Project and career development	Career and organizational development
Career impact	Negative	Bad for domestic career	Important for global career	Essential for executive suite
Professional re-entry	Somewhat difficult	Extremely difficult	Less difficult	Professionally easy
Training and development (language and cross-cultural management)	None	Limited (one week)	Longer	Continuous throughout career
For whom	No one	Expatriates	Expatriates	Managers
Performance appraisal	Corporate bottom line	Subsidiary bottom line	Corporate bottom line	Global strategic positioning
Motivation assumption	Money motivates	Money and adventure	Challenge and opportunity	Challenge, opportunity, advancement
Rewarding	Extra money to compensate for foreign hardships		Less generous, global packages	
Career 'fast track'	Domestic	Domestic	Token international	Global
Executive passport	Home country	Home country	Home country; token foreigners	Multinational
Necessary skills	Technical and managerial	Plus cultural adaptation	Plus recognizing cultural differences	Plus cross- cultural interaction, influence and synergy
Bartlett/Ghoshal	Domestic	Multidomestic/ International	Global	Transnational

Source: Adler and Ghadar, 1990: 246

be given concrete expression determines the success or failure of the (phase IV) corporation (Adler and Ghadar, 1990: 245–254).

The two logics of Evans and Lorange

The third and final contribution comes from Evans and Lorange. Their main question is: 'How can a corporation operating in different product markets and diverse socio-cultural environments effectively establish human resource policies?' (Evans and Lorange, 1989: 144). Basing themselves on the great variety of product–market combinations to be covered and the attendant operations to be performed in settings with a wide cultural diversity, they have developed two logics for shaping HRM policy.

Product–market logic

The various phases of the product life cycle each require a different type of manager. Cost-conscious management will be more important in the maturity phase than it would be in an emerging business, where managers with entrepreneurial skills are more appropriate. This also implies that activities such as recruitment, training and development, and assessment and compensation, will differ from one phase to the other. If we consider that a multinational organization by definition covers a wider range of product–market combinations, and that these combinations will further-more differ from one another with respect to their product life cycle phase, managing human resources would appear to be a highly complex affair, even on the basis of this logic alone. This complexity can, however, be spread out over the various management levels. Assuming that manage-ment will be split into the categories 'corporate', 'divisional' and 'business unit' level, Evans and Lorange propose the following duties for the corporate level:

- key executive appointments and succession planning;
- design and management of appropriate incentive systems;
- cross-fertilization of functional and business experience.

Given the increasing need for corporate integration – specifically with respect to the process of strategic planning – these tasks will only become more important, according to Evans and Lorange (1989: 151). The arguments the authors present to support this view are similar to those previously described for the transnational company.

Social–cultural logic

A company that operates various business units in a wide variety of countries and regions will take on employees who differ from one another in terms of their socio-cultural backgrounds. In addition to differences in the legal (specifically employment and labour law) and educational systems, there are of course also cultural differences in the sense of highly divergent values and norms (Hofstede, 1980b; see also Part 2). Taking Perlmutter as their point of departure, Evans and Lorange have identified two strategies for dealing with such extreme cultural diversity.

1   *Global approach* (Perlmutter's ethnocentrism or geocentrism). In this approach, the company's own specific culture predominates and human resource management is relatively centralized and standardized. Uniform procedures and guidelines in the area of recruitment, selection, assessment, compensation and promotion define a human resource management which is applicable world wide. Typical examples of such an approach are IBM and Shell. It is true that staff are recruited globally, even for management posts, but regardless of the differences in national culture, integration into the dominant company culture is given top priority.

2   *Polycentric approach*. In this approach the responsibility for human resource management is decentralized and devolved to the subsidiaries. Headquarters may provide certain guidelines, but each subsidiary in each country and/or region is free to interpret human resource management as it sees fit. Corporate staff duties are therefore restricted to the three core tasks mentioned earlier. The adaptation to local culture is given priority. The polycentric approach loses out to the global approach when it comes down to the opportunities it presents for integration and coordination (in particular with respect to implementation of global and corporate-wide strategic objectives). On the other hand, the global approach generates higher overheads as a consequence of HRM policies aimed at selection and retention, with large expenditures for management development activities related to indoctrination and socialization.

5   From universal to specific: a framework to account for the differences

In the previous section we summarized a number of models that systematically link various different attitudes held by top management and different organizational configurations to a specific pattern for HRM activities. For the sake of clarity, we used a very common approach by employing a number of typologies – think in this respect of Mintzberg's (1983) configurations. The effectiveness of this approach as a didactic tool is beyond dispute. In real life, however, organizations are not so easy to typify. Is it possible to provide a guide, a framework in which insight can be acquired into the characteristics of a real multinational organization and the way in which these characteristics influence the design of HRM systems and, possibly, the freedom of choice extended to management in devising such systems? An attempt in this direction – albeit a relatively abstract one – was undertaken by Hossain and Davis (1989) in the following form:

$$IPM = F (G, M, A)$$

where

IPM: international personnel management
G: geographic identification
M: multiculturalism
A: attitudinal structure.
(F: is a function of).

As we can see, Hossain and Davis assume that international personnel management is a function of various countries, various cultures and the attitude of top management towards international subsidiaries. Their formulation seems to pay little attention to the business side, in the sense of managing a series of product–market combinations on various different markets at national, regional or even global level.

In the approach taken by Evans and Lorange (1989), on the other hand, the business side is clearly present in the dichotomy between the product–market logic and the social–cultural logic. This dichotomy is not essentially different from that of domestic HRM. Human resource management in companies exclusively targeting the domestic market also has to deal with the fact that the design is determined by the relevant product–market technology combination requirements on the one hand, and by the socio-cultural and politico-legal context on the other.

The relevant variables have been summarized and shown in relation to one another in Figure 4.2. This diagram affords a framework that fulfils two roles. First, it is a diagrammatic summary of what we have discussed so far. Secondly, it is a tool for mapping and analyzing relevant factors in designing HRM policies and activities in a concrete company. Of course, such a company will not match one of Adler and Ghadar's typologies precisely; instead it will be a unique mixture of different typologies brought about by its own specific history (think of the concept of administrative heritage as discussed in Chapter 3, Section 6). In the following sections we will discuss each of the elements in this model in greater detail.

The two dimensions of HRM in both a domestic and an international context

There are two forces that determine the design of HRM policies and activities. Both these forces apply to domestic and international HRM. The HRM design is determined to a large degree by the relevant product–market combination requirements and the technology utilized to meet these requirements (P/M/T dimension). Such requirements are often expressed as:

- efficiency;
- effectiveness;
- flexibility;
- quality; and
- innovativeness.

On the one hand, the P/M/T dimensions represent the harsh economic realities that face a company which must compete in both the domestic

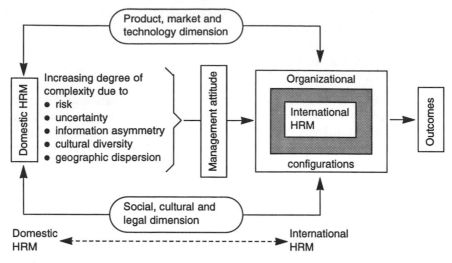

Figure 4.2 *Product–market and social–culture dimensions –
domestic and international HRM*

and international markets. On the other hand, however, 'free' market
forces are in fact embedded in a political, social and cultural framework
(S/C/L dimension). Prevailing values and norms and the institutions which
have been built upon such values and norms channel the outcomes of the
market process in such a fashion that justice can also be done to
requirements of fairness and legitimacy.

By fairness we mean in particular a fair transaction between employer
and employee, in which the transaction concerns not only the exchange of
labour and money, but also of participation and time (Huiskamp, 1992;
Paauwe, 1986; Watson, 1977).

Legitimacy concerns the same elements of exchange, but in collective
form. The focus is no longer on individual market parties, but on interest
groups (for example, employers, trade unions and government) and the
relevant institutions. Of course, these forces (P/M/T and S/C/L dimensions) do not completely determine the design of HRM policies and
activities (deterministic contingency perspective), but their influence is
certainly highly decisive (Paauwe, 1991).

Increasing complexity

Although both dimensions influence domestic as well as international
HRM, there is an important difference: the latter is much more complex.
Companies that operate on international markets have to deal with more
uncertainty, greater risks, information asymmetry,[2] geographic dispersion
and a larger measure of cultural diversity. Naturally there are differences

---

[2] Information asymmetry refers to a situation in which information is available, but is
unevenly distributed among the different parties or stakeholders involved.

between companies depending on their phase of internationalization. Neither should the role of learning effects be discounted.

Management attitudes, strategic choice and room for manoeuvre

Given this increasing complexity, it is the task of management to shape the strategy, structure, organizational culture (organizational configurations) and the most appropriate HRM policies. The attitude of top management is highly important in this process (think of the distinction Perlmutter makes between ethnocentric, polycentric and geocentric) and is reflected in the way in which the organization has developed so far ('administrative heritage' ; see also Chapter 3). Management attitudes, P/M/T and S/C/L dimensions determine the available room for manoeuvre for the parties involved. In Figure 4.2 the shaded area shows this available room for manoeuvre for the design of HRM policies and activities. Depending on the circumstances (conditions, contingencies; Paauwe, 1991), the amount of available room will vary from one organization to the next. Examples of such circumstances are: market position, rate of unionization, degree of labour and/or capital intensity, financial stamina. In the case of an organization occupying a monopoly position, for example, it will be clear that this room for manoeuvre is relatively large. If there are a large number of competitors, however, and stiff price competition in combination with a low level of financial stamina exists, the room for manoeuvre for shaping HRM policies will never be more than minimal (Paauwe, 1991: 111).

Organizational configurations

As we saw in the models proposed by Adler and Ghadar (above) and Bartlett and Ghoshal (Chapter 3), the organizational configuration (designated by typologies such as multidomestic, international, global and transnational) exerts a powerful influence on the design of international HRM. In this context the specific organizational configuration can be seen as the result of historical strategic choices and the resulting structural design.

Product/market/technology dimension

We indicated previously that the requirements arising from these forces are often described in terms of efficiency, effectiveness etc. A more concrete description and analysis of the P/M/T dimension would involve identifying such relevant variables as: factor costs, competitor profiles, product life cycles, market fluctuations, currency risks, inflation figures, interest rates, technological advances and the possibility of exploiting these to further both product and process innovations. For a more detailed summary of these variables, the reader is referred to Porter (1986a), Prahalad and Doz (1987: chs 2, 3), and Dülfer (1990).

Table 4.2   *HRM elements and macro-environmental influences*

HRM elements	Issues	Macro-environmental influences		
		Socio-economic	Institutional	Cultural
Acquisition	Recruitment of personnel	External labour markets	Pressure to recruit locals	Recruitment ethics
Development	Personnel training	National level of education	Public HRD policy	Values attached to competence
Compensation	Wages	Social inequalities	Minimum wage agreements	Motivational forces
	ESOP	Level and distribution of income	Union policies	Social values
Work system	Distribution of tasks	Gender-based division of labour	Regulation of maximum working hours	Individualism/ collectivism
Labour relations	Employee influence	Local authority structure	Corporate law Labour law	Power distance
	Collective bargaining	Inflation rates	Existing agreements	Attitudes towards unions

Source: Gronhaug and Nordhaug, 1992

Social/cultural/legal dimension

If we accept the requirements of fairness (individual level) and legitimacy (collective level) mentioned previously, it becomes important to describe this dimension more concretely, thereby making an effective analysis possible. According to Hossain and Davis (1989: 125), socio-cultural factors are perhaps the most important variables that internationally operating managers must take into consideration. These are variables like language, values (more or less general beliefs, that either define what is right or wrong, or specify general preferences), the position accorded to women, educational factors and labour factors such as employee representation and unionism. A more detailed summary is given by Gronhaug and Nordhaug (1992) and by Dülfer (1990). Gronhaug and Nordhaug (1992: 4) make a distinction between macro-environmental influences and micro-environmental influences. The macro-environment, which is the most important for our framework, consists of relevant conditions (socio-economic, institutional and cultural) in the surrounding region and country of operation. Table 4.2 presents a number of variables to be taken into consideration.

International HRM and outcomes

The HRM activities developed on the basis of the previous analysis (such as staffing, assessment and compensation, training and development) are of course aimed at achieving specific objectives/outcomes. In this context, Beer et al. (1984: 16–19) identify the following HRM outcomes.

- *Commitment*: to what extent do HRM policies enhance the commitment of people to their work and their organization?
- *Competence*: to what extent do HRM policies attract, keep and/or develop people with skills and knowledge needed by the organization and society now and in the future?
- *Cost-effectiveness*: what is the cost-effectiveness of a given policy in terms of wages, benefits, turnover, absenteeism, strikes and so on?
- *Congruence*: what levels of congruence do HRM policies and practices generate or sustain between management and employees, different employee groups, the organization and community, employees and their families, and within the individual?

These outcomes subsequently contribute to achieve long-term consequences such as individual well-being, organizational effectiveness and societal well-being.

These objectives are inspired by a 'stakeholder' approach within the company, in the sense that in the process of determining the objectives, account is expressly taken of the wishes and demands of the internal and external parties involved. Both HRM outcomes and long-term consequences fit in with the HRM dichotomy described previously, in which the design is subject to both the P/M/T dimension and the S/C/L dimension. More recent HRM approaches (for example Guest, 1987, 1989; Legge, 1989) recognize this duality and aspire to achieve congruence between personal and company objectives.

With the objectives/outcomes discussed above, all elements of our framework have been dealt with. Before concluding the chapter we will, in the next section, take a short excursion into the subject of developing transnational managers.

6   The main challenge: developing capable transnational managers

In this and the previous chapters we discussed how the changing international environment forced most companies to develop multidimensional and heterogeneous strategies and structures. This development poses considerable challenges for the managers who have to carry out these strategies and construct these structures. We repeatedly stressed the importance of management processes in developing a transnational company.

In this section we will discuss the roles and responsibilities of transnational managers. Given the heterogeneity and multidimensionality of the transnational organization, it is virtually impossible for one person to possess all the skills necessary to be an effective transnational manager in each and every part of the company. According to Bartlett and Ghoshal the answer to the question 'what is a transnational manager?' is 'a network of specialists, not a single individual' (Bartlett and Ghoshal, 1992a: 124). The roles and responsibilities of transnational managers will be different for different parts of the organization. We will therefore distinguish three different management forms: global business management, worldwide functional management and geographic subsidiary management (based on Bartlett and Ghoshal, 1992b: ch. 7). In a final subsection we will also discuss the necessary capabilities for top management.

Global business management

Effective global business management complies with the demands of global efficiency and competitiveness. Capturing scale and scope economies and coordinating and integrating activities across national and functional barriers are the fundamental tasks of the global business manager. In order to perform these tasks a global business manager has three core roles and responsibilities: worldwide business strategist, architect of a worldwide asset and resource configuration, and cross-border coordinator and controller.

In his role as *worldwide business strategist* the global business manager tries to reconcile the different perspectives of geographic, functional and business management in order to provide an integrated competitive strategy for his particular business. As *architect of an asset and resource configuration* he subsequently coordinates the distribution of key assets and resources to support the competitive strategy chosen. In this role, however, he also has to take the other perspectives into account and will furthermore be guided by the company's administrative heritage (see Chapters 2 and 3) of existing assets and resources. This distribution of assets and resources leads to a flow of materials, components and finished products that has to be coordinated by the global business manager in his role as *cross-border coordinator*. As transnational companies mostly rely on distributed sourcing (see Chapter 2), this is a very complex task.

Worldwide functional management

Effective worldwide functional management responds to the challenge of developing and diffusing innovations on a worldwide basis. Knowledge is transferred by links between functional experts around the world. Most worldwide functional managers play three basic roles: worldwide scanner of specialized information and knowledge, cross-pollinator of 'best practices' and champion of transnational innovation.

As *worldwide intelligence scanner* the worldwide functional manager scans the whole world for opportunities and threats, which may be in the form of a technological breakthrough or an emerging consumer trend. Functional managers are linked through informal networks, so that information is transmitted rapidly. In a transnational company subsidiaries can be an important source of capabilities, expertise and innovations, which can be transferred to other parts of the organization. It is the worldwide functional manager in his role as *cross-pollinator of 'best practices'* who spots these opportunities and transfers them in a way that breaks down the 'not invented here' syndrome. Transnational innovations are the focus of this role of *champion of transnational innovation*. The first form of transnational innovation, which is called 'locally leveraged' (discussed in Section 6 of Chapter 1), follows from the 'best-practices' approach – local innovations that have applications everywhere. A more sophisticated form of transnational innovation is termed 'globally linked' innovation. 'This type of innovation fully exploits the company's access to worldwide information and expertise by linking and leveraging intelligence sources with internal centres of excellence wherever they may be located' (Bartlett and Ghoshal, 1992b: 785).

Geographic subsidiary management

Effective geographic subsidiary management involves first and foremost multinational responsiveness, responding to the needs of national customers and satisfying the demands of host-country governments. However, it also demands defending a company's position against global competitors and leveraging local resources and capabilities. The geographic subsidiary manager's very complex task can be divided into three main roles: bicultural interpreter, national defender and advocate, and frontline implementer of corporate strategy.

In the first role, *bicultural interpreter*, the geographic subsidiary (or country) manager must not only understand the demands of the local customers, competitors and government, but also interpret this information and communicate it effectively to managers at headquarters who might not understand its importance. The country manager must also act in the opposite direction, interpreting the company's overall goals, strategies and values in such a way that they become meaningful to local employees and do not compromise local cultural norms. As a *national defender and advocate*, the country manager should try to counterbalance excessive centralizing pressures from global business managers and make sure that the interests of the local subsidiary are taken into consideration. The country manager's role as a *frontline implementer of corporate strategy* is an especially difficult one. He or she is pressured by local governments, unions and customers on the one hand and constrained by a global strategy that often leaves little room for manoeuvring on the other. This manager's actions 'must be sensitive enough to respect the limits of the diverse local constituencies, pragmatic enough to achieve the expected corporate outcome, and creative enough to balance the diverse internal and external demands and constraints' (Bartlett and Ghoshal, 1992b: 788).

Top-level corporate management

Top-level corporate management has to take all the transnational challenges (efficiency, learning and responsiveness) into account. This means not only creating different management groups and giving them specific roles and responsibilities, but also continuously striving to maintain the 'organizational legitimacy' of each group. Balancing and integrating diverse and often conflicting interests is the key challenge for top-level corporate management. In doing so, there are three basic roles to fulfil: providing direction and purpose, leveraging corporate performance and ensuring continual renewal.

A multidimensional and heterogeneous company runs the risk of falling apart if there is no common vision and a shared set of values to lead it towards common goals. It is the task of top-level corporate management in its role as *provider of direction and purpose* to create this common vision. This is, however, a rather long-term strategy. Top management's role of *leveraging corporate performance* makes sure that the company survives in the short run. To do so, top management balances the different coordination devices (formalization, centralization and socialization) to achieve the mix that maximizes corporate performance. Both a focus on the long-term mission and on short-term performance, however, can lead to a loss of flexibility if put to the extreme. Therefore, the third role of top management is to *ensure continual renewal*. Goals and values have to be adaptive; they are continually questioned and challenged to achieve the flexibility that is vital in a transnational environment.

7   Summary and conclusions

In this chapter we have seen that human resource management is of crucial importance in multinational corporations. HRM requires something more than traditional personnel management, as we saw in Section 2. In this section we also saw that international HRM distinguishes itself from domestic HRM primarily by having to deal with a greater complexity, a large amount of uncertainty and a higher level of operating risk (all due to the characteristics of international business: geographic dispersion and multiculturalism). The basic functions for international HRM are the same as for domestic HRM; it is how they are performed that makes the difference. Section 3 discussed how HRM functions are influenced by operating in an international context. Subsequently, in Section 4 we discussed three models that attempted to link management attitude and organizational configurations to IHRM activity patterns. Section 5 summarized the relevant variables in designing HRM policies and activities in a concrete company. Finally, in Section 6 we discussed the different types of managers needed in a transnational company and outlined their roles and responsibilities.

This chapter concludes the first part of this book. In Part 2 we will discuss national differences in HRM policies and two theoretical models to account for these differences.

PART 2

PERSONNEL AND ORGANIZATION FROM A COMPARATIVE PERSPECTIVE

5 Cross-national differences in personnel and organization

Arndt Sorge

1	Introduction	99
2	Organizational structures in the United Kingdom, Germany and France	100
3	Organizational behaviour	102
4	Analyzing cross-national differences	107
5	The societal effect approach	113
	Dimensions, structure and flow	113
	Central tenets of the societal effect approach	114
	Reciprocal interdependence between dimensions	115
	Complementarity of opposites	116
	Non-identical reproduction of dimensions and their interrelations	116
	Illustrations	118
	Internationalization, European integration and institutional differentiation	122

1 Introduction

Before entering into a discussion of cross-national comparative research and its results, it is necessary to give a first impression of how personnel structures and organizations differ from one country to another. It is impossible to account for all the differences we know about, but a basic and exemplary treatment of some differences is feasible within a limited amount of space. This will be done in Section 2. Since there is some disagreement in the literature on how to interpret cross-national differences, Section 3 will develop a perspective which can be used to integrate divergent approaches into a more general framework, without neglecting the theoretical contributions and empirical findings that various approaches have to offer. In the fourth section of the chapter, we will see how such a framework can be used to analyse cross-national differences.

From the more general framework we will derive what are essentially two main approaches. One of these, the *societal effect* approach, will be described in the final section. This approach is mainly of a sociological nature. The other, which is rooted chiefly in psychology, might be called the *culturalist* approach. The task in Chapter 6 will be to present the latter in greater detail. It is crucial that students try to use both approaches in combination when seeking to understand cross-national differences.

2   Organizational structures in the United Kingdom, Germany and France

What, then, is the empirical essence that emerges from cross-national comparisons? First, only those comparisons are pertinent here which highlight differences that cannot be attributed to different direct outcomes. Organizational and personnel differences between agricultural and industrial societies, for example, are too well understood to be covered in this chapter. Our interest is focused on differences that cannot be attributed to common explanatory variables in organization theory, such as technology, firm size, products made, innovation rates, variability of products made, ownership etc. Intriguing differences are those which arise despite similarities in the factors just mentioned. Let us therefore look at differences between actors and systems, in different countries, that are more or less identical with regard to such factors. In which ways do actors and systems differ, even when the organizations are of the same size and make the same product, with the same technology, for similar types of clients?

The following emerged when the administrative structures of manufacturing sites that are similar regarding size, technology etc. were compared in three countries – France, the UK and Germany. Table 5.1 summarizes a number of quantitative measures describing the shape of organizations. The data were first published by Maurice et al. (1980), reformulated by Lane (1989: 51), and reformulated again by the present author. Most of the variables are expressed as percentages, ratios or index values. The

Table 5.1   *Overall view of administrative structures in the UK, Germany and France*

	Low	Medium	High
Tallness of hierarchy	D	UK	F
Functional differentiation	D	UK	F
Share of white-collar employees	D	UK	F
Supervisory span of control	D	UK	F
Administrative and commercial personnel/workers	D	UK	F
Authority positions/workers	UK	D	F
Authority positions/white-collar workers	UK	F	D

D, Germany; F, France; UK, United Kingdom.

differences between the countries were usually in the order of 10–20 percentage points, which is quite a lot, bearing in mind that we are dealing with organizations that do basically the same thing. German sites came across as having very 'lean' and simple structures, the hierarchy being strong but short. There is a tendency to restrict the growth of any component that is separate from direct production and the line of authority. French organizations tended to have tall hierarchies with large numbers of people in managerial, supervisory, administrative and specialist positions. British firms tended to have medium-sized components on most counts, except that they had the smallest numbers of people specifically classified as having line authority.

Such differences went hand-in-hand with striking contrasts in labour control, management control, payment systems, industrial relations, work careers, personnel policy, competence requirements for jobs and vocational education and training. German organizations put the emphasis on extensive vocational training for most of the employees and positions, continuous development of vertically differentiated qualifications, and stability and autonomy of people in their jobs, within a fairly tight and coherent overall scheme. French organizations emphasized learning by hierarchical advancement, qualification and career distinctions, upward mobility and restriction of autonomy, all within a complex and centralized scheme. British organizations were more loosely coupled amalgamations of components, each with its own identity and displaying a number of status, career and qualification differences between them, but held together by generalist management.

Similar and related differences have tended to crop up time and again, whenever organizations in similar situations were compared in the three countries (Lane, 1989). These attest to sizeable contrasts in the way European countries train people, organize units, pay employees, set up work careers and labour markets, and so on, although the nature of the task in hand is fairly similar. Such comparisons also showed that people working in organizations had different ideas about what kind of arrangement was 'natural', self-evident or ideal. Germans seemed to appreciate professional autonomy in a well-oiled, productive machine. British employees appeared to strive for individual and group prerogatives, and the possibility of negotiated compromise between different interests. The French invariably seemed to go for detailed and complex schemes that permitted sizeable inequalities while allowing extensive upward mobility and fixed individual rights while buttressing the exercise of authority.

Such differences are even more striking when European and Asian organizational and personnel policies and practices are compared. A case in point is the classic study by Dore (1973) on highly similar British and Japanese electrical engineering enterprises. The major conclusion of this study was that there is a multitude of ways to achieve the same industrial, or service production, task. The multiplicity of task achievement is rooted in the fact that institutions of vocational and general education and training, standard organizing practice, industrial relations, labour markets, social stratification and mobility, occupational profiles, relations between men and women, and people's expectations differ a great deal from one country to another.

Differences are derived from a variety of sources: government law, collective agreements, custom and practice, financial incentives and restrictions, ideologies, symbols, preferences and social values. In the case of the chemical production units discussed above (Maurice et al., 1980), it emerged that they themselves had already investigated to what extent their structures differed and could be assimilated. The managers of the sites had been baffled by the number of differences that were impossible to assimilate. They had also concluded that there was no real need to assimilate structures and practices, since they were able to achieve comparable performance in strikingly different ways.

The complex tangle of the interrelated factors mentioned above has been a daunting challenge to a more systematic conceptualization, not only for managers in international companies but also for scholars. Managers are more intimately familiar with operations, but they have a practical job to do. Is it possible to put forward a coherent theory that makes sense of all this diversity? To provide an answer, we need to acquire a more detailed notion of the way organizations, and people in organizations, behave. This is what we will try to do in the following section. Throughout the more theoretical reflections, we will try to show the empirical and practical relevance of such considerations by giving illustrative examples.

3   Organizational behaviour

Formal organizations try to achieve specific goals in an effective or efficient way, and they have clearly demarcated boundaries which distinguish between members and non-members and which separate irrelevant aspects from those which are considered pertinent to the organization. Modern organizational life is understood to be full of instrumental rationality, purposeful endeavour and impersonal relations founded on specific and formalized social roles and rules. However, as Scott (1981) suggested, this is only one definition of organizations, and one in which the emphasis is placed on *rational system* properties. Organizations are also distinctive with regard to the informal and pragmatic regulation of behaviour, based on custom, tradition or spontaneous resolve; to that extent, they have *natural system* properties. What both natural and rational systems have in common, despite the differences between them, is that they distinguish relevant aspects and people *inside* the organization from those outside the organizational ambit. Such boundaries may be blurred, but even when blurred, they are important.

Blurred boundaries imply that organizations must also be viewed as *open systems*. This means that it is not quite clear who precisely is a member, which aspects are relevant and which goals are to be pursued. It is even doubtful whether open systems can be described as 'systems' at all, or whether they can be more properly analyzed as a coalition of 'parties' with different interests, which 'import' such interests, preferences, habits and mentalities into an organization (Lammers, 1987: 410). Organizations are thus characterized by conflicting elements and contradictory definitions. This can be summarized as *substantive pluralism* (see box on pp. 104–105).

Giddens (1986: ch. 4) has made the point that individual behaviour and social structure are in principle reciprocally related. However, to be quite clear, there is the possibility that different social inducements and sanctions make the same type of individual behave in different ways. Similarly, the same set of social inducements and sanctions may provoke entirely different sorts of individual behaviour, depending on individual predispositions. Actors and systems do not simply mirror each other, and relations between them have to be differentiated.

1   Actors and systems are analytically *distinct* categories, each with its own dimensions and characteristics.
2   The independent nature of the categories is, however, compatible with partial *cross-referencing*. System properties may be reflected in the minds of individuals, and individual behaviour may be implied by system properties. The individual has certain organization structures and norms 'in mind', and the organized system has an inter-subjective, if not objective, understanding of the nature of individual perceptions, motives, ambitions and behavioural inclinations.
3   Systematic cross-referencing does not exclude the substantial *partial autonomy* of actors' mindsets with regard to social system structures and vice versa. The system's understanding of the actor generally differs, at least in part, from what the actor himself has in mind.
4   Even substantial partial autonomy of actors and systems does not exclude extensive *reciprocal causal influences*. Actors modify systems, and they are modified by systems in return. Actors try to impose their mental map on the system, and the other way round.

In the working time example mentioned in the box overleaf, it is clear that an explicit working time policy was represented in the minds of the actors and in the plant's generally accepted structures. This is cross-referencing at work. However, there is also partial autonomy, since both the production manager and the Austrian worker saw the time regime as adaptable to the wishes or requirements of workers, under specific conditions; an actor's individual perceptions and the view expressed in the system as such may diverge. Moreover, this divergence is sanctioned by the system, since the production manager supports the Austrian worker. This is a case of actors modifying the system in its concrete details.

The co-existence of these differentiated principles is a consequence of substantive pluralism following Scott (1981), as described above: rational system properties, and the attribution of rationality, emphasize cross-referencing and reciprocal causal influences. Natural system properties are associated with the partial autonomy of actors and systems, because of the inchoate rationality of actors, the tenuous relationship between formal and

Substantive and methodological pluralism

When we try to explain the behaviour of, and in, organizations, we are attempting to emulate norms of clarity: we make efforts to avoid definitional ambiguity and contradiction, pretending that a non-contradictory theory of organizational life is possible, although we know perfectly well that it is not. This idealistic presumption is inherent to the formulation of nomothetic theory, that is a non-contradictory body of statements which have been proven empirically.

But to do justice to the real world, we have to construct theory in a way that allows contradictory elements to creep in. Arguably, whenever words – or language – are used (and who could construct a theory without using words?), contradictions creep in. Try to give a clear, non-contradictory definition of a simple thing, like a 'window', and you will see that you will inevitably get tangled up in ambiguity and contradictions. An approach which does not place a taboo on contradictions within theory-building aims at dialectical theory. This notion used to raise the hair of so-called positivist scholars, who considered it merely an excuse for confusion and arbitrariness. But dialectical theory does not want to avoid norms of clarity and empirical corroboration. Indeed, it submits itself to norms of rational discourse and tries to keep contradictions to a minimum. The minimum is imposed by the tendency of the real world to defy non-contradictory statements. Dialectical theory therefore displays an inherent tension between contradictions and ambiguity on the one hand, and clarity on the other.

Lest you think that such reflections are of academic interest only, consider the following everyday example from a case study. At one factory I investigated, I asked the production manager if workers had fixed or flexible working hours. He said they were fixed for everybody. Every aspect of the factory's policy, by the way, showed an insistence on each and every person adhering to existing formal rules, planning and control systems. Foreigners invariably think that this is a German characteristic. However, things were not that simple. Pointing at an unmanned machining centre, I asked why this expensive instrument was unmanned on a Friday at two o'clock in the afternoon, during regular working hours. The production manager replied: 'Ah well, the worker is Austrian and he goes home for weekends, and he's good, and he makes up the hours he misses on Fridays during the week.' The way the manager replied indicated that he thought this was a perfectly sensible arrangement. You will recognize rational, natural and open systems elements side by side. The production manager was quite unworried by the fact that the plant's policy on working hours contained contradictions. Practitioners are notoriously unworried by contradictions, as long as the controlling people or bodies do not make an issue of them. This is what the above-mentioned tendency of the real world to defy non-contradictory statements boils down to. In this sense, abstractions and dialectics are more down-to-earth than appears at first sight.

Nomothetic theory and dialectical theory are not simply exclusive of each other. The need for dialectics becomes apparent when nomothetic theory-building – clarity and empirical corroboration – is taken seriously. But dialectics which is uncontrolled by norms of clarity and empirical corroboration leads to nonsense. Similarly, unbridled nomothetic theory-building leads to highly artificial statements which appear strange in relation to real life. Nomothetic and dialectical approaches have to balance each other if an understandable and empirically pertinent discourse is to be maintained.

In our example, we first needed to decompose what happened, and try to explain reality by applying different nomothetic perspectives, each with regard to separate facets of this reality. The full reality, however, can only be captured by combining different perspectives, which leads us out of nomothetics and straight into dialectics. This can be summed up in a postulate: meaningful theory also requires methodological pluralism, in addition to the substantive pluralism mentioned above. Different methodologies have affinities with different aspects of reality. In the example, the individual variation of working time was unearthed by applying open-ended interviewing on the basis of direct observation. Administering a standard questionnaire would not have brought it to light; the manager would simply have ticked off 'uniform working time' and 'two work shifts' for factory workers.

The danger with pluralism, of course, is that different perspectives and methods are accumulated, without trying to link them in order to make them fit into a larger scheme. When this happens, consistency comes out as the loser. However, we need a treatment which is pluralistic and consistent at the same time. To reach the largest measure of conceptual agreement in a general paradigm, organization theory has the following to offer: it seems organization theory is marked by the interaction of actors and systems. Interaction means that actors and systems influence each other, in both directions. This interaction can be seen to lead to organizational outcomes. Actors are individuals and groups of individuals who are characterized by specific modes of thinking and behaviour. Systems are organized units with standardized interpersonal relations, rules, norms and structures; properties of systems are located at a supra-individual level. Actors act in certain ways because their mind is made up that way, but also because organizational – and other social – structures, rules, norms and institutions make them act that way.

informal rules and between rules and behaviour, and the extreme ambiguity of both rules and behaviour. Open systems imply extensive causal influences between actors and systems, almost amounting to constant flux, and a large amount of cross-referencing; but the cross-referencing varies according to the different types of actors and implies different sorts of mental maps and sets of social rules.

In the case of the Austrian worker, respect for professional tradition and autonomy play into the hands of the natural system perspective, in addition to the rational perspective which had been at the root of a uniform working

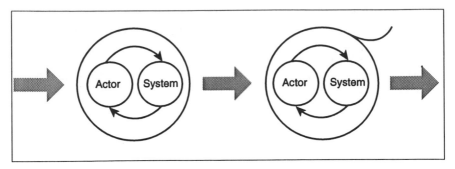

Figure 5.1 *Actor–system configurations*

time regime. Furthermore, the fact that the family life of the Austrian worker was respected by management shows the topicality of the open system view; after all, his wife and children are not employees of the company.

The conjoint influence of these differentiated organizational principles can be represented, graphically, by visualizing organizational life as consisting of feedback links between actors and systems (see Figure 5.1). Actors and systems are linked by feedback loops. Their representation by separate circles emphasizes their distinctness and partial autonomy. The feedback loops stress both cross-referencing and reciprocal causal influences. A set of actors, system properties and loops, surrounded by a circle to denote a pattern of cross-referencing and causation, can then be seen to lead, via the arrow, to organizational *outcomes*, the circle to the right hand of the diagram which also signifies an 'O' (for outcome). This outcome includes the achievement or non-achievement of organizational goals.

But the outcome also includes another set of actors and system characteristics, and the feedback loops between them. This is to express that organizational outcomes not only consist of direct results (production of goods or provision of services, at a certain level of efficiency and effectiveness), but also of a modification and maintenance of the described sets of actors, system characteristics, cross-referencing and reciprocal causation patterns. Nowadays, this fact is referred to as 'self-referencing': actors and systems act upon their own characteristics, not only on external targets (G. Morgan, 1986: 235ff.).

Clearly, the production manager of the plant in the example did not consider achieving production efficiency and effectiveness as the system's exclusive goal. He also wanted to maintain the social identity of the factory as a system, as an outcome in its own right. To do this, a partial adaptation of the working time regime appeared necessary. The manager was confident that such a policy also contributed to effectiveness.

It may therefore be that achieving direct organizational goals goes hand-in-hand with the modification of the characteristics of actors, systems and the relations between them. Organizational life re-arranges such characteristics. With regard to actors, such a re-arrangement can be called *socialization and personal development*. With regard to systems, the re-arrangement is usually called *reorganization*. Pervasive change in all the components (actors, systems, partial autonomy, cross-referencing, reciprocal influences) implies shifts in the emphasis on natural, rational and open systems features, or an innovative recombination of such elements.

The difference between the left-hand and the right-hand circle in Figure 5.1 indicates whether the *identity* of a system-and-actors constellation has changed over time. Maintaining the identity of the actors, systems and interrelations is to some extent necessary for reasonable personal stability and organizational performance. But it is also true that changes in such identities are normal and necessary. We have, here, another dialectic, this time of stability and change. The preservation of stability requires at least some amount of change, and change tends to reconstitute patterns which have already existed in a novel form. The term *non-identical reproduction* has been coined to express this kind of dialectical balance: given sets of actors, systems and their interrelations are reproduced over time, not in an identical fashion, but with modifications. Normal organizational life even requires that the very identity of an actor–system constellation should reside in its non-identical reproduction! Despite the complicated reasoning, this expresses the common-sense insight that the total absence of change is tantamount to the degradation of personal and social identity.

4   Analyzing cross-national differences

To describe and explain cross-national differences adequately, following the comprehensive approach sketched out in the last section, one would have to present no less than an encompassing treatment of the following aspects.

- The 'construction' of actors, consisting of the programming of their minds in the form of values and preferences, and of the way they imagine, and make sense of, system design (under what is here called cross-referencing).
- The design of organizational systems, including structures, norms, rules of the game and other institutionalized regularities; this includes, again under 'cross-referencing', their implications with regard to individual actor mentality.
- Causal influences, either way, and relative autonomy between the construction of actors and the design of systems.
- The social, political, economic and psychological architecture of a society as the sum total of external reference points which function as signposts, in the 'open systems' perspective, for the behaviour of both actors and systems.
- The way in which the dynamic development of outcomes (with regard to self-referenced and other goals) varies or remains constant between societies.

Modes of generating organizational outcomes

Both indirect and direct organizational outcomes may come about in mainly two different ways:

1   Actors work to generate outcomes in a trial-and-error fashion; they try out solutions without conscious reference to an articulate concept, recipe or knowledge basis. Such a knowledge basis may exist, but actors are not able or pressed to formulate it before taking action. This way of generating organizational outcomes may be called the simple mode. This is clearly prevalent in the case of the Austrian worker.
2   Actors do provide a conceptual, theoretical or programmatic basis before taking action. This means that they think about relations between forms of action and goal attainment, and they articulate such ideas. Since actors consciously monitor relations between their own acts and organizational outcomes, let us call this the *reflexive* mode. This mode would have been expressed if the production manager had formally circumscribed and legitimated policy with regard to the Austrian worker.

Reflexivity must not be confused with 'self-referencing'. Self-referenced action may occur under both the simple and the reflexive mode, and reflexivity does include consideration of external targets, for instance market structures, customer behaviour, technology, and social or political pressures. Self-referencing makes the actor or system itself a target, leaving out external considerations. Reflexivity, on the other hand, brings in conscious conceptualization; it may extend to internal and external reference points, and to the relations between them.

There is a tendency, in all manner of social science theory, to consider the simple mode pre-modern because of the emphasis on tradition, whereas the reflexive mode is evaluated as highly modern, in view of its inherent rationality. This expresses a well-known prejudice in social science theory that reflexive modes drive out simple modes in a long-term evolution. But in actual fact, humans are terribly good at reconciling the different modes. The application of one mode may even intensify the application of another. Discrepancies between the simple mode and the reflexive mode are permitted or approved. Actors operate, and systems are designed, essentially to permit two possible combinations of the simple and the reflexive mode, as a matter of everyday life.

One possibility is that reflexively generated theories, concepts or programmes are operative in practice, although this may not quite be the truth. Let us call this method of reconciliation *ideological*. Clearly, our production manager in the example was subject to an ideology of uniform working time. Far from being only a trick played by a political enemy, ideology is in fact, as Gouldner (1976) has shown, a perfectly normal modern phenomenon which arises in the wake of reflexivity (human thought consciously turning its attention to the requirements and results of human action) and rational action. In that way, ideology is a child of the enlightenment and rationality, although an unreasonable one. Its lack of reason is due to the persistence and growth of the simple mode, which is programmatically impossible to reconcile with the reflexive mode.

The other possibility of reconciling the simple and the reflexive mode lies in the *pragmatic* method. Pragmatism acknowledges the impossibility of founding practice on theory, and it turns a tenuous relationship between the reflexive and the simple mode into a creative asset. This is based on the supposition that the reflexive mode would stifle innovative advancement and adaptation to specific circumstances. Our production manager was not a pure ideologist but also a pragmatist. Innovation and adaptation are attributed to the application of the simple mode, in the first instance. The unreasonableness of pragmatism lies in its refusal to articulate and discuss the motives behind action, latent interests, predispositions and traditions.

The interesting thing is, again, that these two possibilities do not exclude each other, as the case of our production manager illustrates. They are dialectically intertwined, which means that they may even reinforce each other. Deployment of an ideology may be pragmatically motivated. There may also be a thoroughly ideological side to the use of pragmatism. It is not difficult to think of examples for both cases. The important thing at this point is to refrain from viewing ideology and pragmatism as mere caricatures of a more systematic and forthright approach. They are two crucial methods for accomplishing something very important: they maintain the identity of organizational and larger social systems in a balance of stability and change. This happens through a process of non-identical reproduction. The process implies maintaining a particular balance of the simple and the reflexive mode of generating outcomes.

It will be obvious that achievement of such an ambitious objective appears to be a near-impossible task. The amount of detailed and coordinated research work required, even for the treatment of a small number of societies, would be overwhelming. The practical difficulties involved in coordinating concepts and methods, making resources available and motivating researchers over a long period of time get in the way. At this point, the all-encompassing perspective developed in the previous section has a tendency to become ideological. However, as we have seen, this is no reason to dismiss it, for it is needed to assure the identity of this set of activities through its non-identical reproduction. Furthermore, researchers have developed a certain pragmatism which they apply to narrow unwieldy study perspectives down to more limited approaches which have the additional advantage of being pragmatically feasible.

It is also clear that there is a temptation to generalize the one-sided conceptual basis of either approach more than warranted, in which case pragmatism slips into ideology. This is perfectly natural, as long as we are aware of such limitations and are prepared to rationalize them. Over-extended generalization of limited approaches is not harmful but productive, provided it serves a specific purpose: a controversial discussion of countervailing approaches can alert us to possibilities of contradiction which are dialectical, that is, they stand for complementarity of approaches. This points the way to the formulation of a more general theory, such as that put forward in the previous section.

Let us then focus on one possible narrowing-down of the more general and complex framework into a more single-minded and handy-to-use approach. This would involve basing research and theory-building on the category of the *actor*. Actors are human individuals or a whole collection of individuals. They can be defined either by common characteristics (quasi-groups) or by integrated social interaction. Individual and collective actors typically feature what may be called a 'programming of the mind', arising from socialization processes which are similar for members of the collectivity. There are various possible commonalities that can be imagined: early childhood socialization may have a distinctive pattern in a society; education and school experiences differ from one country to the next; working careers are also different, exerting a socializing influence on the human mind even though they are not necessarily labelled as education or training. In every example, a socialization process of a specific form and with a specific content contributes to the formation of an individual identity that is typified by the way the individual mind works. This approach is found in exemplary fashion in the work of Hofstede (1980b).

This approach will be covered in greater detail in the following chapter. It will be obvious how it fits in in terms of the present analysis. The cornerstone of the approach is the actor. Hofstede also showed that actors display a particular correspondence between the general programming of the mind and more specific mental programmes related to what he called 'work-related values'. The latter are a cross-reference to system characteristics. They are the imagined desirable and undesirable organization structures and methods, preferred and contested organizational outcomes.

This approach may be called *culturalist* if culture is taken to represent a specific programming of the mind. According to Hofstede, the effect of culture extends from the level of the individual mind to characteristics of organization systems and other structures. Individual mental programming has an influence on the selection of system characteristics; it makes the individual choose between alternative system characteristics, in conformity with its own values and preferences. Such system characteristics will, in turn, stabilize or reinforce a specific programming of the individual mind. The feedback cycle will, furthermore, predispose actors and systems to go in the direction of specific organizational outcomes, notably particular self-referenced outcomes. A universal management principle, for instance management by objectives, will be adapted to existing mental programmes and related system characteristics, thereby acquiring a specific application – or even non-application – within the actor-and-systems constellation of the society in which it is implanted.

Further examples can be mentioned and have been demonstrated by Hofstede. Whether it be in the case of delegation or centralization of authority, individual versus group work, number of levels in the hierarchy of authority, the strength of the position of superiors, methods of motivation to work, communication patterns or other organizational practices, every time a plausible link between mental programmes and system characteristics can be demonstrated in cross-national comparisons. This tends to confirm strong causal influences between actors' and system properties. However, the approach also builds on the open systems concept, since mental programmes are shown to be rooted in wider socialization processes in the society-at-large, and they are definitely open to change. Hofstede has documented instances of what he called *value changes* in great detail. This emphasis on the open systems perspective is combined with an emphasis on the natural systems perspective; the evolution of mental programmes appears to escape rational control by whichever actor. This by no means prevents inclusion of a rational system perspective. Actors are shown to confront obstacles, restrictions and opportunities; this makes them rationally adapt the selection of system characteristics to match given mental programmes and system properties. But the latter two have to be explained in turn in terms of natural and open systems perspectives.

Now, Hofstede would be the last to deny that mental programmes evolve completely autonomously. He would admit that feedback loops may point either way, and may be equally strong in both directions. Yet its conceptual focus on the actor and the preferred research method of individual value surveying has slanted the approach towards methodological individualism. The latter is continuously on the look-out for mental programmes to match system characteristics, actor-and-system constellations and the outcomes which they generate. The mental programme of the actors always matters.

The opposite point of view would be that the mental programme does not always matter, but system characteristics do. The generation of organizational outcomes would be seen to depend, in the first instance, on system characteristics. Whether these would or would not have given rise to the adaptation of mental programmes is a secondary consideration. The main point is that different rules of the game make individuals move in different directions, even if their mental programming is the same. It may well be that different rules provoke the adaptation of individual mental programmes through a process of learning about context-specific factors associated with success (such as physical well-being, social recognition, professional and social advances, and personal development).

Faced, for example, with organizational outcomes in Japan, compared with other societies, such an approach would play down the role of Japanese culture to the extent that this refers to individual mental programmes and general socialization processes. Proponents of such an approach would argue that the specificity of Japanese practices resides in a different construction of professional careers, labour markets (life-long employment), payment systems, industrial relations etc. They would argue that, if Europeans and Americans were to be transplanted into a Japanese-type context, they would generate the same organizational results. The outcome would have to be traced back to the institutionalized rules of the game. Such proponents would also point to instances where Japanese-type management and organization practices have been transplanted success-fully to other countries.

This approach is very *structuralist*, which can be taken to represent the opposite of a culturalist approach. Structuralism is very much in evidence in industrial sociology or more narrowly sociological cross-national com-parisons. It is forever on the look-out for system characteristics as factors at the root of organizational outcomes, whether mental programmes are adapted in due course or not. The evidence in favour of structuralism is by no means weaker than that in favour of culturalism. In their study comparing attitudes and social rules in similar US and Japanese enter-prises, Lincoln and Kalleberg (1990) came to the conclusion – surprising to many but methodologically well substantiated – that work commitment is not greater in Japanese workers, if measured as an individual mental programme. Differences in organizational outcomes are explained by different rules of the game, rather than by ascertainable individual mental programmes. The authors do show how enterprises have to some extent adapted towards congruence with cultural predilections, as they call it; but the main factor is the design of system characteristics, and the role of culture is considered to be indirect and additive.

It is not sensible, however, to develop a structuralist counterprogramme to combat the culturalist programme. That would not be in the interest of authors such as Lincoln and Kalleberg. We are better served with an approach that has strong structuralist foundations, broad enough to take on board many culturalist analyses (within organization theory, such an approach had been proposed by Crozier and Friedberg, 1977). The idea is that the gap, in a purely nomothetic framework, between different sorts of reductionism can be bridged in the manner indicated by Giddens (1986), through what he called *structuration theory*. This is no more and no less than an erudite explication of how actors and systems constitute each other reciprocally. This eliminates the chicken-and-egg problem in the following way:

- It is silly to quarrel about the order of causality or precedence between chickens and eggs *in general*.
- Every chicken has crept out of an egg.
- Chickens cannot reproduce except via eggs.
- The reproduction among chickens is non-identical, since the egg and the young chick are different from the hen. This implies historical variation and evolution of chickens. (The argument neglects cocks and their contribution, in order to comply with recent pressures to choose language and metaphors that help redress the traditional imbalance in favour of the masculine gender.)

5   The societal effect approach

A succinct and understandable introduction to the societal effect approach was written by Rose (1985), a sympathetic outsider who brought out its essence. The classic statement of the approach can be found in Maurice, Sellier and Silvestre (1982), on the basis of a Franco-German comparison reported in greater detail by the same authors in 1977. This comparison focused on four dimensions of the wider social, economic and political spheres of society:

- organization of work and of the enterprise;
- human resources, education, training and socialization;
- industrial and sectoral structures, and relations between such industries and sectors;
- labour markets, as the sum total of events and arrangements which constitute the exchange of labour power for an equivalent, such as intrinsic satisfaction, social affiliation or (last but not least) money.

Dimensions, structure and flow

Every one of the four dimensions can be subdivided into a *structure* and a *flow* aspect. This means the following. First, the structural aspect refers to 'stocks' and properties which characterize the composition of an aggregate of people or of a system. The flow refers to additions and subtractions which occur with regard to a dimension, over a certain period of time. The interesting thing is that structures and flows are not set apart. A flow, for instance labour market mobility between enterprises, has a clear structure, being decomposed into relative shares of types of labour differentiated by age, experience, specialism, education and training, and other salient variables. Inversely, a structure has to be characterized by flows, since the structure is never completely stable. The identity of the structure over time cannot be limited to those elements that remain stable over a period of time; it also includes a relatively stable pattern of addition and subtraction, that is, of flows.

The *organizational dimension* has structures such as formal and informal organization structures, of both hierarchical and functional kinds. On the flow side of the dimension, we find primary and secondary transformation processes which transform inputs into outputs.

The *human resources dimension* has, on the flow side, personnel flows across stages of education, training and socialization more generally. The latter includes job changes, since even a succession of jobs without a manifest training purpose has a definite socialization effect. On the structure side, there are professional structures, the apparatus (schools, instructors, teaching methods etc.) dedicated to training, and the educational system of a society, both inside and outside enterprises.

The *Industrial–sectoral dimension* includes, on the structure side, the subdivision of an economy into sectors and industries, the subdivision of

---

Flows and structures of transformation processes

Any system and subsystem can be said to perform a transformation of inputs into outputs. Such transformation processes therefore also suppose flows, and these flows have structures. There are flows of information, material, semi-manufactured inputs, people, experience, knowledge, competence and other things, and these are all structured in ways that have to be described. Now, the identity of an actor and a system is not determined by a minimum of flows, that is, a restriction of change. Instead, it reposes on an equilibrium of flows, such that structures are reproduced – in a non-identical fashion.

The authors of the societal effect approach do not really use the notion of equilibrium because they would not consider equilibrium a necessary or normal condition of any kind of system. Disequilibria are a normal fact of life. On the other hand, they also highlight the phenomenon that countervailing forces – such as stability and change – hold each other in place, as analyzed above. This may legitimate using the notion of equilibrium, because even in situations of social 'disequilibrium', such as revolts, revolutions, upheaval, malfunctioning of institutions, civil war, power struggles etc., the changes that occur, and the imbalances that exist, tend to reproduce patterns. Therefore, these have to be considered as stable.

---

industries into enterprises of different types (differentiated according to size, age, dependence etc.). On the flow side, we get transactions of commodities and goods between industries and sectors, including ideas and information, rather in the manner of an input–output table. There are also flows of enterprises which leave and enter industries.

The *labour market dimension* has structures such as organisms, contractual, informal and statutory rules, which govern flows in the transaction of labour power. Professional structures also have to be included under the structural aspect, since they affect the supply of, and demand for, labour. Such professional structures also form part of the human resources dimension, which is, in a way, close to the labour market dimension.

More recently, a *technical dimension* has been added; this comprises structural characteristics of physical artefacts, of their mode of development, design and employment, plus flows of information, knowledge and experience which constitute and change technology. Innovation comes under the flow aspect of the technical dimension, being concerned with additions to, and subtractions from, structures of technical experience and knowledge.

Central tenets of the societal effect approach

The intention is not to define a rigid decomposition of the society and the economy into subsystems. The above categorization can easily be supplemented, for instance by capital markets. The precise structure of the subdivision is not central; it has been derived in a fairly pragmatic way. Proponents of the societal effect approach do not think that dogmatic classifications, which are sometimes proclaimed as basic to disciplines, are very helpful. The important thing is to grasp the relations between events, arrangements, structures and flows, across any classification scheme. This means that it is important to explore the *societal* aspect of any social, economic and political phenomenon we are concerned with. The definition of society, then, does *not set society apart* from the economy, or the polity, or what have you. The societal effect is concerned with lateral, reciprocal, relations between any subdivided components of reality. In a nutshell, this means that what happens in a specific sphere, be it technology, social stratification, labour markets, enterprise organization etc., has to be explained with reference to a set of cross-relations with as many other spheres or dimensions as possible.

Through these cross-relations, there is what the American sociologist Talcott Parsons termed 'interpenetration', meaning that the economy has a social and a political subsystem, and similarly for any other category. In the terminology of the societal effect approach, this is referred to as 'reciprocal interdependence' (*encastrement* in French), which denotes the fact that any 'separate' sphere of political, social, economic and technical life also forms part of every other sphere. In essence, it is therefore impossible to keep spheres of human life apart; through the interpenetration of spheres, a societal effect is ever present.

Let us now consider what the approach has to say about these cross-relations. In addition to the cross-relations already mentioned, that is, between spheres of human life, there are two other types: cross-relations between actors and systems, and between actor–systems constellations at different points in time. Let us first deal with cross-relations between the dimensions described above, as one possible way of categorizing major components of economy and society.

Reciprocal interdependence between dimensions

The first central tenet of the approach is that characteristics of any of the four dimensions mentioned above are related to specific, parallel characteristics of every other dimension. This means that specific patterns of work organization and enterprise structures are linked with specific patterns of human resource generation, of industrial and sectoral structures, and of industrial relations. What happens in one dimension has implications for what happens in the others. If a society, for instance, shows a tendency to deepen the hierarchical differentiation of enterprises, there will be a related differentiation with regard to human resources and in industrial relations structures, and it will also be related to the importance of concentrated industries in that society. The implication is that such characteristics are specific for a society, and the identity of the society is constituted through stable couplings of characteristics across the dimensions mentioned.

This is the more static aspect of the approach, which tries to summarize features that are relatively stable over time. These can be formulated following a more nomothetic logic of theory-building: if work is organized in a particular way, this will be interdependent with related human resources, industrial-sectoral and industrial relations patterns. Note that it is not one-way determination or causality which is implied, but *reciprocal interdependence between dimensions of social, economic and political life*. It has been suggested that, for instance, vocational education and training patterns 'explain' organizational characteristics. But this is not the way the approach should be understood. Its proponents insist on interdependence rather than dependence. Societal effect analysts do not pretend to put in place a new kind of 'grand theory', however. Rather, they see themselves as developing an approach based on *different* 'grand theories' rolled into one. Neither do they see themselves as developing just another 'theory of the middle range', which can be translated as nomothetic theory represented by inter-linked 'if A, then B' statements.

Complementarity of opposites

This takes us to the second basic tenet: actors reproduce characteristics on any dimension of society, and the interrelations between such dimensions. This happens because structural properties and rules of the game, that is, the 'systems' properties, tend to load the individual 'choices' that actors make in a specific way. It also happens because the actors learn to see particular 'choices' as generally favourable, and develop a specific 'programming of the mind'. In contrast with the culturalist perspective, the emphasis is on the interactive relationship between systems characteristics and mental programming. But the interactive relationship may be marked by both correspondence and opposition: faced with hierarchical organization patterns, the actors may learn to internalize corresponding assumptions and find them legitimate. But they may also develop a dislike for them, and attempt to evade them while trying at the same time to comply with them. This means that expressed value preferences and manifest behaviour may both converge and diverge. Under this tenet, the emphasis is on the *complementarity*, or *mutual affinity, of opposites*. Here, we see dialectical rather than nomothetic theory-building at work.

Non-identical reproduction of dimensions and their interrelations

This brings us to the third tenet, which defines the *reproduction* of characteristics on every dimension mentioned, and their interrelations, as *non-identical*. Thus, although open and natural systems properties imply erratic, or at least unpredictable variations in the course of evolution, such changes are in line with existing system properties. Let us take a simple example. Until the mid-1960s, the prevalence of greater numbers of skilled workers in German factories went hand-in-hand with much more restrictive access to selective secondary education; more young people went into

Work ethic and work discipline

The example of Japanese workers given by Lincoln and Kalleberg (1990), and mentioned above, illustrates the point about complementary opposites: the Japanese do not view the company more favourably than the Americans, but the social rules of the game load their behavioural 'choices' towards manifest company loyalty, even if they hate it. Similarly, surveys tend to show that German workers in no way attribute greater importance to the work ethic, work discipline and the centrality of work in life; the reverse is usually true. Yet it is a well-known cliché that Germans work hard and maintain work discipline. Is this all nonsense? Germans work comparatively few hours per year, on average, and have fewer working years per lifetime than most other countries; this would make us believe that at least part of the cliché is nonsense. On the other hand, company studies do show work discipline in operation. However, its persistence is due to the construction of social relations in the workplace and the employment sphere, which is also reflected in the 'mental map' of the individual of legitimate and advantageous expectations, forms of behaviour and outcomes. The simple fact is that Germans tend to hate work and yet comply with the ground rules of the workplace because they appear legitimate. This may culminate in a love–hate relationship as a frequent phenomenon. Anyone who has seen Germans work will find the interpretation entirely plausible.

Not the mental maps of individuals, nor their values, nor the system characteristics to which they attach themselves, nor the relations between them can ever be free of conflict or contradictions. This shows the limitations of a nomothetic approach and of a perspective which stresses the 'static' side of the societal effect. Conflicts and contradictions exemplify the necessity to use, in addition, a dialectical perspective. Social systems at every level are simultaneously closed, naturally evolving and open. Similarly, complete societies are even more strongly marked by closure, natural evolution and openness, all at the same time. A dialectical perspective stresses that openness, and the natural properties of systems in the wider sense, account for the ever-present tendency to change and modify in ways that transcend the relatively stable patterns put forward in the first two tenets of the societal effect approach. This transcendence has an uncomfortable habit of blurring nomothetic statements that were meant to be so beautifully precise and general.

apprenticeships, rather than going to selective secondary schools. In France, access to selective general education was more generous, but fewer people went into apprenticeships or vocational education.

The example may be taken to imply a simple nomothetic logic: if selective secondary education in Germany is expanded, this will mean greater convergence with French patterns, and a concomitant reduction of apprenticeship as a major socializing arrangement. That would have been change, but change to be expected on the basis of a nomothetic proposition alone. Life does not work that way, however, and what happened in

Germany was different. To be sure, there was not simply a haphazard or accidental deviation from 'relatively stable' patterns. What Germany got was an increase in secondary education *before* apprenticeship, such that growing numbers of ex-grammar school and secondary modern or secondary technical school (*Realschule*) graduates took up apprenticeships. The change was that the sharpness of the 'choice' between selective education and apprenticeship training had been reduced, but earlier patterns had been reasserted, since apprenticeship continued to be an attractive education and training choice. Change and continuity are therefore united in the non-identical reproduction of previous patterns.

France has since greatly increased the status and quantity of vocational education, but mainly by upgrading vocational schools and diplomas. It has made vocational education more attractive by giving it *baccalauréat* status, and other measures. But training by apprenticeship has continued to dwindle. Thus, France has asserted the particularity of its own education and training arrangements in a way which is parallel to Germany but nevertheless different.

Note that convergence between France and Germany did not come about for very clear reasons: the novel education and training arrangement is distinctive for its creative combination of old and new patterns, with no mechanical shift along a known continuum of 'choice'. What is novel is the new combination, rather than the sheer rate of increase in secondary education. This insight can be generalized. In the societal effect approach, it lays the basis for the view that true 'convergence' hardly ever takes place, since any change tends to consist of non-identical reproduction; we are not in reality dealing with change upon a continuum of nomothetically established alternatives.

Illustrations

Let us now discuss a number of findings in the light of the societal effect approach and start with the simpler, more nomothetic side, to expound the first major tenet of the approach. We tried to sum up comparative findings on France, Germany and the United Kingdom in a set of three law-like statements focusing on the interdependence of the organizational and the human resources dimension (Maurice et al., 1980: 80ff.).

1   *The higher the practical professionalization of workers, technical employees and supervisors and managers, the less technical and authoritative tasks are split off from shop-floor roles and organized into differentiated jobs, and the less such activities are differentiated internally in the white-collar area.* This relationship explains how different measures for job specialization, organizational differentiation and professionalization in the three countries are obtained. France features the greatest amount of specialization and differentiation, and the smallest amount of practical professionalization; Germany has the smallest amount of specialization and differentiation, and the greatest amount of practical professionalization; the UK is somewhere in between. The explanation could be extended

to include interdependence with other dimensions, but this has been left out for the sake of brevity, not because it is of lesser importance. Contrary to many clichés, the professional autonomy of shop-floor production workers is most highly developed in Germany, and production management is therefore more technical than authoritarian.

2 *The larger the discrepancy in training and competence between production and maintenance components of the shop-floor, the greater the separation between production and maintenance activities and careers.* This combined organizational and human resources effect is strongest in the UK. This society has brought forth a characteristic difference between the autonomous maintenance craftsman and the production worker as a more restricted and less responsible worker. The effect lays the basis for functional, human resources and career differentiation 'higher up' in the pyramid of the enterprise, between line and staff personnel, job categories and careers. This 'lateral' differentiation is very strong in the United Kingdom, intermediate in France and smallest in Germany. As a result, managerial authority is most isolated from technical responsibility in the UK, whereas the two are most intimately linked in Germany. The British manager is more of a pure, or general, manager, whereas the German manager is more of a technical (or commercial, or administrative) leader. Leadership implies joint involvement in similar tasks, whereas management means a separation of operative and managerial tasks. Such findings are summarized in the following hypothesis.

3 *The greater the human resources and career differences between managers and technical experts, the greater the differences between line management and specialist functions.* Such differences between societies are recreated even in the midst of technical and economic change. After about 1977, all three countries introduced computer numerically controlled (CNC) machine-tools in factories on an increasing scale. This made it easier to combine automation with productive flexibility, and to let shop-floor workers share in work planning and programming tasks, more than under previous forms of automated metal-cutting. Yet the precise impact of such new machines depended less on the potential of the technology itself and more on the continuation of previously existing characteristics of the various dimensions.

German companies accordingly exploited the potential for 'shop-floor programming' of machine tools more purposefully than British companies (Sorge and Warner, 1986), and French companies continued earlier patterns of hierarchically more differentiated human resource generation, work organization and internal labour markets (Maurice et al., 1986). This happened because of the type of non-identical reproduction of actor–systems constellations put forward. There were changes, to be sure. French companies adopted a policy of recruiting and training a higher calibre of metal worker, but they were taken on in addition to workers with less training, so that the received hierarchical differentiation patterns were preserved. Similarly, although British companies invested more in skilling direct production workers, the investment mainly targeted more restricted 'company skills' rather than the broader apprenticeship skills linked to maintenance craftsman status.

The relevance of the societal effect approach in the midst of dynamic change is also illustrated by the differential evolution of the French and the German machine-tools industries. Actor–systems constellations better prepared German industry for developing and manufacturing universal, flexible CNC machines and control systems, giving them a better position in the machine-tool market and leading to better outcomes in terms of market share and employment. The French machine-tool industry entered a severe crisis and shed employment on a larger scale after a series of redundancies, bankruptcies and takeovers by competitors from abroad. Interestingly, the French manufacturers that survived or did better were those which produced more single-purpose CNC machines. French industry had already possessed more manufacturers of single-purpose machines, whereas German industry had previously been stronger in universal machines.

So it was that a successful outcome was marked by a different type of success in each country: in Germany, success was attained through the manufacture of universal machines, while France achieved it by manufacturing single-purpose machines of a more specialized kind. And this was valid both for the period preceding and for the period after the rise of CNC, as a major metal-cutting innovation. All this attests to the reproduction of societal patterns, even when the up-and-coming innovation is basically the same everywhere, and even when a large number of technical, industry structure, human resource and organizational changes are in evidence. The simple fact is that such changes are not quite the same in every society, even when they are technical. They evolve not as something which is factually neutral, but as something internalized into the existing features of a society.

Another interesting case of the impact of the societal effect from a dynamic perspective is a comparison between French and Japanese machine-tool makers and users. In the French case, the linking of electronic controls with mechanical equipment and processes was slower and more precarious, in view of the practice of separating jobs, functions, competencies and industries, and the more inferior status of the machine-tools industry in many respects. In contrast, the Japanese practice of mixing professional experience of different types within the internal labour markets of firms and industrial groups, and the absence of status differences between industrial sectors and professional bases made for a quick move into the 'mechatronic age', a specifically Japanese term referring to the amalgamation of electronic controls and mechanical production processes (Maurice et al., 1988).

Even if this Franco-Japanese comparison highlighted differences similar to the Franco-German comparison in the machine-tool industry, this is not at all to suggest that German and Japanese institutions and practices resemble each other more closely. For instance, the German inter-firm labour market for engineers is well developed, whereas there is no inter-firm labour market for engineers in Japan. Germany has highly developed professional specialisms at all levels, generally valid apprenticeships (training methods, contents, exams and certificates) and practically oriented education; Japan has none of these, indeed quite the opposite. But on the basis of totally different institutional regimes, Germany and Japan are both able to achieve something which appears to be more difficult in France: to stabilize technical people in technical functions over a longer period of their career. This happens on the basis of reward structures, a common and overlapping basic qualification, the role of continuous learning, and a continuous human resource dimension. In France, the human resource and organizational dimensions are more segmented, both laterally and hierarchically; career mobility and rewards promote an escape from technical specialism into generalism and management. The Japanese engineer is more of a multi-specialist, the German engineer a specialist who extends his domain into other specialisms, while the French engineer is a potential generalist who tries to escape the specialism in which he initially finds himself. Hence, German enterprises have a propensity to be 'mechatronic' which is not too far removed from that of Japanese firms, but on the basis of radically different education, training, labour market, industrial and organizational systems. In contrast, the French firm is either electronically or mechanically based, and a forward integration of mechanical firms and professions into electronics is more precarious.

All these examples reiterate the point that organizational outcomes differ quantitatively and qualitatively from one society to the next. This is true both with respect to direct outcomes (the nature of precise organizational goals, the extent to which they are achieved and the way in which they are achieved) and indirect outcomes, represented by the simple or reflexive reproduction and change of actor–systems constellations. For instance, it is clear that the average French machine-tool manufacturer now differs more sharply from the average German and Japanese competitor, following the advent of a basic technology which is the same in all three countries, and after the development of a market situation which is very international. Manufacturers in different countries have carved different slices out of a global market, with different measures of success. In France, manufacturers of universal flexible machines have disappeared or have been taken over. In Japan, makers of universal standard machines have boomed, while in Germany such makers have maintained their position until recently.

The importance of societal settings has also been documented for the patterns which specifically apply to R&D departments in the electronics industry. Multi-specialism in Japan appears to favour applied market and production research and development. Conversely, the fragmentation of organizations and careers and the generalist approach to engineering in France appear to favour a high calibre of basic research and development which is more de-coupled from production implications and marketing concepts. Hence, the internationalization of competition and the advent of a similar basic technology may imply that enterprises in different countries develop different strengths and weaknesses, focus on different market segments and localize different functions in different countries. Although there is 'institutional learning', whereby firms in one society try to emulate 'best practice' from another country, an important countervailing tendency nevertheless remains strong. And even when firms and societies do learn from each other, internationally, they will usually achieve comparable direct outcomes in ways which are institutionally different. This is illustrated by the contrast in the institutionalized methods employed by the Japanese and German firms to 'mechatronize'. In the Japanese case, the internal labour market and interprofessional job chains are central; in Germany, professionalized multi-specialism and an inter-firm labour market remain important.

What kinds of outcomes firms achieve, and how successful they are in which market segment or activity, can then be explained by the society in which they are embedded. The same point was made for the evolution of the automobile industry in the major manufacturing countries. There has been a further segmentation of market segments; and which kinds of manufacturers did well in which kinds of segments is explained by the societal setting which they already inhabited. Of particular importance are, again, the above-mentioned dimensions of organization, human resources, the labour market and industrial structures (Streeck, 1992: ch. 6).

Internationalization, European integration and institutional differentiation

To sum up this particular point, the societal effect approach argues that internationalization and universal technical change lead to different outcomes in each society, within an intensification of the international division of labour. How this division of labour develops can only be explained by reference to societal characteristics that are relatively stable, even in the midst of change. This change triggers development of societal specificity, rather than bringing about convergence between societies. That is also the clear message which the approach offers to all those who think that European integration will reduce the differences between separate European countries. Such a message suggests that the societal effect approach will continue to be relevant and applicable for new research into cross-national differences. It will be central to any exploration of the new emergent sectoral, industrial and functional profiles of different countries.

The approach rests on the assumption that societies will grow increasingly different in their industrial and activity portfolio, because the institutionalized constructions of their various systems already differed. Internationalization of economic activity and technical innovation, and institutional differentiation of societies are, therefore, two sides of the same coin. But the approach also suggests that, to the extent that societies and firms try to achieve similar direct outcomes, the international learning which takes place precludes direct transfer of institutionalized practice. If direct outcomes are to be similar, the systems and actors needed to achieve them have to be constructed in ways that have a bearing on systems and actors already there. Whichever way you turn it, institutional (indirect outcome) and direct outcome convergence are fundamentally incompatible. Either you assimilate institutions cross-nationally, or you assimilate performance with regard to direct outcomes.

6 The 'culture' factor in personnel and organization policies

René Olie

1	Introduction	124
2	Cross-national organizational research	125
	Universalism	125
	The cultural approach	125
	The ideational and the institutionalist perspective	127
3	Culture: a definition	127
4	Cultural diversity and the work organization	130
	Cultural diversity of Western conceptions of management	131
5	Hofstede's work on national culture	135
6	Consequences of national cultural differences for managerial behaviour and personnel practices	138
	Motivation	138
	Leadership and decision-making	140
	Organizational design	141
7	Conclusions	142

1 Introduction

Anyone who crosses national borders will immediately notice a number of differences between the people of each country. Differences in lifestyle, dress, speech, ways of greeting others and other forms of interpersonal interaction are some of the more visible contrasts that may strike the visitor. After a while one may even become aware of differences between various national traditions and ways of thinking about such aspects as family, education, religion, politics etc. Such idiosyncrasies, which we often label collectively as culture, are fundamental to a particular way of life. As such they are highly relevant for organizations that operate across borders. Consumer preferences and attitudes, for example, are determined to a large extent by the social environment. As a result, companies operating in these markets must often develop distinct marketing approaches adapted to local consumer needs and preferences. Companies sometimes have to change to other colours, labels or names. For example, the colour green is generally taboo in the Far East; gold, on the other hand, is viewed as a symbol of value and prestige in Latin American countries. Similarly, a brand name may have unfavourable connotations in a foreign language and need to be changed.

At another level, one may ask whether cultural differences also require different ways of organizing. Are there, for example, different 'human resource' problems which require organizations to develop distinct organizational practices? More broadly stated: are organizations culture-free or are they culture-specific? In this chapter we will deal with this question by 'comparing' firms from different nations and by looking at the extent to which national variations in organizational approaches can be attributed to national cultural differences.

2   Cross-national organizational research

Universalism

The role of national culture in organizational functioning and its influence on management has not always been acknowledged to the same extent as nowadays. In the 1950s and 1960s, when researchers influenced by the internationalization of business organizations began to study management and organizations in different parts of the world, there was a strong belief in universal principles of management. The idea was that there were principles of sound management which applied regardless of the national environment. This is known as the *convergence hypothesis*. The principal notion was that the 'logic of industrialism' had a homogenizing effect upon business organizations, irrespective of the country they were located in. Scientific progress and the consequent creation of more and more highly developed forms of technology and production processes would eventually drive all industrial societies towards the same end. As societies became more and more alike, a universal type of business organization would evolve.

The belief in convergence waned in the 1970s and was replaced by a growing interest in the national distinctiveness of organizations and the cultural roots of organizational functioning. The cultural approach emphasizes national differences between organizations, differences which have cultural factors at their root. We will discuss this cultural approach below.

The cultural approach

Compared to other approaches to organization and management which stress universal tendencies, the cultural approach emphasizes national distinctiveness. Central to this approach is the belief that each society is distinctly different from any other society, and that this distinctiveness is reflected in the way organizations are structured and function. The special nature of organizations can only be understood in terms of their relationship to the wider societal system of which they are a part.

The rise of Japan as an industrial superpower was a particular stimulus for the renewed interest in cultural and societal-specific factors. When Western – mostly American – researchers started examining the characteristics of the Japanese business organization in the 1970s and the early

1980s, they found striking differences between the Japanese approach and the dominant organizational approach in Western countries. There was much less convergence between Japanese and Western organizations than expected. Marked differences, for example, were found with regard to employment policies, worker orientation and reward systems. As opposed to American organizations, the Japanese offered stable tenure, often in the form of lifetime employment. Japanese workers and management were furthermore characterized by a strong collective orientation, illustrated by the wish to put the company first and the emphasis on team effort. Significant features of the Japanese reward system were the gradual promotion to higher-level jobs, the relatively minor salary differences between the members of a particular intake, and job rotation. Another feature was the distinctive decision-making process in Japanese firms, characterized by extensive consultation, participative management and the many points of view which were expressed throughout the process. For example, proposals for new policies, regulations or expenditures are circulated through the firm. Although many of the distinctive qualities of Japanese management have in fact evolved in recent decades, many authors agree that the cultural context of Japan makes possible and encourages certain patterns of organizing (Smith and Misumi, 1989). Characteristics such as the strong collectivist orientation fit in well with the Japanese societal culture, where values such as group loyalty, dedication and balance and harmony among group members are highly valued.

Convergency and distinctiveness

Although cultural patterns may encourage different ways of organizing, this does not imply that other factors, such as size, technology, variability of products or services (the contingency factors) or the level of industrialization, are irrelevant. The cultural approach more or less suggests that *ceteris paribus* (task, size and environment being equal), organizational characteristics may differ according to the cultural characteristics of the country in which the organization is located. Convergency as postulated by the contingency approach, and distinctiveness due to cultural factors, may be viewed as two forces influencing the organization in two different areas, as is argued by Child (1981). The contingency approach, for example, has mainly been concerned with the influence upon formal structure and strategy. The cultural approach, by contrast, principally postulates the effects of national culture at the group or individual level, such as leadership styles, decision-making processes and worker motivation. Thus, as Child states, while organizations may be expected to show convergency in some respects, such as in organizational structure, they may exhibit diversity in other respects. Other researchers, however, have shown that the influence of national culture may not be limited to micro-level variables, but may also affect the structuring of organizations and the strategic process (e.g. Hofstede, 1980a; Schneider and De Meyer, 1991).

The ideational and the institutionalist perspective

Generally, there are two complementary perspectives on cross-national variation, each of which chooses a different starting point. The first perspective, the *institutionalist* or *structuralist* tradition, has primarily been concerned with the structural aspects within organizations, such as the division of labour and career, status and reward structures that are generated by national institutions, such as educational and professional training systems, the system of industrial relations, or the overall organization of industry in a society (Maurice et al., 1980). Values and ideas are derived or secondary (Child and Tayeb, 1983). This perspective is taken by the *societal effect approach*, which we explored in Chapter 5 (see Sections 4 and 5).

In this chapter we will focus on the *ideational* perspective, which draws attention to cultural distinctiveness in terms of values, ideas and beliefs shared by people in a society. In Chapter 5 this approach was labelled *culturalist*. This school of research tends to focus on cultural dimensions that are situated at the level of the personality. Values and ideas form the core of a societal culture. Members of a society learn these shared characteristics by going through different stages of various socialization processes. Common early childhood experiences in customs, education, language and religion are formative in determining the basic assumptions of a given culture. In time cultural values and ideas will shape national institutions which, in turn, reinforce and perpetuate dominant value patterns. Work organizations are also seen as reflecting culturally based preferences.

3   Culture: a definition

In a review of cross-cultural organization studies, Ajiferuke and Boddewyn state: 'Culture is one of those terms that defy a single all-purpose definition and there are almost as many meanings of culture as people using the term' (Ajiferuke and Boddewyn, 1970: 154). Most cross-cultural research has suffered from methodological inadequacies and weak conceptualizations of culture, employing culture 'simply as a synonym for "nation" without any further theoretical grounding' (Child, 1981: 304). A central issue, therefore, is to define the concept in order to prevent culture from becoming an omnibus variable representing a range of social, historical, political and economic factors.

Despite the many definitions of the concept, most authors agree on the following characteristics of culture. First, culture is not a characteristic of individuals, but of a collection of individuals who share common values, beliefs, ideas etc. These groups or collectivities include family groups, occupational groups, regional groups and national groups. While some of these categories overlap, each group has ways of behaving, thinking and perceiving that are common to all those who belong to this group or

Definitions of culture

Although there appears to be widespread acceptance at a general level of definition, there is little agreement about either an exact definition of culture or the operationalization thereof. The American anthropologists Kluckhohn and Strodtbeck (1961), for example, identified 164 different definitions of culture in the early 1950s. One of the first definitions comes from the anthropologist Taylor, who defined culture in 1871 as 'that complex whole which includes knowledge, belief, art, morals, law, custom and any other capabilities and habits acquired by man as a member of a society'. A more recent definition is provided by Kluckhohn and Strodtbeck (1961): 'Culture consists of patterned ways of thinking, feeling and reacting, acquired and transmitted mainly by symbols, constituting the distinctive achievements of human groups, including their embodiments in artifacts; the essential core of culture consists of traditional (i.e. historically derived and selected) ideas and especially their attached values.' Clifford Geertz (1973), another American anthropologist, defines culture as 'an historically transmitted pattern of meanings embodied in symbols, a system of inherited conceptions expressed in symbolic forms, by means of which men communicate, perpetuate and develop their knowledge about and attitudes towards life.' Finally, the Dutch organizational researcher Hofstede, whose work we will draw heavily from in this chapter, defines culture as: 'the collective programming of the mind which distinguishes the members of one human group from another'.

category, but which differ from all those who belong to other groups or categories.

Secondly, culture is learned. People learn the culture of a group or collectivity when they become a member. Children are born into a society and a family and are taught the values and norms of that society and family. They go to school and learn the skills needed to practise an occupation or profession. At an even later stage they become members of organizations and acquire the culture of this organization. At all these different levels, the culture of the group is transmitted from generation to generation: from parents to children, from teachers to pupils, from supervisors and peer group members to organizational novices. This process is called *socialization*.

A third and related aspect of culture is its historical dimension. A particular nation's culture, for example, develops over time and is partly the product of that nation's history, its demographic and economic development, its geography, and its ecological environment. A warm climate, for example, limits inhabitants to a completely different lifestyle than a cold climate. A society faced with the continuous threat of ecological disasters, such as flooding or earthquakes, usually adopts world-views which are consistent with the exigencies posed by the environment. The societal norms that evolve over time lead to the development of institutions such as family patterns and religious, educational, political and

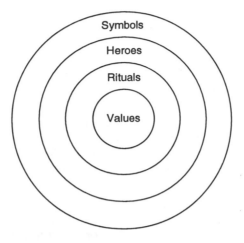

Figure 6.1 *Four different layers of culture (Hofstede, 1991)*

legal systems which reflect these shared ways of acting and thinking. In turn, these institutions reinforce and sustain the social norms and beliefs that have generated them. For example, social inequality as a societal norm is more generally accepted in France than in the Netherlands. We see the same difference between the French and the Dutch educational systems, which, in their turn, confirm and perpetuate the societal norm. For this reason, national culture is very stable and will typically change only slowly.

Finally, culture has different layers. The Greek-American cross-cultural psychologist Triandris has divided culture into objective and subjective cultures (Triandris, 1972). *Objective* culture includes human artifacts such as architecture, art, roads etc. *Subjective* culture, on the other hand, refers to a group's characteristic way of perceiving its social environment and includes norms, roles and values in particular. Many researchers have excluded the objective part of culture and focused almost exclusively on the subjective part, that is, the values, norms, ideas etc. Hofstede (1991) distinguishes four different layers of culture, ranging from the more visible and superficial manifestations of culture to deeper and less tangible elements, comprising ideas, values, beliefs and so on (Figure 6.1).

The first level consists of symbols. *Symbols* are words, gestures and objects that carry a particular meaning for the members of a society. Official national symbols like a country's flag, its national anthem, king or queen are examples of such cultural symbols. *Heroes* constitute the second level of culture. These refer to persons, alive or dead, real or imaginary, who embody characteristics that are highly prized in a society and who may serve as role models. The third level of culture consists of rituals. *Rituals* refer to the social rules and norms that need to be followed in a certain environment. Examples of such rituals are the ways in which we greet relatives, friends or colleagues, which may differ considerably from nation to nation. The deepest level of culture distinguished by Hofstede consists of shared values. *Values* represent collective beliefs, assumptions and feelings about what is good, normal, rational, valuable, and so on. Since this level is believed by many culturalists to represent the core of a national culture, we will focus our discussion of national culture differences on this level.

Values may be either conscious or unconscious, although most of the time we are unaware of their influence and take them for granted. Normally we only become aware of our own values when we meet people from other cultures with different sets of values and ways of perceiving and approaching the world. Usually we tend to view such differences as deviant, believing that our way of thinking is the most appropriate and sensible. This is called *ethnocentrism*. In international collaboration such a belief increases the potential for conflict.

Values may have a considerable influence on conceptions of identity and the role of individual rights and duties as opposed to collective ones. For example, in most West European countries and in North America, children are raised in the belief that they have to be self-sufficient as adults. Children are taught to make their own decisions and are encouraged to clarify their own needs and opinions and solve their own problems. The houses in which these children grow up often reflect this individualism. Each member of the family, including the children, often has a separate bedroom in order to maximize personal privacy. This stands in marked contrast to most other societies in the world, where children are taught that they belong to social groups, like the extended family, which will look after them and to which they owe their loyalty. People thus learn to identify closely with the goals and interests of these social groups. While property in Western societies belongs to individuals, property rights in other societies are often shared with other members of the group. Normally, houses do not allow for private places for individuals. Rooms are shared with other relatives.

4   Cultural diversity and the work organization

As mentioned, cultural values may find expression in a great number of national institutions, including work organizations. Initially, national culture shapes the organization through the values, attitudes and expectations which the founders or other key leaders and employees bring into the organization. Since they have all been raised in a particular environment, they will shape the organization according to the dominant preferences, values and norms of that environment. For example, in a society characterized by distinct inequalities in the child–parent, pupil–teacher, or subject–king relationship, it can be anticipated that work organizations will also reflect this tendency. In most Asian countries, it is common to accept the authority of one's elders. In these countries it can therefore be expected that superior–subordinate relationships in the organization are also characterized by a large power distance and by the centralization of authority.

A second way in which national culture shapes the organization is through institutions in that country and through the culturally derived expectations of external stakeholders such as shareholders, consumers, unions, the national government and the public at large. For example, participative legislation which grants employees a say in organizational decision-making may be the result of certain values of cooperation and equal sharing of power and influence in that country.

Cultural diversity of Western conceptions of management

A concrete example of national differences and their effects on management is provided by Laurent (1983). Laurent developed a questionnaire consisting of 56 different statements measuring managers' implicit theories of management. The questionnaire was initially administered to groups of management students and upper-middle-level managers from a large number of European and US business firms attending management education programmes at INSEAD, a European management institute located in France. At a later stage, the results were replicated in a study among managers of national subsidiaries of two US multinational companies. From statistical analysis four dimensions emerged that differentiated national cultures in terms of their managerial ideologies. These were:

- organizations as political systems;
- organizations as authority systems;
- organizations as role-formalization systems; and
- organizations as hierarchical-relationship systems.

The first index, organizations as political systems, measured to what extent managers agreed or disagreed with statements like: 'Through their professional activity, managers play an important political role'; 'Most managers seem to be more motivated by obtaining power than by achieving objectives'; and 'Most managers have a clear notion of what we call an organizational structure'. The results are shown in Table 6.1. Managers from France and Italy tend to interpret their organizational experience in power terms. They are more aware of their political role in society, emphasize the importance of power motivation within the organization and report a fairly hazy notion of organizational structure. Danish and British managers, on the other hand, show the opposite pattern: a relatively weak political orientation both within and outside the organization, and a fairly clear notion of organizational structure. The remaining five countries fall in between these two extremes, with the Netherlands being very close to the British/Danish position.

The second dimension, organizations as authority systems, also consists of three questions. These measure whether hierarchical structure is

Table 6.1 *Organizations as political systems*

772 managers from nine countries[1]	Denmark	UK	Netherlands	Germany	Sweden	USA	Switzerland	France	Italy
Sample size	54	190	42	72	50	50	63	219	32
Percentage agreement with: **40.** Through their professional activity, managers play an important political role in society	32	40	45	47	54	52	63	76	74
Percentage agreement with: **49.** Most managers seem to be more motivated by obtaining power than by achieving objectives	25	32	26	29	42	36	51	56	63
Percentage disagreement with: **33.** Most managers have a clear notion of what we call an organizational structure	22	23	36	31	30	42	38	53	61
Percentage average agreement/disagreement	26	32	36	36	42	43	51	62	66

[1] Belgium has been excluded from this table because of its indecisive rate, more than 20 percent for two items (40 and 33).

Source: Laurent, 1983

Table 6.2 *Organizations as authority systems*

817 managers from ten countries	USA	Switzerland	Germany	Denmark	Sweden	UK	Netherlands	Belgium	Italy	France
Sample size	50	63	72	54	50	190	42	45	32	219
Percentage agreement with: **14.** The main reason for having a hierarchical structure is so that everyone knows who has authority over whom	18	25	24	35	26	38	38	36	50	45
Percentage agreement with: **52.** Today there seems to be an authority crisis in organizations	22	29	26	40	46	43	38	64	69	64
Percentage agreement with: **43.** The manager of tomorrow will be, in the main, a negotiator	50	41	52	63	66	61	71	84	66	86
Percentage average agreement	30	32	34	46	46	48	49	61	61	65

Source: Laurent, 1983

Table 6.3   *Organizations as role-formalization systems*

817 managers from ten countries	Sweden	USA	Netherlands	Denmark	UK	France	Belgium	Italy	Germany	Switzerland
Sample size	50	50	42	54	190	219	45	32	72	63
Percentage agreement with: **1.** When the respective roles of the members of a department become complex, detailed job descriptions are a useful way of clarifying them	56	76	71	87	86	87	89	90	89	91
Percentage agreement with: **13.** The more complex a department's activities, the more important it is for each individual's functions to be well defined	66	69	79	85	85	83	84	94	93	94
Percentage disagreement with: **38.** Most managers would achieve better results if their roles were less precisely defined	50	54	52	67	68	72	71	69	73	71
Percentage average agreement/ disagreement	57	66	67	80	80	81	81	84	85	85

Source: Laurent, 1983

conceived of as being designed to specify authority relationships, whether managers feel that there is a crisis of authority in organizations today, and whether they have an image of the manager as a negotiator. The results are presented in Table 6.2. Once again, the two Latin European countries, France and Italy, together with Belgium, form one cluster, showing more personal and social concepts of authority as regulating relationships among individuals in organizations. The opposite end of the continuum is represented by US, Swiss and German managers, who report a more rational and instrumental view of authority as regulating the interaction between tasks or jobs.

The third index measures managers' perceptions of organizations as role-formalization systems, that is, the relative importance of defining and specifying the jobs and roles of organizational members. As is shown in Table 6.3, managers from Sweden, the United States and the Netherlands showed a significantly weaker preference for detailed job descriptions, well-defined tasks and precisely defined responsibilities than managers from the remaining seven countries.

The last dimension, organizations as hierarchical-relationship systems, shows a close correlation between the belief that conflict should be eliminated from organizations on the one hand, and the conviction that a manager should know more than his subordinates and that organizations

Table 6.4   *Organizations as hierarchical-relationship systems*

817 managers from ten countries	Sweden	USA	Netherlands	UK	Denmark	Switzerland	Germany	Belgium	France	Italy
Sample size	50	50	42	190	54	63	72	45	219	32
Percentage agreement with: **19.** Most organizations would be better off if conflict could be eliminated for ever	4	6	17	13	19	18	16	27	24	41
Percentage agreement with: **24.** It is important for a manager to have at hand precise answers to most of the questions that his subordinates may raise about their work	10	18	17	27	23	38	46	44	53	66
Percentage disagreement with: **2.** In order to have efficient work relationships, it is often necessary to bypass the hierarchical line	22	32	39	31	37	41	46	42	42	75
Percentage agreement with: **8.** An organizational structure in which certain subordinates have two direct bosses should be avoided at all costs	64	54	60	74	69	76	79	84	83	81
Percentage average agreement/ disagreement	25	28	33	36	37	43	47	50	50	66

Source: Laurent, 1983

should not be upset by such practices as bypassing the hierarchy or having to report to two bosses on the other hand. Managers from Belgium, France and Italy adhere more strongly to these beliefs than their colleagues from the northern European countries and the United States (Table 6.4).

Although limited in scope, Laurent's study reveals important national variations in managers' views of their role and authority in organizations and the way these organizations need to be structured. In particular, sharp differences can be noted between the two Latin European countries and Belgium on the one hand, and the other countries in the sample on the other hand. On three of the four dimensions, managers from these countries exhibit contrasting management attitudes. The research findings indicate that French and Italian managers, more so than managers from non-Latin countries, tend to view organizations as political, authority and hierarchical-relationship systems. These different conceptions are likely to influence the behaviour of managers in organizations and the way organizations in these countries are structured. As Laurent argues, the contrasting results obtained from Swedish and Italian managers with respect to the final index, may, for example, suggest that matrix-type organizations as opposed to classical hierarchies might have better prospects in Sweden than in Italy.

5   Hofstede's work on national culture

The most comprehensive study on national cultural differences to date has been conducted by Hofstede. Unlike most of the previous studies on cross-national differences, which involved only a limited number of countries, Hofstede used a huge database involving 53 countries/regions to identify four dimensions which bear a strong resemblance to the three core issues that Inkeles and Levinson (1969) had distilled from the literature on national character. These three core issues were:

- relationship to authority;
- conception of self, including the individual's concepts of masculinity and femininity; and the relationship between the individual and society;
- primary dilemmas or conflicts, and ways of dealing with them.

As we will see, the second issue actually consists of two parts: the concept of masculinity and femininity, and the relationship between the individual and the community. The four dimensions in this study were thus found through a combination of theoretical reasoning and statistical analysis of survey data collected in the period between 1967 and 1973 among employees of subsidiaries of the US computer company IBM. By surveying employees in different countries who all worked for a single multinational corporation and, moreover, were similar in age, sex and occupation, Hofstede eliminated any differences that might be attributable to varying practices and policies in different companies. In spite of the obviously homogenizing effects of IBM's corporate culture, Hofstede found significant differences in value orientations between organizational members of different national origins. These national differences explained more of the differences in work-related values than did the position within the organization, profession, age or gender. The four dimensions along which managers and employees appeared to vary, are:

1   power distance;
2   uncertainty avoidance;
3   individualism versus collectivism;
4   masculinity versus femininity.

The scores of the 50 countries and three regions in Hofstede's sample on these four dimensions are shown in Table 6.5.

Recently, Hofstede, in cooperation with Bond (Hofstede and Bond, 1988), has examined national values from a non-Western point of view. They identified a fifth value dimension called 'Confucian dynamism'. Values on this dimension reflect persistence, categorization of relation-

Table 6.5 *Values of the four indices for 50 countries (with rank numbers)[1] and three regions*

		Power distance		Uncertainty avoidance		Individualism		Masculinity	
		Index (PDI)	Rank	Index (UAI)	Rank	Index (IDV)	Rank	Index (MAS)	Rank
Argentina	(ARG)	49	18–19	86	36–41	46	28–29	56	30–31
Australia	(AUL)	36	13	51	17	90	49	61	35
Austria	(AUT)	11	1	70	26–27	55	33	79	49
Belgium	(BEL)	65	33	94	45–46	75	43	54	29
Brazil	(BRA)	69	39	76	29–30	38	25	49	25
Canada	(CAN)	39	15	48	12–13	80	46–47	52	28
Chile	(CHL)	63	29–30	86	36–41	23	15	28	8
Colombia	(COL)	67	36	80	31	13	5	64	39–40
Costa Rica	(COS)	35	10–12	86	36–41	15	8	21	5–6
Denmark	(DEN)	18	3	23	3	74	42	16	4
Ecuador	(EQA)	78	43–44	67	24	8	2	63	37–38
Finland	(FIN)	33	8	59	20–21	63	34	26	7
France	(FRA)	68	37–38	86	36–41	71	40–41	43	17–18
Germany (FR)	(GER)	35	10–12	65	23	67	36	66	41–42
Greece	(GRE)	60	26–27	112	50	35	22	57	32–33
Guatemala	(GUA)	95	48–49	101	48	6	1	37	11
Hong Kong	(HOK)	68	37–38	29	4–5	25	16	57	32–33
Indonesia	(IDO)	78	43–44	48	12–13	14	6–7	46	22
India	(IND)	77	42	40	9	48	30	56	30–31
Iran	(IRA)	58	24–25	59	20–21	41	27	43	17–18
Ireland (Rep. of)	(IRE)	28	5	35	6–7	70	39	68	43–44
Israel	(ISR)	13	2	81	32	54	32	47	23
Italy	(ITA)	50	20	75	28	76	44	70	46–47
Jamaica	(JAM)	45	17	13	2	39	26	68	43–44
Japan	(JPN)	54	21	92	44	46	28–29	95	50
Korea (S)	(KOR)	60	26–27	85	34–35	18	11	39	13
Malaysia	(MAL)	104	50	36	8	26	17	50	26–27
Mexico	(MEX)	81	45–46	82	33	30	20	69	45
Netherlands	(NET)	38	14	53	18	80	46–47	14	3
Norway	(NOR)	31	6–7	50	16	69	38	8	2
New Zealand	(NZL)	22	4	49	14–15	79	45	58	34
Pakistan	(PAK)	55	22	70	26–27	14	6–7	50	26–27
Panama	(PAN)	95	48–49	86	36–41	11	3	44	19
Peru	(PER)	64	31–32	87	42	16	9	42	15–16
Philippines	(PHI)	94	47	44	10	32	21	64	39–40
Portugal	(POR)	63	29–30	104	49	27	18–19	31	9
South Africa	(SAF)	49	18–19	49	14–15	65	35	63	37–38
Salvador	(SAL)	66	34–35	94	45–46	19	12	40	14
Singapore	(SIN)	74	40	8	1	20	13–14	48	24
Spain	(SPA)	57	23	86	36–41	51	31	42	15–16
Sweden	(SWE)	31	6–7	29	4–5	71	40–41	5	1
Switzerland	(SWI)	34	9	58	19	68	37	70	46–47
Taiwan	(TAI)	58	24–25	69	25	17	10	45	20–21
Thailand	(THA)	64	31–32	64	22	20	13–14	34	10
Turkey	(TUR)	66	34–35	85	34–35	37	24	45	20–21
United Kingdom	(UK)	35	10–12	35	6–7	89	48	66	41–42
United States	(USA)	40	16	46	11	91	50	62	36
Uruguay	(URU)	61	28	100	47	36	23	38	12
Venezuela	(VEN)	81	45–46	76	29–30	12	4	73	48
Yugoslavia	(YUG)	76	41	88	43	27	18–19	21	5–6
Regions:									
East Africa	(EAF)	64	(31–32)	52	(17–18)	27	(18–19)	41	(14–15)
West Africa	(WAF)	77	(42)	54	(18–19)	20	(13–14)	46	(22)
Arab countries	(ARA)	80	(44–45)	68	(24–25)	38	(25)	53	(28–29)

[1] Rank number: 1=lowest; 50=highest.

East Africa: Ethiopia, Kenya, Tanzania, Zambia.
West Africa: Ghana, Nigeria, Sierra Leone.
Arab countries: Egypt, Iraq, Kuwait, Lebanon, Libya, Saudi Arabia, UAE.

Source: Hofstede, 1991

ships, thrift, sense of shame versus personal steadiness, reciprocity, saving 'face' and respect for tradition. Since this dimension is not as developed with regard to organizations as the other four dimensions, and does not seem as relevant when comparing Western organizations, we will restrict the following discussion to the initial four dimensions.

1 *Power distance*. One area in which societies differ and to which they have found different solutions is that of social equality between their members. Hofstede defines power distance as 'the extent to which members of a society accept that power in institutions and organizations is distributed unequally'. Inequality of power in organizations is usually formalized in hierarchical superior–subordinate relationships. Hofstede found large power distance values for Latin countries (both European Latin and Latin American countries), and for Asian and African countries. Northern Europe and the Anglophone countries scored low on this dimension.

2 *Uncertainty avoidance*. The dimension of uncertainty avoidance involves the fundamental issue of how a society deals with uncertainty and conflicts. This dimension reflects a society's tolerance for situations of uncertainty and ambiguity and the extent to which it tries to manage these situations by providing explicit and formal rules and regulations, by rejecting deviant ideas and behaviour, by accepting the possibility of absolute truths and the attainment of expertise. High scores on this dimension occur for the Latin American, Latin European and Mediterranean countries, as well as Japan and South Korea. In these countries the inclination to avoid situations of uncertainty is strong. The scores of the German-speaking countries in Europe – Austria, Switzerland and Germany – are medium high. Asian countries, African countries and the Anglophone and Northern European countries score medium to low.

3 *Individualism versus collectivism*. Individualism describes the relationship between the individual and the group or society at large. It reflects the degree to which people in a country learn to act as individuals rather than as members of cohesive groups. In countries where collectivism predominates, the emphasis is on social ties or bonds between individuals, while in individualistic societies, the ties between individuals are loose and people are supposed to look after their own interests.

In general, wealthy countries score high on individualism, while poor countries score low. One notable exception is Japan which, in comparison to most Western countries, shows relatively strong collectivist features.

4 *Masculinity versus femininity*. This dimension refers to the extent that dominant values in a society emphasize masculine social values like a work ethic expressed in terms of money, achievement and recognition as opposed to feminine social values, which show more concern for people and quality of life. Masculine societies define male–female roles more rigidly than do feminine societies. Japan and Austria are highly masculine; the Scandinavian countries and the Netherlands are highly feminine.

The fact that only four dimensions were identified does not mean that these are the only dimensions possible to describe cultural variations. In

Hofstede's research, however, they appear to be the most significant dimensions for describing differences between societies. Hofstede's dimensions have provided an important theoretical and empirical framework for the prediction of many kinds of behaviour in cross-cultural organizational settings. In the following section we will discuss in more detail some of the consequences for organizations in these different value systems.

6   Consequences of national culture differences for managerial behaviour and personnel practices

The role of management in organizations largely consists of the following tasks: motivating, supervising and controlling people, defining goals, planning and strategy development. Since these management tasks concern essentially human rather than technical activities, they are likely to be influenced by the values and norms of participants and hence by cultural factors. We will limit this discussion to those tasks that are the most relevant for the management of personnel: motivation, leadership and decision-making. In addition, we will discuss the effects of national culture on organization design.

Motivation

Motivation can be described as a readiness to exert high levels of effort, contingent upon the success with which this effort satisfies some individual need. The discussion above makes clear that employees from different national settings may not share similar needs and motivational systems. In fact, nations differ in the level of importance that employees attach to different needs, and how well employee needs are met through work. To illustrate this we will apply a widely used theory of motivation developed by the American psychologist Maslow (1970). Maslow postulated a hierarchy of needs. These needs are: physiological (hunger, thirst etc.), safety (security and protection), social (affection, belongingness, acceptance), esteem (self-respect, achievement, status, recognition), and self-actualization (achieving one's potential and self-fulfilment). According to Maslow, as each of these needs is substantially satisfied, the next becomes dominant. The previous discussion about national cultural variation, however, makes clear that needs are partly culture-bound. Putting self-actualization plus esteem above social needs and security reflects the dominant North American value system characterized by weak uncertainty avoidance, strong masculinity and very strong individualism. In such societies, people can be expected to be ambitious in their work, to have a desire to succeed, and to strive for advancement. In countries with sharply different value systems, we can expect employees to be motivated by different needs. This is illustrated in Figure 6.2, which again uses Hofstede's 50 countries and three regions (see also Table 6.5).

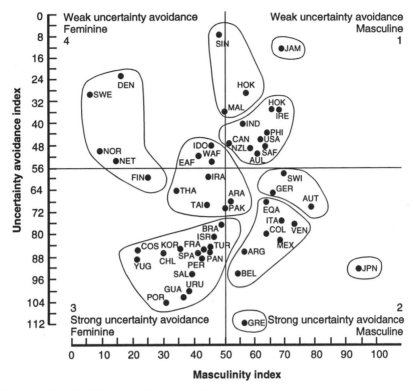

Figure 6.2 *Positions of 50 countries and three regions on the masculinity/femininity and uncertainty avoidance dimensions (for abbreviations see Table 6.5) (Hofstede, 1991)*

Countries in quadrant 1 (upper right-hand corner) score low on uncertainty avoidance and high on masculinity. In these countries the employees' individual needs are likely to be characterized by achievement motivation, that is, performance plus risk. Countries in quadrant 2 are both uncertainty avoidance cultures and masculine, characterized by security motivation, that is, performance plus security. The countries in quadrants 3 and 4 distinguish themselves from those in the other two by a focusing on quality of life and on relationships between people rather than on performance, achievements, money and possessions. Thus, it can be expected that employees in countries in the third quadrant (strong uncertainty avoidance + feminine) will emphasize both social needs and security, while employees in the fourth quadrant (weak uncertainty avoidance + feminine) will be motivated by social needs plus risk.

If employee needs are found to differ from one nation to the next, then evaluation and reward systems have to differ along with them. Thus, if performance, achievement and making money are the dominant values in a society, reward systems have to be geared to these values. While in one society organizations should provide monetary rewards, challenging work, recognition and promotion, in other societies a work environment which offers security, a sense of belonging and work that is basically interesting and satisfying may be more rewarding for employees, and it would be a mistake to try to motivate employees by offering them only financial incentives. Furthermore, while individual performance and evaluation systems will be preferable in an individualistic society, in more collectivist cultures group-based performance measures may be more appropriate. Organizational practices that have a highly individualistic orientation could be dysfunctional in a collectivist culture where group-based incentives are more salient.

Leadership and decision-making

Leadership, broadly described as the ability to influence a group toward the achievement of goals, is another management task. One way of classifying leadership behaviour is by the degree of participation subordinates have in decision-making. This is related most closely to the dimension of power distance. In a culture with large power distance, employees more or less expect and/or prefer the leader to make decisions, solve problems and assign tasks. Under conditions of small power distance, on the other hand, employees expect a greater say in how they do their jobs. Too much authoritarian behaviour and too few opportunities to participate may create problems. In this case participative leadership would be the appropriate style, while in the former more autocratic leadership styles can be expected.

It is important to note that the power distance norm is present in the values of both the leader and those being led. Thus, power distance is not only reflected in the superiors' preferred leadership style, but also in the type of leadership that subordinates favour in their boss. For example, in Hofstede's study, subordinates in France found bosses displaying persuasive-paternalistic behaviour as the most positive, whereas in Germany this assessment was given to bosses displaying participative characteristics. As with theories of motivation, most leadership theories are of American origin. Because the United States is a moderately small power distance country, US-based theories typically advocate democratic leadership styles while simultaneously emphasizing certain management prerogatives. Whether theories developed in this cultural environment work well in other countries depends on how much they differ from the United States with respect to power distance. In this respect, Hofstede has indicated management by objectives (MBO) as a management tool which motivates personnel by setting mutually agreed objectives between a boss and his subordinates. This technique, however, presupposes that the power distance between the boss and his subordinates is not too large, one reason why MBO never became popular in large power distance countries like France.

While power distance is one factor determining decision-making, other dimensions may also exert an influence. While fact-based and rapid decision-making procedures will prevail in masculine-oriented countries, decision-making in feminine cultures may make more frequent use of intuition, and show a concern for consensus.

Organizational design

In the preceding sections we discussed research conducted by Laurent (1983) showing that managers from different countries have different conceptions about the organization. Much of his findings can be related to differences in power distance and uncertainty avoidance. According to Hofstede these dimensions are the most important ones for organizations. They relate to two basic features of organizational design: the concentration of authority and the structuring of activities, the latter defining the degree of formalization, specialization and standardization in an organization. According to Hofstede, different combinations of power distance and uncertainty avoidance lead to different implicit models of what an organization should be. Four organizational types can be distinguished: the pyramid, the machine, the village market and the family (Hofstede, 1980a). These are shown in Figure 6.3.

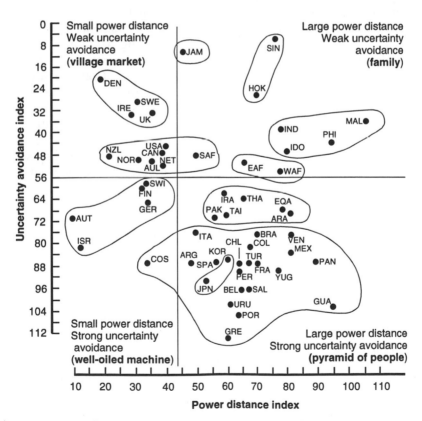

Figure 6.3 *Implicit models of organization (for abbreviations see Table 6.5) (Hofstede, 1991)*

In large power distance and strong uncertainty avoidance countries, organizations will tend to be structured as *pyramids*: decision-making and control from the top. The opposite form, the *village market*, found in countries with small power distance and weak uncertainty avoidance, is characterized by the lack of a decisive hierarchy and flexible rules. In this 'implicitly' structured organization, neither work processes nor relationships between people are rigidly prescribed. Problems in this organizational form are not solved primarily by the exercise of authority or by formal rules, but through negotiation. We can expect to find the first type in countries like France and Italy, while the latter type will prevail in the United Kingdom and other Anglo-Saxon and North European countries, including the Netherlands. Small power distance combined with strong uncertainty avoidance creates the image of an organization as a well-oiled *machine*. Like the pyramid, this organizational model is characterized by a focus on rules, but it does not share the tendency toward centralization of authority. Given the national value pattern, the impersonal bureaucracy will be the preferred organizational type in Germany and other Central European countries. The fourth model, the *family*, is a combination of large power distance and weak uncertainty avoidance. This organizational model is thought to be the preferred organizational approach in a number of Asian countries: strong personal authority combined with few formal rules. Lammers and Hickson (1979), summarizing a number of cross-national studies, arrived at a classification of organizations in national types which are very similar to those put forward by Hofstede, with the exception of a particular configuration for the German-speaking countries. The implication of these different 'implicit' models of organization is that, characteristics of the task environment and other contingency factors being equal, organizations in one country will tend to be structured as a well-oiled machine, while in another country they will have a pyramid structure, in accordance with the culturally derived preferences of managers and employees in these countries.

7　Conclusions

In this chapter we have explored how national culture shapes organizations and organizational behaviour. One conclusion that can be drawn on the basis of the research presented in this chapter is that more cultural variation exists within the Western world than one would imagine on the basis of trends towards internationalizing consumer markets and professionalization of management. Behind the façade of superficial uniformity, fundamentally different conceptions of organization and management are often hidden. The implication of these nationally bounded collective maps is that management is not universal. For human resource management this means that cultural diversity often calls for different policies geared to the needs of the people involved. Human resource management methods and systems developed in one society cannot always be transferred and applied in another. Messages of sound management promoted by such books as Peters and Waterman's *In Search of Excellence* may work well in contexts which are similar to the United States, but not in other cultures. This explains why management techniques like management by objectives, matrix organizations, humanization of work programmes, or performance-based reward structures are not as successful in some countries as they are in the United States.

7 Compensation and appraisal in an international perspective

Ed Logger, Rob Vinke and Frits Kluytmans

1	Introduction	144
2	Purposes, functions and types of compensation	145
	Purposes and functions of compensation	145
	Types of compensation: compensation components	146
3	Factors which affect differences in compensation	147
	Internal business factors	147
	Differences in prosperity and spending power	148
	Social factors	148
	Conclusions: compensation differences between countries	152
4	International compensation from a total remuneration perspective	153
5	Compensation trends	155

1 Introduction

The wide gap between wages paid for comparable positions in different countries is obvious. But an accurate comparison of these wage differences often poses many problems. Different economic systems, development levels, political and institutional contexts, traditions and cultures make it difficult to find a uniform method for comparision. Yet, having a knowledge of these differences is very important in that compensation practices may considerably influence staff performance and motivation. Moreover, wage cost control will contribute positively to the output of the organization as a whole.

Not only do the wage sums differ, the wage structure also varies according to country. In some countries, employees receive a relatively low cash income and a high portion of deferred income in the form of insurance and/or pensions. In other countries this deferred portion may be much smaller. Since these differences are largely culture-based, forms of income known in the one country cannot automatically be transferred to the other, where there may be different traditions and practices. If a transfer is made, it can have unexpected and undesired consequences.

As stated, it is generally very difficult to draw a true comparison between wages paid in different countries, the more so since research into wage differences has been taken up only recently. The coming about of global product markets has not yet resulted in global compensation practices. For this reason, the emphasis in this chapter will be placed not so much on the actual wage differences as on the factors that influence these differences. Section 2 sets out the functions and types of compensation; Section 3 discusses these factors in greater detail and provides examples. In Section 4, we will look at what are called 'total remuneration systems', which enable companies to put into practice a general pay policy while allowing for country-specific elements. Despite the differences between the countries, we can distinguish a number of universal trends in compensation, the most important of which are listed in the final section.

2   Purposes, functions and types of compensation

Purposes and functions of compensation

Before discussing the factors that cause wages to differ between countries, we first have to ask ourselves what goals management proposes to achieve in formulating their compensation policy. Compensation serves several major purposes (Logger and Vinke, 1989; Schuler, 1987; Thierry et al., 1988). First, a compensation programme should enable the organization to attract potential job applicants. To do this, the level of compensation must be commensurate with local or regional standards. Secondly, the programme should be internally equitable and externally competitive in order to retain suitably qualified employees. Internal equitability is important in preventing social and personal conflicts within the organization. Thirdly, the programme should stimulate employees by rewarding behaviour/performances that is/are essential to the organization's success. Fourthly, the programme should be in line with the existing status hierarchy in the organization and in society in general. Last, but not least, the programme should enable the organization to optimize its total wage level.

In addition to these principal objectives, companies may want to achieve a number of related goals, such as compensating for inconveniences (irregular working hours and/or poor or dangerous working conditions) or supporting a change of strategy by adjusting the pay system to correspond with the company's new course. When pursuing these objectives, companies will inevitably be faced with a multitude of conflicting requirements with which their compensation system is supposed to comply.

Obviously, an extra complicating factor must be added if a company has a cross-border compensation policy, particularly where there are employees who work in different countries on consecutive assignments (expatriates). An analysis of this interesting issue is provided in Part 3 of this book, in Chapter 12. Also in multinational companies, however, a balance needs to be struck between uniform basic rules and requirements on the one hand and country-specific elements on the other for the staff employed in the various different countries.

Types of compensation: compensation components

Employee compensation is not only about cash in hand. It comprises a wide range of components. A first distinction can be made between intrinsic and extrinsic compensation. Intrinsic compensation concerns the non-pecuniary compensation which is related directly to the nature of the work. Interesting work and good career prospects may compensate for comparably low pay. We see that at the outset of their careers, young employees are not only attracted to the rate of pay, but in selecting their first employer also take into account such matters as corporate image, trainee programmes and their scope for development (Vinke, 1993).

In this chapter, we confine ourselves to discussing some forms of compensation: compensation of a financial nature, or whose value can be expressed in money (extrinsic compensation). These forms of compensation are also referred to as *primary* and *secondary terms of employment*. The secondary terms cover all non-pecuniary components whose value can nevertheless be expressed in terms of money. Another distinction can be made between direct and indirect compensation. Direct compensation is the employee's fixed and variable annual income. Indirect compensation consists of all kinds of deferred income, such as pension and insurance (health insurance, disability insurance, unemployment and so on), and of benefits like a company car, expense allowances and days off.

The sum of the direct and indirect compensation makes up the organization's total compensation programme (Figure 7.1). These components may further be itemized into different compensation forms (fixed or variable, performance-related or otherwise). Countries have been found to show large differences on this point. Table 7.1, for instance, sets out the differences between fixed (time-related) pay and variable (performance-related) pay in different countries.

While performance-related pay is common in some countries, like Luxembourg and former East Germany, it is still an exception in a country like the Netherlands. However, we must add that not too much weight should be attached to these figures, as they only reflect a specified point in time. Developments in this field follow one another rapidly. A survey of

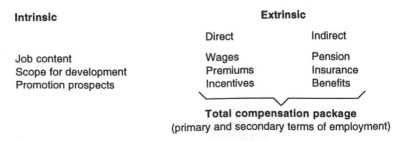

Figure 7.1   *Compensation components (after Sullivan, 1972)*

Table 7.1 *Relation between time-related and performance-related pay in different countries (row percentages)*

Country	Time-related pay	Performance-related pay
Netherlands	85	15
Denmark	61	39
France	65	35
Ireland	56	44
Italy	75	25
Luxembourg	50	50
UK	55	45
Former USSR	44	46
Former East Germany	47	53

Source: Vinke and Thierry, 1985

personnel managers in 12 countries shows that they consider the conditioning of pay upon performance, creativity and profits as an essential and necessary initiative to give companies a competitive edge (IBM survey, done by Towers Perrin in 1992). So it may be expected that these figures will quickly change to reflect more variable pay systems. Still, as we will see in Section 3 below, the differences found between countries are often dictated by tradition and culture, which are not easily ignored.

3   Factors which affect differences in compensation

What factors must we investigate in order to understand the compensation gap found for comparable jobs? Any attempt at answering this question brings to light a large number of factors, all of which may be reduced to three main categories:

- internal business factors;
- differences in prosperity and spending power between countries;
- social factors.

Internal business factors

Internal business factors are those factors which are trade-related and/or organization-related and which affect pay levels. Differences occur between lines of trade and industry which can be put down to the usual level of compensation in a particular trade or industry. For example, capital-intensive industries often have more leeway in terms of payroll costs, so pay levels there often exceed those found in labour-intensive sectors. Whereas a 10 percent pay rise in these sectors will have a direct knock-on effect for cost prices, causing them to rise by almost the same rate, capital-intensive trades will feel much less of the impact. The margin for wage costs is also dependent on the added value and profits generated. So compensation levels in a particular trade or industry and between countries must also be related to productivity. A labour shortage or surplus is another factor influencing pay rates. A shortage generally causes rising pay levels. However, the inverse case, where wages fall because of a surplus, is less frequently seen. In this sense, wages are quite inflexible.

As stated, organization-related factors also have a bearing on pay levels. Some organizations offer their employees a large measure of security in exchange for lower pay. These differences are often connected with differences in strategy. A cost-efficient strategy will put more pressure on pay levels than will a quality-oriented or innovation-oriented policy. A carefully constructed corporate image may also affect wages. An organization wishing to project a dynamically active image will sooner adopt a compensation policy directly based on the results generated by all corporate levels than will a traditionally bureaucratic organization, where the emphasis is put on job security, fixed career moves and predictability.

When comparing wage differences between countries, then, we also have to take account of the large differences between industries and organizations within each individual country. Such differences are the result of specific factors which cannot be attributed to country-specific variations.

Differences in prosperity and spending power

When comparing wage differences between countries, the picture becomes blurred by differences in prosperity and spending power. Table 7.2 shows the relation between gross salaries paid at three different management levels in various countries. Since the same method has been used to assess these job levels, the comparison is between salaries paid at similar job levels. The Netherlands has been taken as a reference point and set at 100. However, this comparison has little value because a Swedish krone may have less buying power than a Greek drachma. And it does. When we adjust the table using a spending power parity, an entirely different picture emerges (Table 7.3).

A senior executive staff member in Greece has 30 percent more spending power than a comparable Dutch senior executive, and as much as 50 percent more than his Swedish colleague. The reduced ranking of the Scandinavian countries in particular as compared to Table 7.2 has mainly to do with tax rates and the prices of consumer goods in those countries. The United States's higher ranking (where the maximum tax rate stands at 28 percent) is the reverse result of the same phenomenon.

Any comparison of compensation levels must therefore take spending power into account, lest we find ourselves comparing apples and oranges. Then again, we should also be aware that these tables only use direct income components and disregard any type of indirect compensation.

Social factors

Organizational and management practices are closely linked to social factors. Indeed, wage bargaining often takes place at the national or

Table 7.2   *International income levels: the annual fixed income*
(Netherlands=100)

Country	Junior middle management	Senior middle management	Senior executive level
Austria	137.2	147.9	138.0
Switzerland	147.?	147.5	136.8
Germany	139.9	144.9	148.9
Italy	95.5	121.8	118.8
Spain	113.2	120.4	120.7
Denmark	112.0	110.9	99.7
Belgium	107.2	109.1	106.0
France	98.7	100.1	93.5
Netherlands	100.0	100.0	100.0
Sweden	100.2	99.3	85.1
Ireland	93.3	90.1	92.0
Finland	90.7	86.4	76.8
USA	85.0	83.1	81.0
Portugal	73.9	82.8	81.8
UK	79.0	81.4	79.5
Norway	93.2	80.0	67.1
Greece	57.3	63.1	67.0

Source: Hay Management Consultants, 1992

Table 7.3   *International income comparison: the annual net*
cash income, adjusted by spending power parity

Country	Junior middle management	Senior middle management	Senior executive level
Germany	154	164	217
Spain	154	159	195
Italy	114	157	201
Austria	133	155	195
Portugal	126	144	178
USA	127	136	185
France	126	132	164
Switzerland	126	130	165
UK	106	113	150
Greece	99	110	130
Belgium	108	107	133
Netherlands	100	100	100
Ireland	95	97	121
Norway	87	75	82
Finland	75	71	87
Denmark	58	68	89
Sweden	66	60	80

Source: Hay Management Consultants, 1992

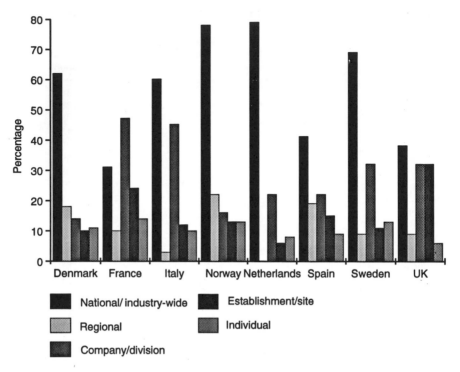

Figure 7.2   *Levels of basic pay negotiations for manual workers (Price Waterhouse, 1991)*

industry level and is thus affected by all sorts of social trends. Figure 7.2 depicts the relationship between the different regulatory frameworks within which wage bargaining for manual workers takes place. Switzerland and Germany are not included because bargaining there nearly always takes place at the national or industry level.

Despite the fact that the 1980s have seen important changes in the manner in which wages and other terms of employment are established, this graph shows that pay and other terms of employment for manual workers are still largely determined at the national or industry level. Only in France does the company level exceed the national/industry-wide level of regulation. The graph concerns manual workers, and although pay determination at the individual or local level increases as one goes up the hierarchical ladder, even for managerial staff over a third of organizations in most countries, and well over half in some, set their basic pay nationally or on an industry-wide basis (Price Waterhouse, 1991). Again, this is a random picture, as the same survey also concludes that the general trend now is for further decentralization of the bargaining framework. This certainly reflects the wish of personnel managers quoted above increasingly to link pay decisions to strategic issues and, notably, performance.

Apart from the direct influence which society and existing negotiating frameworks have on pay determination, society also exerts a more subtle influence in that a country's culture often greatly affects such pay aspects as:

- the extent to which pay differences are considered acceptable;
- the appreciation of different forms of pay;
- the acceptance of different forms of compensation and appraisal.

Since we have no clearly defined picture of this influence, we can only piece together something of an outline sketch.

By definition, compensation practices based on results, like performance-related pay and share option plans, embody an element of insecurity. In cultures where 'uncertainty avoidance' is not much of an issue (especially in the Anglophone countries), these types of compensation are more widely accepted than in cultures where uncertainty avoidance is considered of basic importance. In Germany, for instance, performance-related compensation is not very popular precisely because of this element of uncertainty. We find a similar correlation when we look at the power distance in countries. If the distance is great, as in Italy, then high-level and low-level positions will show a wider compensation gap than in, say, the Scandinavian countries, which have a more egalitarian culture (see Table 7.4).

(Performance) appraisal practices also tend to be based on assumptions which are far less universal than one would expect. Exporting these practices may well end in fiasco. Thus, an incentive scheme for salespeople in a Danish subsidiary of an MNC was turned down because it favoured a specific group and ran counter to the Danes' egalitarian spirit (Schneider,

Table 7.4 *International differences between high-level and low-level positions (as a ratio)*

Country	Gross difference factor		Net difference factor	
	1987	1992	1987	1992
Italy	4.98	5.97	4.06	4.62
Portugal	2.62	4.97	1.94	3.86
Denmark	4.00	4.94	2.55	4.19
Germany	4.32	4.86	3.26	3.74
Spain	4.24	4.82	3.08	3.49
Belgium	4.01	4.43	2.60	2.93
Netherlands	3.86	4.24	2.79	2.50
UK	3.90	4.17	3.15	3.58
USA	4.12	4.17	3.80	3.66
Switzerland	3.62	4.03	3.12	2.95
France	4.11	3.98	3.37	3.37
Ireland	3.08	3.97	2.10	2.70
Sweden	3.87	3.50	2.81	2.67
Finland	3.44	3.14	2.29	2.42
Norway	2.69	2.59	1.65	2.18

Source: Hay Management Consultants, 1992

1988). So it seems that performance appraisal criteria to be used in individualistic cultures should to a large extent be individual in nature. In collectivist cultures, like Japan, group appraisals will be preferred.

The varying appreciation of a management method such as management by objectives (MBO) again illustrates the impact of dominant cultural values and views. This technique caught on well in Germany because it followed the call for decentralization and less emphasis on hierarchy; moreover, it was a formal method. The method was less successfully transferred to France, however, due to the French ambivalent nature towards authority. MBO was viewed as an exercise of arbitrary power and a manipulative ploy of management. With power concentrated in the hands of the boss, subordinates would be held responsible without having the power to accomplish goals. The notion of a boss and subordinates cooperating in reaching a decision together is quite foreign in that culture (Schneider, 1988).

Thus, cultural differences between countries greatly influence opinion as to what is considered acceptable and proper in terms of compensation and appraisal practices. But we should be aware that these differences are quite broad and that the picture which emerges may vary from region to region. The typical national stereotype seems to be disappearing gradually. What emerges is the awareness that people with similar motivations and views can be found in every country. The difference lies rather in their number per country. This trend has been confirmed by a survey conducted by CCA International/Europanel in 1990. The survey identified 16 'socio-styles' in Europe, ranging from 'Europrudents' and 'Eurodefenders' to 'Eurorockies' and 'Europrotesters'. These groups showed great similarity in lifestyle and preferences. The Eurorockies were the biggest group: young people with less schooling who, motivated by money, wish to become rich and consume in an 'every man for himself' society. This group is especially strongly represented in Norway, Belgium and the Netherlands. By contrast, Germany and Switzerland have many Euromoralists and romantics, who wish to lead retiring lives and attach greater weight to the quality of their lives and that of others. Each of the other groups also had its own distinctive characteristics. Although we should be careful in using these profiles, they do make clear that with national boundaries disappearing in Europe, a more European culture will develop, but one in which many cross-border differences in lifestyle will continue to exist.

Conclusions: compensation differences between countries

Returning to the question of what factors cause the differences in compensation for similar positions in different countries, we can draw the following conclusions. First, these differences are obviously the result of differences in prosperity and spending power. A related factor in this respect is the different tax and social security systems. Secondly, the institutional frameworks within which wage bargaining takes place are quite different. The more negotiations are conducted at the national or industry level, the more society will influence such negotiating rounds directly. Increased decentralization of the negotiating framework down to the company level will result in company-specific issues becoming relatively more important. Thirdly, cultural differences between countries have quite an important impact. These differences do not so much influence the rates of pay as the apportioning of the total sum between wages, incentives and benefits (Townsend et al., 1990) and the appreciation of different compensation and appraisal methods. Finally, there may be considerable differences between organizations and industries. They may be the result of a deliberate line of policy or differences in strategy, but also of differences in productivity, labour/capital ratios and the situation on the relevant labour market.

4   International compensation from a total remuneration perspective

For companies that operate internationally, the differences noted above are a formidable obstacle to adopting a uniform compensation policy. What we see in practice is that companies adjust their policies to local culture. But there are examples of companies operating in countries with a less advanced pension and benefits system which have concentrated their compensation policy specifically on these secondary compensation elements with a view to recruitment. In the past few years, MNCs establishing branch offices in Greece have introduced various secondary terms of employment, such as insurance and pension schemes. Other businesses were forced to follow suit to remain competitive. In this way, internationally operating organizations may take the lead in improving a country's social security system.

As an increasing number of companies become involved in international operations, it is essential that their compensation policy should remain balanced and comparable when crossing borders. This may be accomplished by looking at compensation from what is called a *total remuneration perspective*. An assessment of the value of the total remuneration package should not only consider the fixed and variable income portions. Secondary terms of employment also represent a value, and differences in tax and social security contributions must also be weighed. Consequently, a comparison must be based on the total package, the total remuneration, that is to say, the sum of all fixed and variable income components plus the secondary terms of employment as expressed in money. In this way, different compensation packages may still have an equivalent total remuneration value and companies will be able to accommodate the different (culture-based) wishes of their employees, with costs remaining at the same level.

In order properly to interpret the concept of total remuneration, we must distinguish between three aspects:

Table 7.5 *International comparison of a specified managerial position (in Dutch guilders)*

	Netherlands	Germany
Total fixed income	159,700	198,500
Variable income	21,900	23,400
Total cash	181,600	221,900
Company car	20,300	15,900
Expense allowance	4,800	—
Health insurance	3,000	—
Telephone allowance	400	—
Total pay	210,100	237,800
Pension	26,700	18,500
Extra health and disability insurance	8,400	6,500
Early retirement	8,400	—
Total remuneration	253,000	262,800

- employer's costs: the sum needed by the company to grant an employee a certain benefit;
- gross benefit: the sum received by the employee, or a provision or benefit expressed in money;
- net benefit: the gross benefit after taxes and social security premiums.

These categories roughly correspond to such questions as 'what does an employee cost?', 'what does he or she earn?' and 'what does he or she receive?' The tax authorities determine what remains of an employee's gross benefit once all of that individual's gross data are known. However, companies have a considerable influence on the structure of the package: some benefits are tax-deductible, others are taxed. By deciding on a certain package structure, companies more or less determine the ultimate tax rate payable.

Since the value of benefits is not always clear in terms of money, we must use a model to arrive at a denominator. In general, every benefit is translated into a premium or lease sum. In many cases, the employer's costs are equivalent to the employee's gross benefit. For instance, the costs incurred by the employer in paying a fixed expense allowance, telephone allowance or any other tax-free payment, usually correspond to the employee's gross benefit. This is different for a company car. Only the private mileage is treated as a benefit. Business mileage must be attributed to the employee's performance of his duties, and cannot be regarded as 'compensation'.

To illustrate how this approach to an overall comparison may work out in practice, Table 7.5 sets out the difference in compensation between a German manager and a Dutch manager holding similar positions. It shows that the German manager is paid a higher fixed income than his Dutch colleague. But this is partly compensated by the more favourable second-ary terms of employment of the Dutch manager. By making a comprehensive comparison of package values, we may prevent superficial differences from becoming the basis for action.

5   Compensation trends

Despite the differences, we can discern a number of universal compensation trends, the most important of which we have listed below.

1   There has been a general tendency toward more strategic compensation policies where required performance like customer service and creativity is linked with the rate of compensation. This trend coincides with increased decentralization of the framework within which compensation levels are established: less national and industry-wide and more company-specific.
2   There have been calls for tailor-made compensation policies so as to accommodate the individual wishes and needs of employees. As a result, terms of employment will be less uniform.
3   In connection with the previous point, individual employees are increasingly likely to insist on exercising more influence on the structure of their terms of employment package. Progressive employees will increasingly demand responsibility for structuring their own employment package.
4   As a logical outcome of the above trends, more insight will be required into the value of the total remuneration package and its component parts. This will secure comparability as differences grow wider.

Thus, on the one hand, European integration and the ensuing market developments will level out differences in compensation, albeit that those between the North and South may remain noticeable for some time. On the other hand, the advancing individualization and increasingly marked differences in lifestyle will, in terms of quality (the diversity of compensation forms), lead to larger differences in compensation packages. Finally, it is expected that governments will be less ready and individual employees will be more keen to take responsibility for the care components (like pension schemes or extra-legal health insurance) in their employment packages. At the same time, corporate policy will become a more dominant factor.

For all these reasons, clearly communicated information on compensation levels and types will become increasingly important if compensation packages are to continue to motivate and inspire employees within companies.

8 Human resource development and staff flow policy in Europe

Marcel van der Klink and Martin Mulder

1	Introduction	156
2	Framework and key concepts	157
	HRD and staff flow policy	157
	Educational system	159
	Labour market	159
	Coordinating education and the labour market	160
	Influence of companies on education	162
	Staff flow policy, HRD and the division of labour	162
	Summary	163
3	German and British practices compared	164
	Vocational training	164
	Company training	165
	Staff flow policy	166
	Division of labour	167
	Conclusions	168
4	France and the Netherlands compared	169
	Vocational training	169
	Company training	170
	Staff flow policy	171
	Division of labour	172
	Conclusions	173
5	Flow policy and HRD for managers	174
	Appendix: Comparison of the structure of company training in France, Germany, Japan, the Netherlands, the United Kingdom and the United States	175

1 Introduction

This chapter deals with the role and content of human resource development (HRD) and staff flow policies adopted by companies in different European countries. It is important for international companies to have an understanding of the variations between the HRD practices encountered in different countries. Such an understanding is essential if they are to tune central corporate policy in terms of HRD and staff flow to the nationally rooted practices of their local branches. In Section 2 we will define the concepts of HRD and staff flow policy and provide a framework to explain the differences between countries. This model takes into account the organization-specific influences, but also includes country-specific influences arising from the educational system and the labour market. Sections 3 and 4 present a comparison between HRD practices and flow policies adopted in four European countries: Germany, the United Kingdom, the Netherlands and France. Section 5 centres on staff flow policy and HRD for managers in different European countries.

2   Framework and key concepts

HRD and staff flow policy

Human resource development (HRD) refers to the entire range of educational, training and development facilities available in an organization, which enhance the desired learning processes in employees (Nadler, 1980). HR interventions are aimed at achieving planned human resource output in terms of productivity, quality, innovation, satisfaction and willingness to change (Mulder, 1993). A company's success can partly be put down to its HRD policy. The skills and expertise of the workforce are a prerequisite for the company's ability to adapt to changing circumstances. Given the speed at which changes are taking place, corporate success increasingly hinges on a successful HRD policy (Carnevale et al., 1990).

An important aspect of personnel management is 'staffing'. In its restricted meaning, the term refers to the measures, instruments and facilities used by a company to recruit the most suitable workers for every job. In a wider sense, staffing not only covers the recruitment and selection of personnel, but also personnel and career development. Following Beer et al. (1984) (see also Vander Meeren and Kluytmans, 1992), Bolweg (1989) has recently introduced the term 'staff flow policy' to describe this phenomenon. It aptly denotes what staffing is all about: optimizing the flow of personnel in, through and out of the organization. Flow policy fits in with the organization's strategic policy. The idea is that:

- an adequate flow policy is aimed at realizing the company's strategic goals;
- flow policy contributes towards the company's success;
- the instruments and activities developed under a flow policy make up a coherent set;
- line management is responsible for the implementation of an adequate flow policy (Vander Meeren and Kluytmans, 1992).

Organizations with properly operating flow policies recruit staff from the external or the internal labour market, or they sometimes prefer a combination (see below). The practical operationalization of a flow policy very much depends on the company's objectives and the situation on the labour market.

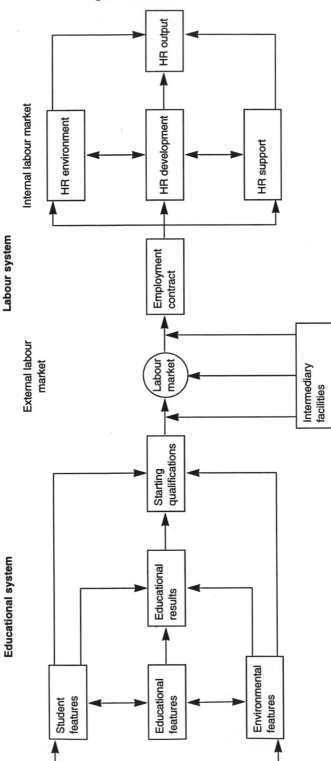

Figure 8.1 *The relationship between the educational system and the labour system (Mulder, 1994)*

The societal effect approach has demonstrated the cross-relations between the structure and functioning of an organization and the characteristics of the societal environment in which the organization operates (Maurice et al., 1980). We will come across this mutual influencing of organization and societal environment when analyzing HRD and staff flow policies in different countries. As we will see in Sections 3 and 4, the content and implementation of these policies differ according to country. Country-related factors like social and economic policy, the labour market and the educational system account for the differences found. Figure 8.1 shows a framework in which staff flow policy and HRD policy have been related to a number of institutional factors. The framework will be explained step by step below.

Educational system

The educational system, and notably the tapestry of vocational training courses available in a country, substantially influences the nature and quality of the initial competencies of school-leavers, and also affects the distribution of competencies among the working population. The substance of these starting competencies is highly dependent on how the vocational tuition system has been organized. Broadly speaking, vocational training is of two kinds: full-time or dual. In full-time courses, students spend most of their training at a vocational school or college. Only a (limited) part of the training period is spent as a trainee in a company. Dual vocational training shows exactly the reverse situation. It is largely provided on the job. Coupled with the theoretical knowledge learned at school or college, the working experience gained on the job enables apprentices to acquire the competencies needed to practise their profession. Full-time vocational training places the emphasis on the acquisition of (abstract) knowledge. Dual vocational training offers the opportunity to become better qualified through working experience. Less attention is given to the acquisition of general and abstract expertise.

Labour market

School-leavers enter the labour market in possession of starting competencies. An important feature of the labour market is its division into segments (Grootings and Hövels, 1981), although little is known about the fine lines between them (Van Hoof, 1987). We will not go into this in further detail, but confine ourselves to dividing the labour market into four segments: a primary and secondary segment, and an internal and external segment (Van Iersel, 1985).

The *primary segment* comprises positions with favourable terms of employment and working conditions, a relatively high level of job security and attractive prospects for promotion. Those wishing to enter this segment must have professional qualifications. Some positions require specific vocational training for admittance to the profession. If no specific diplomas are required, applicants must often be educated in a particular professional field at a specified level. In these cases, the educational record is rather seen as an indication of a certain intellectual level and the employee is taught the missing skills through company-specific training (on the job). The jobs found in the *secondary segment* offer little or no prospects for promotion, unfavourable terms of employment and little job security. There are hardly any training requirements and the jobs usually involve routine manual work. Only rarely do companies invest in additional training courses. Whatever training is provided is usually aimed at increasing productivity or improving performance levels in the same job, rather than linked to any move on to a different or higher position, or to any career path.

A further distinction may be made between the external and internal labour market. The term labour market usually conjures up the picture of job-seekers applying for jobs and employers recruiting and selecting from this pool of applicants, filling their vacancies. This is, however, what we call the *external labour market*. It includes a comparatively large number of newcomers (school-leavers), jobless people and women returners. There is also an *internal labour market*, that is, a labour market inside companies themselves and from which outside job-seekers are excluded. This is the case when an employer recruits for a particular position exclusively from among (groups of) current employees. Additional training – usually on the job – and/or the working experience gained in the company give employees the opportunity to move on to other positions. This move often coincides with a rise in the internal status hierarchy. The employees benefit in the sense that they can improve their terms of employment working in the same company; the employer benefits to the extent that valuable employees will remain loyal to the company and their competencies will not be lost. This internal flow-through of employees can be shaped into a policy. Such a policy should focus on personnel development (continuous education and stimulation of employees to gain working experience) and the development of career paths, which may be linked to a training policy.

Coordinating education and the labour market

The labour market can be seen as the link between education and the business community. The labour market usually displays coordination problems (Hövels and Peschar, 1985): the job-seeker's training fails to match the requirements of a company, or companies cannot find the employees they need for their production processes. Whether the problem lies in the training or in the nature of a job is often difficult to determine. What is clear is that the acquired competencies do not match those that are required. The discrepancies may be qualitative or quantitative. *Quantitative discrepancies* concern the relationship between supply and demand. In the 1980s, the supply of labour exceeded the number of vacancies in all EC countries. This resulted in high unemployment, especially among newcomers to the labour market (young people, women returners), who lack any relevant working experience. At the same time, however, the reverse situation may occur: a lack of qualified staff and ensuing long-standing vacancies can put the brake on corporate growth.

International HRM and the shortage of international managers

Despite the economic recession, Unilever made a larger profit in 1992 than it did in 1991. For the first time in the company's history, profits exceeded 4 billion guilders (a substantial portion of which has been generated by its European and North African operations). An important growth market for the company is China. Thus far, the company has not been very active there. Unilever explains that it has too few managers in China effectively to expand its business activities. The company is now trying to select 'high potentials' from among the Chinese themselves and offer them training programmes in preparation for a further expansion of Unilever's activities in China.

Qualitative discrepancies occur when the competencies required for the jobs on offer do not quite match the competencies of job-seekers. In times of soaring unemployment, under-utilization is common; in other words, competencies exceed job requirements. For no apparent reason, employers will test the competencies of job applicants against stricter criteria. Prolonged under-utilization may lead to demotivated staff and loss of the organization's innovation potential. Qualitative discrepancies, moreover, are the result of the different speeds at which the educational system and business organizations develop. Technological changes in some sectors are taking place so rapidly that vocational training seems to be forever lagging behind (Van Hoof, 1986). Unclear innovation goals, the sometimes powerful influence of politics on the decision-making process and the lack of skills to implement innovation ideas are only a few factors adversely to affect the pace and quality of curriculum reform (Dalin, 1989). In some cases, intermediary facilities have been created, better to coordinate education and work (Kraayvanger and Van Onna, 1987).

It should be said, however, that qualitative discrepancies do not always automatically require adjustments to the educational system. Work may be restructured by reshuffling duties and positions so as to maximize the use of the labour force available. Also, long-term under-utilization of workers' competencies may be avoided by adding responsibilities to existing jobs.

The qualitative matching problems signalled above are partly the result of the relative autonomy of the educational and production systems. Both systems have different decision-makers. Both systems have different social functions, which only partially overlap and sometimes conflict. For instance, full-time vocational training tends to provide a broad education, which is not always in line with the interests and wishes of the business community. In the Netherlands, as in France, much weight is attached to young people receiving a broad social education, which means that part of the educational period is set aside for social training (see, for example, Van Kemenade, 1981).

Influence of companies on education

In order to bridge the gap between education and work, companies can adopt different strategies. At the national level, they may exert influence on the (standing) consultations between the government, social partners (that is, employers and employees) and educational representatives. These structures are usually set up to establish professional profiles for future practitioners. At the local level, companies may exert influence by participating in local consultations or concluding cooperation contracts with training institutions which see many of their students being hired by these companies (Römkens and De Vries, 1986). Under these contracts, companies provide trainee posts for students and supply equipment in order to bring the skills acquired at school more in line with the company's needs and requirements. Offering internships to teachers may also be an effective instrument to bring about change (Frietman and De Vries, 1987). A third instrument for change has recently become available at the international level. Under the umbrella of the European Union, plans have been made to form a European Professional Qualifications Council. At the European level, attention is being paid to the international comparability of educational qualifications (Oliver-Taylor, 1993). Nevertheless, it may be years before companies will be able to influence effectively the curriculum and structure of vocational education, as the European member states still have full autonomy in shaping their educational systems.

Staff flow policy, HRD and the division of labour

Automation has a considerable impact on the substance of jobs. Dequalification and requalification trends may occur, depending on the practical application of new technologies, which is in turn primarily decided on by management (Christis et al., 1981). When introducing new technologies to an organization, management to some extent has an organizational choice either to reinforce or cross the dividing line between manual routine jobs on the one hand, and planning, preparatory and supervisory jobs on the other. A rigid division of labour will cause a decline in the professional competencies of manual workers and reduce the number of options open to them to become better qualified (Valkenburg and Hulskes, 1983).

However, new technologies may also give an impetus to integrate manual, planning and preparatory work into newly formed 'all-round' jobs (Kern and Schumann, 1984). Successful integration (also known as functional flexibilization) hinges on the competencies potential of employees. Adequately educated staff with general expertise will be easier to retrain to meet changing job requirements than employees with little or no professional skills or experience. In the latter case, companies will be forced to keep to their existing, rigidly Taylorist division of labour, even though this will prevent them from rapidly and flexibly responding to market changes.

Summary

The preceding sections clearly show that there is a connection between staff flow policy on the one hand, and environmental and institutional factors and a company's characteristics on the other. We will now discuss this relationship in more detail.

If a comprehensive system of vocational training is absent, companies will resort to creating narrow jobs requiring few specific professional skills. What skills are needed can be quickly acquired on the job. This type of situation only reinforces the Taylorist division of labour. Companies are unwilling to invest a lot in developing the competencies potential of their employees, particularly if employees seem only too willing to change jobs in pursuit of higher wages, allowing the new employer to reap the benefits of training without contributing to its costs. This situation is characterized by an unsophisticated system of vocational training, business organizations with a rigid division of labour and few investments in HRD and in-company training.

Conversely, companies will more readily switch over to new forms of labour division (integration of duties into multifaceted jobs), enabling them to respond flexibly to fluctuations in the demand for customized quality goods, as they can draw from a large pool of well-educated all-round employees. Companies will be more willing to invest in HRD and in-company training if they have the guarantee that their employees will not immediately defect to a better-paying employer. The validity of such a guarantee depends on the availability of well-qualified employees and thus on a comprehensive network of vocational education. It also depends on whether pay negotiations are conducted at the industry level, so employees with equivalent required qualifications will receive equal compensation, and it will not 'pay' to change jobs. This situation highlights the interrelationship between a well-developed system of vocational training, a tendency to innovate, and willingness to invest in human resource development.

From the company's point of view, we can conclude that social factors like education or the manner in which pay is negotiated provides opportunities as well as constraints in terms of staff flow policy and HRD policy. However, other organization-specific factors like the division of labour and the nature of the production means play a large part as well. A good example of this has been given by Glynn and Gospel (1993). On the basis of a historical analysis of industrial development in the United Kingdom, they show that British companies are mainly geared to manufacture comparatively cheap mass products. Highly standardized production processes have severely shrunk the demand for skilled employees. Although forms of vocational training have been and are still being developed, companies make relatively little use of the professional skills of school-leavers as a consequence of the nature of the production process and the Taylorist division of labour. British companies have not been keen to invest in human resource development. This practice has over the decades resulted in a shortage of well-qualified all-round employees. The consequences of this shortage are now being felt, as companies come under increasing pressure from the marketplace to develop advanced production techniques and more flexible working structures. These organizational changes can be implemented only if there are a sufficient number of highly qualified staff available. The present shortage of qualified workers seems largely due to the long-standing predominance of the Taylorist division of labour in British industry.

3   German and British practices compared

Vocational training

There are two educational systems in the United Kingdom, one for England and Wales and one for Scotland and Northern Ireland. We will confine ourselves to discussing the system in England and Wales. Compared with Germany, the English system of vocational training is rather underdeveloped. Some authors go as far as to say that there is a serious lack of training in England (Lane, 1989: 70–74; Lauglo and Lillis, 1989). The majority of young people who enter the labour market have no vocational training at all (OECD, 1990). Vocational education has quite a low status compared to other forms of education.

Compared to England and many other European countries, Germany has a sophisticated system of vocational training. Having completed one of the many types of secondary education, the majority of young people go on to receive some form of vocational training. In Germany the emphasis lies on the dual system, which is a combination of school and in-company training. Additionally, part-time and full-time vocational training courses are provided.

Conrad and Pieper (1990) set the number of dual training programmes at 400. The courses emphasize the flexibility of the graduates. All graduates receive a nationally recognized diploma. The graduate's flexibility and the formal recognition of his competencies improve his chances of success on the external labour market. Moreover, the responsibility for the dual system is shared. The employers' and employees' organizations and the government design the curriculum together. The government finances the educational component, which takes place at school. Responsibility for the work component is mainly vested in the employers. Until recently this interrelationship between training and work meant that there were few qualitative coordination problems in Germany. However, the reunification has resulted in a growing number of former East German employees being put out of work and lacking the qualifications to find new employment in the technologically advanced industries of former West Germany. Added to this, there are also quantitative coordination problems. Student numbers in a dual system vary according to the economic situation. In times of recession, employers are less eager to provide trainee posts, so students move to full-time vocational education.

Until recently, England also had an apprenticeship system, although it was restricted to certain regions and professions. However, rising wages coupled with the powerful influence of the trade unions on the curriculum made this system unpopular with the employers. In the 1980s, the apprenticeship system was replaced by Youth Training Schemes. A drawback of YTS is that the training is too company-specific, does not result in a generally recognized certificate, and thus fails to improve the prospects for success on the external labour market (Eyraud et al., 1990). A growing number of adults take part in this type of training.

Coordination between education and work in England leaves much to be desired. To overcome this problem, the Technical and Vocational Educa-tion Initiative was launched in the early 1980s. Under this system, schools contact companies to arrange trainee posts for students and teachers and seek sponsors for vocation-oriented projects and excursions. Attempts are also being made to adjust the curricula adopted by institutions of higher education to the needs of the labour market. Employers are urging colleges to focus more on non-technical competencies such as communicative skills and the ability to solve problems and work efficiently.

Company training

In Germany, all major companies have their own training centres, while smaller companies have set up joint training facilities. These facilities are used within the context of the dual system and for the training of employees. A wide variety of courses are on offer in these centres (Conrad and Pieper, 1990). In 1987, German companies spent a total of 26 billion Deutschmarks on company training and management development (this is exclusive of their contribution to the dual system). The lion's share of this sum is used for off-the-job training programmes for highly educated staff who will be appointed to management positions (Conrad and Pieper, 1990). A smaller portion is spent on training skilled and semi-skilled employees. Training primarily targets young male employees of between 21 and 30. For the group of skilled and semi-skilled employees, companies more and more deploy training instruments in the workplace itself. Offering courses off the job increasingly meets with business-economic objections, such as rising costs and training activities which are difficult to fit into the production process. Educational arguments have also been put forward: on-the-job training notably appeals to the older employees and less skilled staff and is a more efficient way of acquiring key competencies (Münch, 1990; Onstenk, forthcoming). Moreover, on-the-job training resembles the type of training received by many young people in Germany. The German government is pursuing an active policy in the field of company training. With the aid of pilot projects and research programmes, attempts are being made to develop new ideas and disseminate them throughout the country.

Less is known about the training situation in UK companies. We will mention only a few important aspects. Fewer efforts have been made in the area of company training than in Germany. The government has adopted an exceptionally restrained policy on this point, leaving it to businesses to take the initiative. They in turn generally do not view training and education as their responsibility. Thus, thanks to the government's policy and the position taken by the business community, comparatively little progress has been made in the training sector. Large companies offer in-company courses and smaller businesses retain the services of education colleges (Lane, 1989: 76). For manual workers, on-the-job training is the most important form of training. This is partly due to the lack of other training instruments (Onstenk, forthcoming). At the end of the 1980s, small-scale initiatives were taken to broaden the limited competencies profile of employees by providing additional training. The idea is to render employees qualified to work in two or more workplaces (Lane, 1989), which is an important condition for the implementation of types of functional flexibility.

Staff flow policy

Recruitment by German companies often starts with the selection of school-leavers who seek a place in the dual training system. Personal characteristics play a role in the selection process. Male indigenous students stand a better chance than women and ethnic minorities. Having completed the apprenticeship period, apprentices in large companies are more likely to be offered a job in the company where they were trained than apprentices in small and medium-sized companies. Large companies use staffing forecasts and on that basis establish the number of dual training places. Small and medium-sized businesses usually act on a direct need. If ex-apprentices are not offered a job, they can still apply to other employers because they have a recognized diploma. They do run the risk, however, of ending up in a less qualified position (Onstenk, forthcoming). The prospects for promotion for manual workers in the internal labour market of German companies are largely determined by a combination of starting qualifications, the nature of the work and additional training. A promotion to floor manager is possible for manual workers if they have taken a two-year part-time course and acquired the 'Meisterbrief', which is again a generally recognized diploma.

Less internal mobility is found in British companies. The fact that training is considered less important and companies have implemented a rather rigid division of labour has resulted in a very modest development of competencies in companies. Qualitative upgrading of the workforce is mainly realized by dismissing employees and recruiting adequately trained personnel from outside the company (Van Ruysseveldt, 1991). Alternatively, companies temporarily hire outside experts (Ramsey et al., 1992). In both cases, companies turn to the external labour market.

Division of labour

There are a few important differences between the two countries as to how work is organized (Lane, 1989; Ramsey et al., 1992; Van Ruysseveldt, 1991). British companies are characterized by strictly delineated jobs requiring few specific competencies. Moreover, there is a sharp division between management, technical staff and production workers. Communication between the different levels is difficult, which is reflected in poor after-sales service (Lane, 1989: 50). Managers have only limited technical expertise. This results in a permanent need for technical staff, who are hired in great numbers from outside the company. The strict division of labour exerts a downward pressure on the costs of training. Companies are primarily concerned with mass production at low cost. Productivity increases are largely realized by rationalizing production processes, often coupled with redundancies. British companies only rarely use new technologies to develop essentially new forms of the division of labour. Ramsey, Pollert and Rainbird (1992) attribute this phenomenon to the low competencies level of manual staff and their direct superiors. The lack of competencies is felt on both the internal and the external labour market. The operation and servicing of expensive equipment either prompts companies to create special jobs and/or hire outside experts. There are indications that broader jobs are being created (extension and rotation of tasks), but there is still no sign of any true integration of planning, supervisory and manual tasks as found in Germany. In Germany, the organization of work accommodates the broad competencies of students graduating under the dual system. German companies moreover endeavour to make their employees as all-round as possible. This is done by allowing employees to rotate between two or more jobs. Also, employee autonomy in the German workplace is much more advanced than in the United Kingdom. There are two explanations for this. First, the employees have had a broad education, allowing them to control the quality of their own work. Secondly, students in the dual system are trained to feel responsible and adopt a professional working attitude, so that intensive supervisory control is not required. The division between direct superiors, technical staff and manual workers is less sharp. The employees working in those positions partly have a common educational background, which enhances cooperation between them despite the formal hierarchical differences. In order to become a manager, employees must attend a two-year part-time course after their dual training, leading to the 'Meisterbrief'. Because managers and manual workers have the same technical expertise, communications between them takes place at a more equal level than in the UK. Due to the greater emphasis on training, most German companies are less concerned with mass production and attach more weight to flexible quality production and proper after-sales service. German companies also make more intensive use of new technologies. They create fewer separate jobs for the operation and normal servicing of equipment than do their British counterparts. Having a general knowledge of the production process, German employees are better able to anticipate a possible disruption of production and set a diagnosis, so problems can be more quickly resolved, either by them or by the technical staff.

Conclusions

We may conclude from this comparison that there is in fact a connection between the nature and structure of the vocational education system on the one hand, and the division of labour in companies on the other. The absence of a comprehensive system of vocational training in the UK only reinforces the stringent division of labour found in industrial companies. And vice versa, this strict division of labour suppresses the need for qualified staff, effectively eliminating any incentive to develop a comprehensive system of vocational training. In Germany, we also notice a relationship between the division of labour and vocational training, although this relationship is fundamentally different from the one found in England and Wales. The competencies provided by vocational training enable companies to reduce the rigidity of division of labour and to design all-round positions, permitting a more flexible organization of the production process. These business innovations in turn encourage investments in vocational education and in-company training. From the comparison it can also be inferred that the importance attributed by employers to professional qualifications has a bearing on their involvement in vocational education. Since there is less need for qualified staff in the United Kingdom, contacts between vocational training institutions and employers' organizations are less well developed than in Germany. In Germany, employers' and employees' organizations and the government are closely involved in organizing the vocational education system. It can be said that German employers have a strategic interest in the developments occurring in vocational education.

Finally, the comparison highlights the connection between HRD policy and staff flow policy adopted by a company on the one hand, and the division of labour and acquisition of competencies in vocational education on the other. In light of the broad qualifications profile of the average German employee and the career prospects associated with his all-round job, companies consider it useful and profitable to invest in company training and provide career paths. They view HRD and staff flow policies as the cornerstones of their personnel management. The combination of few professional skills, narrow jobs and traditional organizational structures make British employers less eager to invest in HRD and to adopt staff flow policies. British companies seem to consider redundancies and the recruitment of better-qualified employees a more important instrument to improve the quality of their workforce than investing in company training and developing career paths.

4   France and the Netherlands compared

Vocational training

In France and the Netherlands, the emphasis is on full-time vocational education, although dual forms have been developed.

Only 13 percent of young people in France take part in dual training courses. It must be added that these courses have a low status. About one-third of all young persons enter the labour market without any formal professional qualifications (Lane, 1989: 68–70). The central government has of old exerted a profound influence on the organization and programming of full-time vocational education. The influence of employers is negligible. Compared with the countries discussed above, an exceptionally large number of young people in the Netherlands participate in full-time and part-time vocational education (Cedefop, 1990). Dual education and school education exist alongside each other. However, a majority of students are trained in school rather than on the job. In the 1980s, partly at the request of the business community, substantial investments were made to improve the dual system (apprenticeship). These investments resulted in a doubling of the number of apprentices. Qualitative improvements have been achieved in that training has been made less sensitive to cyclical fluctuations and supra-company training centres have been set up (common training activities) to prevent the practical component of the training becoming too company-specific (Hövels, 1987). Moreover, consultation structures have been developed (per trade or branch of industry) so as to involve the social partners (that is, employers and employees) in the organization of vocational education. As in Germany, school training is the responsibility of the national government, while employers are responsible for the practical component. In recent years, substantial curriculum reforms have been introduced better to tune the programmes of full-time vocational training courses to the labour market. In the Dutch vocational education system, the emphasis is placed on providing a general education for a specified profession. In terms of coordinating education and work, this system has its pros and cons (Verhoeven, 1991). The benefit is that students acquire more professional qualifications than are required for a specific position. This means that they do not necessarily need additional training with every change of duties. A drawback is that the emphasis placed on general competencies implies long periods of vocational training so that students are comparatively old when they leave school. Although students get to know many relevant aspects of professional practice because of their long school careers, they cannot always be put to work immediately in a specific job. Acquiring company-specific competencies remains necessary in many cases.

In France, the lack of involvement of the social partners in vocational education has led to considerable qualitative coordination problems. A survey of 3,000 leading industrial employers has shown that 72 percent believe that the French educational system fails adequately to prepare young people for business life (Oechslin, 1987). There also appears to be little connection between vocational training and the positions which young people subsequently occupy. Due to economic and political events (economic stagnation and a socialist government), the social partners have been encouraged to be more involved in vocational education in recent years. The government has stressed the need to improve full-time vocational education and intensify company-specific forms of training in order to respond to future economic developments (Cedefop, 1990).

Company training

French companies are statutorily obliged to spend a portion of their payroll costs (1.5 percent) on company training and to report on training to the government in writing. There is no such obligation in the Netherlands (see Appendix at the end of this chapter). Investment in company training is left entirely to the employers. Some sectors have educational funds to which employers make financial contributions pursuant to agreements with the trade unions. In France, company courses are primarily attended by lower and upper managerial and technical staff. Substantially fewer efforts are made to provide training for manual workers (Lane, 1989: 75). French companies mainly provide in-company training, probably with a view to the company-specific competencies of the employees. In-company training tailors their competencies more to the needs of the company. In terms of content, the training closely matches the employees' (narrowly defined) jobs. Little attention is paid to the acquisition of competencies in excess of those required for the job. Given its very company-specific nature, the training certainly does not improve the external mobility of the employees. Another important aspect of French company training is that it places the emphasis on (informal) on-the-job training, particularly for the lower corporate echelons. It is customary practice that the floor managers supervise the training. However, since they have little technical expertise, the quality of this type of training could be called into question.

Dutch companies make increasing use of outside training courses. This has reduced the number of courses offered by the companies themselves (Warmerdam and Van den Berg, 1992). Participation in supra-company courses not only increases the prospects for promotion but also safeguards the external mobility of employees. What we see is a growing integration of training efforts and career development. Prompted by economic (cost-saving) and educational reasons, there is a trend in the Netherlands towards on-the-job training of manual workers (de Jong, 1991). Although there are indications that floor managers sometimes have too little technical and educational expertise to be able to supervise training properly (Kessels and Smit, 1991), quality problems appear to be less pressing than in French companies.

The Appendix shows some of the features of company training provided in the countries discussed in this chapter, as well as information about the situation in Japan and the United States.

Staff flow policy

As pointed out earlier, many young people in France have jobs which do not match their training. Even if the training and the job are compatible, companies still prefer to appoint young employees to positions in the secondary segment, usually to unskilled positions on a temporary basis. Employers adopt this strategy so that they have an adequate pool of employees which they can tap for the primary segment of their organization. Once permanent contracts have been concluded, the young employees may be eligible for additional company-specific training, usually in the form of (informal) on-the-job training, after which they may be promoted to higher positions (Lane, 1989).

In the Netherlands, companies tend to require increasingly higher qualifications, which is partly the result of the large-scale application of new technologies. Warmerdam and Van den Berg (1992) observe that companies increasingly hire skilled young people (MBO level at minimum, that is, intermediate vocational education) for less complex jobs. Companies also prefer to conclude temporary contracts first before they offer any permanent contracts.

French employees have to rely on the internal labour market for promotion (Eyraud et al., 1990). The well-developed hierarchy in many companies has resulted in intricate career paths. Promotion requires working experience and, to a lesser extent, company-specific training. A promotion to floor manager is possible, provided that the employee has sufficient experience (years of service). The more company-specific experience an employer has, the more valuable he is for the company, but the less chance he has of finding a similar position on the external labour market. In recent years, companies have sometimes been seen to prefer recruiting skilled workers for skilled work from outside the company rather than training their own employees (Lane, 1989). This strategy reduces the investment in company training and adversely affects the career prospects of employees.

Dutch employees not only have internal career opportunities, they also have the possibility of improving their position via the external labour market. However, there are indications that the latter route is becoming less important. More than in France, the prospects for promotion in the Netherlands depend on the formal qualifications (diplomas) of the employees. Access to the primary segment of Dutch companies remains the privilege of well-educated employees who perform the more complex key activities of the organization. This has led to the introduction of the term 'core employee'. Companies seemingly prefer to fill vacancies for core employees by recruiting on the internal labour market (Kluytmans and Paauwe, 1991). Activities which do not come within the core operations of a company are often performed by temporary employees.

Division of labour

The division of labour in French and British companies shows strong resemblances. Industrial companies in France are quite hierarchically structured. The organization seems to be based on the principle of control: a great deal of power at the top, little autonomy in the workplace. The cooperative working climate in German companies, where floor managers and manual workers work closely together, is less common in France. French companies tend rather to regulate the work via written communication (Rojot, 1990). Managers have a notably narrower span of control than in the UK or Germany. Lane (1989: 42) explains this situation by pointing out that French managers place little trust in their employees.

In the Netherlands, the division of labour is less strict. On the basis of the research available, we can also conclude that Dutch companies apply advanced technology more intensively and effectively than do French companies. This large-scale use of new technologies does not, however, automatically change the rigidity of the division of labour. Many companies stick to classic organizational structures. Tillaart (1993) signals an increasing division of labour in large retail chains, coupled with numerical flexibilization and limited company-specific training. Research into the processing industry shows a great deal of variety. There, the application of new technologies has led to a reduction in the competencies needed for the position of operator and a growing need for general competencies such as accuracy and the ability to concentrate. Technical failures must no longer be resolved but have to be reported to the technical staff (Valkenburg and Hulskes, 1983). However, Van der Klink's research (1989) seems to indicate that the introduction of new production methods in the processing industry does not necessarily result in a downgrading of professional skills. In some companies, trainee operators are taught how to resolve failures themselves or else assist the technical staff. In the graphics industry, the general policy is to have flexible employees. Ideally, every employee should be suitable for two jobs (Kayzel, 1985). The emphasis on general usability is also noticeable in the food and tobacco industry (Feijen, 1993) and various other sectors. However, the limits of functional flexibility are in sight. Recent research on Dutch businesses in different sectors by Warmerdam and Van den Berg (1992) shows that the functional flexibilization launched in the workplace in the 1980s has partly been reversed due to staffing problems. Functional flexibility requires all-round employees. It turns out that training (current) employees up to that level is not always possible. Because of the scarcity of qualified employees on the external labour market, companies have had to appoint lower-qualified personnel, which has only added to the training ability problem. The researchers conclude that staffing problems, in particular, have prompted companies to return to forms of partial flexibilization tailored to the abilities of their employees.

Production innovation is progressing less smoothly in France than in the Netherlands. Rojot (1990) describes the laborious introduction of quality circles in French companies. Implementing quality circles means that employees must be granted access to information about the production process. But information is also the gateway to power, all of which is hardly compatible with the traditional French corporate structure. Additionally, quality circles require all those involved to be willing to communicate in order to achieve improvement. The hierarchical structure and sharp division between different job levels render direct communication quite difficult. The lack of sufficiently qualified employees in the workplace, the lack of trust in their abilities and the rigid division of labour have meant that companies, when applying new technologies, have preferred numerical flexibilization (Rojot, 1990). In the past few years, in some sectors, attempts have been made to introduce new forms of work designed to improve the quality of jobs (Lane, 1989: 189–192).

Conclusions

The comparison between France and the Netherlands brings to light a number of links between various factors. The first link concerns government intervention in the field of corporate training policy. A remarkable situation is found in France, where the central government obliges companies to appropriate part of their payroll costs for company training. In this manner, the government tries to stimulate companies to increase the level of competencies of their employees. There is no such obligation in the Netherlands, where the government leaves it entirely up to companies to decide to what extent they wish to provide company training. Sweeping measures like the one imposed in France are not really necessary in the Netherlands because employees are usually better qualified than French workers.

Secondly, there is a link between education and the division of labour similar to that found in the comparison between Germany and the United Kingdom (though less clear-cut). As a result of the large pool of generally qualified employees, it seems comparatively easy for Dutch companies to introduce innovative work structures. French companies, in contrast, face substantial, and interrelated, obstacles, namely: less generally qualified employees; influx at low job levels; promotion on the basis of work experience and company-specific competencies; the strict division of labour in a highly hierarchical organization.

Finally, staff flow policies have a different structure in the two countries. In France, employees receive less vocational education and/or are hired at low job levels. If they seek promotion, they will have to look to the internal labour market. Promotion is related to working experience (years of service) and the acquisition of company-specific competencies. From the employers' point of view, this staffing policy is beneficial in terms of control: loyalty is rewarded in the form of promotion. From the employees' point of view, the acquisition of company-specific competencies reduces their chances of finding a similar job outside the company. Dutch employees usually have broader qualifications which are generally recognized, so their careers depend less on the company where they work. They can easily change jobs and, more than in France, promotion is based on objective criteria such as the acquisition of higher formal qualifications.

5   Flow policy and HRD for managers

To conclude, we will briefly discuss staff flow policy and HRD for managers in the four European countries mentioned. The following outline is based on research conducted by Evans, Lank and Farquhar (1989). They refer to the policy adopted in German companies as the 'functional career model'. Companies annually recruit from university and technical college graduates. Elite recruitment also takes place to some extent, particularly from candidates with a doctorate. Those taken on are offered a two-year dual course, which at the same time serves as a trial period, before receiving a contract for an indefinite period of time. During the two-year trial period, job rotation and additional training are combined. This results in broad competencies and indicates for what type of position the candidate is best suited. Once the permanent contract is there, promotion takes place within the employee's own professional classification. Appraisal is primarily based on competencies. There is little horizontal mobility. Especially in large companies, career development coincides with increased specialization. Not all candidates find this prospect attractive. Those who do not, switch over to smaller firms, where management positions are more general and less technical.

The 'generalist model' is predominant in the UK (Evans et al., 1989). Candidates spend a trial period of between five and seven years, during which they are expected to rise in their own technical or functional hierarchy. Only then may they be selected for management positions. The subsequent use of management development programmes stimulates their mobility on the internal labour market. A drawback of the generalist model is the late selection of prospective managers, which sometimes prevents promotion to top positions. This has led some companies to advance the time of selection.

French companies recruit their managers from graduates from a handful of leading institutions (the *grandes écoles*). Evans, Lank and Farquhar (1989) term this type of recruitment the 'elite-political model'. The political fight for top positions is essentially based on visible performance, finding sponsors, creating coalitions and the ability properly to interpret signals. Managers are immediately appointed to high-level jobs. In order to acquire competencies, French managers have to rely primarily on informal on-the-job training.

Evans, Lank and Farquhar report that Dutch companies adopt either of the following two strategies to recruit their managers: the 'functional model', as is applied on a large scale in Germany; or the 'generalist model', which is found in British companies.

Appendix: Comparison of the structure of company training in France, Germany, Japan, the Netherlands, the United Kingdom and the United States

The details of the structure of company training in six different countries given below are derived from studies by: Birtwhistle, 1990; Carnevale et al., 1990; Dore and Sako, 1989; Force, 1992; Méhaut, 1990; Mulder and Luijendijk, 1990; Mulder et al., 1989.

France

Legislation   Statutory obligation for employers to invest in personnel training (1.5 percent of the payroll costs).

Educational leave   Right to educational leave (and right to training, qualifications and career assessment).

Offered by   Private sector 78 percent, public sector 14 percent, semi-government 8 percent (basis: 1989).

Quality measures   Contractual terms and conditions. Act setting out the minimum terms and conditions to be met by organizations participating in public sector programmes.

Certificates requirement and diplomas   The Ministry of Education and the National Committee for Recognition and Diplomas issue diplomas. Diplomas are recognized in the national negotiations for collective bargaining agreements.

Participation   7.4 million employees (1989); 34 percent of the working population.

Costs   FFR 53 billion (1989); 2.9 percent of the payroll costs.

Germany

Legislation   Three federal statutes:

- Vocational Education Act;
- Act on the Advancement of Employment;
- Act on Correspondence Courses.

Educational statutes at the state level.

Educational leave   ILO Convention 140 ratified in 1976. Educational leave has been regulated by state laws and under collective bargaining agreements. Courses may be vocation-oriented but are mainly designed to develop personnel. Duration: about 5 days a year.

Offered by   Large companies have training departments. Small and medium-sized companies use outside organizations. Initiative: 44 percent by companies; 39 percent by outside agents (17 percent unknown) (basis: 1988).

Quality measures   The quality of company training is overseen by the companies themselves. Quality measures have also been laid down in statutory provisions and collective bargaining agreements.

Certificates requirement and diplomas   Company training consisting of parts of training programmes offered under the dual system leads to formally recognized certificates. The greater part of company training does not lead to a generally recognized diploma. Within the context of training to increase employment, a number of diplomas are issued by agencies that provide training, Chambers of Commerce, private organizations and trade sectors which are recognized by the government.

Participation   6.4 million employees (1988), or 18 percent of the working population, who are mainly apprentices financed by the business community.

Costs   DM 35 billion (1988).

Japan

Legislation   Within the context of lifetime employment, training and development is seen as a natural element within the organization.

Educational leave   There are no statutory rules. Many employees take courses for their own account.

Offered by   Large companies have their own training departments. There are many private training institutions providing technical courses.

Quality measures   There is an extensive assessment and diplomas tradition. The most important actor is the government. In some cases, employers' organizations play a role in setting professional standards. Professional organizations hardly do so.

Certificates requirement and diplomas   There is a tradition of issuing diplomas, in which the government plays the largest part. Many state examinations take place. Some professional organizations wish to have more powers in this field.

Participation   Dore and Sako (1989: 107) found that 75 percent of the working population took profession-oriented training courses in 1986. Since large companies are over-represented in their survey, this is probably too high an estimate.

Costs   Yen 877 billion (1986). In 1984, 0.3 percent of payroll costs.

The Netherlands

Legislation   No statutory obligations: some sectors have training funds available paid for by employers.

Educational leave   No statutory obligations: 66 percent of the collective bargaining agreements contain clauses on educational leave (varying from between 1 and 8 days a year).

Offered by Private sector 58 percent, public sector 11 percent, semi-government 31 percent (basis: 1986).

Quality measures Recognized Educational Institutions Act. Assessment of institutions by CEDEO. Contract assessment of VETRON institutions.

Certificates requirement and diplomas A quality care system is being developed. The certificates requirement does not extend to individual staff members of the institution.

Participation 1,000,000 employees (1990); 18 percent of the working population.

Costs NLG 3.5 billion (1992); 1.7 percent of the payroll costs.

United Kingdom

Legislation Employers are obliged to provide training to increase health and safety in the workplace. Some professions are regulated by law where employees must have had training in order to receive an employment contract. Statutory right to training with a view to workers' participation. Enhancement of influx.

Educational leave No statutory obligation to grant educational leave; employers and employees make arrangements in mutual consultation.

Offered by Training and Enterprise Councils (TECs) in England and Wales; Local Enterprise Councils (LECs) in Scotland and Ireland; in collaboration with local educational and training institutions. Contract teaching provided by Colleges of Further Education. In general, there has been a free educational market (since 1979).

Quality measures This is the responsibility of the National Training Task Force and Industry Training Organizations. They control the quality of courses on offer and monitor the improvement of company training.

Certificates requirement and diplomas Diplomas are issued as National Vocational Qualifications. Vocational diplomas are being worked on.

Participation In 1988, 48 percent of employees took part in some form of training. In 1991, 15 percent of the working population attended job-oriented training (in four-week sections).

Costs £16 billion (1986–7).

United States

Legislation No national statutory obligations.

Educational leave No statutory obligations. Statutory obligations are being advocated (Carnevale et al., 1990).

Offered by Private sector 17 percent, public sector 65 percent, semi-government 17 percent (4 percent unknown) (basis: 1992).

Quality measures   Competition between different professional organizations. ASTD advocates self-assessment; IBSTPI advocates certificates requirements.

Certificates requirement and diplomas   Different professional organizations adopt different stands; self-assessment or certificates requirements (see above).

Participation   40.9 million employees (1992); 44 percent of the working population.

Costs   US$ 45 billion (1992).

PART 3

MANAGING AN INTERNATIONAL STAFF

9 Composing an international staff

Malcolm Borg and Anne-Wil Harzing

1	Introduction	179
2	Analysis of international transfers	181
	Reasons for international transfers	181
	International transfer policies	183
	Extensive and planned international transfer of personnel	183
	Assigning key managers abroad	184
	Policy of not having expatriate managers	184
	Ad hoc policy	184
	PCN, HCN and TCN	185
3	The international transfer cycle	185
	Phase 1: recruitment and selection	187
	Phase 2: the assignment period abroad	190
	Phase 3: repatriation	192
4	Profiles of international managers	194
	Transfer archetypes	194
	Transfer archetypes and international transfer functions	198
5	The process of (re)designing international staffing policies	201
	Phase 1: analyzing the situation and involving top management	201
	Mapping the present situation	201
	Establishing improvement potentials	202
	Creating commitment among top managers	202
	Phase 2: designing the staffing policy	203
	Phase 3: implementing the staffing policy	203
6	Summary and conclusions	204

1 Introduction

International transfer of personnel is a multi-faceted and fascinating subject. It has a strong bearing on a company's success and is of crucial concern for the person who is transferred internationally. The successful outcome of a transfer is important for the manager who initiated it and for the manager in charge of personnel. For the family involved a transfer might mean permanent change. It may be the first of many transfers

Figure 9.1 *Long- and short-term instruments used to bridge both geographical and cultural distances*

around the globe and the beginning of a lifelong stay abroad as an expatriate family. The subject of international transfers is 'transdisciplinary', covering such aspects as general management, sociology, psychology and even politics. A great deal has been written on international transfers from the individual and psychological/sociological viewpoint. In this chapter we will focus primarily on the general management and business perspectives.

A practical approach is to regard the international transfer of personnel as a means of bridging geographical and cultural distances. The direct personnel contacts it engenders undoubtedly make it a very effective, although costly, way of doing so. There are other ways, however. Figure 9.1 indicates some of the long- and short-term instruments which can be used in order to bridge geographical and cultural distances.

In the case of assigning managers from the parent firm to a key position abroad, the effect on bridging geographical and cultural distances can be short term and long term at the same time. International conferences are also a common way of bridging such distances. The agenda for an international conference, that is, the network and the contents, is entirely the responsibility of the corporate management group. This type of activity provides solid grounds for discussing different strategic and organizational matters, but unfortunately does little to foster an understanding of local business and cultural aspects. Travelling managers have relatively superficial contacts with subsidiary personnel, so their long-term impact is likely to be small. They can, however, be highly effective in the short term because they can provide solutions to immediate problems. The opposite is true for MBA training and recruitment and career planning. The impact of both these measures only becomes evident after a long time and they are therefore mainly effective in the long term.

In the rest of this chapter we will concentrate on the international transfer of personnel. Our purpose is, first of all, to provide an analysis of international transfers from the company perspective and, secondly, to analyze the international transfer cycle, both from the company and from the expatriate perspectives. Furthermore, we will take a look at the different types of expatriates and their function in international staffing. These analyses are the basis for a consultant's view on how to improve and design international staffing policies in multinational corporations.

2   Analysis of international transfers

In this section we will discuss three essential questions in the field of international transfers. First of all, why do firms bother to send their managers abroad? The first sub-section below attempts to provide some answers to this question. Secondly, can we distinguish different company policies with regard to international transfers? The answer is yes: companies generally demonstrate a preference for parent-country nationals (PCN), host-country nationals (HCN), third-country nationals (TCN) or a particular combination of these different groups. The policies are discussed in the second sub-section, while the final discussion will centre on the advantages and disadvantages of employing the different groups of employees.

Reasons for international transfers

There are few theoretical clarifications or concepts regarding the organizational function fulfilled by international transfers. Edström and Galbraith (1977) seem to be the only ones who have formulated a theory explaining why companies make this type of transfer. They found three general company motives.

The first was to '*fill positions*' when qualified host-country nationals were unavailable or difficult to train. It was thus a question of assigning managers abroad for the purpose of transferring technical and administrative knowledge. According to Edström and Galbraith, such transfers chiefly involve lower-level positions of a technical nature. Employees sent abroad to fill such positions accept only one or two assignments before returning to the parent organization.

Companies may also fill a vacant position with a view to maintaining the bureaucracy, that is, exercise control through rules and regulations. In the MNC this takes place by means of administrative and financial control systems. Persons working in bureaucracies must accept the legitimacy of the organization's authority as well as learn its rules and regulations. In addition, they must acquire the technical competence required for their position. The selected parent-country national can in principle immediately meet these requirements and function as a representative who also passes on know-how, technical skills, administrative systems etc. Training of host-country nationals can also be regarded as a control and coordination mechanism, since it brings about consistency in the manner in which tasks are performed within the company. Thus it seems that a company may use international transfer of managers to make the bureaucracy run more smoothly – a way of oiling or servicing the machinery – or to implement changes in the formal design of the MNC.

The second motive, '*management development*', was that a transfer gives managers international experience and trains them for future important tasks in subsidiaries abroad or with the parent company. This kind of transfer takes place even when qualified host-country nationals are available. Managers might be transferred to subsidiaries abroad where they can acquire special skills, e.g. superior marketing skills at the German subsidiary or inflationary accounting at the Brazilian subsidiary. These types of transfer are usually reserved for parent-company nationals who specialize in technical or administrative areas or for selected host-country nationals. Their number is moderate and they generally make several moves, that is, more than two.

Management development is a motive for training managers to occupy positions, either at the parent organization or at subsidiaries abroad, which require international experience. The purpose is to train managers who can gradually take up more advanced posts within the parent company or at a subsidiary abroad. Since it is difficult to select successful international managers beforehand, that is, before the assignment abroad, a large number of managers are sent out so that those who are successful may be selected for further assignments, whereas the rest are repatriated or resign.

The third motive, the strategy which most closely resembles the geocentric company concept as discussed in Chapters 2, 3 and 4 of this book, concerns the international transfer of managers for reasons of '*organizational development*'. The idea behind this motive is that managers become less ethnocentric if they come into contact with a variety of cultures. It is assumed that the large-scale transfer of managers of different nationalities between the subsidiaries abroad, and between the parent company and its subsidiaries, will socialize managers and create international communication networks. This would allow for more decentralization than the traditional bureaucratic strategy. Control by socialization implies that 'the functional behaviour and the rules for determining them, [are] learned and internalized by individuals thereby obviating the need for procedures, hierarchical communication and surveillance' (Edström and Galbraith, 1977: 251). Transfers should be frequent, since they are in and of themselves processes by which individuals who already have the appropriate attitudes are selected and self-selected. A large number of managers should be transferred so that 'at each subsidiary there are pockets of internationalized, company-socialized local employees . . . who buffer the expatriate from the full force of the culture shock, yet absorb him into the management team . . . and impart the company culture to the expatriate' (1977: 258). However, in reality we see little of this kind of policy. Ondrack (1985: 17), for instance, who explicitly used the Edström and Galbraith typology for analysis, found in a case study of four MNCs that, contrary to his hypothesis, 'despite the global nature of their international operations, none of the firms . . . have a truly geocentric approach to personnel'.

Organizational development is a means of establishing an additional mode of control in the MNC. The control is achieved by 'acculturation', socialization and interaction among managers of different nationalities from various parts of the MNC. Thus, transfers to fill positions and transfers to promote organizational development are both directly associated with organizational control, whereas management development is not. So we see that, in fact, two of the three major organizational functions of international transfer policies involve a focus on control, either formal/bureaucratic control or informal control by socialization.

These motives for international transfer are comparable to the different purposes of international staffing, as distinguished by Adler and Ghadar (Chapter 4). They distinguish: project 'To get the job done' (position filling), career development (management development) and organizational development (same term). According to Adler and Ghadar (1990), organizational development occurs mainly in global companies (transnational in 'our' terminology), management development in both global (transnational) and multinational (global in 'our' terminology) companies and position filling in both multinational (global) and international (multidomestic/international in 'our' terminology) companies. In the first part of this book we have seen that truly transnational companies are still very rare. We should therefore not be surprised at the small number of transfers for purposes of organizational development. Most transfers still involve position filling and occasional management development.

International transfer policies

Companies have different ways of handling international transfers of personnel. Some companies have formal systems, while others have no policy whatsoever on this subject. The different transfer policies we will discuss below are simplified and will rarely be found in the pure form delineated here. In general we can distinguish four transfer policies: extensive and planned international transfer of personnel, the assignment of key managers abroad, a policy of not having expatriate managers and, finally, an ad hoc policy.

Extensive and planned international transfer of personnel

Some corporations have identified the supply of competent international managers as a critical success factor or a competitive weapon. They spend considerable resources, both financial and human, on the (international) transfer of personnel. These transfers take place in all directions, from headquarters to subsidiaries, from subsidiaries to headquarters and between subsidiaries. Furthermore, individuals from all nationalities and from each level of the company are transferred. There are policies and central departments which support these extensive transfers. Some companies have trainee programmes where junior managers are transferred for a period of 6–12 months as part of their training. Other companies, like IBM, transfer professionals in different areas for knowledge development purposes. Examples of companies pursuing a policy of extensive and planned international transfer of personnel are Unilever, Shell and McKinsey. This approach is broadly comparable to the geocentric approach to staffing as discussed in Part 1 of this book.

Assigning key managers abroad

The approach in which trusted managers are assigned to key positions in subsidiaries is a common one in many firms, among them manufacturing companies with many plants throughout the world. This policy has been adopted widely in the 'mother–daughter' organization form, for example. It is a simple control strategy which builds upon the idea that 'a trusted person on site' will make the same decision as the parent-company managers would have done. Parent-company personnel are also widely assigned to start-up activities, for example, the building of a plant or the start-up of newly acquired companies. European and especially Japanese companies practise this policy more than US companies (Tung, 1988). The strategy is broadly comparable to the ethnocentric approach to staffing as discussed in Part 1.

Policy of not having expatriate managers

The idea of reducing the number of expatriate managers has many advocates. One argument in favour is that there are many negative aspects associated with expatriates: high costs, limited promotion opportunities for native managers at the subsidiaries, low morale caused by an imposed leadership style, culture shock, high risk of failure and repatriation problems. Another argument is that the control and coordination effect might nowadays be achieved by other means. Companies can try to find other ways of managing foreign activities, for example, extensive travel and international conferences. We will come back to both these arguments later. IBM, for example, has a policy of not assigning parent-country managers to key positions, the top management in each country normally consisting of locals. As mentioned before, however, IBM does assign managers to specialist functions and for training purposes. This strategy is broadly comparable to the polycentric approach to staffing as discussed in Part 1.

Ad hoc policy

The ad hoc strategy implies that transfers are made without the help of major guidelines or that such major guidelines are ignored. Most large corporations will probably claim to have policies on international transfers. Such policies are very difficult to implement, however, and in the majority of cases have little to do with the actual situation. The usual course of events in an ad hoc transfer policy is that line managers at headquarters assign a few key managers to subsidiaries abroad.

PCN, HCN and TCN

The policies we discussed above imply a preference either for parent-country nationals (PCN), host-country nationals (HCN), third-country nationals (TCN) or a combination of these different groups.

- A PCN is a national of the country of the MNC's headquarters.
- An HCN is a national of the country of the subsidiary.
- A TCN is a national of a country other than the MNC's home country or the country of the subsidiary.

A discussion of the advantages and disadvantages of employing these different groups of employees will clarify the applicability of the different transfer policies. Some of the advantages and disadvantages mentioned most often (Negandhi, 1987; Phatak, 1989; Dowling and Schuler, 1990) are summarized in Table 9.1.

Over time certain circumstances have evolved which could be expected to make expatriate managers (PCN and TCN) redundant. First, the development of telecommunications has greatly improved both written and oral communication. Nowadays it is possible to telephone directly all over the world, making it easier to communicate with headquarters when there is uncertainty about a decision. Secondly, improved and expanded business flights allow speedy travel, so that executives from headquarters are able to visit the subsidiary and help local management with technical and administrative issues. Finally, universal competence in languages has improved communication between different nationalities. Today most business people, at least in the industrialized world, speak English.

Although we might expect that expatriate managers are a vanishing breed in modern organizations, it seems that expatriation is still a very viable approach within MNCs. Table 9.2 summarizes part of a study by Tung (1988) involving expatriate managers in 169 companies (105 US, 29 European and 35 Japanese). The results show that PCNs account for between 29 percent and 85 percent of the senior positions in the foreign affiliates.

The lowest proportions of host-country nationals and consequently the highest proportions of expatriate managers are found where the cultural distance can be expected to be largest – between US and European MNCs on the one hand and their Far East subsidiaries on the other, and vice versa (Japanese subsidiaries in Western countries). Moreover, Japanese MNCs generally have the highest proportion of expatriates, whereas US organizations have the lowest. So we see that although current trends suggest the opposite, MNCs still make extensive use of expatriate managers, especially PCNs.

3   The international transfer cycle

Now that we have discussed some fundamental questions in the field of international transfer, we will take a closer look at the international

Table 9.1 *The advantages and disadvantages of using PCN, HCN and TCN*

	Advantages	Disadvantages
PCN (parent-country national)	Familiarity with the home office's goals, objectives, policies and practices Technical and managerial competence Effective liaison and communication with home-office personnel Easier exercise of control over the subsidiary's operation	Difficulties in adapting to the foreign language and the socio-economic, political, cultural and legal environment Excessive cost of selecting, training and maintaining expatriate managers and their families abroad The host countries' insistence on localizing operations and on promoting local nationals in top positions at foreign subsidiaries Family adjustment problems, especially concerning the unemployed partners of managers
HCN (host-country national)	Familiarity with the socio-economic, political and legal environment and with business practices in the host country Lower cost incurred in hiring HCN as compared to PCN and TCN Provides opportunities for advancement and promotion to local nationals and, consequently, increases their commitment and motivation Responds effectively to the host country's demands for localization of the subsidiary's operation	Difficulties in exercising effective control over the subsidiary's operation Communication difficulties in dealing with home-office personnel Lack of opportunities for the home country's nationals to gain international and cross-cultural experience
TCN (third-country national)	Perhaps the best compromise between securing needed technical and managerial expertise and adapting to a foreign socio-economic and cultural environment TCN are usually career international business managers TCN are less expensive to maintain than PCN TCN may be better informed about the host environment than PCN	Host countries' sensitivity with respect to nationals of specific countries Local nationals are impeded in their efforts to upgrade their own ranks and assume responsible positions in the multinational subsidiaries

transfer cycle. Although the primary focus is on parent-country nationals, this international transfer cycle in principle also applies to third-country nationals and to a lesser extent to host-country nationals. We can distinguish three phases in this international transfer cycle: recruitment and selection, the actual period abroad and repatriation or transfer. We will not discuss the second phase, the actual period abroad, in any great

Table 9.2 *Senior managers in US, European and Japanese MNCs (row percentages)*

		PCN	HCN	TCN
US MNC	Western Europe	33	60	7
	Latin America	44	47	9
	Far East	55	38	7
European MNC	United States	29	67	4
	Western Europe	38	62	0
	Latin America	79	16	5
	Far East	85	15	0
Japanese MNC	United States	83	17	0
	Western Europe	77	23	0
	Latin America	83	17	0
	Far East	65	35	0

Source: Compiled from Tung, 1988

detail. This is not because it is not important: it is in fact the most crucial phase. However, most issues that come up during the assignment abroad have to do with either general management principles or cultural differences, both subjects which are discussed extensively in other books and which are not that specific to expatriate management. To some extent cultural differences have also been discussed in Part 2 of this book.

Phase 1: recruitment and selection

When discussing the recruitment and selection of international managers, the first question naturally is: what are the ideal characteristics of an international manager? One author (Heller, 1980) puts it like this:

> Ideally, it seems, he [or she] should have the stamina of an Olympic swimmer, the mental agility of an Einstein, the conversational skill of a professor of languages, the detachment of a judge, the tact of a diplomat, and the perseverance of an Egyptian pyramid builder. . .

In this section we will first discuss two popular studies which have concerned themselves with these considerations, and then look at the situation that seems to persist in practice. More information on the ideal profile of an international manager – one which might be used in the recruitment and selection process and in the process of training and development – is given in Chapter 10.

The first study we will discuss was carried out by Tung (1981). Based on a review of the literature on the selection of personnel for assignments abroad, she identified four groups of variables that contribute to success or failure on the job:

1   *Technical competence on the job.* As in the selection and placement of personnel in domestic operations, this factor is one of the primary determinants of success (Hays, 1971). It may even be more important for assignments abroad because the individual is located at some

distance from headquarters, the hub of technical expertise, and cannot consult as readily with his or her peers and superiors on matters related to the job.

2   *Personal traits or relational abilities.* This refers to the ability of the individual to deal effectively with his superiors, peers, subordinates, business associates and clients. In assignments abroad, this variable greatly influences the probability of successful performance. It is not limited to simple knowledge of another culture. The crucial thing is the ability to live and work with people whose value systems, beliefs, customs, manners and ways of conducting business may be greatly different from one's own.

3   *Ability to cope with environmental variables.* In domestic operations the ability to identify and cope with environmental constraints, such as governments, trade unions, competitors and customers, is crucial to effective performance. This same requirement is no less valid in assignments abroad, with one important distinction – environmental constraints are 'now variables in the sense that obviously constant factors at home are now different abroad' (Farmer and Richman, 1965: 373). The political, legal and socio-economic structures which constitute the macro-environment in the host country may be very different from the systems with which the expatriate is familiar. This poses problems of adjustment. The expatriate has to understand these systems and operate within them.

4   *Family situation.* This refers to the ability of the expatriate's family (the partner in particular) to adjust to living in a foreign environment. Researchers and practitioners are becoming increasingly cognizant of the importance of this factor to effective performance abroad. The situation often becomes even more complex if the partner (male or female) has had to give up a job or even a career to accompany his or her partner abroad. We will come back to the problems of dual-career families in the chapter on women in international management.

A second important contribution is the study by Mendenhall and Oddou (1985). According to these authors there is insufficient knowledge about the relevant dimensions in expatriate acculturation, leading to the use of inappropriate selection procedures. They distinguish four dimensions as components of the expatriate adjustment process:

1   *The self-orientation dimension*: activities and attributes that serve to strengthen the expatriate's self-esteem, self-confidence and mental hygiene.

2   *The other's orientation dimension*: activities and attributes that enhance the expatriate's ability to interact effectively with host-nationals.

3   *The perceptual dimension*: the ability to understand why foreigners behave the way they do, the ability to make correct attributions about the reasons or causes of host-nationals' behaviour.

4   *The cultural toughness dimension*: this dimension can modify the importance of the first three dimensions. In culturally tough countries

(countries that are culturally very different from the home country), the first three dimensions become even more important than in culturally similar countries.

The expatriate selection process should focus explicitly on the strengths and weaknesses of the applicant on these four dimensions.

In both these and other studies we notice an emphasis on the fact that expatriate selection is a multi-faceted subject and that interpersonal skills are very important. In practice, however, most companies use technical competence and knowledge of company systems as selection criteria (Barham and Devine, 1990; Brewster, 1988; Harvey, 1985; Mendenhall et al., 1987; Miller, 1972; Tung, 1981). According to Miller (1972) there are two major reasons for this: first, the difficulty of identifying and measuring the relevant interpersonal and cross-cultural skills, and secondly, the self-interest of the selectors, who will try to minimize the personal risk involved in selecting a candidate who might fail on the job. Technical competence will almost always prevent *immediate* failure on the job. A more practical reason for the lack of attention to factors such as relational skills, cultural empathy and partner/family support in selection

---

Selection for expatriate postings – typical MNC procedure

Deciding on a person for a job abroad is by and large the same process as deciding on an appointment at home. The line manager, and other managers, have identified and decided to appoint a certain person for a job in order to achieve a certain task, for example making the subsidiary more market-oriented, decreasing the costs, integrating the activities with another company, or integrating an acquired company into the corporation. In due time top management or the business area management group decide on the appointment. Subsequently the personnel department is consulted, or perhaps the company has a central department (if it is a large corporation) which takes care of the many practical problems. In the majority of cases little use is made of sophisticated methods. The line manager involves the personnel manager from the assigning company (which in most cases will be in the company's home nation). The corporate personnel manager then contacts the personnel manager abroad (if such a position exists).

---

lies in the actual selection procedures adopted by companies. Brewster (1991) notes widespread reliance on personal recommendations for expatriate postings from either specialist personnel staff or line managers. This results in more or less pre-determined selection interviews in which negotiating the terms of the offer takes precedence over determining the suitability of the candidate. The boxed description confirms this observation. It depicts standard procedure in most multinationals and is based on a consultant's experience.

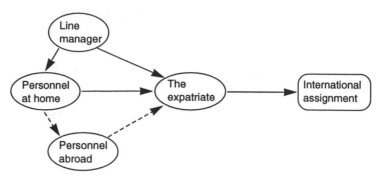

Figure 9.2   *Actors helping the expatriate to move abroad*

Figure 9.2 illustrates how the line manager, personnel at home and personnel abroad support, assist and help (almost push) the expatriate abroad. The time span before the transfer is normally very short, from a few weeks to some months before the transfer. This implies that in the majority of cases there will be no formal and elaborate selection and recruitment procedures, since the job is rarely advertised. The personnel department therefore has very little say with respect to the suitability of the candidate. Some typical complaints from personnel departments are:

'Recruitment should be more open and the job should be advertised.'

'The personnel manager should interview the candidate (or candidates) in order to test whether he/she is suitable for transfer abroad.'

The training of international managers has received ample attention, both from researchers and from cross-culture training consultants. We will return to this subject in greater detail in Chapter 10. In practice, pre-departure training usually has to be limited to a very short period of time – often just a few weeks – because of the many business problems to be solved. In addition there are practical issues to attend to such as compensation, legal matters, housing and schools for the children.

Before turning to the next phase in the international transfer cycle, we will take a short look at the reasons given by expatriates for wanting to go abroad. In a study by Borg (1988), managers were asked to choose the three most important motives for accepting/applying for their assignment abroad. The results, which are compared with those found in an earlier study, are given in Table 9.3.

It seems that new experiences and opportunities, both in the business and in the personal sphere, are very important. However, the glamorous picture of the expatriate way of life (large houses, generous salary allowances and, in many non-Western countries, even a staff of servants) also appeals to many would-be expatriates.

Phase 2: the assignment period abroad

An assignment abroad normally lasts about three years. The first six months abroad are perceived by most expatriates in a similar way. At the

Table 9.3   Managers' motives for going abroad

Motive	%	Present study Rank	Torbiörn (1976) Rank
Desire for new experience – 'Wanderlust'	96	1	3
Better economic conditions on employment abroad	84	2	1
Increased prospects of future promotion with employment abroad as a background	82	3	2
Employment abroad indicates immediate promotion	70	4	4
Employment abroad gives possibility for improvment within his or her field	48	5	6
Desire to escape from personal problems at home	21	6	8
Dissatisfaction with prevailing home conditions	19	7	5
Restricted career possibilities within the parent company	15	8	7
Other	25	—	—

Source: Borg, 1988

beginning of the assignment everything is new and exciting, but after about three months a kind of 'culture shock' sets in, which may be expressed in frustration over details such as the difficulties involved in getting a new telephone line installed or the manners of the local personnel. Carefully designed selection procedures and pre-departure training could of course temporize some of the culture shock. After another two months the expatriate starts to adapt to the foreign culture and gradually moves to a more neutral state. After a period of four to five years the expatriate is naturalized to some extent (Torbiörn, 1982). It is an advantage if the personnel department at home and at the subsidiary are aware of this adjustment process.

With regard to day-to-day practice in the foreign country, a common reflection about expatriate managers – which is rarely described in the literature – is that the expatriate position makes people very creative and hard working. They are sometimes able to do things as an expatriate which would not be considered by a native manager. Expatriates see other opportunities and may not see the barriers. They may also be excused for breaking the rules – at least in the first period of the assignment.

During the assignment, the expatriate focuses on the task at hand, that is, the assignment itself. In the majority of cases the expatriate is transferred to achieve a change, make the company more customer-oriented, build up a sales organization, make production more efficient etc. Generally it is a good idea to keep an eye on the future, however. 'Out of sight – out of mind' is unfortunately a very common truth in most companies. Some large companies have a system for keeping in touch with the expatriate, but usually it is up to the business area, division or strategic unit to take charge of this. Some companies have found a comparatively easy way of solving this problem by asking someone at home to send newspapers and information in general to the expatriates and encouraging the expatriates to keep informed about the home country. This may considerably facilitate the next phase of the international transfer cycle: repatriation.

Phase 3: repatriation

After a number of years – usually about three – the assignment period ends and the expatriate is repatriated. In the case of failure the expatriate returns earlier of course. In Chapter 10 we will take a closer look at the reasons for expatriate failure. Figure 9.3 shows the actors the expatriate uses when he/she is repatriated.

The problem of repatriation is twofold: readjustment and re-establishment (Borg, 1982). Readjustment means adjusting to one's native culture again. Returning expatriates often experience a second culture shock (see also Chapter 10). Readjusting to one's native culture can sometimes prove to be even more difficult than adjusting to a foreign culture. The foreign culture is new and confusing . . . but exciting. Returning home means 'getting back to normal', and friends, relatives and colleagues are often not really interested in the expatriate's experiences.

Re-establishment is finding a suitable position on return. Normally an expatriate is still employed by the home base and has the right to a position. Unfortunately, however, it rarely happens that repatriates are offered suitable positions on return. In many cases they are forced to arrange things themselves by contacting the line manager who sent them abroad in the first place and/or the personnel department at home or abroad. A typical repatriate complaint is:

> 'The line managers should cooperate more and not keep the repatriates within the business area. There may be suitable jobs in other parts of the corporation (if it is a large one).'

It may also be argued that the professional knowledge acquired abroad is not very useful at home. In fact it is often asserted that expatriates lose

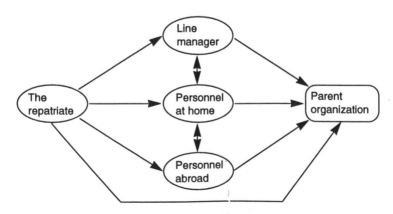

Figure 9.3 *Actors the expatriate uses when repatriated*

Table 9.4   *Why managers choose to resume a domestic career*

Motive	%[1]
There was a possibility of promotion within the home organization	56
Consideration for the education of the children	54
Discomfort for the employee or his family caused by the conditions in the host country	36
Consideration for relatives, friends etc. in Sweden[2]	35
Need to keep abreast of one's own profession	31
Employment was found in another firm	21
Failure with the appointment in the host country	17
Uneasiness with the employment in the host country	4
Other	7

[1] Percentage of managers who chose a certain alternative. The respondents were allowed to choose three.
[2] Sweden represents the home country in Borg's study.

Source: Borg, 1988

competence while abroad – this is especially true when they have been assigned to developing countries. Abroad the expatriate had more responsibilities and often felt like a 'big fish in a small pond'. It goes without saying that if both re-establishment and readjustment are difficult, the re-entry can be very problematic.

If the expatriate has been successful in his task, and if he and his family[1] are amenable to staying abroad, another assignment can be considered and the international transfer cycle starts anew. With regard to transfer to another subsidiary and geographical location, Borg (1988) found that career patterns were not very specialized. During his first assignment, the expatriate may have been the managing director, while in his next assignment he becomes the financial controller. The weak patterns of specialization are probably related to the fact that there is very little chance of a similar position becoming vacant in a similar geographical area at the same time that the expatriate concludes an assignment.

Concerning the expatriate himself, we might ask what his reasons are for choosing either a domestic or an international career after the first assignment. The motives for returning to the home country (Sweden in the case of Borg's study) indicate why an expatriate might choose a domestic career. Table 9.4 ranks managers' perceptions as to why expatriates in general choose a domestic career. To summarize, a promotion, the children's education and discomfort with conditions in the host country are the most common reasons given for returning home to a domestic career.

Borg (1988) found that approximately half of managers assigned abroad continue to pursue international careers. The managers' perceptions of why expatriates remain abroad in general are shown in Table 9.5. The strongest motive for remaining abroad has to do with the financial benefits,

[1] The overwhelming majority of the expatriates is male. Chapter 11 is devoted to issues specific to female expatriates.

Table 9.5   *Why managers choose to continue an international career*

Motive	%[1]
The economic conditions for overseas employment are more favourable than employment in Sweden[2]	83
Employment on overseas assignments is more stimulating than employment in Sweden	69
Re-adjustment to Swedish work conditions would be too difficult	34
The number of suitable positions in Sweden is limited	33
Family reasons – the family prefers to live abroad	32
The company 'keeps them' overseas	11
Difficulties in finding suitable positions in Sweden due to the lack of information about vacant positions at home	11
The possibilities for promotion are greater abroad than in Sweden	6
Other	6

[1] Percentage of managers who chose a certain alternative. The respondents were allowed to choose three.

[2] Sweden represents the home country in Borg's study.

Source: Borg, 1988

which was the second strongest incentive for going abroad in the first place – perhaps the strongest if one believes that financial motives are suppressed at an interview. (Note that the question concerning the expatriate's motives for going abroad was put directly: 'Why do you want to go abroad?', whereas here the question is put indirectly: 'Why do you think managers choose an international career?') The second reason, namely that employment abroad is more stimulating, has to do with the fact that at headquarters jobs are more specialized due to a larger and more bureaucratic organization than is to be found in a subsidiary, where the expatriate manager is perhaps the managing director.

4   Profiles of international managers

The previous section focused on the international transfer cycle. In this section we will take a closer look at the expatriates themselves. First, we will see that different transfer archetypes can be distinguished, then we will relate these transfer archetypes to the organizational functions of international transfer which we discussed in Section 2 above.

Transfer archetypes

A study by Borg (1988) investigated 200 managers who had been transferred abroad for the first time. After 13 years the picture depicted in Figure 9.4 emerged.

The *naturalized* managers were those who remained on the foreign assignment or left the company during or after the assignment. This

	One assignment abroad	Several assignments abroad
Ending up abroad	Naturalized (25%)	Cosmopolitan orientation (22%)
Ending up at home	Local orientation (38%)	Unsettled (15%)

Figure 9.4   *Ultimate destination of managers assigned abroad: situation at the end of the investigation period (Borg, 1988)*

category accounts for 25 per cent of the managers. The naturalized archetype is illustrated below.[2]

> *Mr A was 32 years old when he was sent on his first assignment to Madrid in 1971. After upper secondary school he was employed in a provincial bank for five years before coming to Swedish Tools, where he held the position of assistant manager in the accounting department for four years. At that time, Swedish Tools were implementing new administrative and accounting systems within the group and needed managers to introduce the new routines at their foreign subsidiaries. Mr A was unhappy with conditions in Sweden and was seeking adventure as well. He had been in Spain just one year when he met the Spanish woman who has become his wife. He has now worked in the accounts department of the Spanish subsidiary for 13 years. Mr A feels at home in Spain with his wife and three children, and enjoys the financially advantageous conditions there. He considers his job to be like any other job and does not consider foreign assignments as a 'nomadic' activity. He does not wish to return to his native country.*

The *locally-oriented* managers, about 38 per cent, were repatriated after one assignment. These managers return to the location they had before going abroad. The following case illustrates the local category.

> *Mr B was 35 years old when he was sent abroad. He took an MS degree in Mechanical Engineering at the Swedish Royal Institute of Technology (KTH). He was immediately appointed as a shop-floor technician at the Machinery Company. After three years he was promoted to group technician and after another three years he became an industrial engineer. In 1972, after having worked for the Machinery Company for nine years, he was asked to go to Brazil to fill the post of technical manager. His main*

[2] Note that, in all the case examples which follow, the company names have been changed.

motive for accepting the offer was that he considered it a promotion. He also saw opportunities for change, adventure and a chance to improve his technical skills. Mr B believed that his main role as an expatriate Swede was to facilitate the transfer of technical and administrative knowledge and to start up new activities.

In 1977, after four years abroad, he returned to Sweden and took up the post of technical manager in one section of the parent company, which he still held six years later. The main reason for returning was that Mr B and his family had trouble adjusting to the new environment. Another reason was his concern for his children's education. Mr B and his family are very pleased with Sweden and conditions in general and have no desire for further assignments abroad.

Unsettled managers, the smallest category, with only 15 percent, were those who filled two or more assignments abroad and were then repatriated. They are called 'unsettled' since their orientation is difficult to establish. Most of them have a local orientation (only a few of them would consider going abroad again). The following case illustrates an 'unsettled' manager.

Mr C studied business administration, economics, law and some other subjects at the University of Lund. He was thereafter employed at the headquarters of the small Chemical MNC and worked there for two years before being assigned to the Netherlands and appointed head of the sales department. Mr C thought that the post abroad offered immediate promotion and better prospects in Sweden later on. After three years, after threatening to resign if he was not appointed managing director of the Dutch company, he was transferred to Paris. He was considered too inexperienced for the managing director post, and in retrospect, Mr C believes that this judgement was correct.

The relationship between the French subsidiary and the parent company was poor, and better relations were sought by placing Mr C in the subsidiary as the only Swede. However, shortly thereafter Mr C was transferred to Houston in order to close down a newly acquired subsidiary which had proved to have no prospects. After ten months he was re-assigned to Paris and became deputy managing director again, with the task of teaching the newly appointed French managing director the parent company's policies, structure, production lines etc. After seven years abroad Mr C and his family returned home because he found permanent 'ambassador duty' abroad very demanding. His family was also dissatisfied with France and the French. Mr C was given the post of financial division manager on his return. Mr C plans to go after new promotions either at home or abroad, and is at present considering joining another corporation.

The *cosmopolitan-oriented* managers, 22 per cent of the total, were those who took up several assignments abroad and remained there (or left the companies as cosmopolitans). The case of a cosmopolitan manager is presented below.

Mr D spent six years at the Stockholm School of Economics but did not graduate. He then went to Argentina and worked for almost a year at Swedish Mechanics as an apprentice employed according to local laws, that is, not on a contract basis. In 1971 he was assigned to Dallas on a contract. His main task was to ensure that the activities were conducted in accordance with the wishes of the parent company. In 1974 he was assigned to Singapore, which Mr D regarded as a promotion and an excellent opportunity to familiarize himself with Asia. He remained in Singapore for seven years, together with his Argentinian wife, whom he had met during his stay in Argentina, and their three children, who were born in the USA. After his assignment in Singapore, Mr D was assigned to the parent organization in Sweden for a short period of two and a half years. This sojourn at home was considered necessary to avoid losing touch with Sweden and the parent organization, of which Mr D had very little experience. After this short assignment, Mr D and his family were pleased to learn that he had been transferred to the Brazilian subsidiary, where he became financial executive and deputy managing director. The transfer to Brazil was considered a step forwards in his career. Mr D is prepared to undertake assignments anywhere in the world if the company so demands. However, he prefers to stay away from Sweden since it would be impossible to live on one salary there. Also, he considers the educational opportunities for the children to be superior abroad.

A comparable classification is given by Black and Gregersen (1992) (see Figure 9.5).

The four transfer archetypes described by Borg (1988) are defined in terms of destination and mobility. However, in order to merit characterization as archetypes, they should have distinctive features or attributes in other respects as well. Figure 9.6 summarizes the features Borg found in his study. It also shows the exit rates (the percentage of managers that had

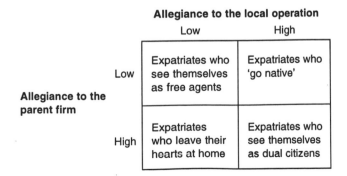

Figure 9.5   *Forms of expatriate allegiance (Black and Gregersen, 1992)*

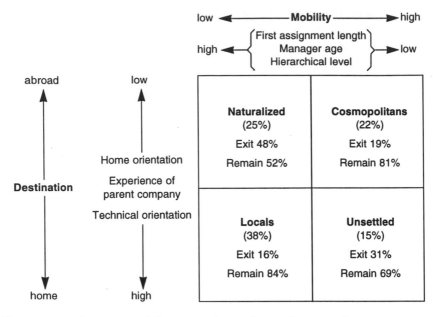

Figure 9.6   *Summary of features of transfer archetypes (Borg, 1988)*

left the company at the end of the investigation period) of the different transfer archetypes.

In the next section we will see that these different types of expatriates perform different international transfer functions.

Transfer archetypes and international transfer functions

Table 9.6 combines the transfer archetypes and the organizational functions which international transfers of managers are assumed to fulfil, as discussed in Section 2. The relative contributions of each archetype (after the first assignment) are indicated on a scale from low through moderate to high.

The *naturalized* managers are those who took up only one assignment during the investigation period. They are not likely to move in the future and are therefore regarded as less mobile. Some naturalized managers are still with their companies and thus continue to fill a post. After three to five years, however, which can be considered an average period with the inclusion of a contract extension, the expatriate is likely to have completed his or her tasks. In the case of position filling, these tasks might include the transfer of technical and administrative knowledge. Host-country nationals at the subsidiaries should therefore have acquired some of the expatriate manager's technical and administrative knowledge. Moreover, after such a

Table 9.6   *Transfer archetypes and organizational functions*

Transfer archetypes	Organizational functions		
	Position filling	Manager development	Organizational development
Naturalized	Low	Low	Moderate
Locals	Low	Moderate	Low
Unsettled	High	Moderate	Moderate
Cosmopolitans	High	High	High

Source: Borg, 1988

period the expatriate has probably lost some of his technical and administrative capacity, since it can be difficult to keep up with progress at the parent company from abroad. As indicated in Table 9.6, then, naturalized managers tend to score low on the position filling function. Management development does not seem to apply to naturalized managers, due to their low mobility. The experience acquired by these managers during their first assignment was not used to fill other key positions at the parent company or at other subsidiaries. In terms of organizational development, the socialization effect diminishes, since the manager loses touch with the parent company and has few opportunities to socialize with new executives there. Of course, the managers still understand executives from headquarters better than a host-country manager would, but the mere suggestion that a shift in their loyalties has occurred immediately makes them a less powerful means for organizational development. That is why the naturalized archetype has only a moderate score for organizational development. The overall conclusion for this category is that, after the first contract period, managers only fulfil the three organizational functions which motivate international transfers to a very limited extent.

As with naturalized managers, *locals* have only held one position abroad and few of them are likely to accept additional foreign assignments. With regard to being transferred back to the parent company, it is unusual for an individual to be recalled in order to fill a position, that is to say, a vacancy at headquarters. Locals, therefore, score low on position filling after their first assignment. With regard to management development, the transfer back does not mean immediate upward mobility, but the experience acquired by the locals abroad is likely to have given them moderate management development, especially in the area of personal development. The expected contribution of locals to the organizational development function is estimated to be low. They are resocialized into the parent company organization and rarely retain any contact with the foreign subsidiary. During their first assignment, managers in this category were of course probably the most effective group in terms of organizational development, since they seem to be those closest to the parent company.

The *unsettled* managers undertook two or three assignments during the period of investigation, and the majority accepted two consecutive assignments before returning to the parent company. If position filling is the motive behind the additional assignment abroad, the managers involved can once again make use of their technical or administrative knowledge. Since managers in this category are highly mobile – perhaps the most mobile of all – they can be expected to score high on the position filling function. As evidence of management development, we observe that some managers have taken up positions which they would not have obtained without prior expatriate employment. However, these managers have stayed abroad for a much longer period than necessary for management development, and many of them have had serious repatriation problems. Management development is therefore assumed to be moderate in this group. The contribution made by the unsettled category to organizational development is also judged to be moderate. Their mobility is a positive quality, but a relatively high proportion of this group leaves the company on return from abroad.

Cosmopolitan managers are also highly mobile. They undertook at least two assignments in the period of investigation and are expected to remain abroad. Their contribution to position filling is large, and they are able to utilize the experience gained at one subsidiary when moving on to another. The management development function also scores high. Cosmopolitans gradually develop both personally and professionally and can therefore take up increasingly advanced positions abroad. Cosmopolitans are perhaps not as loyal to the parent company as locals, but they nevertheless constitute a selected and self-selected group who have proved to be successful and reliable. This group of managers can be very useful to an MNC, as they not only have broad contact patterns within their companies but probably also with other international managers around the world. The cosmopolitans, therefore, also score high on organizational development.

We can perhaps assume that the international transfer of managers functions in two ways. The first is by assigning a trusted manager from the parent company who identifies with it and tries to do his best in harmony with the parent company; this immediately improves communication between headquarters and the subsidiary. *On their first assignment*, then, all managers are transferred with a view to filling a position and fostering organizational development. The local category is probably the most effective in terms of organizational development since this category seems to be closest to the parent company.

Secondly, international transfer is also the process by which professional expatriates (cosmopolitans) can be identified who have the aptitude and the desire to move frequently and who have proved successful in handling headquarters–subsidiary relationships, subsidiary–environment relationships, and the management of the foreign subsidiaries. The control made possible by the international transfer of managers arguably depends on reliable managers who are on their first assignment, and on a professional, mobile cadre of expatriates who are selected, self-selected and developed over time in MNCs.

5   The process of (re)designing international staffing policies

As we discussed earlier in this book, the basic principle of HRM is that human resource practice should support company strategy. If the company is in a period of strategic change, it would do well to redesign its present international staffing policy. An international staffing strategy may be designed in such a way that it helps to establish the common frame of reference required to implement strategic change. In this section we will propose an approach for (re)designing and improving international staffing policies, taking both the company and the transfer pattern into account. Keep in mind that the three phases discussed below interact with each other and that several feedback loops might be necessary.

Phase 1: analyzing the situation and involving top management

Mapping the present situation

The starting point is to draw up an international 'personnel inventory' of the number of expatriate managers in each position. Surprisingly, few companies have bothered to take stock of their international personnel, but even if they have, the data are seldom analyzed.

The next step is to assess the current situation. What is the current transfer policy (see Section 2 above)? What are the lessons that can be drawn from the current and past situation of the firm? What are the other organizational design parameters which bridge geographical and cultural distances (see Introduction)? Do the current transfer practices support the company's strategy and objectives? Is the transfer policy consistent with the organization structure and the company control systems? The second step is to assess the dominant frame of reference among the top managers of the company regarding international staffing policies. It may prove that they have borrowed their frame of reference from another company, or that they have never really thought about it.

Two warnings must be heeded here. First, make sure that the staff member or the external consultant performing the diagnosis takes a *general* management view. International staffing policies have to be integrated with overall corporate strategy. Be on the lookout for both an isolated personnel perspective and a short-sighted concentration on business. Secondly, try to avoid presumptions about the existence of a 'one best' staffing policy. A 'geocentric staffing policy' is often considered to be the ideal because of the assumption that 'all employees should have the same promotion opportunities regardless of passport' and that 'international mobility' is positive in general. This policy, however, does not fit each and every situation, and a mismatch may lead to frustration in the implementation process. The result might well be the adoption of an 'ad hoc' strategy. Presumptions about a 'one best' staffing strategy, then, will certainly not support a useful diagnosis.

Perhaps the best way of performing the diagnosis is to interview top managers within the company and analyze strategic documents and plans. All important geographical divisions within the company should be covered. Preference should be given to line managers (and not to staff at HQs), because they are able to provide first-hand information.

Establishing improvement potentials

Once the present situation has been analyzed it is time to establish the potential for improvement. When companies fail to take full advantage of effective international staffing policies, this can lead to:

- individuals not developing the desired frame of reference for the company;
- departure of managers;
- difficulties in recruiting the best personnel for international transfers;
- the expatriate being offered meaningless or, indeed, no work upon return, which will lead to dissatisfaction and may give the company a poor image as an employer;
- the knowledge acquired abroad not being transferred to colleagues and other business units;
- high costs necessary to handle premature re-entry, unsuccessful repatriation, etc.

Unfortunately, there are few studies in which the costs for both the company and the individual expatriate have been calculated. Furthermore, many of the drawbacks cannot be expressed quantitatively. It is, however, certainly worth the effort to try to measure the drawbacks in terms of costs and to describe them as improvement potentials. Such estimates, however rough, are very likely to make an impression on both top management and the personnel department. A cost analysis of ineffective international staffing policies can be presented in a positive fashion: how can effective international staffing policies help the company to earn more money, to expand its market shares, to open up new markets etc.?

Creating commitment among top managers

The commitment of top managers is highly important in facilitating acceptance and an easy implementation of the staffing policy. A very effective way to create commitment is to find a line manager in top management who is interested in this subject and ask him or her to put together a project group to investigate and diagnose the present situation. As mentioned before, commitment and involvement can be created in the analysis phase by involving all important top managers in the diagnostic process, for example by having them participate in interviews. If it is difficult to create consensus on the most desirable policies for international staffing, it is even more difficult to implement them. One reason is that the policies are often supervised by staff managers. Line managers or business managers, who have the power to act, frequently do not carry through on the policies determined. Staff managers, for example the personnel department, have very little power to stop a transfer and usually virtually no power to initiate transfers of personnel. Another obstacle to consensus is that managers have different views and values regarding international staffing. Managers who have been abroad themselves see things differently from those who have not etc. A vital part of creating consensus and commitment, then, is to involve line management in the decision-making process and to assess the dominant frame of reference among top managers regarding international staffing policies.

Phase 2: designing the staffing policy

Once consensus has been reached on the diagnosis of the present situation and the improvement potentials, it is time to start designing a new and improved international staffing policy. The diagnosis might serve as input for a 'brainstorming' workshop. Research and ideas from other companies can of course also form valuable inputs for this workshop.

Developing and implementing international staffing policies takes a lot of creativity and hard work. The first step is to develop general guidelines for such a policy, rather than presenting a completely worked-out solution. These guidelines can then be tested and refined during implementation.

The definitive staffing policy should at the very least include the following elements:

- the purpose of the staffing policy;
- the benefits related to corporate strategy;
- the kind and number of employees that should be transferred;
- a recruitment and selection policy;
- a transfer policy;
- a training and development policy;
- a compensation policy;
- a complete set of steps which can be undertaken to implement these policies;
- an estimate of the costs involved.

When developing the international staffing policy, it will be necessary to make a 'forward-directed analysis', that is, attempt to incorporate foreseeable changes in the future.

Phase 3: implementing the staffing policy

The implementation phase is the most difficult part of the process. The personnel department may have decided on a number of international staffing policies and documents, but members of the top management team can always invalidate such decisions by sending 'the wrong person in the wrong direction'. The result is that the staffing policy appears useless and that managers feel justified in ignoring it. One way of handling this is the 'grandfather principle', a strategy in which all transfers are accepted by the next level up in the organization. Another way of facilitating the implementation is to put together a 'road show' at the various subsidiaries or units in order to 'sell' the benefits of the staffing policy. In many cases the personnel managers in the subsidiaries have very little knowledge of the subject. They need more information if they are to acquire enough power to be able to assist in implementing an international staffing policy.

A general piece of advice is: do not develop the staffing policy first and then try to implement it. In the first place, it is unlikely that anyone, even a project group, can develop a workable staffing policy by doing nothing more than think about it. Secondly, by involving the key managers in the diagnosis and design of the policy, half the job of implementation is done.

6 Summary and conclusions

This chapter has taken a general look at international staffing. We provided an analysis of the reasons for international transfers and described the different transfer policies, the international transfer cycle and the different transfer archetypes. We also offered some advice on improving staffing policies. In the following chapters we will look at three subjects related to international staffing. We will start by analyzing the process of cross-cultural training and development in multinational companies. Then, we will consider the problems women encounter in (international) management. Finally, we will deal with a very practical problem that often puzzles personnel managers: how to compensate international managers.

Advice for potential international managers

- Work with the home industry/society before going abroad.
- Do not try to escape from personal problems.
- Keep in touch with the home company.
- Do not stay away longer than three to four years.
- Have a job arranged on return.

---

10 Training and development of international staff

Kerstin Baumgarten

1	Introduction	205
2	Outline of the present situation	206
3	Training and development of expatriates	209
	Identification and analysis of cross-cultural training needs	210
	Training needs analysis	210
	The search for profiles of international staff	211
	The goals of cross-cultural training	213
	Methods for cross-cultural training	213
	Available training methods	213
	Choosing a training method	216
4	General view of the training of international staff	219
	Training and development: a process, not an event	219
	Integration of training and development in the other areas of HRM	220
	Inclusion of the partner in cross-cultural training	221
	Inclusion of HCNs in cross-cultural training	222
5	The problem of re-entry into the home culture	223
6	Closing the circle	226
7	Summary and conclusions	227

1 Introduction

The training and development of international staff is an issue which should be gaining more importance within the field of human resource development, as companies develop from purely domestic firms into multinational or even transnational corporations (see Chapter 2). However, much of the current writing on the internationalization of firms and on the formation of global organizations focuses primarily on marketing resource application, technology transfer and organizational configuration as they relate to information flow, strategy and control requirements. Relatively little attention is paid to human development needs that arise during the evolution from a domestically postured business to one that operates from a truly global perspective. Adler (1986) points out this same flaw when she notes that in many functional business areas, strategies are currently being used that would have been unheard of or inappropriate only two decades ago, but that at the same time many firms conduct their worldwide management of people as if neither the external economic and technological environment nor the internal structure and organization of the firm had changed.

Within the new 'global' management of people, the training and development of international staff plays a very important role. Owing to factors such as increasing international competition and the resulting need to market products world wide, international mergers and acquisitions, and new market access opportunities (Eastern Europe, China, the former Soviet Union etc.), more and more managers and other staff will be confronted at least once in their careers with the opportunity to take on an international assignment and thus temporarily become an expatriate working and living in a foreign country. Such an assignment poses challenges in terms of new tasks and responsibilities, but also in terms of adaptive capabilities and cultural sensitivity.

Considering the above, we would expect companies to send their expatriates out on foreign assignment well equipped. To what extent this is true will be discussed in Section 2 of this chapter, in which we outline the present situation as regards the expatriation of international staff. In Section 3 attention will be focused on the procedural aspects of preparatory training for international staff, with an emphasis on training needs analysis, instructional goals and choice of training method. In Section 4 a more general view of the training and development of international staff will be introduced. Subsequently, in Section 5, we will describe the problems that can arise during the re-entry phase in the home country after the completion of an assignment. Finally, in Section 6, we will take a look at the ideal deployment cycle.

2   Outline of the present situation

According to Adler (1991), companies can no longer afford to send any but their best people abroad, and neither the companies nor the individuals can afford to let the best fail. Throughout the literature on the topic of expatriation, however, we see very high estimates of the percentage of foreign assignments that fail. Studies have shown that 16–50 percent of US expatriates fail on their foreign assignment (Baker and Ivancevich, 1971; Black, 1988; Dunbar and Ehrlich, 1986; Mendenhall et al., 1987; Tung, 1981). European and Japanese expatriates seem to fare better. Their failure rates, surveyed by Tung (1981), are significantly lower than the failure rates in the US samples: 59 percent of the European sample reported failure rates lower than 5 percent, 38 percent of the sample reported failure rates of 6–10 percent, and 3 percent reported failure rates between 11 and 15 percent. The criterion for failure used in the studies cited above is the return of the expatriate to his home country before the assignment has been successfully completed. The percentages cited therefore do not include expatriates who fail to perform satisfactorily but who nevertheless are not sent home early. It can be expected that if these cases were included in the above figures, the failure rates would be significantly higher than those cited.

Given the worrying situation concerning the success of many international assignments outlined above, and given the assumption that the more rigorous the training (and selection) procedures, the lower the incidence of poor performance or failure on foreign assignments (Tung, 1979), one would expect companies to do their utmost to prepare their staff adequately for international assignments. Surprisingly this is not the case: 70 percent of US expatriates and 90 percent of their families are sent abroad without any cross-cultural training (Baker and Ivancevich, 1971; Black and Mendenhall, 1990; Lanier, 1979; Tung, 1981).

On top of the fact that many companies do not provide any training at all, most of the companies that do offer training provide only brief environmental summaries and some culture and language preparation, mainly concentrating on the development of technical competence and other job-related skills (Lanier, 1979). Furthermore, in 80 percent of the cases when training is provided, the partners are not included in the training programmes. This is a worrying finding if one considers that research has indicated that the inability of the partner to adapt to the foreign environment is one, if not the most, important cause of expatriate failure (Mendenhall et al., 1987). To aggravate the situation even further, most training is of very short duration, generally lasting only a few days.

Japanese and European firms seem to offer more, and more extensive, training than US firms, a finding which may be explained in part by the fact that US firms have a higher employee turnover which undermines their willingness to invest in people. Tung (1982) found that 69 percent of the respondents in her West European sample sponsored training programmes to prepare candidates for foreign assignments, and the same percentage applies to the 267 largest companies in Japan as surveyed in 1982. However, in a survey of Dutch multinational companies and organizations carried out by the University of Utrecht (Baan, 1992), the following conclusions were reached. On average only 25 percent of aspirant expatriates receive preparatory training prior to departure. Most respondent firms (70 percent) favour preparatory training only for expatriates sent on assignments outside Europe and the United States. An exception are assignments to Eastern Europe: 40 percent of the respondents feel that preparatory training is needed for this region. However, the content and quality of the training programmes cannot be extracted from surveys such as the ones cited above. Given the failure rates presented in the beginning of this chapter, chances are that much can still be improved.

Why does there seem to be such a relatively widespread neglect of preparatory training for international assignments? The most frequently mentioned reasons in the literature (Hogan and Goodson, 1990; McEnery and DesHarnais, 1990; Mendenhall and Oddou, 1985; Murray and Murray, 1986; Ronen, 1989; Tung, 1981) are the following.

- Training is not thought to be effective. Many managers believe that international expertise can be learned only through experience (business travel and assignments abroad). As a result, top management often gives little support to cross-cultural training programmes.

- The period of time between selection and the expatriate's departure is short, leaving little time to expose him or her to in-depth training prior to departure.
- The temporary nature of most assignments does not warrant budget expenditures for training. This idea is especially widespread among US companies. In Japan the need for preparation, even for short assignments, has long been recognized.
- The individual dimensions needed for successful acculturation are not well enough known to devise sound training programmes. In order to be able to design effective training programmes, HRD staff feel that they first need to know which competencies are needed for success and whether these competencies can be acquired through training.
- There is a belief that technical skills are the main success factors on assignments abroad. Relational skills and other intercultural competencies are not seen as being of importance for success on foreign assignments, resulting in a lack of awareness of relevant selection criteria and training goals.

That this last assumption is especially misleading can be concluded from a list of the main reasons for the failure of foreign assignments of US expatriates assembled by Tung (1981). In descending order of importance:

- the inability of the manager's partner to adapt to a different physical or cultural environment;
- the inability of the manager to adapt to a different physical or cultural environment;
- other family-related problems;
- the manager's personality or emotional immaturity;
- the manager's inability to cope with the responsibilities posed by the work abroad;
- the manager's lack of technical competence;
- the manager's lack of motivation to work abroad.

As can be noted, the manager's lack of technical competence scores rather low on the list of main causes for failure of foreign assignments (which seems logical because, as we have seen, the expatriate-to-be is mainly selected for his technical competence). The inability of both the manager and his partner to adapt are far more important factors of failure. It seems that the long-standing belief that management is a scientific art and that an effective manager in New York or Los Angeles will therefore also do fine in Hong Kong or Tokyo has to give way in the face of overriding evidence to the contrary. International staff cannot be expected to perform as well on a foreign assignment as they do in their home country without proper preparation. What is 'proper preparation', however? What are the real training needs of expatriate staff? What training options are there and which are effective? How can one choose between the many options? These and other issues concerning the training and development of international staff will be addressed in the next section.

3   Training and development of expatriates

In order to improve the quality of preparation of international staff for their foreign assignments, it is important to follow a systematic approach in the development, implementation and evaluation of training. In Figure 10.1 a simplified training cycle is depicted which can serve as a basis for such a systematic approach. The cycle starts with the identification and analysis of the training needs of the target population and the translation of these training needs into training goals (aims to be achieved during the training formulated in behavioural terms). At this point in the cycle the question of 'what' one wants to achieve with the training has been answered, but what has not yet been established is the 'how'. The answer to the latter question is provided during the design phase, in which the content, the methods, the media and the teaching sequence required to achieve the stated training goals are determined. Once the training materials are ready and the course is planned, the training course can begin and the outcomes can be evaluated. Evaluation should not only take place after implementation, however, but formatively at all four stages of the cycle.

Below we will discuss the training and development of international staff based on the training cycle presented in Figure 10.1. Emphasis will be placed on the identification and analysis of training needs and on the

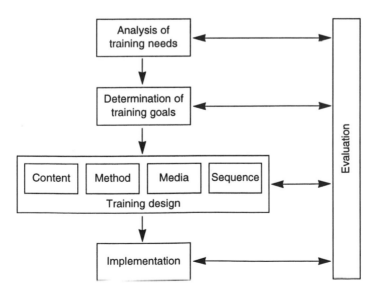

Figure 10.1   *Systematic training cycle*

training design, since these phases demand special attention in the case of international staff. The other phases depend less on the target population and are therefore not discussed in greater detail in the context of this chapter.

Identification and analysis of cross-cultural training needs

In Section 2 we indicated that companies fail to make greater investment in preparatory training because of the widespread belief that the competencies needed for success on foreign assignments are not well enough known to devise sound training programmes. In other words, because they lack a thorough understanding of the training needs of international staff, many companies either do not invest at all in preparing their expatriates, or they resort to relatively easy solutions, such as superficial cultural briefings. In order to improve the way in which we prepare international staff, then, we must first reach a better understanding of the target population's training needs.

Training needs analysis

The aim of training needs analysis is to identify and describe discrepancies between the existing performance levels of a certain group of employees, and the desired levels. Important in this analysis is the recognition that not all discrepancies in performance are the result of insufficiently developed competencies which can therefore be resolved through training. There may be equally viable causes in the organization itself, for example, or among management, requiring solutions other than training.

A proper training needs analysis consists of three interrelated components: organizational analysis, job/task analysis and person analysis (Goldstein, 1986). The organization analysis studies the organizational variables which might result in potential training needs. For example, there may be a certain organizational culture which all managers are expected to uphold. The job analysis describes the job to be carried out by the target population in behavioural terms, and specifies the tasks involved in carrying out the job. In the task analysis, information is collected regarding the competencies needed for effectively carrying out the various tasks. For example, one of the tasks of an international manager during his assignment may be to develop his local subordinates. Hence he might need training in subordinate development skills prior to departure. Person analysis is concerned with how well the employee performs the competencies which have been identified during the task analysis. Does the assignee have prior experience? Which of his competencies are strongly developed and which are less developed? The individual profile of each trainee should be taken into account during the training needs analysis at the personal level.

As far as the job/task analysis of expatriates is concerned, we can assume that certain tasks are carried out by all expatriates, so that we can identify

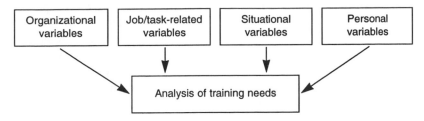

Figure 10.2 *Variables that influence the training needs of international staff*

the general competencies required by the entire target population. There are many situational variables, however, which influence specific assignments, such as the specific economic and political circumstances of the host country. In order to be able to function appropriately under these specific situational variables, the expatriate may require special competencies which are not necessary for the successful completion of every foreign assignment.

One can thus conclude that the job/task analysis of international managers can take place at two levels. At the more general level, the competencies required by every international manager must be identified and analyzed, resulting in potential training needs for the entire occupational group. At a more specific level, the situational variables influencing the tasks of a specific international manager on a specific assignment must be taken into consideration, as these help to identify the special competencies and, hence, the specific training needs required.

Figure 10.2 shows the various types of variables that have to be taken into consideration during the identification and analysis of training needs of international staff.

Analyzing the training needs of expatriate staff is clearly a complex process in which many variables play their part. However, if this phase of the training cycle is carried out with care, the other steps of the cycle will rest on solid foundations and will be relatively easy to perform.

The search for profiles of international staff

A big step towards determining the potential training needs of expatriates is to identify the competencies needed for international success and summarize them in an 'ideal profile', which can then serve as a basis on which to construct a training needs analysis for a specific assignee on a specific assignment. The profile can be tested against the information gained from an analysis of the organizational, job/task, situational and personal variables of the specific organization, assignment and assignee. On the basis of this analysis, competencies can be added to or deleted from the ideal profile and the remaining competencies translated into specific training needs for the assignee in question.

There are numerous research reports and surveys cited in the literature aimed at determining the competencies needed for international success. A review of these reports has resulted in a list of more than 80 competencies, ranging from listening skills to a sense of humour, from mental alertness to leadership skills (Baumgarten, 1992a). Based on this enormous amount of information, a hypothetical profile for international managers was developed and subsequently validated by means of a survey carried out among a stratified sample of 117 (ex-)international managers of a Dutch multinational company, 94 (80 percent) of whom returned the completed questionnaire (Baumgarten, 1992b). The survey asked the respondents to indicate the relative importance of various competencies for success on foreign assignments. The six competencies of the hypothetical profile that were perceived as being most important for the success of international managers are (in descending order of importance):

- leadership skills;
- initiative;
- emotional stability;
- motivation;
- ability to handle responsibility;
- cultural sensitivity.

Since the sample was heterogeneous in terms of both functional specialization and region of assignment, a separate analysis of the relevant sub-populations was carried out. As expected, breakdown of the data by functional specialization of the respondents and geographical area of assignment resulted in clearly different profiles for the various sub-populations. Four of the dimensions, however, turned out to be of importance for all international managers, regardless of the functional specialization or region of assignment. These were: leadership, initiative, emotional stability and motivation. Other dimensions were of special regional importance, for example, the ability to handle stress in Africa, Latin America and Asia, and to demonstrate empathy in Latin America and Southern Europe. Dimensions which varied among the various functional specializations (technical, commercial, financial and general management) were: technical skills, flexibility, cultural sensitivity, the ability to deal with responsibility and subordinate development skills.

As we can see, the research described above supports the assumption made in the section on training needs analysis that there are both 'general' (shared by all international managers) and 'specific' competencies needed for success on international assignments, and that there are therefore both general and specific potential training needs. Four of the competencies included in the hypothetical profile turned out to be 'general' competencies or potential training needs, whereas the importance of the other competencies varied across the various sub-populations. As we mentioned above, if profiles such as the ones resulting from this study were validated by further research, an important basis would be laid for the analysis of the training needs of international staff.

The goals of cross-cultural training

The next step towards the achievement of effective cross-cultural training programmes is the translation of training needs into training goals and objectives (see Figure 10.1). A goal is a fairly general statement of intent, whereas objectives are very specific statements of what the student should be able to do at the end of the learning session, under which conditions, and to which standard (Romiszowski, 1981).

What is the common goal of all cross-cultural training programmes? Very generally speaking, we can assume that the general goal of cross-cultural training is to improve the chances of success of international staff and their families on their foreign assignment. 'Success', however, is a rather vague term which has been frequently used in the preceding sections, but which requires further specification.

How can one distinguish a successful from an unsuccessful assignee? There seem to be three main indicators of international success: the degree of personal adjustment, the degree of professional effectiveness and the degree of interpersonal adjustment and effectiveness (Brislin et al., 1986). An expatriate can be considered personally adjusted if he (or she) feels happy and satisfied with the situation abroad. He is professionally effective if he performs the daily tasks, duties and responsibilities on the job abroad in a competent manner, and he is interpersonally adjusted and effective if he takes an interest in interacting with nationals of the host culture and is capable of doing so. The goal of cross-cultural training should therefore be to equip the trainees with knowledge, skills and attitudes which enable them to achieve the above-mentioned adjustment and effectiveness. The specific knowledge, attitudes and skills which have to be learned depend on the training needs of the target group or individual and must be derived from the needs analysis.

Methods for cross-cultural training

Once the training needs have been identified and translated into specific objectives, we know 'what' we want to achieve with training. What we do not yet know is 'how' to achieve these objectives. Decisions concerning this question are made during the design phase (see Figure 10.1), during which are determined the specific instructional content needed in order to achieve the stated objectives, the methods and media to be used and the sequence in which the material will be offered to the trainees. In the remainder of this section we will emphasize the choice of training method, since there are special considerations which must be taken into account with respect to international staff.

Available training methods

The literature provides various classification systems for the different methods of cross-cultural training. Many of these taxonomies do not make

Table 10.1 *Overview of the available training options for cross-cultural training*

Instructional strategies	Specific methods
Simulations	Role playing Case studies Instructional games
Programmed instruction	Cultural assimilator
Expositive instruction	Lectures (area briefing) Tutorials Reading assignments Audio/visual presentations
Sensitivity training	T-group
Behaviour modification methods	Drill-and-practice Modelling
Field experiences	Field trips Assignments to micro-cultures Meetings with experienced international staff
On-the-job training	Coaching Job rotation

a clear distinction between training methods and training outcomes, however. For example, 'cultural awareness training' is not a training method, but rather a desired outcome (cultural awareness), which can be achieved by means of various training methods. That is why the outline of available methods for cross-cultural training presented in Table 10.1 does not categorize the methods according to their possible application, but rather into generally accepted categories. The first category consists of instructional strategies (column 1): simulations, programmed instruction, expositive instruction, sensitivity training, behaviour modification methods, field experience and on-the-job training. These basic instructional strategies can be used to achieve both cross-cultural training goals and training goals in general. In column 2 more specific methods are indicated, all of which are especially suitable for the training of international staff. Short descriptions of the training methods summarized in Table 10.1 are set out below.

When cross-cultural training first began, it took a purely cognitive, intellectual, instructional approach. The most frequently used instructional strategy in this period (up to the 1960s) was expositive instruction. In the late 1960s humanistic influences made their way into cross-cultural training, and the emphasis shifted to the individual being trained. Strategies such as sensitivity training were favoured in this period, with the emphasis on 'learning how to learn' . Since then the field of cross-cultural training has matured and currently the best of both approaches is integrated. Present cross-cultural training thus usually combines both informational and experiential approaches.

Methods for cross-cultural training

Role playing: Participants are asked to imagine themselves in situations presented by the trainer and subsequently to act out simulated roles. Feedback follows immediately after each role play.

Case studies: An approach to management development that was pioneered at the Harvard Business School. This method stresses situation or problem analysis by the trainee, who is asked to determine possible courses of action for the solution of the problem presented in the case. The individual outcomes are thereafter generally discussed in a group context.

Instructional games: Essential characteristics of instructional games are the competition factor and a simplified representation of a real-life situation. The early games focused almost exclusively on the development of basic business skills. More recent games also focus on interpersonal and communication skills.

Cultural assimilator: A computer program (or written material) which aims at increasing the trainee's ability to see situations from the perspective of members of another culture. The underlying idea is that individuals can learn to make attributions that are appropriate to a different cultural environment. In order to achieve this aim the assimilator focuses on key problems and key differences, summarized in critical incidents. These incidents describe interactions between individuals from two cultures followed by four reasonable alternative attributions to their behaviour. Only one explanation, however, is correct from the viewpoint of the host culture. The trainee is asked to make a choice among the alternatives and is then given feedback.

Lectures: Oral, one-way transmission of information.

Tutorials: Here the transmission of information is not exclusively one-way. Both the teacher and the learner participate actively in the learning process.

Reading assignments: Suggested reading material on relevant topics which may be studied by the learner by means of self-tuition.

Audio/visual presentations: Presentations of this kind are used for the transmission of information that cannot be fully transmitted by, for example, oral lectures or reading materials.

T-group: Participants are expected to unfreeze from their habitual roles and adapt to a novel situation by developing new and often unexpected roles. These behaviour changes are subsequently studied by the other participants of the group.

continues

Drill-and-practice: A very intensive method in which practice and feedback are alternated frequently in such a way that undesired behaviour has little chance of establishing itself. This method is frequently used in the context of language training.

Modelling: The basic assumption of this method is that learners, by observing models perform desired behaviours and being reinforced doing so, will adopt these same behaviours if they can practise them and are positively reinforced during this practice. Modelling may take place on-the-job, through observation of peers or superiors who demonstrate desired behaviours and who are rewarded for their actions.

Field trips: A pre-visit may be made to the country of the assignment.

Assignments to micro-cultures: Trainees are placed in a situation for a limited period of time in which they are forced to interact with people whose way of life and values are different from their own.

Meetings with experienced international staff: The informal setting of such meetings allows for the exchange of much valuable information and experience.

Coaching: The trainee is provided with feedback regarding his or her performance, aiming at improvement. Managers who coach well model the correct behaviours, assign specific and challenging goals, and provide trainees with frequent and immediate feedback.

Job rotation: Under this system employees spend designated periods of time in different kinds of positions and business areas. A unique advantage of this method is that it allows the trainee to develop an appreciation for the specific role of his or her job in the overall organizational structure.

Choosing a training method

The previous section provided a brief introduction to the various training options available for cross-cultural training. We have not, however, indicated how to go about choosing between these many options. A responsible choice requires us to consider many different factors and to base our decision on these factors. We will discuss a number of these factors below.

In the first place, the choice of training method is very much dependent on whether we can in fact train staff in the specific competencies. Not all competencies can be acquired through the same training method. For example, while the expatriate may be able to acquire some basic conversational language skills just prior to departure by means of drill-and-practice, basic flexibility in thought and action may require much more time and more sophisticated methods. Researchers have tried to discern which methods are the most effective for which (type of) objective (Burack and Smith, 1982; Carrol et al., 1972), but much more research (also experimental) is needed if we are to obtain clear guidelines for the relative effectiveness of the various training methods in achieving the various types of training goals.

As long as these guidelines are not available, we will have to resort to other methods of choosing between the many available training options. Recognizing that this choice depends upon the training goals and that these goals, as we have seen above, are a result of the trainee's training needs, we might consider the variables influencing the training needs as important sources of information to be used when choosing a training method. An especially important cluster of variables in the case of international staff consists of the situational factors of the assignment (see Figure 10.2). It is therefore no coincidence that it is exactly this cluster of variables on which approaches to the choice of training method have been based in the literature.

Before discussing situational factors, we should first recognize that not all foreign situations are the same. Members of certain cultures can adapt more easily and are more effective in some regions than in others. Torbiörn (1982), for example, found that for Scandinavians the most difficult regions of the world in which to live and work are (1) Africa, (2) the Middle East and (3) the Far East. North America and Australia are relatively easier to adapt to. Secondly, the tasks to be accomplished by international staff vary. Some tasks are very technical, involving little interaction with locals, while other jobs require a high degree of inter-action with the local population. Using these two factors (similarity between the host and home culture, and degree of interaction required in the host culture), Tung (1982) presented a contingency framework for choosing an appropriate cross-cultural training method and its level of rigour. Essentially, she argues that the lower the required degree of interaction and the greater the similarity between host culture and home culture, the more the content of the training should focus on task- and job-related issues as opposed to culture-related issues, and the lower the level of rigour should be. This framework does not, however, help the user determine which specific training methods to use, since it does not indicate in depth the relative rigour of the various available methods.

Black and Mendenhall (1991) propose that a sounder basis for choosing an appropriate training method may be found in Social Learning Theory. Bandura (1977), one of the leading authors of Social Learning Theory, argues that learning takes place in two ways: first through the effect of reinforcement on behaviour, that is, appropriate behaviour is rewarded and undesirable behaviour punished, and secondly through imitating or modelling the behaviour of others. Bandura (1977) further proposes that there are two main forms of modelling: symbolic and participative. In symbolic modelling the trainee does not actually practise the modelled behaviour, but watches the model and rehearses mentally. The two main types of symbolic modelling are verbal symbolic modelling (the trainee hears or reads about the behaviour and observes the behaviour in his or her mind) and observational symbolic modelling (the trainee actually sees the behaviour being modelled). In the second major form of modelling, participative modelling, the observer actually practises the modelled behaviour. Again there are two types: in verbal participative modelling the trainee participates in modelling the behaviour by describing what he or she would do in a similar situation, and in behavioural participative modelling the learner participates physically in the modelling process. We indicated above that training methods vary as to their relative level of rigour. We have not yet defined the concept of 'rigour', however. Within the framework of Social Learning Theory, rigour can be defined as the trainee's degree of cognitive involvement. Recognizing that the various forms of modelling introduced above require different levels of cognitive involvement, the various training methods can be classified as to their relative level of rigour as depicted in Figure 10.3.

As indicated above, the required level of rigour of the training method depends upon the situational factors of the assignment. The greater the novelty of the host culture, the higher the degree of interaction with the host culture and the greater the novelty of the job to be carried out, the more rigorous the training method should be.

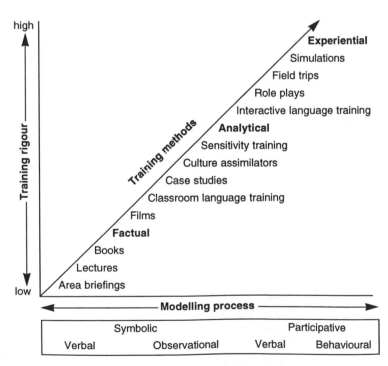

Figure 10.3 *Modelling processes, rigour and training methods (Black and Mendenhall, 1991)*

4   General view of the training of international staff

Having exposed some of the procedural aspects of cross-cultural training in Section 3, let us now turn to a more general view on cross-cultural training which ties together and gives meaning to the components of the training cycle discussed above.

Training and development: a process, not an event

As revealed in Section 2, cross-cultural training is often seen as a one-shot remedy applied just prior to departure. On top of this, it is usually of a very short duration. Yet in order to increase the effectiveness of cross-cultural training, it is important to recognize that training, and especially development, should not be seen and approached as an event, but as a process.

If we return to our examination of the competencies included in the profiles needed for success on foreign assignments (pp. 211–212 above), we must conclude that many of these competencies lie in the area of attitudes, abilities and even personality traits: leadership, initiative, motivation, emotional stability, cultural sensitivity, ability to deal with responsibility etc. Even if we assume that such competencies can be acquired through training, it rapidly becomes clear that many of them cannot be acquired on a short-term basis. They need time to develop and become strong. This implies that a training course of very short duration just prior to departure cannot be effective in changing and/or developing competencies related to attitudes, abilities or personality traits. The most that can be achieved in such a 'one-shot training event' is the development of basic skills and a certain increase in knowledge. In order to achieve more than a superficial increase in their effectiveness on foreign assignments, potential international managers will have to acquire competencies which are more difficult to develop through training. We therefore recommend starting to develop these competencies early on in a manager's career, using a phased, cumulative approach.

The *first phase* of training and development should begin soon after initial selection has taken place and the candidate has been accepted into the company for a position with international prospects. Development in this phase should focus on strengthening those abilities needed for an international career and on reinforcing the manager's motivation to work abroad. Modelling and coaching by superiors with international experience are two important development mechanisms in this first phase. The *second phase* of training and development should take place after the manager has been selected for an international career. In this phase the focus should be on strengthening all required competencies for the fulfilment of an international assignment. Besides coaching and modelling, more rigorous training methods should be applied in this phase. After the manager has been selected for a specific assignment, the *third phase* of training and development should be implemented. In this phase the manager is trained in specific skills needed for his assignment and the necessary knowledge of specific cultural issues in the host country, logistical information and business practices and procedures is imparted. According to Adler and Ghadar (Chapter 4), continuous training and development throughout a manager's career would typically only take place in global (transnational in 'our' terminology) companies.

An interesting example of training which precedes selection for an international career is that which is applied by a large Dutch multinational company. Young managers who have been with the company for two to three years are sent, along with their partners, on a week-long workshop in which they are confronted with the pros and cons of expatriate life. The aim of this workshop is, first of all, to increase the trainees' ability to make a responsible choice either for or against an international career, and secondly to create an environment in which there is space for the discussion of possible doubts and, if necessary, alternative careers.

The advantages of a cumulative approach to preparatory training are two-fold. In the first place, because training and development takes place over a period of several years, the company tackles not only those training needs that can be met in the short term (technical skills, language skills etc.), but also those training needs in the area of abilities and attitudes whose development requires a much longer period of time. By spreading the development of international managers over a number of years, then, the company will automatically avoid the mistake of offering only very condensed, information-transmitting training just prior to departure, the effectiveness of which is highly dubious. The second advantage of the proposed approach is that the distinction between selection and training may become blurred, a benefit which will be discussed in more detail in the next section.

Integration of training and development in the other areas of HRM

The training and development of international staff should be integrated into the other activities of human resource management. An instrument which can make an important contribution to such an integration consists of profiles which are described in terms of the key competencies necessary for success, such as those introduced in our earlier discussion in Section 3 above. If these profiles are used as a basis for deducing training needs and training goals and, at the same time, as a basis for deducing selection and appraisal criteria, a common language will be created which can link the various areas of human resource management. The result is that communication is fostered, not only between these various areas of human resource management, but also with the manager himself. He is appraised, selected and trained in accordance with the same set of competencies. Links between appraisal outcomes and training interventions or selection decisions, for example, become more transparent and easier to accept since they can be explained rationally.

Turning specifically to the integration of training and selection, both Siveking, Anchor and Marston (1981) and Harris and Moran (1991) recommend including as much training as possible in selecting expatriates. The first advantage of such an integration, they argue, is that on the basis of the information received during training, the candidates can make more responsible decisions as to whether or not to accept an international career or a specific assignment. An example of a training programme with this goal was given in the previous section. A second advantage of the integration of training and selection of expatriate staff is that the selectors can observe the candidates during the training sessions and can therefore make informed selection decisions. Because the cumulative approach proposed above spreads training over the career of the manager, such observations can be made on a regular basis and will therefore become increasingly reliable and less threatening.

Inclusion of the partner in cross-cultural training

A very important factor in the training and development of international staff is the inclusion of the partner in preparatory training. In Section 2 we mentioned a study by Tung (1981) in which she investigated the reasons for the failure of international managers from the United States and Europe. She concluded that the inability of the manager's partner to adapt to a different physical or cultural environment is the major cause for failure of international assignments. On the basis of this finding, one would expect companies to focus on the training of accompanying partners. That this is not the case has become clear from the estimate, also cited in Section 2, that in 80 percent of the cases in which pre-departure training is provided, the partners are not included in the training programme.

If companies wish to lower the failure rate of international assignments, they must face up to the potential threat posed by an unknown and unprepared partner. This implies that the partner has to be included in both the selection process and the training and development procedure. Two factors are of special importance in this context.

First, the partner has to be given support while deciding for or against a life abroad. At present most companies expect the candidate to discuss the implications of such choices with his or her partner. The partner facing this situation, however, often cannot make an objective assessment of her or his own motivations and competencies. In the first place, most partners find it difficult to stand in the way of such an assignment (promotion), and allow their own concerns to take a back seat (Adler, 1991). Secondly, at the point in time when they have to decide, many partners are simply not sufficiently well informed about the context of the assignment in order to be able to take a responsible decision. In the third place, many partners lack knowledge about their own competencies. A combination of training and selection activities could provide at least a partial answer to these difficulties. A possible option would be the training mentioned above, during which potential candidates and their partners are exposed to the pros and cons of international life before making a decision.

Secondly, the partner must be well equipped for her or his international life prior to departure. It is widely recognized that companies prefer to send couples abroad rather than single individuals. Companies thus apparently expect the partners to fulfil an important function during the assignment. The partner is expected to function as a source of support for the expatriate (and the rest of the family), in addition to fulfilling more complex social functions than in the home country. Yet many companies seem to forget that in an international move, the partner has in fact the most difficult role of all of the family members (Adler, 1991). While employees have the basic company and job structure which carries through in the various assignments, and children have the relative continuity and routine of school, partners must give up their friends, activities and, very often, their careers, thus losing both the structure and the continuity of their lives. On top of this, partners are often more exposed to the local culture (and hence culture shock) than the other family members who live a more insulated life. It should be clear that, in order to cope with their own difficulties and to be able to support other family members, the accompanying partners have to be well equipped. Appropriate training and development should provide them with the necessary 'tools' .

Inclusion of HCNs in cross-cultural training

Although we have not yet mentioned host-country nationals (HCNs), the training and development of this group of employees is very important if we consider the role they are expected to play in a multinational or even transnational organization (see Chapter 2). But even if an organization is not yet thinking in 'transnational' terms, the training of HCNs should receive more attention. The reason is simple: the ultimate success of an expatriate assignment depends not only on the expatriate himself or herself but also upon the local people with whom he has to work.

Regarding a training design for HCNs, an important lesson which can be drawn from past experience is that companies must avoid the mistake of simply exporting parent-country training and development programmes to other countries. Training and development programmes for HCNs must be culturally adapted to meet local conditions. Furthermore, the management development programmes for HCNs need to be linked to the strategic situation in each country as well as to the overall strategy of the firm (Scullion, 1992). As far as the content of the training is concerned, it may focus on the development of technical or managerial skills, but it can also serve to introduce the HCN to the parent corporate culture and the cultural background of the parent country.

Besides formal training, assignments to headquarters are also very valuable as a tool to develop HCNs. Until recently, however, there were very few opportunities for HCNs to acquire developmental experience at headquarters or to fulfil assignments in other countries. This contributed to many companies failing to attract and retain high-potential HCN managers and staff. At present more companies are seeking to develop HCNs through development transfers to corporate headquarters. This type of international transfer exposes HCNs to corporate headquarters' culture and supports them in developing a corporate perspective rather than simply reflecting their own local interests. Furthermore, it has been argued that this approach can be very effective in the development of global management teams, which are essential for the operation of a truly global firm.

We can therefore conclude that in addition to the training of expatriates and their families, companies should also take care to train HCNs. In fact, training represents a long-term investment in both the individuals and in the organization as a whole. Through training, HCNs become more capable of effectively cooperating with expatriates. Moreover, they increase their own chances of promotion, thus enabling the organization as a whole to make better use of all its human resources.

5 The problem of re-entry into the home culture

While companies pay relatively little attention to training and developing international staff and their families prior to departure, they give even less consideration to supporting expatriates upon their return to the home country. Whereas the potential problems of adapting to a new (and foreign) working and living environment are widely recognized (even if this is not always reflected in the amount of pre-departure training offered), the many difficulties which can occur during the re-entry period have only recently been brought to the fore (Adler, 1991; Harris and Moran, 1991).

It is a well-known and widely studied fact that culture shock may play an important role during the adaptation phase to a new culture. In the initial phase in the host country, expatriates are excited by their new environment. This initial euphoria gives way to disillusionment, a phase which reaches its lowest point at the moment that 'culture shock' occurs – the frustration and confusion that results from being bombarded by uninterpretable clues (Adler, 1991). Following culture shock, expatriates start adapting and generally begin to feel more positive. Figure 10.4 represents the 'mood' of expatriates during their stay in a foreign culture.

The occurrence of culture shock is instinctively recognized as a natural reaction in the transition from familiar to unknown surroundings. When assignees return to their home country, however – in the eyes of many, from an relatively unknown to a known environment – no such culture shock is expected to occur. The returning expatriate and his family are expected to pick up the threads of their old life and settle in quickly without major difficulties. After all, they are 'coming home'. But what if the 'home' is no longer home? Not only do firms frequently fail to recognize the potential shock of re-entry, but the returnees themselves

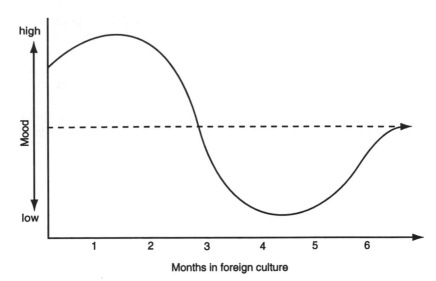

Figure 10.4 *The culture shock cycle (Adler, 1991: 233)*

expect an easy return. They do not consider the possibility that they themselves have changed as a result of their foreign experiences, and that there have also been changes in the parent organization and in their home country.

Returnees describe going through stages similar to those characteristic of culture shock, the first being a highly optimistic mood which lasts only a very short time, then a descent to an emotional low point and finally another rise to their normal mood (Figure 10.5).

Besides personal re-entry, professional transition back to the home organization may cause problems. This is especially the case in organizations which do not consider international experience critical to overall corporate success. For many returnees, the short-term career impact turns out to be negative rather than positive, as they expected. The returnee also has to adapt to the culture of the home organization, which may be very different from the culture he or she had grown accustomed to during the assignment. Suddenly the returnee is just one among many again, having lost the special status, responsibilities and freedom accorded by expatriate professional life.

Adler (1991) points out three factors which are important contributors to successful professional re-entry:

1   *Communication during the assignment.* Returnees who maintain close contact with the home organization while abroad will be more effective and satisfied in their re-entry jobs. Management should therefore regularly inform expatriate employees about current organizational policies, projects, plans and staffing changes. Frequent personal contact between assignees and home-country managers in both the home and the host country is also very important.

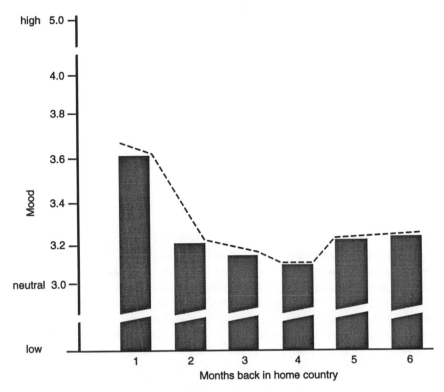

Figure 10.5   *Re-entry adjustment curve (Adler, 1991: 234)*

2   *Career planning which takes account of re-entry.* The return of many
    expatriates is triggered by the completion of the assignment rather than
    by the availability of a suitable position in the home organization. Not
    many companies have sophisticated international career path systems
    guaranteeing a suitable position upon return. Plans for international
    assignments should not only include the demands of the foreign
    project, but also the broader career perspective of the expatriate.
    Before the assignment actually takes place, it should be clear what is
    going to happen upon completion.
3   *Recognition of the value of the foreign experience.* Home organizations
    (and thus home managers) should recognize and value the former
    expatriate's foreign experience. They should recognize that they can
    profit from this foreign experience, that it can contribute to home
    organization learning. To achieve this, the returnees themselves first
    have to recognize the value of the skills they have acquired abroad.
    Secondly, a constructive dialogue has to take place between returnees
    and home-country managers in which the optimal utilization of these
    acquired skills is discussed.

    Training (coaching!) can play an important role during the re-entry
phase, focusing in the first place on personal re-entry in the form of both

practical support (housing, schooling etc.) and counselling which addresses the natural 'shock' associated with re-entry and the need to re-define personal roles (partner's career re-entry, new 'old' social system etc.).

Secondly, training can play an important role in professional re-entry into the home organization. It may, for example, play an important role in validating the expatriate's foreign experience. On the one hand, home-country managers may need training in order to be able to recognize and utilize the foreign experience of their returning expatriates; on the other hand, the returnees themselves may be greatly aided by debriefing and re-entry training sessions.

6   Closing the circle

As we have seen above, training and development plays an important role in the international deployment of staff. In Sections 3 and 4, the emphasis was placed upon preparatory training for foreign assignments, and in Section 5 the focus shifted to the importance of training during the re-entry phase. No specific attention has been given to the role of training in the intermediary phase, that is, during the assignment itself, even though training may play an important role during this phase, especially in the form of arrival orientation. Familiarization with the environment (language, housing, shopping, transport etc.) may have to be acquired on site, at least in part, because some subjects may be understandable only through actual experience. The same is true for familiarization with the work unit, with fellow employees, and with the actual job. Coaching by superiors and/ or colleagues often proves very valuable in this context.

The ideal deployment cycle can thus be depicted as presented in Figure 10.6. The employee is accepted into a position in the home organization that offers him international prospects. Once he has shown that he possesses the basic abilities and motivation needed for an international career, he is selected and receives further training. After selection for a specific assignment, country-specific preparation follows, both for the future expatriate and his partner. On the assignment he (and his partner) receive on-site orientation and briefings, as well as support and monitoring from the home organization. Upon completion of the assignment he is given support during the re-entry process, and finally reassumes a position in the home organization.

It should be clear that this 'ideal cycle' can only take place if the home organization is committed to supporting its expatriates in all phases of their deployment, and if these training and support activities fit well into a broader development plan. In Section 5 we pointed out that career planning plays an important role in the ultimate success of an assignment and readjustment upon return. In other words, assignments (and recalls) should not be ad hoc actions, but should follow logically from a career development plan. In order to be able to implement such a plan, companies must decide what the ultimate purpose of such assignments is.

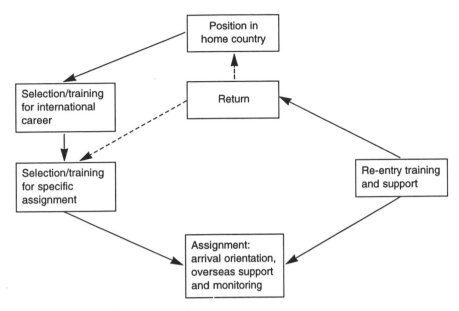

Figure 10.6   *Deployment cycle*

Are staff mainly sent on assignment for staffing purposes, for control and coordination of foreign operations, and for the transfer of know-how, or are management and organizational development the main purposes? If the latter is the case, assignments must be prepared, supported and brought to completion based upon a systematic staffing policy.

7   Summary and conclusions

In this chapter we have discussed the training and development of international staff. The main conclusions are summarized below:

1   Despite the fact that many expatriates fail on their foreign assignments and despite the fact that preparatory training increases the chance of success, surprisingly few companies provide such preparatory training.

2   Two important reasons for not providing such training are that companies do not believe in the effectiveness of training and that they do not know enough about the individual competencies needed for success in order to be able to design appropriate training.

3   In order to develop and design effective preparatory training for international staff, companies must implement a systematic approach which includes thorough analysis of the training needs of the target population, the translation of these training needs into training goals, and a careful training design.

4   Profiles in terms of competencies needed for success on international assignments may form an important basis for the development of

effective training for international staff. More research is needed in this area.

5 Training and development of international staff should be approached as a process and not as a one-time event just prior to departure. Many of the competencies needed for international success lie in the area of abilities and attitudes and therefore require development and strengthening over an extended period of time. The recommended approach is to begin preparing managers for international assignments early on in their careers by means of a phased, cumulative approach.

6 Training and development of international staff should be integrated into the other areas of HRM. Integration with the process of selection may prove particularly effective. Profiles based on key competencies could be a very useful instrument in such an integration.

7 The partner of the expatriate must not be forgotten in the preparatory process. She or he has to be well informed in order to be able to decide for or against an international assignment and must be well equipped to fulfil the new role. Furthermore, the training and development of host-country nationals should not be neglected, as they have important roles to play both in the interaction with expatriate staff and in the development of a truly transnational organization.

8 The re-entry process should receive more attention in the future. It is frequently underestimated at present, since returnees are not expected to encounter many difficulties upon returning 'home' .

9 Training and development of international staff must be viewed in the light of the complete deployment cycle, and will be most effective when linked to systematic career development plans.

11 Women's role in (international) management

Hilary Harris

1	Introduction	229
2	The changing role of management	230
3	Women in management	231
	The global perspective	231
	The changing role of women in employment	233
	Global changes	233
	The United States	234
	Europe	235
	Asia	235
	Developing countries	236
4	Barriers to women moving into senior management	237
	Causal factors at entry level	237
	Causal factors of women's career pathing options	238
	Motivation/commitment	238
	Managerial/leadership behaviour	240
	Perceptual problems in selection and appraisal	241
	Impact of organizational systems	242
5	The role of women in international management	243
	Organizational factors	243
	Socio-cultural factors	244
	Host country cultural barriers	244
	Dual-career issues	246
	Advantages for female expatriate managers	249
	Avenues for change	250
6	Summary and conclusions	250

1 Introduction

One of the few verifiable facts in the field of expatriate management research is the paucity of women expatriate managers. A number of surveys in the past ten years have put the number at between 2 and 5 percent (Adler, 1984b; Brewster, 1988; Reynolds and Bennett, 1991). This figure relates only to women sent abroad by the home country organization and does not take into account women who obtain jobs in foreign countries as a result of independent job-search methods.

This chapter looks in detail at the process of (international) management as it relates to women; taking into account organizational, individual, economic and socio-cultural perspectives. It first considers the changing role of management and the skills needed for effective international management, together with international management selection procedures and career development issues. Secondly, it discusses the potential impact on women of an increasing emphasis on internationalization by looking at issues facing women managers both within home country environments and in the international arena. As women have to get through to (senior) management positions in their home country before they will be taken into account for international positions, a large part of this chapter will be devoted to the reasons for their failure to do so.

2   The changing role of management

We have already seen in Chapter 4 that a key factor in developing a transnational capability lies in companies' approaches to international human resource management (HRM), and in particular the identification and development of effective international managers. Beyond superior technical and managerial skills, the profile of the international manager includes adaptability, sensitivity to different cultures, language and relationship skills and the ability to work in international teams (Barham and Devine, 1991).

The above profile denotes a move away from a reliance on traditional management qualities, to 'soft skills' such as interpersonal and cross-cultural adaptation abilities, which emphasize the human relations aspect of international management and the ability to handle unfamiliar situations. This new emphasis is interesting in relation to women's role in international management, for there is substantial evidence that women have superior skills in this area.

Rosener (1990), for instance, argues that women adopt an 'interactive leadership style, particularly well suited to the versatile and rapidly changing business environment of today'. Women's ability to work well with people, developing 'smooth and cooperative relationships' is also stressed by Wentling (1992). Sharma (1990), meanwhile, sees the main attributes of their approach as collaboration and cooperation, team work, intuition and creativity. We will come back to this later in this chapter, especially in Section 4 in our discussion of managerial/leadership behaviour.

Women's greater inherent skills in this area may well be a result of socio-cultural factors, in that traditional familial roles have reinforced nurturing and people-oriented behaviour in women. A similar phenomenon may be at work in organizations. Kanter (1977), for instance, argues that the women's adoption of cooperative management styles is more a result of their inferior status within organizations, and such a style would be adopted by other minority groups as well.

However, despite the emphasis in theory on 'soft skills' for effective international managers, research into actual selection practices amongst multinational organizations indicates a clear reliance on technical competence and knowledge of company systems, often as a response to the perception of international selection as a high-risk operation (see also Chapter 9).

A more practical reason for the lack of attention to factors such as relational skills, cultural empathy and partner/family support in selection lies in the actual selection procedures adopted by companies. Research into company practices reveals widespread reliance on personal recommendation for expatriate postings from either a specialist personnel staff member or line manager. This results in more or less predetermined selection interviews with little formal testing of potential expatriates, restricted use of personality and psychological tests and a general suspicion of the validity of cultural awareness and adaptability tests. We have already referred to this phenomenon in Chapter 9.

Selection criteria and procedures for international assignments become especially critical if such experience is seen to be a prerequisite for access to senior management positions. In the current context it is difficult to assess the exact importance of international management experience (in terms of managing an operation abroad) to future career development. There are strong indications, however, that international experience will be taken as a prerequisite for senior management appointments as a result of the imperatives of the increasingly global marketplace. Given that women traditionally make up only a tiny percentage of expatriate managers, what are the implications for them of this increasing emphasis on international management experience?

3 Women in management

Women's participation in international management assignments is influenced by a complex set of cultural, social, legal, economic and political factors which affect women both within their home countries and host country environments. Later in this chapter we shall look in more detail at the effect of host country cultural barriers on women expatriate managers; at this stage, however, we need to examine more closely the factors affecting women in management within their home country environment to determine the extent to which this may affect women's ability to gain entry to international assignments and to perform effectively as international managers.

The global perspective

A useful global perspective is provided by Adler (1986/87) when reviewing the situation female managers face across a wide range of countries. She observes that the possibility of increased representation and impact of women in management and the selection of effective strategies for bringing about change depend fundamentally on each culture's perception of the dominant constraints.

Women in Japan and Saudi Arabia, for example, may focus on cultural patterns when explaining the situation with regard to female managers, whereas American women look primarily to the legal structure and Chinese women in Singapore and the People's Republic of China may emphasize current economic conditions and political leadership. (Adler, 1986/87)

However, it is important to note that whatever each culture's perception of the dominant constraints, socio-cultural norms constitute the basis on which political, economic or legal actions are founded.

Adler argues that underlying nationally based explanations are two fundamentally different assumptions about the ideal role of women in management. The first is an *equity* model based on assumed similarity, and the second is a *complementary contribution* model based on assumed differences (see Table 11.1).

Under the equity model female professionals are viewed as identical to male professionals and therefore able to contribute in the same way. The emphasis is on enabling women to gain equal access to the world of male management and on a process of assimilation of women to male norms.

Table 11.1 *Assumptions made about women's role in management*

	Equity model	Complementary contribution model
Fundamental assumptions	*Similarity*	*Difference*
Men's and women's contributions	Identical	Complementary
Fairness based on	Equity	Valuing difference
		Recognizing and valuing
Strategic goal	*Equal access*	difference
Assessment	Quantitative	Qualitative
Measured by	Statistical proportion of women at each hierarchical level	Assessing women's contribution to organizational goals
Process	Counting women	Assessing women's contribution
Measurement of effectiveness		
Women's contribution	Identical to men	Complementary to men
Norms	Identical for men and women	Unique to men and women
Based on	Historical 'male' norms	Women's own contribution
Referant	Men	Women
Acculturation process	*Assimilation*	*Synergy*
Expected behaviour	Standardized	Differentiated
Based on	Male norms	Female norms
Essence	'Dress for success' business suit	Elegant, feminine attire
Example	*United States*	*France*
	'The melting pot'	'Vive la différence'

Source: Adler, 1986/87: 5

The complementary contribution model, by contrast, is based on the assumption of difference, not similarity. It emphasizes equivalent recognition of men's and women's different patterns and styles of contribution rather than focusing on statistical representation as in the equity model. Analysis of progress is based on the extent to which organizations encourage unique contributions from men and women and build synergistic combinations of these contributions.

Adler stresses that these models are not complementary; for instance, under the equity model, seeing various groups as 'different' can be seen to be calling them 'inferior'. Likewise, under the complementary contribution model, not to see women's uniqueness negates their identity and contribution to the organization.

Rothwell (1991) makes a similar distinction in her analysis of women and employment in Europe. She raises three key discussion points on the basic themes relating to women's employment; which she sees as applicable to all parts of the world, not just Europe:

- Are women aiming to become more integrated, to become more like men, to compete more successfully in the capitalist system?
- Or are women aiming to obtain greater recognition for 'female' qualities, skills and attributes and establish that a 'woman-shaped pattern of life' has as much validity and claim on national resources and status as a man's?
- Or do we attempt to put greater emphasis on a common humanity and seek to maximize choices for both women and men in the belief that a more just society is likely to evolve? (Rothwell, 1991: 24)

These themes raise fundamental questions concerning the role of paid employment in overall life-career development. The first theme, echoing Adler's equity model, views paid employment as the sole means of achieving maximum individual career satisfaction. The second theme, most closely related to Adler's complementary contribution model, proposes that women should be allowed equivalent recognition for responsibilities and challenges outside the formal economy as for paid employment. The third perspective extends this option to men as well and would appear to represent a more equally based society in terms of role-choice flexibility. Elements of all three themes are evident when looking at individual case studies of men and women in management; however, the extent to which one or the other will predominate at the overall societal level will be determined by each country's unique socio-cultural background.

The changing role of women in employment

Global changes

One of the most significant features of the global labour market in the last half of the twentieth century has been the increasing labour force participation rate of women – defined as the total labour force (male/female) divided by the population of working age (15–64) at mid-year.

Whilst male participation rates in the OECD area declined from 88.3 to 82.4 percent between 1973 and 1991, female participation rates rose steadily over the same period from 48.3 to 60.5 percent (OECD, 1993).

Changes in participation behaviour linked to the state of the labour market in terms of unemployment rates, the level of vacancies and other effects do not explain the long-term growth trend of female labour force participation. According to an OECD report on the integration of women into the economy , the forces behind this phenomenon are extremely wide-ranging and include

> demographic changes, alterations in marriage and divorce patterns, increasing education, changing social attitudes, new consumption patterns, inflationary pressures which increase the need for two-wage earner families, government equal-opportunity policies and changes in the economy, such as the increase in part-time jobs which may have enabled workers with specific characteristics, such as the aged, youth and women responsible for dependents, to enter the labour market. (OECD, 1985)

The report also highlights the importance of structural change leading to a varied pattern of employment growth by sector, together with the role of the public sector in expanding job opportunities for women. In terms of structural change, the service sector became the major source of net job creation and is now the sector with the highest concentration of female workers. The public sector has also provided many opportunities for female participation, especially in the creation of part-time jobs. It is interesting that one of the key features of employment patterns over the last two decades has been the growth of part-time employment, concentrated primarily in the service sector. The vast majority of part-time workers are women, due to a large extent to the constraints placed upon them by family responsibilities and lack of adequate childcare facilities.

Women are therefore entering the workforce in ever-increasing numbers but are still primarily concentrated in the service sector and undertake a disproportionate amount of part-time work compared with male workers. Despite these overall trends in increasing labour force participation for women, considerable variations exist between countries in terms of women's progress into managerial positions as a result of differing cultural, social, legal, economic and political histories.

The United States

Progress for women within the United States has come about much more as a result of political action rooted in the powerful civil rights and women's movements of the late 1960s and early 1970s. Responsive governmental legislation, including the use of quotas, and affirmative action programmes did much to improve the representation of women in the workforce and in other areas of public life. Under more than a decade of Republican administration, legislative initiatives diminished as a result of a move to the political right, bringing with it pressure to return to 'traditional' family values which espouse the notion of a woman's place as being in the home. Some observers have viewed the embracement of conservative values by the ruling legislative party as a major barrier to women's progress in terms of equality of employment opportunity. It would appear, however, that on a broader societal level, women are accepted into the workforce and have continued to make inroads into management as a result of improved educational opportunities, work experience and individual self-confidence. Whilst entry into management ranks may appear more egalitarian within the United States than in Asian countries, the influence of the equity model exerts pressure on women to conform to a male pattern of working which discriminates against women with family responsibilities. In contrast with Asia, women managers in the United States do not have access to cheap sources of domestic help and are therefore faced with greater difficulties in combining home and work responsibilities.

Europe

Europe can be said to combine elements of both the equity and complementary contribution models. Within the member states of the European Union, a broad span of socio-cultural norms are in evidence, with a tenuous North/South split in terms of attitudes towards women's role in society. Northern countries such as the United Kingdom, the Netherlands and Denmark espouse full participation of women in the workforce, whilst more traditional cultural patterns exist in Southern countries such as Spain, Portugal and Greece. Progress within individual member states is, however, influenced by EU policy, which is directed by a strong commitment to social justice for all individuals within the European Union. As a result, many legislative and political initiatives have been instigated on a Union-wide basis aimed at preventing discrimination against women and minority groups and at ensuring equality of treatment in all aspects of public life. Compulsory compliance with European Union directives has led to greater legislative progress on equal employment opportunity issues than would perhaps have been the case amongst several member states. How far legislative change has affected societal attitudes to women is still very much a matter of debate.

Asia

Women in Asian countries can be seen to be affected to a much greater degree than European and American women by strong cultural norms which denote the woman's place as in the home with the man's being in the workplace. Despite these cultural barriers, increasing economic pressures have brought about a growth in women's labour force participation rates, particularly with the rapid expansion of the service economy. It is interesting to note that women have made most progress within the banking and finance sector, which can be attributed to a reflection of 'the traditional role of the Asian woman as keeper of the household purse-strings' (Asian Institute of Management). It can be noted, therefore, that there is a cultural perspective to this phenomenon. Additionally, socio-cultural factors can be seen to be at work in relation to women's progress into management in Asia when it is noted that the majority of women executives in this region come from high social status family backgrounds which give them access to superior educational opportunities and provide entry routes through familial recommendations. These women are also able to afford domestic help, which frees them from many of their traditional household duties.

Developing countries

The situation for women in the developing world presents additional problems in terms of their gaining access to the sphere of paid employment. Whilst economic activity rates of women are generally rising, Momsen (1991) finds that there is no clear relationship between higher levels of development, urbanization and increased female employment. Indeed, she points to India and parts of Africa where urban growth has led to a decline in overall female labour force participation. Two key problems are identified by Momsen:

- *Domestic responsibilities*. For women in urban areas who are entering the workforce, changes in household composition mean that they are often facing heavier domestic responsibilities than before. This arises through smaller family size, less help from relatives, increased cost and decreased availability of domestic help and increased educational opportunities for children, so that the burden of domestic work falls on one particular woman in the family. 'It is estimated that married women in Malaysia who do housework and are in paid employment outside the home spend, on average, 112 hours per week working, while the equivalent figure for the United States is 59 hours' (Momsen, 1991).
- *Sexual harassment*. Sexual harassment may be a greater problem in the Third World than in developed countries as a result of traditional societal norms about women's family role, seeing women who move outside this role to take jobs as 'loose' women. Men at work, when unaccustomed to meeting women in that situation, may revert to gender-based social expectations and treat women at work as sexually available.

Momsen underlines the fact that many barriers to women's participation in the urban modern sector relate to the fact that modern industry is spatially separated from the home and involves a standard fixed pattern of working hours that are usually longer than in the industrialized world. In many ways the situation facing women in the developing world is similar to that experienced by women throughout the industrialized world at the time of the exodus from rural to urban communities during the last century. The progress of women was seen then to be hindered by a combination of economic, social and cultural factors giving rise to specific political and legal regimes. Progress in the developing world will not come about merely as a result of increasing educational opportunities for women, but only from a far-reaching change in cultural attitudes brought on by the spread of industrialization and shaped by individual country political and economic histories.

4   Barriers to women moving into senior management

In the light of more and more women entering the workforce, their failure to attain the highest management positions is particularly puzzling. This phenomenon has become known as the 'glass ceiling' or 'glass wall', to denote an impenetrable barrier which is invisible and which prevents upward – and in the case of the 'glass wall', also lateral – movement. Solomon (1990) explains these terms as the phenomena experienced by women and minorities as they attempt to climb upwards in the managerial ranks or move sideways to line positions which have traditionally been held by the dominant work group, in most cases white males. One argument put forward against the 'glass ceiling' theory is that women have not been in the pipeline long enough to reach top management levels. This, however, does not do justice to the complexities of the issue, for studies of men and women's progress up organizational career ladders show blockages for women appearing at much earlier stages than men (Broderick and Milkovich, 1991; Davidson and Cooper, 1987). It is necessary, therefore, to look for causal factors which affect women's choices and options at both entry level and during subsequent stages of their careers.

Causal factors at entry level

Despite a trend towards increased participation in non-traditional occupational areas, women's choices and options at entry level are still very much influenced by socio-economic factors contributing to occupational segregation and wage differentials. Ragins and Sundstrom (1989) argue that initial choices by women in terms of employment can be affected by sex role stereotyping in early socialization. Such socialization leads women to self-select in terms of job versus career and choice of gender-typed occupation and gender-typed speciality. These choices exclude women at the first stage of their careers from positions or areas of power which the authors argue are essential for career progression.

Occupational segregation can be seen to have a direct effect on women's pay and promotion prospects. Women entering traditional gender-typed occupations may find themselves in such archetypal female 'ghetto' occupations as secretarial work which offer few possibilities of lateral and vertical transfers (Pringle, 1989). Historical devaluing of women's work means that traditional women's occupations tend to be symbolized by less pay, power and prestige, which may negatively affect women's career progress.

Causal factors of women's career pathing options

Underlying causes of occupational segregation and wage differentials fail, however, to account for the fact that even within strongly gender-typed occupations such as teaching or the social services, women do not necessarily hold a proportionate number of senior management positions. In the United Kingdom, for instance, latest figures for full-time teachers in secondary schools show that, although women make up 63 percent of all teaching posts, they hold only 43 percent of head teachers' positions (Department of Education and Science statistics for 1990). This would suggest either that women are less able or less willing or that they encounter more obstacles than men in their career progression within organizations. Given that women nowadays enter employment with the same level of educational attainment as men, especially in gender-typed occupations, the literature on male/female differences in values and attitudes to work and male/female managerial/leadership styles, together with issues of perception of male/female attributes and the impact of organizational systems, may provide some clues to more deeply rooted causes of the 'glass ceiling' phenomenon.

Motivation/commitment

The effect of *sex role identity and gender-related behaviour* feature prominently in discussions relating to women's motivation to succeed in the workforce. Powell (1988) argues that early socialization from parents, schools, the media and peer groups contributes to the development of a sex role identity which will affect occupational aspirations and expectations. Aspirations will be constrained both by a need to restrict career hopes to 'sex-appropriate' activities and by the strength of occupational segregation in a given sector. Expectations are viewed in highly sex-typed terms for females. A study by Heilman (1979) amongst high school seniors in the United States found that males expressed greater interest in two male-intensive occupations, architect and lawyer, when told that the projected proportion of women was 10 percent or 30 percent than when told it was 50 percent. Their expectations of future success at a career were not, however, affected by its projected population of women. Women on the other hand expressed greater interest in each career and expected they would be more successful at it when the projected proportion of women was 30 percent or 50 percent than when told it was 10 percent.

Devanna (1988) in her review of research into *male/female differences in motivation* reports that there were 'no innate differences, but rather that men and women are more likely to respond differently to motivational questions depending upon the circumstances or context in which the questions are framed.' In this context, Devanna contests Horner's (1972) theory that women possess a latent and stable personality trait which leads them to 'fear success'. According to Horner, this trait is acquired early in life as a result of attitudes from male peers and parents as to what constitutes appropriate gender role behaviour. Devanna argues that this is in fact more a case of 'fear of failure' and demonstrates appropriate behaviour in line with expectancy motivation theory. Viewed from this perspective, Devanna suggests that the women in Horner's original study (who talked of changing their career goals from those directed at high-status male occupations to those more in keeping with social perceptions of female roles in the workplace) would see that women had not yet succeeded in these fields and would thus reassess the probability that they would succeed to a lower level.

Ragins and Sundstrom (1989) examine the hypothesis that the under-representation of women in upper management is due to the fact that women have relatively *low levels of aspirations*. They point to current research evidence which shows that although women may have lower expressed career aspirations, this is not the case in terms of other aspirations, such as those related to family and home. They argue that it is therefore misleading to take the evidence of low aspiration levels among women at face value, as low career aspirations represent only part of their full aspirations, and that women may express relatively low aspirations because of actual barriers to their advancement; in other words, they may make their aspirations consistent with realistic expectations about promotion and advancement for women (Kanter, 1977). Powell et al. (1984), however, reported a quite striking result from their study of effects of sex on managerial value systems. In what appeared to be total contradiction of sex role stereotypes, they found that female managers place a greater emphasis on their careers in comparison with their family or home lives and feel less anxiety about any effect of career on home life than males. Their explanation for this phenomenon was that, given that women have more barriers to overcome in holding managerial positions than men, a woman with the same age, education, salary and managerial level as a man may have made more sacrifices and have a greater commitment to her career than a man to be in that position. From the perspective of the influence of socialization in sex role stereotypes, men could be seen to experience greater sex role expectations to be successful at work than women and could come to hold managerial jobs even though they had less of a career orientation than women in equivalent positions.

In conclusion, the complex interplay of sex role socialization and individual behaviour in terms of work decisions is still the subject of much discussion amongst researchers. Freedman and Phillips (1988), in a review of the literature on gender-related differences in work values and motivation patterns, conclude that study results are equivocal at best and fail to deal adequately with potentially confounding variables such as age, organizational level and education, amongst other things, which they feel could provide highly plausible alternative explanations for any observed sex differences. Despite a lack of agreement as to the causal relationships between sex role socialization and male/female differences in work behaviours, the bulk of research evidence would suggest that sex role identity does impact on male/female behaviours in relation to occupational aspirations and expectations. The impact of proportional numbers of males and females in occupational categories is particularly relevant in the highly male-dominated area of expatriate management.

Managerial/leadership behaviour

Given that women have the same motivation to succeed as men in similar circumstances, why do so few achieve executive status? Are women innately less suited for management?

In line with Adler's complementary contribution model and Rothwell's vision of a 'woman-shaped pattern of life', the *unique management style* of women is expounded by a number of writers, amongst them Marshall (1984), who argues that the literature on management implicitly alludes to masculine qualities which are equated to 'good' management. Marshall views women as having different managerial/leadership styles, with an emphasis on interpersonal, intuitive and cooperative skills, but argues that these are often seen as deficient in contrast to the predominant male style. However, as we have seen in Section 2 of this chapter and in previous chapters, such qualities are being emphasized increasingly as particularly suited to the needs of international management.

Rosener (1990) details the ways in which women's interactive leadership style is particularly well suited to contemporary business. Women 'encourage participation, share power and information, enhance other people's self-worth and get others excited about their work'. Sharma (1990) describes the feminine management style as being distinct and non-traditional. The main attributes of women's approach are collaboration and cooperation, teamwork, and intuition and creativity. Tom Peters, one of management's most celebrated gurus, is reported as having discovered the future potential of women's leadership styles and even as claiming that men need to learn 'women's games'.

A study carried out by Vinnicombe (1987) at Cranfield School of Management used the Myers–Briggs type indicator (MBTI) to look at differences in male and female working styles and found that, whilst 56.9 percent of male managers exhibited preferences for the 'traditionalist' managerial type, significantly more women fell into the 'visionaries' and 'catalysts' types. Whilst 'visionaries' are supposed to be 'natural' strategic managers, the strengths and weaknesses of 'catalysts' are seen to link directly with the stereotypical model of the female manager. The effectiveness of 'catalysts' in an organization is summed up by Bates and Kiersey (1984: 149–150):

> Catalysts are excellent in public relations and shine as organizational spokespersons since they work well with all types of people. They can sell the organization to its customers and can make employees feel good about themselves and the organization. They are excellent in the top position if given free reign to manage, but they may rebel and become disloyal if they perceive themselves as having too

many constraints. They can easily nurture a following which is loyal to them personally rather than to the organization. They may have authority-figure problems and thus may intentionally undermine the organization if they see authorities as being in conflict with their personal values and belief systems.

Vinnicombe (1987) sees this description as relating to Gloria Steinem's observation that women tend to define power differently, that is as the ability to use their own talents and to control their own lives. In working with people, they are much more collaborative and cooperative and far less hierarchical and authoritative than men. She argues that there is a great need for organizations to recognize the worth of different managerial working styles and that it is the predominance of the 'traditionalist' style which is squeezing women managers out of organizational life.

These views, however, must be balanced against claims that there are very few or *no differences between male and female leaders*. Dobbins and Platz (1986), in a review of the literature, concluded that men and women were not generally perceived to exhibit differing amounts or kinds of leadership behaviour. Similar findings were reported by Powell (1988), who undertook an extensive review of research on management styles and discovered that the similarities between the approaches by far outweigh the differences. Indeed, Powell felt that the only real difference between men and women in management may be in the environment in which they operate. This echoes Kanter's observations about women's interpersonal relationship styles being a result of their inferior position in the organization. It may be that this observed similarity is due to the fact that Adler's equity model, in which women aim to become integrated into the predominant (male) style of management, is more pervasive in the United States and the United Kingdom, where most of the research was carried out.

Perceptual problems in selection and appraisal

The inherent assumption that if women 'overcome their own individual disadvantages' and become equal to men in terms of education, experience and motivation they will achieve the same levels of promotion as men, is contested by Adler (1993). She posits that institutional discrimination exists in which assumptions about who is suitable to be a manager are based on societal assumptions about women and men. This results in a situation where organizations do not perceive women as naturally acceptable in positions of real power and authority. The strength of ingrained assumptions about gender roles means that few people question the perpetuation of such a system.

The effect of gender schemas developed from the stereotypes grown over a lifetime is demonstrated in two studies by Heilman et al. Looking at perceived causes of work success in organizations, Heilman and Guzzo (1978) found that equally qualified women received unequal rewards for their job performance in comparison with men as a result of a perception that women's success was a matter of luck as opposed to ability. Heilman and Saruwatari (1979) postulated that gender stereotypes lay behind the problems encountered by 'attractive' women when applying for traditional male jobs.

Impact of organizational systems

Organizational factors affecting women's career development have been extensively researched, most notably by Kanter (1977). Characteristics such as the underrepresentation of women in management, tokenism, whereby a solitary member of a minority group, i.e. women, is promoted to a senior position, and unequal opportunities for promotion were reported to have a major influence on women's behaviour and attitudes towards managerial ambitions. Such an analysis, however, assumes that organizations are gender-neutral and does not take into account the possibility of institutional discrimination as posited by Adler (1993).

Two issues are particularly important in this respect: first, the concept of power and gender in organizations, and secondly, the effect of exclusion from an organization's informal networks on women's career progress.

Ragins and Sundstrom (1989) explore the relationship between power and gender in organizations from a longitudinal perspective, arguing that power develops over time and grows out of an accumulation of resources during a person's career. They argue that for women the path to power resembles an obstacle course. Adler (1993) argues that one reason current (male) managers limit the number of women managers is simply that they do not want more competition. The extent to which they can influence the situation depends on their power and authority within the organization, with the most senior managers being able to determine organizational rules in ways that will impede women's progression to the highest ranks of management.

Marshall (1984) stresses the importance of an organization's informal networks in fostering conformity to reduce uncertainty and risk, thereby excluding unusual categories of employees such as women. The importance of informal networks in aiding career progression has been widely acknowledged. Women face additional obstacles to men in this respect as their exclusion from networks does not allow them to build vital contacts and networking skills. Once again, this situation is changing, with evidence of the development of women's networks and a growing awareness of the necessity of networking amongst managerial women.

As a result of many of these underlying factors, researchers conclude that women managers experience additional stressors in the work environment in comparison to men. Davidson and Cooper (1987) identify these stressors as prejudice and sex stereotyping, overt and indirect discrimination, lack of role models, tokenism and work/family issues. These pressures result in many women becoming blocked on the management ladder or 'opting-out' by leaving the organization altogether.

5   The role of women in international management

Given the significant problems facing women managers on the domestic scene, what opportunities or threats does an increase in demand for international management experience create for women?

The fact that greater barriers exist for women in expatriate management is demonstrated by a comparison of the numbers of female managers in the United States (approximately 40 percent) and the United Kingdom (approximately 27 percent) and the numbers of female expatriate managers emanating from the same two countries (estimated at about 3–5 percent). Very little research has been carried out concerning female expatriates, mainly due to their scarcity. Organizational reactions to women expatriate managers tend, therefore, to reflect assumptions about the ability and suitability of women working in foreign countries. Adler (1993) argues that often, as a result of a historical scarcity of local women managers in most countries, firms have questioned whether women can function successfully in cross-border managerial assignments. Another reason for a negative appraisal of the potential of women expatriate managers may be a tendency for organizations to confuse the role of female expatriate managers with that of the expatriate partner, whose failure to adapt has been one of the most commonly cited reasons for premature expatriate returns (Brewster, 1991). However, the far more ambiguous role of the expatriate partner entails very different problems of adjustment from those faced by female expatriate managers.

If we look beyond these initial misapprehensions, a combination of organizational and socio-cultural factors can be seen to play a large part in the minimal representation of women in expatriate management positions. This section will briefly examine some of the major determinants of women's entry to and successful completion of international assignments.

Organizational factors

One constant that should be borne in mind is the effect of sex role stereotyping and gender schemas on women's access to international management positions. Research evidence points to widely used 'pools' of employees with high potential within companies from which future international managers are picked. Initial assessment of 'high potential' takes place at a very early stage in an employee's career. First postings for people identified in 'high potential pools' are often not implemented until the individuals have acquired a certain level of maturity and management experience within the domestic environment; the age range would therefore be late twenties to mid thirties. As a result of our earlier discussion of the causes of the 'glass ceiling', it can be seen that women face additional barriers; first, in being picked as showing 'high potential', and secondly, in being able to comply with the service requirements.

Earlier in this chapter, the issue of women's reported superiority in relational and cross-cultural skills was discussed. It was shown that, despite evidence that such skills are predictive criteria of success in expatriate positions, organizations still look for technical competence as the main criterion in expatriate selection procedures (Brewster, 1991). Growing criticism of reliance on the 'hard skills' of management within both the domestic and international business environment may well provide the impetus for a more balanced selection procedure in this respect.

Edström and Galbraith (1977) posit that some MNCs use international transfers of managers as a method of control based on socialization. In this process 'socialized' managers create international, verbal information networks which will influence the distribution of power in organizations. The authors see the process of socialization being achieved by frequent transfers, forcing the manager to sacrifice many of the advantages of a stable domestic life, becoming more committed to the organization, growing to rely on organizational culture and losing attachments to other social systems so that the organization is the only constant factor in life. Under such circumstances, women are doubly disadvantaged. First, as we have seen, women are often excluded from informal organization networks and consequently have less access to positions of power in organizations (Marshall, 1984; Ragins and Sundstrom, 1989). Secondly, the requirement for frequent transfers and 'sacrifice' may well be more difficult for women to comply with than men, given their traditional family responsibilities.

Although the impact of informal organizational systems remains inadequately documented, revision of selection procedures to encompass broader 'feeder' channels and to emphasize skills related to international assignment success could trigger a substantial increase in the number of women being offered foreign postings. However, male resistance to women expatriate managers in such a traditionally male-dominated area may be much stronger than at the domestic level.

Socio-cultural factors

Women in general face additional constraints to men in deciding to take up international assignments. Our earlier mention of Devanna's (1987) observations concerning contextual influences on motivation for men and women are particularly relevant to the international scenario where socio-cultural factors become especially problematic.

Host country cultural barriers

A major limiting factor to international management participation for women has traditionally been managers' perceptions of whether women can undertake assignments abroad. In a survey of 60 major North American MNCs, more then 50 percent expressed reluctance to select female managers for foreign assignments. One of the major reasons given was that foreigners are prejudiced against female managers (Adler, 1984a).

Subsequent research by Adler (1987) amongst US women expatriates working in South-East Asian countries challenges the validity of this assumption by finding a very high rate of success amongst women international managers, largely due to the fact that women were seen as foreigners who happened to be women, not as women who happened to be foreigners – a subtle, but highly significant distinction. Female expatriate managers were therefore not subject to the same limitations imposed on local females.

Examples of interviewees' responses from Adler's study are:

Japan: 'It's the novelty, especially in Japan, Korea, and Pakistan. All of the general managers met with me . . . It was much easier for me, especially in Osaka. They were charming. They didn't want me to feel bad. They thought I would come back if they gave me business. You see, they could separate me from the local women.'

Pakistan: 'Will I have problems? No! There is a double standard between expats and local women. The Pakistanis test you, but you enter as a respected person.'

The question of host-country cultural prejudices as a major barrier to women's employment in expatriate positions appears to have been debated only from the point of view of women going to traditionally male-dominated cultures. Little research has been carried out into women's experiences when transferring to countries with similar or more relaxed cultural values, for instance British women expatriates working in North America or Europe, or female expatriates from Pacific Rim countries working in Australia or North America, where the literature would argue there should be fewer problems of acceptance for female managers/professionals.

The question of how men are affected by cultural differences in the area of international management is an important issue in this respect. There is increasing research into cross-cultural adaptation and its links to expatriate adjustment and performance. A related question revolves around the subject of culturally determined managerial behaviours and their relationship to performance during assignments abroad. According to the 'cross-cultural' school of thought, the effectiveness of a particular managerial behaviour is a function of the culture in which the behaviour is performed. The basic logic for such a position is that because managerial attitudes and values differ from one culture to another, so do effective managerial behaviours.

Despite conflicting research results as to the extent to which cross-cultural differences can affect expatriate management performance, it is important to note that these issues relate to the expatriate management population as a whole. One can then question the validity of the argument put forward by very many companies that women will not perform successfully in expatriate management positions as a result of host country cultural sanctions against females. It is necessary to examine the exact nature of these claims; for instance, to which countries do they refer, what is the basis for the claims – women's actual experiences, the opinions of host-country managers, of existing male expatriate managers or of home-country managers? Unless women can be seen to be directly prevented from entering and working in a country as a result of cultural sanctions, it would appear that they would be subject to the same problems as men in terms of cross-cultural effectiveness. Evidence from the literature would support the claim that women are potentially better suited to international management in view of their superior interpersonal and communication skills. However, Adler's survey of women expatriates in the Pacific Rim region found they had experienced numerous instances of corporate resistance to sending them abroad. For example:

> According to one woman being considered for an assignment in Malaysia: 'Management assumed that women don't have the physical stamina to survive in the tropics. They claimed I couldn't hack it.'

Several women were offered positions only if there were no suitable male candidates for the post:

> Japan: 'They never would have considered me. But then the financial manager in Tokyo had a heart attack and they had to send someone. So they sent me, on a month's notice, as a temporary until they could find a man to fill the permanent position. It worked out and I stayed.'

Firms often expressed their hesitancy by sending women in temporary or lower-status positions:

> Hong Kong: 'After offering me the job, they hesitated, "Could a woman work with the Chinese?" So my job was defined as temporary, a one-year position to train a Chinese man to replace me. I succeeded and became permanent.'

Lack of confidence on the part of organizations can communicate itself to foreign colleagues and clients, thus making it even harder for women to be taken seriously (Adler, 1987). It may well be, therefore, that worries about women being accepted as expatriate managers stem more from male managers in the home country organization blaming other cultures for their own prejudices, as postulated by Moran (1985), than from a correct interpretation of reality.

Dual-career issues

The Adler survey (1984a) also highlighted the potential barriers posed by work/family considerations, in particular the issues facing dual-career couples. The traditional profile of the expatriate manager has been male, married and accompanied on the assignment by his family. This profile is now changing, with the US Department of Labor predicting that by 1995, 81 percent of all marriages will be dual-career partnerships (Reynolds and Bennett, 1991). Such dynamics imply that fewer employees will be willing to relocate, either domestically or internationally, without assistance for their partners. Given the evidence that both dual-career couples and women expatriate managers are increasing (Brewster, 1991), international firms will need to address the issue of dual-career couples in international transfers, as well as the specific case of the husband as partner in these transfers. There has been relatively little research on the topic, with much of the research confined to domestic transfers (Rapoport and Rapoport, 1976), whilst the research on international transfers has considered the role of the partner in the success or failure of the expatriate, only from the perspective of a non-working partner (Brewster, 1988).

The problems of spousal adjustment in international assignments would appear to be magnified when considering women expatriates and their partners. In this respect, male partners face additional role transition obstacles in terms of adjusting to the role of secondary breadwinner or homemaker, if they cannot find work in the foreign location. Socio-cultural norms relating to career models make it easier for women to make these transitions than men, with potentially damaging repercussions for men making negative or neutral career moves (Sekaran, 1986). Additional socio-cultural barriers include the likelihood of the male partner finding himself the lone man in a group of women and the unavailability or inappropriateness of traditional volunteer activities which women undertake in foreign locations, thus limiting the extent of productive activities for males (Punnett et al., 1992). Successful transitions are even more difficult across national boundaries as a result of practical barriers such as work permit restrictions which make it impossible for a partner to work, and differing requirements in relation to professional qualifications, which can affect career advancement.

On an individual level, partners accustomed to working and having a career may be particularly frustrated if they cannot work. These problems are likely to add to an already stressful transfer situation and may perhaps increase the possibility of failure. It is likely that the emotional stress will be even greater in the case of a male partner as a result of the aforementioned socio-cultural norms (Punnett et al., 1992).

Few companies have any formal policies in relation to dual-career couples. Reynolds and Bennett (1991) describe some of the most common ones used by US organizations:

- Career and life planning counselling. Assists the couple in clarifying and prioritizing long- and short-term personal and professional goals in the context of the assignment abroad.
- Inter-company networking. Identification of job openings in other companies. Setting up 'job banks' for accompanying partners.
- Job-hunting/fact-finding trips. Companies differ in the amount allowed and expenses provided.
- Continuing education. Tuition reimbursement and assistance with school entrance formalities at institutions abroad.
- International partner assistance programmes. Various outplacement firms and community organizations abroad (with corporate and government support). Offer job counselling, networking groups and assistance programmes in business centres abroad.
- Intra-company employment. Opportunities created for partners by companies which do not have anti-nepotism rules.

- Commuter marriage support. Ensures coverage of regular visitation trips, housing, telephone and related expenses.
- Short-term assignments. Designed for high-potential employees to go abroad for professional development reasons if there is no other resolution of the dual-career problem.

It should be noted that the literature suggests that most of these activities are based on the assumption that the 'trailing partner' is female. An exploratory study of women expatriates with partners, carried out in Canada, asked the women which activities would be most useful in assisting partners to find career-oriented activities in the foreign location. The results are shown below.

- Longer preparation time for the move.
- Realistic pre-departure information on foreign job opportunities.
- Pre-move trip to make employment contacts.
- Help in obtaining requisite visas, permits etc.
- Career-oriented employment networks.
- Executive search services.
- Letters of introduction, office space, secretarial support, other job-hunting services.
- Financial and social recognition for assistance to the employee.
- Preference for available jobs within the organization.
- Creation of career-oriented position at appropriate level.
- Dual transfers where both partners work for the same organization.
- Job-sharing when both partners are in the same field.
- Similar support when returning home (also for those who meet partners abroad).
- Provision of unemployment benefits, pensions etc.
- Funds for career-oriented research work.
- Funds for career-oriented education.

Whilst there appears to be a willingness to look for solutions to the dual-career issue for male employees, companies still tend to use dual-career problems as a reason for not selecting potential female expatriates. This behaviour is essentially illogical if the assumption is made that dual-career couples fall into a pattern of 'superordinate partners' (Powell, 1988). In this case both partners value both work and family activities and set the goal of achieving satisfaction in both domains for both partners. In such a case the potential male expatriates will experience as many constraints as females.

Punnett et al. (1992) have suggested priorities for future research into this topic.

- The costs of ignoring dual-career couples internationally: e.g. costs associated with transfer refusals, less than optimal choices, poor performance, expatriate failure.

- The decision-making process used by dual-career couples in considering international assignments: e.g. the perceived positive and negative aspects.
- The impact of current social values on willingness to accept or decline international transfers: e.g. upward mobility or success, homemaking, childrearing.
- The dynamics of the process: e.g. decisions and trade-offs relative to age, sex, career stage, family.
- The reality of success/failure: e.g. success/failure rates for various groups, the relationship to factors such as the partner's ability to work, finding work, undertaking other productive activities.
- Country-specific concerns for dual-career couples and male partners: e.g. social barriers to apparent role reversals, legal barriers to work.

It is evident that much work needs to be done in this area to provide a clearer picture of the needs and experiences of both male and female partners in dual-career relationships and to enable organizations to design effective programmes to deal with these complex issues. Currently, work/family considerations are still likely to be more of a problem for married women than for married men. Despite changing socio-cultural trends, it is still rare for a man to give up a job to accompany a partner abroad. The situation is, however, dynamic and within a relatively short space of time companies which ignore this problem may well find themselves with a very small pool of potential recruits, comprising mainly single people or older, more traditional, male expatriates.

Advantages for female expatriate managers

In the light of the many disadvantages faced by women expatriate managers, the advantages are harder to define. Adler (1993) summarizes some potential advantages from her research studies as follows.

- *Visibility*. Many of the women in Adler's study of expatriates in the Pacific Rim countries reported the advantage of being highly visible, as foreign clients were curious about them and anxious to meet them. They were also more easily remembered.
- *Interpersonal skills*. The female managers in the study also discovered a number of advantages relating to their interpersonal skills; local men, for instance, appeared to be able to talk to them more easily than to other male expatriates about a wide range of topics.
- *Novelty*. Because of the rarity of women in expatriate management positions, many foreign clients assume that the women who are sent must be 'the best'. This situation is likely to change with the appearance of more and more expatriate women managers.
- *Domestic help*. Some of the role overload experienced by female managers in general can be alleviated on expatriate assignments by the availability of domestic help.

Avenues for change

Increased participation for women in expatriate management is a possibility if both organizations and women adopt a flexible approach to
international assignments. Adler (1993) cites several approaches for both
organizations and individuals.

Organizations

- Avoid assumptions as to the likely motivation to go and the likely
  success rate of women expatriates.
- Provide flexible benefits packages which will cater for single employees
  and dual-career couples as well as the traditional 'married male with
  family' expatriate.
- Define the expatriate assignment in such a way that the chances
  of success are high: that is, establishing full-status, permanent
  assignments.

Women

- Adopt an 'educative' approach to organizational resistance to sending
  women abroad; do not assume it is the result of direct prejudice.
- Ensure excellence in the professional field to aid selection. Also, try to
  be in the right place at the right time.
- Address private life issues directly. Use networks wherever possible.

The growth of international business is a continuing phenomenon and, by
its nature, will need to incorporate the most talented human resources. It is
unlikely that these will be found within the ranks of male employees only.
Adler (1993) looks to the transnational corporation as a fitting role model
in terms of hiring and promoting women to significant international
management positions as a result of competitive advantage considerations.
These trends indicate that women will take a more active part in
international management in the future; the question is: how rapidly and to
what extent?

6　Summary and conclusions

This chapter has looked at the process of international management as it
relates to women, taking into account individual, organizational, economic
and socio-cultural perspectives. It has examined the impact of increasing
internationalization of business in terms of the types of skills required for
effective international managers and has contrasted the theory with the
actual practice adopted by many MNCs. The extent to which international
experience will become a prerequisite for access to senior management
positions has also been debated.

The role of women in international management was reviewed by
looking first at major influences affecting female managers' representation
and contributions at home country level. Secondly, additional barriers
facing potential female expatriates were examined, including host country
cultural barriers and problems of dual-career couples.

Opportunities for increased representation of women in expatriate management were highlighted by research evidence contradicting the myth that women would not be successful in expatriate assignments. The extent to which women will participate in this arena depends, however, on the willingness of both the organization and the individuals involved to adopt a flexible and positive approach to existing constraints.

12 Compensation and appraisal of international staff

Ed Logger and Rob Vinke

1	Introduction	252
2	International staff: a different compensation perspective	252
	Term of the assignment	253
3	Compensation of international staff	255
	Objectives of compensation	255
	Methods of compensation	256
	The budget system	256
	The balance sheet or home-net system	257
	The local going-rate system	259
	Differences per country	260
4	Appraisal of international staff	261
	Adding an extra dimension to the appraisal	261
	Appraisal criteria	262
	Current points of appraisal	263
5	Developments in the field of Euro-compensation	264
	International compensation policy	264
	ECU points	266
6	Summary and conclusions	269

1 Introduction

This chapter deals with the appraisal and compensation of international staff. First, the special position of international staff will be looked at. Subsequently, we shall discuss the different compensation methods used in multinational companies, such as the budget system, balance sheet system and local going-rate system. Section 4 sets out the criteria for appraising international staff and discusses the problems which may be encountered during the appraisal. Finally, we shall report on recent developments in this field and draw special attention to the concept of Euro-compensation.

2 International staff: a different compensation perspective

The term international staff refers to those who hold management positions with international organizations. International staff members are not only confronted with cross-border decisions, but are also expected to cross the frontiers themselves.

Chapter 8 shows that base pay still varies considerably from country to country. Additionally, differences in terms of performance pay or such other benefits as pensions and company cars may further increase the income gap. In the past few years, notably in Europe, attempts have been made to reduce the differences in tax and social security contributions. Although there is still a long way to go, some progress has been made. Against the backdrop of frontiers and differences which are becoming increasingly diffuse, and anticipating the globalization of what used to be domestic markets, international organizations have begun to feel the need to formulate a policy or review existing policies regarding staff who work or will be working abroad for a short or long period of time.

The manner in which organizations currently compensate their assigned staff will be described below. It should be borne in mind that the traditional expatriates of large multinationals are increasingly being re-placed by a more internationally-oriented management corps. These employees must not only be internationally versatile, they also have to be fitted into a compensation policy different from the old policy aimed at individuals and consisting of one-off reimbursements for expatriate 'dis-comforts'. Thus, companies are increasingly seeking new forms of compen-sation, first to rule out the 'excrescences' of expatriation and, secondly, to be able to treat international assignments as inherent to a staff member's career, so that no special compensation is required. The final section of this chapter will set out alternative methods of compensation which may, to some extent, offset the disadvantages of the old pay systems.

This chapter primarily deals with the material aspects of international compensation. One should not forget, however, that an international posting may in itself be a reward. In the first place, it can be a direct reward in that the foreign activities are an added challenge or perhaps already constitute a promotion. And secondly, it can be an indirect reward since the assignment may decisively influence an employee's future career opportunities inside or outside the organization.

Term of the assignment

The nature of the assignment to a large extent determines the method of compensation. An important factor is the term of the assignment.

1   *Short-term assignment.* The assignment may be for a relatively short period, such as in the case of a feasibility study. This type of assignment does not usually exceed six months. In general, assignments of up to one year are considered short-term. Family members do not generally accom-pany the employee on the assignment.

2   *Long-term assignment.* If the assignment is for more than one year, it will usually result in the employee and his or her family 'moving house'. Depending on the individual situation (age, family, social status and so on)

and the extent to which the new local situation differs from the old one, extra efforts will have to be made to turn the assignment into a success. An assignment from the Netherlands to a developing country is likely to entail greater change than an assignment, say, to Germany. Distance is of less importance in this respect. For example, being transferred from the Netherlands to Spain may entail greater adjustment than being transferred to the United States.

3   *'Permanent' assignment.* This is when an employee signs what should, in principle, amount to a permanent employment contract with a foreign subsidiary. The assignment may conceivably fall short of the company's or the employee's expectations, so the contract is usually made for a fixed period of time. Still, the intention is for the employee to stay on.

Base pay and perquisites vary according to these three categories. Generally, one can say that the longer a planned assignment abroad is, the more the principles and local environment of the host company should determine the compensation of the employee. Employees who fall into the first category are not usually called expatriates. Their assignment is of such a short duration that pay and benefits remain linked to compensation in the home country. After all, the employees must still pay the on-going costs, such as rent or mortgage, insurances, costs for keeping the family etc. incurred in their home country. The assignment could be seen as a long business trip which 'has got out of hand'. However, the expenses incurred for food, clothing, housing and the like will often be 'liberally' reimbursed. Obviously, for longer short-term assignments, companies will allow their employees to visit their families once or twice during the term of their assignment.

Expatriates are those employees who are on long-term assignments. However, many international companies do not make a distinction between long-term and permanent assignments and thus have a number of 'permanent' expatriates on their pay-roll. In principle, this situation should not have any special consequences in terms of pay, because many multinationals take the view that their expatriate compensation policies are aimed at guaranteeing that the individual employee is in any case not worse off, but also not much better off, if assigned abroad. The latter is a strong understatement, which hardly reflects reality. On the contrary, there are employees who strive to become expatriates because they are so well paid. Expenses which exceed the level in the home country are almost always reimbursed, in most cases without the cheaper expenses being deducted. To be added to this are the costs of the employee and his or her family going home (by air) on leave or during a holiday. 'Additional' costs further include housing, removal, language courses and education of the children and, last but not least, measures to support the partner's position. In the next section we shall discuss in detail the compensation methods used for long-term assignments, including the local going-rate system, which should, basically, be suitable for permanent assignments.

We have already noted that an employee is called an expatriate in the case of a long-term assignment. It should be added, however, that an

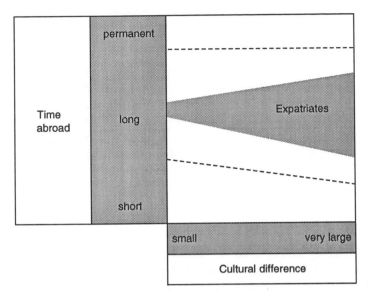

Figure 12.1   *What is an expatriate? (Hay Group)*

employee stands a greater chance of being considered an expatriate when assigned to a country whose culture differs significantly from that of his or her own (for example, from the Netherlands to Zambia rather than, say, France). In countries with fewer cultural differences, the assignment will have to be for a longer period if the term expatriate is to apply and any special (that is to say, more liberal) compensation to be paid. Figure 12.1 illustrates this point.

3   Compensation of international staff

Objectives of compensation

As with national compensation policies, international compensation policies are not an end in themselves, but a means to achieve certain company objectives. Robock and Simmonds (1983) argue that an effective compensation policy for international staff should strive to meet the following objectives:

1   Attract and retain employees qualified for service abroad.
2   Facilitate transfers between foreign affiliates and between home-country and foreign affiliates.
3   Establish and maintain a consistent and reasonable relationship between compensation of all of the employees of any affiliate, whether posted at home or abroad, and between affiliates.
4   Arrange reasonable compensation, in the various locations, in relation to the practices of leading competitors.

To this we might add:

5   Be cost-effective.

Of course, these objectives will often be conflicting. A generous pay package will certainly attract and retain employees, but will not be very cost-effective. Consistent and reasonable compensation of all employees within an affiliate will often not facilitate transfers between foreign affiliates if the general level of compensation is very different between countries (see discussion of the local going-rate system below). In the next section we will discuss various methods of compensation that all attempt to meet one or more of the objectives stated above.

Methods of compensation

There are many methods to compensate international staff. The bottom line will always be that the assigned employee must be compensated for what he or she misses out on. Economic factors play a role, but also the quality of the employee's social life. As a rule, the assignment abroad is preceded by fresh negotiations between the employer and employee, particularly where the assignment is likely to interrupt the employee's career. Almost all compensation methods, however, are variations of the following three systems:

- the budget system;
- the balance sheet or home-net system;
- the local going-rate system.

The balance sheet system will be most extensively dealt with, since it is used by the majority of companies.

The budget system

This system takes in all costs incurred by the employee in both countries (the home country and host country). These costs, and the effects of the local tax system, form the basis on which the employee's income is calculated. The system is extremely expensive to keep up because of the many adjustments which need to be made, notably in high-inflation countries. This method used to be popular in the colonization era, which probably explains why nowadays it is only used by a few large, paternalistic British companies, and then especially in developing countries. An assignment from Britain to India will, for example, result in lower expenses for clothing, food and other fixed or variable private expenditure. These costs are meticulously compared and totalled. Admittedly, account is also taken of the employee's on-going expenses in the home country. The net total is subsequently grossed up and incorporated in the (British) salary. The result is that the company completely controls the expatriate's prescribed spending pattern in an attempt to maintain the British standard of life. Problems may occur if products or services are not locally available, so the costs of importing these products are also included in the detailed calculation.

This system has been subject to criticism from expatriates. The fact that the employer determines what items will and will not be included in the budget is often seen as paternalistic. Moreover, once expatriates know what items are included in the budget, they will certainly try to get other (expensive) items on the list. They feel that they know best what they will need in the host country. Checking these items is hardly feasible without an independent company representative paying regular visits to compare local prices and needs, which would, of course, be very expensive. An added drawback is that the system may well stir up ill-feeling among host-country nationals, when 'luxury' goods such as imported cheese and whisky are considered as basic essentials for the expatriate employees.

The balance sheet or home-net system

The premise underlying the balance sheet system is that the same net sum must be available in both countries. In this context, 'net' does not mean net salary after taxes and social security contributions. It means the freely disposable income. The idea is that spending power must be identical in both countries. Consequently, allowances will have to be made for cost of living, housing and generally accepted spending patterns.

The original gross income in the home country is reduced step by step by all premiums and costs. It is essential to define beforehand what costs and premiums should be included in the comparison. So mortgage costs (or their tax consequences) or car expenses may or may not contribute to the ultimate net result, which is the freely disposable income. After that, a cost-of-living parity may be applied. Let us take as an example an assignment from the Netherlands to Denmark, which will result in a new income expressed in Danish kroner and calculated as follows.

gross income in the Netherlands	DFL 90,000
less pension premiums	3,200
less social security contributions	18,800
less income tax	22,200
less health insurance premiums	2,500
less housing costs	9,000
less car expenses	12,000
net income in the Netherlands	DFL 22,300

Subsequently, a correction may be made to maintain the spending power of the net disposable income (food, clothing, personal care, household utensils, leisure activities and so on). The spending-power parity between the Netherlands and Denmark has been set at 1.2, meaning that the same net amount buys 20 percent more in the Netherlands. At a rate of 27 Dutch cents to one Danish krone, DFL 22,300 results in DKK 99,100 (= 22,300 ×

1.2/0.27). The ultimate gross (Danish) income will be calculated in reverse order.

net income in Denmark	DKK 99,100
add car expenses	44,000
add housing costs	28,000
add health insurance premiums	8,500
add income tax	142,900
add social security contributions	2,100
add pension premiums	12,000
gross income in Denmark	DKK 336,600

In this example, we arrive at nearly the same income as we would have, had we simply translated the gross Dutch income into Danish kroner (DFL 90,000/0.27 = DKK 333,333). This outcome can be explained by the fact that although items like food, clothing and household utensils are more expensive in Denmark (the spending power of the net Danish income is lower before correction), the costs – and thus the additions – of housing, health insurance and income tax/social security, in particular, are lower in Denmark (note the different way of financing social security; in Denmark, this is done almost entirely through taxation, while in the Netherlands a large portion is funded by social security contributions). Obviously, this will not always be the case.

The benefit of the balance sheet or home-net system is that the expatriate is guaranteed his home-country spending power. Moreover, it results in transparent and explainable differences between the salaries of expatriates who hold equivalent positions in different countries. A major drawback of the system is that it may cause large salary gaps within one and the same subsidiary, particularly between parent-country nationals and host-country nationals.

Companies applying this system are faced with two important questions. First, in recalculating the salary from gross to net and vice versa, should the costs actually incurred in the individual cases be included or should standard items be used? Considerations of efficiency and privacy would advocate the second option, doing justice to individual exceptions would require the first. Large companies hardly have any choice but to opt for standard items. If they do not, the administrative hassle would quickly get out of hand.

The second question is: in grossing up the net income in the host country, should strictly identical items (same car and housing) be included or should the aim be to achieve a social position comparable to that in the parent country? To illustrate this dilemma, consider the example of the assignment of an American (top) manager to the Netherlands. Can he maintain his Cadillac, house and swimming pool, tennis court and four acres of land in the Netherlands, or will he have to 'settle' for a Mercedes of the 500 series and a detached villa set on 1,000 square metres of land in Wassenaar, or a penthouse in the centre of Amsterdam? In view of the costs, companies will nearly always choose the second option, which does not mean to say that an assignment from the United States to the Netherlands, or even Tokyo, may not still be very problematic for the individual in question.

But it does not end there. On top of the gross income, a wide variety of allowances may be paid, such as:

- allowances to cover the specific costs associated with a country;
- allowances to cover personal discomfort or general hardship.

The first category may include the school fees of the employee's children, provided that the fees clearly deviate from those paid in the home country. Membership fees of social clubs are also often translated into a fixed allowance. For countries where taking on private personnel is common practice, standard sums are set. The second category concerns hardship allowances paid to compensate for a very warm or very cold climate, poor communications, language problems, food shortages, political risks, seclusion, viral epidemics, earthquakes and so on. A general allowance may also be paid to compensate for family separation. In the above example of the Danish assignment, it is highly improbable that the second category, compensation for discomfort and hardship, is even so much as discussed. Even so, there are international companies which set the total sum of allowances at a fixed percentage of the salary. This percentage will, of course, vary according to country, and be revised at least once a year.

A long-term stay abroad may often only be completed successfully if the employee is allowed regularly to visit the home front. The majority of arrangements or contracts contain provisions specifying the number of paid visits that may be made (often by air). There are no general standards, but the number of visits will naturally depend on the family situation and the distance between the home country and host country, both geographically and in terms of culture. Expatriates who are joined by their families are usually granted a minimum of one visit a year. Of course, this is also a major subject of negotiation before the assignment starts.

Using the balance sheet method does not necessarily mean that the employee will hold the same income position in the host country. The Dutch income calculated above may have been reasonable or conform to market standards for similar positions in the Netherlands. In Denmark, it could well be considered very low or very high. In our example, a Danish income of DKK 370,000 would have been more realistic from a market point of view. Thus, the system may generate income differences between local employees and expatriates as it fails to include market-induced compensation levels. If companies wish to take market standards into account, they should preferably use the local going-rate system.

The local going-rate system

Under the local going-rate system, the expatriate is paid according to standards in the host country. This prevents the situation where junior staff are paid substantially higher salaries than the expatriate, who is compensated in conformity with the standards of income in his parent country.

Cases in point are countries like Germany and Switzerland, where the general level of compensation is significantly higher than in other European countries. This method is considerably less popular in the reverse case. Employees would not like the prospect of being assigned to a less prosperous country under this system, as it will result in profoundly lower salaries. Thus, the local going-rate system is mostly used for assignments to countries with clearly higher compensation levels. The fact that the host country could, at the same time, have lower levels of perquisites and benefits could be a reason for an expatriate to insist on maintaining the home-country package for this part of the salary. Companies are generally willing to accommodate this requirement. Again, the base salary is usually increased by various allowances to compensate for extra housing costs, international schools and family visits.

Differences per country

Basically, the way in which companies compensate their expatriates hardly differs from country to country. The balance sheet system has been the most common system so far. The organizations which render advice on what sums of compensation and extra allowances should actually be paid almost always have branch offices in many countries. They regularly adjust their compensation schedules to be able to provide an up-to-date picture. It is hardly feasible for companies to maintain such (expensive) systems themselves. In determining the actual compensation to be paid, the organizations still take as a basis the question from which country to which country the employee is transferred.

The local going-rate system is little used internationally. But with tax and social security systems increasingly converging, the system may well catch on. However, a proper comparison between countries will require the use of a job evaluation system which can be applied internationally. After all, companies need to have an insight into the usual income position of host-country nationals in equivalent jobs.

Remarkably, employees who are posted abroad on a permanent basis are often also eligible for expatriate treatment. Using a strict local going-rate system without too many allowances would seem more appropriate in those situations. In fact, international companies have begun to adjust their assignment policies by better defining this 'permanent' category and by treating them more like local employees with regard to compensation.

The belief long held by parent companies that one or more important positions abroad should necessarily be occupied by staff from headquarters is on the wane, although it is still current in companies of Japanese or Anglo-Saxon origin. In other countries, assignments are increasingly looked upon from a management development angle. Business expertise very much depends on the years spent abroad. In that light, companies have begun to review their compensation policies. Clearly, the time has come to find other methods of compensating international or European managers and employees from a career point of view. We shall discuss this trend in more detail in Section 5. Section 4 deals with the problems surrounding the appraisal of international staff members.

4 Appraisal of international staff

Adding an extra dimension to the appraisal

A temporary or permanent transfer to a neighbouring or far-off country, either with a comparable or a totally different culture, will undoubtedly contribute to the employee's experience. The experience gained by managers and specialists alike is of great value to the company. Understanding of local problems, knowledge of local methods and techniques and a better insight into the interrelation between local and central corporate interests are but a few of the many accomplishments where expertise gained can be translated into improved future performance.

In order to find out whether the newly gained experience has in fact benefited the company, a proper appraisal must be made. Besides, an appraisal is also important to the employee in material terms. A favourable appraisal will usually result in a pay rise, bonus or promotion. Properly appraising an employee is not easy; appraising expatriates adds an extra dimension to the problem. In most cases, the final appraisal is done in the parent country, where the appraisers have little or no knowledge of local circumstances, and the context of the performance may be lost. Achieving the same results in an unknown country may well require large efforts in terms of flexibility and creativity, both of which are difficult to quantify.

In view of the geographical and communicative distance between the expatriate and the appraiser, local management are often called in to give their opinion. They are supposed to be familiar with the expatriate's performance and be able to explain the local situation and environment-related factors. Their comments are, however, dictated by their local cultural background. Thus, a manager who is used to guiding and supervising a group through involvement and participation could receive a negative appraisal in a local culture where managers are expected to show strong leadership and be the ones that come up with ideas and initiatives. In such an environment, the appraisal will presumably be to the manager's disadvantage, although he may have made every possible effort and his performance would be termed excellent in the home country. The opinion of an 'ex-expatriate' would be needed to put the situation right.

Depending on the cultural gap, the first six months of an assignment will be used for introduction and adjustment, before the expatriate will be able properly to fulfil his duties. Those first six months will centre on communication, that is to say, mastering the language and getting to know the culture. It is advisable to specify in advance the most important performance areas for the term of the assignment, and indicate who will appraise each area.

Appraisal criteria

In a number of fields, there are differences between national and international staff members working in similar positions. These differences are in many cases qualitative in nature. Thus, the criteria for appraising international staff should take in not only the differences but especially the similarities between them. After all, the international staff member must remain part of the national organization in terms of appraisal too. Table 12.1 shows the main criteria that are used. It should be noted that companies may, on the basis of these main criteria, determine whether the candidate is suitable for assignment, and subsequently, if the candidate is assigned, appraise whether he or she has performed to satisfaction. In Chapter 10 we pointed out the importance of the link between selection and appraisal criteria. The same criteria may be applied to investigate training needs, all of which will result in a more integrated HRM policy.

Every main criterion is usually divided into a few sub-criteria. It is also decided where the emphasis will be put. A combination of criteria may be used, depending on the employee's job description. However, everyday practice shows that detailed criteria such as those listed in Table 12.1 are sometimes less strictly applied and companies confine themselves to making such broad statements as: 'to close down the foreign subsidiary within one year subject to the appropriate legal restrictions'. The targets are linked to a compensation package, and it should be noted that there

Table 12.1 *Criteria for appraisal*

Qualifications
  Training
  Experience
  Technical skills
  Social and language skills

Targets
  Directly derived from the company's objectives
  Directly derived from the subsidiary's objectives
  Directly derived from local objectives
  Individually dictated

Attitude so far
  Flexibility
  Interpersonal understanding
  Ability to cope with stress
  Openness to change

Job performance
  Result areas
  Communication and decision-making
  Personal development
  Personal growth
  Individual growth targets
  Application of (newly gained) expertise

has been a striking shift in the types of challenge that are rewarded nowadays. We will look at this in more detail in the next section.

Current points of appraisal

In any appraisal today, the following skills and qualities are considered decisive (Mitrani et al., 1992), particularly in executive staff (directors and top managers) and the more so if they have been assigned abroad.

Qualities required of executive staff
- Strategic thinking: the capacity to grasp rapidly changing environment-related trends and market possibilities, competition threats, and to be aware of the strong and weak points of the corporate organization, so as to be able to formulate an optimally strategic response.
- Initiating change: the capacity to convey a strategic vision so as to make others feel involved and motivated, and to encourage innovation and a sense of business among employees.
- Relationship management: the capacity to establish relations and exert influence on complex networks of third parties whose cooperation is a prerequisite for corporate success and over whom the company has no formal control, such as customers, shareholders, trade union representatives, government institutions, legislators and lobby activists in different countries.

Similarly, the criteria applying to managers apply even more strongly to managers who have been assigned abroad:

Qualities required of managers
- Flexibility: the capacity to change structures and processes in order to implement changed strategies.
- Implementing change: the capacity to effectuate changes.
- Interpersonal understanding: the capacity to understand and respect others.
- Empowerment: to share information and promote the ideas of others, delegate responsibilities, supply feedback and undertake any such actions as are required to make employees feel more capable and motivated.
- Team support: the capacity to cause employees to cooperate effectively.
- Versatility: the capacity to adjust rapidly and perform effectively in a new environment (abroad).

All other employees are usually expected to be flexible, inquisitive, have the capacity to learn, be performance-oriented, be able to work under time pressure, be open to cooperation and be customer-oriented. All this does not mean that qualities which have not been mentioned are not important, but they are not essential to successful performance.

5   Developments in the field of Euro-compensation

In the previous sections we noted that what was acceptable in the past is increasingly not so nowadays. Compensating expatriates on the basis of the best of both worlds has become not only expensive for companies, as the number of employees calling themselves expatriates is on the increase, but also unacceptable in and of itself. There are increasingly fewer situations where a hardship allowance or an overseas allowance would be in order, although hardship allowances will of course probably remain necessary, in Africa for instance. Assignment abroad and contacts with other cultures have come to be seen as inherent in the job. Inherent in the job also means that changes in work routine are not coupled with extra compensation, but are already regarded as part of the reward. According to Adler and Ghadar (Chapter 4) these less generous, more global packages would be used mostly in multinational (global in 'our' terminology) and global (transnational in 'our' terminology) companies, while other companies would use one of the systems described in Section 3 above and give extra money to compensate for foreign hardships.

In this section we will first discuss some general ideas on developments in international compensation policy and then concentrate on what is called Euro-compensation. Despite the quite large discrepancies between base pay and perquisites in the different European countries (see also Chapter 8), Euro-compensation seems a more realistic option for the short and medium term than a comprehensive world-wide compensation system. The fact that West European exchange rates have been comparatively stable for a long time (although nothing is certain since the collapse of the ERM in 1992), and the existence of a common currency (the ECU) are important facilitators for a system of Euro-compensation.

International compensation policy

Although the European Union's decision to eliminate the internal borders of the European labour markets may not see quick results, an internal labour market is nearing. This is particularly so for highly qualified employees who geographically speaking belong to the more mobile group of workers. Companies in countries with lower pay levels are more and more facing competition from foreign companies on the labour market. It may mean that we are on the road to Euro-compensation. Still, many obstacles are yet to be overcome. What is clear is that multinationals (especially those of European origin) are spearheading the drive for change. But so far they do not seem to be putting their ideas into practice. They probably still regard the gaps between the countries as unbridgeable, or perhaps they find the divergent legislation (tax, non-transferable pension entitlements) too much of an obstacle. It seems as if they are

Table 12.2 *Important international employment conditions*

	Cash	Professional expenses
	Fixed annual income	Telephone allowance
	Variable income	Company car
Currently disposable	Tax-free payment	Personal expense allowance
	Loan	
	Health insurance	
	Allowance	
	Deferred income	*Insurance*
Commitments	Pension	Supplement to sickness benefit
	Voluntary early retirement	Disability
		Widow's/widower's pension

waiting for the fence to come down sufficiently for them to jump over. As it stands, many organizations still use the following guidelines.

- The compensation package must reflect national custom (culture); if it is not common practice domestically to grant a bonus, no bonus is granted, no matter what home-country practice is.
- The relative level of compensation (for example, whether a position is classified as senior or junior) must in principle be the same in all countries; absolute compensation levels may differ, however.
- Differences in taxation and social security are not translated into different compensation levels.

In other companies, however, compensation may already be done differently:

- The company applies the same strategy in all countries in terms of performance-related compensation such as variable income or stock purchase plans.
- The total compensation level (see Chapter 8) of a section of the employees, or all of them, is based on the same spending-power parity.
- The company sets minimum requirements for rules and values governing pensions, life assurance and health insurance.

The latter combination of factors reflects a more global orientation towards compensation. All employees, whether they are parent-, third- or host-country nationals, are treated in the same way.

Table 12.2 specifies a number of important international employment conditions. The company may formulate a policy for each segment, subject to the applicable statutory restrictions. For each (element of a) segment, regardless of whether it concerns an international or a Euro-compensation system, companies must choose any of the following three alternatives.

- *A fixed value in all countries.* This means, for example, that the same net income or personal expense allowance is paid in all countries, or that the make and type of the car is the same everywhere.
- *A relative value in all countries.* This means that the benefit granted depends on other values. For example, all commitments may be

defined in terms of fixed income. The ultimate pension may be set at 60 percent of the last earned salary, irrespective of what any state pension may offer. Under a supplements scheme, statutory benefits could perhaps be supplemented up to 90 percent in all countries.

- *A relative market position in all countries*. This means that the organization will take a relative position in all countries. It may, for example, opt for salary positions which would be labelled as market average. As regards health insurance allowances, it may choose a system which belongs to the top 25 percent of all local systems.

It is of course essential, in taking such policy decisions, that jobs are compared which are similar in terms of responsibilities. In evaluating 'job size', and thus the salary, several criteria may be used.

- Complexity of markets.
- Number of product/market combinations.
- Extent of international distribution.
- Technological level.
- Branch of industry.
- Number of management areas to be administered.
- Extent to which organizations are independent.
- Size of the company in terms of turnover and workforce.

On the basis of these criteria, international companies can develop a global compensation policy. Determining job size is essential to be able to compare properly between the different countries. In particular, cash and professional expenses vary greatly according to job levels. The following schedule sets out an example of a particular job size. The employment package for 'internationally' compensated staff could be as given in Table 12.3. A few components (for example, health insurance allowance) are related to the relative position in the host country; other components (for example, variable income) have the same relative value, while still others represent a fixed value.

All this does not necessarily mean that the global standard used by a company is always valid in all countries. In countries with pay levels in excess of the global corporate standard, the local pay level will take priority. If it did not, companies would lose the battle for talented managers. Consequently, the salaries paid for comparable management positions may vary considerably within one and the same group of companies. However, a massive drain of talented managers from one country to the other is unlikely. For many, the emotional and cultural obstacles are still too high.

ECU points

Current expatriate policies are too complicated and expensive to facilitate compensation within a European context and adequately reward cross-border performance. In order to control flexibility in terms of employment conditions, the pay packages should consist of a fixed part which is not

Table 12.3   *Example of employment package for 'internationally' compensated staff*

	Cash	Professional expenses

Currently disposable	Annual fixed income
	  average income usually paid
	  in the trade
	  Netherlands: DFL 100,000
	  Denmark: DKK 395,000
	  Britain: £28,000
	Variable income
	  15 percent of the fixed
	  income if targets are met
	
	Health assurance allowance
	  average allowance usually
	  paid in the host country
		Telephone allowance
		  full reimbursement of all costs;
		  tax consequences to be borne
		  by the employee
		
		Company car
		  point of reference are cars in
		  the same range as 'make X –
		  type Y'
		Personal expense allowance
		  the same net allowance
		  equivalent to DFL 1,500 in all
		  countries

Commitments	*Deferred income*
	Pension
	  supplement to state pension
	  up to a maximum of 65
	  percent of the last earned
	  income; the pension age is 65
		Insurance
		Supplement to sickness benefit
		  supplement to state benefits
		  up to the full fixed income
		  during the first year of illness;
		  supplement up to 85 percent
		  in the second year
		Disability
		  after the third year of illness,
		  benefits will be supplemented
		  up to 65 percent of the
		  income in all countries,
		  regardless of state benefits
		Widow's/widower's pension
		  the payment to widows/
		  widowers amounts to 65
		  percent of the old age pension

open to negotiation and a variable part to be negotiated by the employees. The variable part in particular should remain controllable. The package may take a form which could as easily be applied in the case of mergers or assignments abroad as in the case of special rewards. This type of package consists of what are called flexipoints. The following steps will show how flexipoints are allocated.

Steps	*Contents*
Step 1	Define the organization's compensation position
Step 2	Convert TOTREM into ECU
Step 3	Define negotiation space
Step 4	Specify benefits package
Step 5	Determine TCP-FLEX
Step 6	Allocate flexipoints

Step 1: Define the organization's compensation position   The position which the organization intends to hold on the pay and benefits market is

clarified and defined. After that, pay and benefits components are 'translated' into total remuneration (TOTREM). In other words, the total economic value of the integral employment conditions package is defined first.

Step 2: Convert TOTREM into ECU   The TOTREM package defined in step 1 must be converted into the European ECU currency. If the Netherlands is set at 1,000, at current exchange rates, the weights for Germany and the United States would be set at 1.2 and 1.8, respectively. The location weight (LW) is also important. It is an estimate of the cost of living for a given work location. For example, Paris has been set at 1.3 and Tokyo at 2.2. The third element comprises versatility and potential growth (VP). In the end, the total results in a multiplication score. The total compensation points (TCP) are standardized at 1,000 and give a unique score for each employee, for example, managers A, B and C, as follows.

Manager	LW	VP	TCP
A	1.3	1.0	1,300
B	1.0	1.0	1,000
C	1.2	1.2	1,440

Step 3: Define negotiation space   It must be determined for each organiza- tion (or division) what part of the pay package is not open to negotiation (say 500 TCP). If the organization holds a position at average level, and determines that 10 percent below that level is acceptable, then 50 TCPs will be available for further definition.

Step 4: Specify benefits package   The same operation as in step 3 is now applied to the benefits package (say 160 TCP). The choice of base pay and benefits may vary. An organization which attaches weight to a strongly caring employment package will opt for a higher TCP portion in benefits than an organization wishing to lay the emphasis on monetary rewards.

Step 5: Determine TCP-FLEX   The individual variable part must be determined, whereby TCP-FLEX is equivalent to TCP minus base pay and benefits and, if desired, plus market adjustment, variable compensation, periodic increases and so on. Employees in comparable positions may subsequently fill in their packages.

Manager	TCP-FIXED pay	TCP-FIXED benefits	TCP-FLEX cash	TCP-FLEX benefits	TOTAL TCP
A	500	160	640		1,300
B	500	160	140	200	1,000
C	500	160	340	440	1,440

Step 6: Allocate flexipoints The actual allocation of flexipoints will, in practice, be subject to a number of conditions. Some of them are laid down by law and may vary according to country (for example, the statutory minimum of 20 days off). Eventually, the flexipoints allocated to the employee in question will be directly linked to the spending limit of an employee's credit card. In this way, it will be easy to reward directly an exceptional performance by increasing the number of flexipoints, without having to perform a thousand-and-one calculations. At present, employees receive extra compensation if they are posted abroad for some time. It is quite conceivable that this situation will change to one where an employee receives a standard compensation for the job-related willingness to be mobile, and where he or she exactly knows, if they are assigned abroad, how many flexipoints the location weight and versatility will generate. Negotiations between the parties will no longer concern details of the employment package, but rather focus on the number of flexipoints.

6 Summary and conclusions

In this chapter we have discussed the problems associated with the appraisal and compensation of international staff. A number of compensation systems have been reviewed. Future expatriates will, in many respects, be different 'persons' from those a decade ago. The phenomenon of expatriation will become more of a rule than an exception. An increasing number of managers and experts are eligible for expatriation. This means that the term will lose its special ring and the compensation will be less 'different' accordingly. The compensation systems discussed in Section 5 are a step in this direction.

This chapter was the last of the third part of this book. The fourth and final part will deal with industrial relations and industrial democracy.

PART 4

INTERNATIONAL BUSINESS, INDUSTRIAL RELATIONS AND INDUSTRIAL DEMOCRACY

13   International human resource management and industrial relations: a framework for analysis

Willem de Nijs

1	Introduction	271
2	Personnel management and industrial relations in international perspective	272
3	The international corporation as a special policy domain	273
4	Two schools of thought as a point of departure	277
5	The system model of national industrial relations	280
6	The system model and international industrial relations	285
7	Barriers to effective international regulation	287

1   Introduction

It is almost impossible to imagine a country in which companies do not have to take account of a whole range of regulations governing the way in which they are permitted to apply the factor labour in the production process. It seems that even in the most widely diverse national systems, there are parties other than company management which influence the form and content of personnel policy or human resource management in some way and to some extent. For example, issues which involve wages, employee participation, training and dismissal cannot be dealt with without taking into account a variety of collective agreement provisions, stipulations governing co-determination and statutory regulations set forth by the government. At the national level, then, there is an inextricable link between the nature and form of personnel management as practised in companies, and the culture and structure of industrial relations in the country concerned (De Nijs, 1992a). In this sense, industrial relations provide an important context factor: in its concrete interpretation of personnel policy, company management must in some fashion take account of rules and regulations which have been negotiated with other employee representatives or which the government has imposed.

It is, however, not the case that personnel management and industrial relations influence each other directly; instead, they form part of a complex and dynamic whole. Labour is regulated as much by personnel management as by industrial relations, e.g. through rules governing remuneration, promotion, recruitment, employee participation etc. Company management functions as a strategic player in shaping the relationship with its personnel and in regulating the factor labour. From this perspective, we can view personnel management as the strategy which company management develops in order to regulate the factor labour within its own organization. It is, in other words, an instrument which management uses in order to structure industrial relations within its own company as it sees fit. If we alternate between the industrial relations perspective and the personnel management perspective, we arrive at the following essential proposition: the objective of personnel management is identical to that of industrial relations in a more general sense. Personnel or human resource management targets those substantive aspects of the employer–employee relationship which also form the core of industrial relations processes, namely the regulation of the employment relationship through consultation and negotiation between employers, employees, their organizations and government agencies.

2 Personnel management and industrial relations in international perspective

The interrelation between personnel/human resource management and industrial relations means that, in the majority of countries, company management is rarely able to act autonomously in determining personnel policy. Personnel management in each industrial nation has been embedded in society at large. That means that this policy domain is subject to societal rules, norms and values. Personnel management has been and is influenced by multiple 'policy centres' such as trade unions, co-determination bodies and government authorities. The degree of societal 'embeddedness' and the concrete way in which this happens in each individual country varies enormously, however. This is one of the most important reasons why, in actual practice, personnel management is subject to the same national variation with respect to content and form (De Nijs, 1989, 1992b).

This brings us to an essential point within the field of industrial relations associated with the special realm of human resource management in international companies. Specifically, it is precisely these companies whose national subsidiaries are constantly being confronted with and intruded upon by the multitude of country-specific regulations which not only differ from one another in a formal and technical sense, but which are often also the expression of specific and deeply rooted cultural traditions and beliefs in the field of industrial relations. One important problem which international companies must solve is how to deal with these differences within their own 'walls'. Although each multinational corporation has a different approach to solving the problem of centralization versus decentralization of personnel management, no single MNC can afford to ignore the influence of the local culture and structure of industrial relations on personnel management at its various subsidiaries. In addition to providing a 'meeting place' for various national practices, the multinational corporation forms an interesting object of study for another reason. Until now the argument has been that the interrelation between personnel management and industrial relations manifests itself principally within strictly national contexts. Personnel management has been subject to a country's own norms, rules, customs and practices. The question automatically arises whether, in the wake of the increasingly international organization of production and services, an international regulatory system has been created, in the same fashion as nationally organized economic activity prompted specific national systems. Seen within this context, the multinational corporation is more than a passive institution which 'runs up against' a wide range of configurations in industrial relations through its subsidiaries; the MNC is also a strategic actor in what may be an internationalizing system of industrial relations, within which personnel management is subject to and possibly measured against international norms and regulations.

The various chapters in this part focus on the interrelations between personnel management and industrial relations in international companies. Before beginning our actual analysis in subsequent chapters, this chapter will present a more general framework for analysis. After a short historical sketch of the MNC as a special policy domain within industrial relations (Section 3) and a presentation of the two theoretical perspectives which dominated scholarly analyses of the MNC for many years (Section 4), we will draw the contours of a framework for analyzing industrial relations in multinational corporations. As a starting point we will use the system model of industrial relations (Section 5), which we will then 'stretch' to include industrial relations at an international level (Section 6). In the final section we will deal with the practical and theoretical relevance of this model.

3 The international corporation as a special policy domain

The phenomenon known as the international corporation is almost as old as the economic order from which it arose – industrial capitalism. Many large and well-known multinationals such as Philips, Shell, General Electric, Standard Oil and ITT developed their international structure around the turn of the century. Not only companies but also associations of employers and employees rapidly made their appearance on the international stage. The best known examples were the 'Internationals', organized under Karl Marx's inspiring leadership; the first of these was held as early as 1864. The 'internationals' were the first more-or-less structured gatherings of national trade unions in which an attempt was made to join forces on an international scale in the struggle against the rise of world capitalism, as it was still called in those days. The present international associations of employees, such as the ICFTU (International Confederation of Free Trade Unions), WFTU (World Federation of Trade Unions) and CWCL (Christian World Confederation of Labour), are descendants of the collective organizations which developed at the beginning of this century. Even at this early stage, the creation of these organizations seemed to meet the most important criteria for the construction of an international system of industrial relations, namely the presence of actors organized across national borders in order to coordinate policy and strategy. At first glance the early birth of the international organization appears to confirm what seems to be a basic pattern of industrial capitalism, described by Piehl (1974) in the following terms: 'Just as the national organization of capitalism has led to the national organization of worker representation, so too shall multinational corporations as an expression of international capitalism, lead to the internationalization of trade unions.' Upon closer inspection, this pattern has not become evident at the international level to the same degree. The national representative organizations were, after all, right there from the very start of what became an increasingly complex network of relationships and institutions, one of whose goals was to impose rules governing the use of labour by employers in a way that would be acceptable to all of the parties concerned. This ultimately resulted in specific national systems of industrial relations in which each party (employers, employees, their respective organizations and the government) attempts to involve the others in furthering its interests in a sustainable and structured fashion. There has been no evolution of this type at the international level, however. It has only been in the past few years that efforts in this direction have been made, and even these have been restricted primarily to one specific region of the world economy, namely the European Union.[1] Since the 1980s, the first hesitant steps have been taken towards establishing a European system of industrial relations in which 'European employers', 'European trade unions' and a 'hoped-for European government' consult one another in 'European institutions', sometimes reaching agreements on socio-economic issues within the European Union. Every once in a while this leads to European directives and regulations with which the member states are obliged to comply (see Chapter 16).

The question which arises is why the pattern mentioned above has been so slow to carry through to the international level, and then only to a very

---

[1] In 1993 the European Community changed its name to the European Union. (See also Chapter 16.)

limited degree. Our initial answer may sound rather paradoxical, but it is a fact that multinational corporations and international trade unions did not consider each other as their 'natural' opponents for a long time. Indeed, within the various international unions, the 'multinational' was not seen as a specific policy domain or area of negotiation. The tone within international trade organizations was actually set almost immediately by Marx's Internationals. These were in fact no more than informal political bodies which discussed vague and general resolutions and called for international solidarity. They did indeed recognize the need to establish an international counterweight to the expansion of world capitalism, but the object and bearer of this economic process of internationalization remained outside the unions' line of vision. The international unions never became more than non-committal 'discussion groups' which were rapidly split into factions by proponents of various ideologies. To be honest, we should of course mention the fact that the trade unions were still engaged in a struggle to gain recognition at the national level, and that is where their priorities lay at the time. But even later, once they had firmly established themselves on the national front, there was no priority given to the international organization of employees and the promotion of their interests at the international level.

By the late 1960s multinational corporations began to appear as an item on the policy agendas of national and international trade union organizations. This happened at a time when it was more or less 'the done thing' to uphold radical and critical views on the functioning of the market economy and, by association, on corporations as well. In scholarly circles this led to what at the time seemed to be a definitive split into two opposing schools of thought (see the next section). International companies were held more or less responsible for global inequality, for supporting dictatorial regimes, and so on. The increasing amount of attention focused on multinational corporations by the trade unions during this period was also prompted by major international restructuring efforts leading to company closures and reorganizations within subsidiaries of multinational corporations.

Until the 1960s, multinational corporations were almost exclusively an American problem. Most multinational corporations had the United States as their home base and concentrated their direct investments on the European Continent. Europe was in the midst of its post-war reconstruction, and the trade unions greeted the arrival of US subsidiaries with open arms, as they brought jobs and prosperity to Europe. The 1960s and 1970s saw tremendous growth in foreign direct investment by European and Japanese multinational corporations. They ultimately surpassed the United States in this respect, transforming the latter from largest 'home country' to most important 'host country' for direct investment. The establishment of the European Economic Community (EEC) in 1958 and the expansion of this organization in the late 1960s were also important steps toward encouraging the internationalization and globalization of European companies. As a result, trade unions and sometimes even governments were forced to face up to the more negative aspects of multinational corporations. Instead of employment importers, they were seen as employment exporters as they transferred production on a massive scale to the so-called low-wage countries. Union calls for collective action against multinational corporations increased. Voices were raised in favour of international collective bargaining; global enterprise councils were occasionally set up and the EEC was put under pressure to create modified policy frameworks.

National unions battle with MNCs

This was also the period in which individual national unions undertook coordinated action in a few multinational corporations. The most successful was the joint action undertaken by Belgian, German and Dutch unions against the chemicals concern AKZO in 1972. That year AKZO had revealed plans to shut down a number of subsidiaries in the three countries mentioned, due to overcapacity on the world market for synthetic fibres. In response, workers at a production facility in Breda, the Netherlands, occupied the plant with the blessing of the trade unions. Employees at other foreign subsidiaries affected were also mobilized and, through close cooperation with foreign trade unions, employees were able to have the original plans altered in their own favour. Similar action was undertaken at other multinational corporations such as Honeywell, Rhône-Poulenc and Goodyear (although these were less successful), and Philips – at the time still considered one of the more progressive multinationals – was even prepared to enter into an annual round of consultations on its European plans with the European Trade Union Confederation (ETUC) and representatives of a number of the International Trade Secretariats. At the time this was considered a transitional step in the direction of a formal, inevitable system of collective bargaining at European level. The field of international industrial relations had become unsettled and trade unions seemed to be arming themselves for a final confrontation with multinationals. Since then history has shown that the battle has yet to begin, let alone that it has been won. What were once identified as victories turned out to be short-lived in the face of the long-term strategies of the multinationals, which not only benefited from changes in the political and economic climate but also succeeded in escaping from the witness box.

The radical and critical tendencies began to ebb, slowly but surely, at the end of the 1970s, giving way to more pragmatic views in the 1980s. This turnabout was also stimulated by the accelerated pace with which a new integrated European market was being created. The idea of a single market with complete freedom of movement for capital, labour, goods and knowledge came to be seen as an obvious and necessary condition for economic growth and for the preservation of Europe as an economic heavyweight on the global scene. 'Le défi américain', already parried by 'le défi japonais', was to be followed by a European challenge which at times could have been described as 'Europhoria', a tendency which has died down since then. In this context, multinational corporations were considered the necessary bearers and implementers of the process of internationalization so coveted by Europe. The internationalization of European trade and industry began to thrive as never before, evidenced by the number of international mergers, takeovers, strategic alliances and networks between companies. The share contributed by multinational corporations to employment within the various separate national economies, for example, increased enormously. This meant that effective socio-economic policies at a national level were running up against the outer edges of international strategies of multinational corporations. And this, I believe, brings us to the most important factor behind the recent efforts at European level to design a new regulatory framework for international enterprises: the necessity expressed by the member states for supranational political integration – indeed some parties even advocate creating some sort of European government. The completion of the internal market in 1992 has in any case stimulated the need for socio-economic coordination at the European level. A European currency and a European central bank will undoubtedly lead to a loss of national autonomy in the financial and economic spheres. The creation of a forum for European political coordination seems to fulfil the final and most important condition for the creation of a European system of industrial relations: the establishment of structural international relations between international enterprises/ employers' associations, international trade unions and a 'European government'. At present the process of institutionalization within the European Union, with the creation of its own bodies, rules and directives (see Chapter 16), can be described as laborious, leading to a tense relationship with the national systems of consultation and negotiation.

4   Two schools of thought as a point of departure

As stated above, the issue of multinational corporations and industrial relations only began to attract the attention of a wide range of scholars in the 1960s. This happened more or less in conjunction with a growing social awareness (particularly within the trade unions) of the influence exercised by these companies on the socio-economic functioning of society. The political and ideological spirit of the times had a major impact on scholarly attempts to devise a global framework for analysis and interpretation. As with other important themes within the study of industrial relations, theoreticians split into two fairly rigid ideological camps. The *radical school*, based on Marxist sources of inspiration, was diametrically opposed to the *institutional* school, which more closely resembled the social system theory. The two theoretical camps scarcely engaged in constructive dialogue, because choosing one or the other scholarly perspective immediately implied a certain political position and vice versa. While the radicals automatically associated themselves with the 'real' interests of workers and trade unions, the institutional school was all too rapidly and unjustly associated with those who might benefit from maintaining the status quo and, as a consequence, a system in which class inequalities essentially persisted. These two approaches not only had different substantive views on multinational corporations, but they also recommended different policy approaches for gaining more control over MNCs. This distinction became evident in the way each camp labelled such enterprises. In the radical camp, the term used was 'international concern' or 'monopoly', because this best expressed the main problem: the fact that these companies exploit the differences and contrasts between the various different countries where they are established or are planning to set up operations. The institutional camp preferred the more neutral and, in any event, broader term of 'multinational corporation', which implies that the most important characteristic is that a company of this type has multiple subsidiaries in more than one country and that it is this which sets it apart fundamentally from the national enterprise.

The most important differences between these two perspectives on the topic of multinational corporations will be discussed in turn.

1 *Assessment of the significance of the multinational corporation.* In the institutional approach the multinational is principally considered as a qualitatively new phenomenon within the market economic system, and therefore it requires a separate approach. By contrast, the radical school assumes that the international company must be considered as the logical consequence of the development of capitalism, which historically has had a disregard for national boundaries. Indeed, the multinational is the purest expression of capitalism, because it is the product of the two most important logics within this system: the tendency to concentrate economic forces or form monopolies, and the global search for circumstances most conducive to the accumulation of capital.

2 *The evaluation of the multinational versus the national corporation.* The institutional approach sees the multinational corporation as fundamentally different from, or even the opposite of, nationally organized corporations in orientation and interests. In this connection, scholars often point out the supposedly large difference in *cash flow* between the two types of companies. Cash flow is defined as that portion of the gross yield which is reinvested in the firm after expenditures have been deducted. National enterprises supposedly concentrate on gaining the biggest possible short-term profits, whereas multinational corporations target long-term growth and attempt to build up their own financial resources as much as possible. According to the radicals, on the other hand, there is no fundamental difference between the two types of companies, either in characteristics or interests. Both are the products of capital flows and are therefore subject to the same inherent laws and contradictions of 'capital'.

3 *The role of the government and 'politics' in general.* Proponents of the institutional approach often see a sharp contrast between multinational corporations and the national state. Such companies do not, after all, fall

under the jurisdiction of the national government. Their international strategies can even undermine the success of national policies, for example in the area of the labour market, employment, trade and industry, and the economy in general. The radical camp acknowledges these types of problems but asserts that in essence there is no question of a contradiction between national states and multinational corporations. In this context, both governments and companies are viewed as institutions that cannot escape the logic of capital. For example, national governments aid multinationals in creating a world market, and will go as far as to create new political and economic structures in order to develop optimal conditions for international business strategies. In this respect, the radicals often gleefully refer to the creation of the European Union and developments within this organization.

4 *Assessment of the position occupied by international companies within nationally organized systems of industrial relations.* The institutional approach sees the multinational primarily as an actor who threatens the internal stability of the national system. To counteract this threat, a new form of institutionalization must be devised at an international level. Some suggestions have been: codes of behaviour for MNCs, legislation and collective bargaining and co-determination for employees at an international level. The radical school, on the other hand, is not as preoccupied with the idea that multinational corporations may pose a specific threat to internal stability, because in their view industrial relations systems based on capitalism are unstable to begin with. In this sense, multinational corporations are considered a progressive force because they speed up the inevitable decline and fall of capitalism. That is why the radicals do not prefer the creation of new policy or control networks at international level. The only effective approach is to reinforce the counterweight offered by trade unions at the international level by means of confrontation and worker control.

These differences in approach are not only relevant from the perspective of scholarship. Traces of both approaches can be found in the aspects of strategy and policy that some (international) unions emphasize. The institutional approach, for example, is associated primarily with an indirect strategy, whereas the radical approach prefers counteraction directed specifically at the multinationals themselves. Current practice has shown, however, that trade unions and employees make use of both strategies, alternately or simultaneously, depending on the specific problem and goal to be achieved.

In the following section we will concentrate on developing a concrete framework of analysis for the issue of multinational corporations and industrial relations. As our point of departure we will make use of a model developed by Dunlop (1958) for the analysis of industrial relations. This model is closely tied to the institutional approach and consists of system-theoretical insights reinterpreted for the field of industrial relations. We have chosen this model because it in fact presents an 'empty' descriptive conceptual framework which makes no actual pronouncements on the

strategy, values, objectives and interests pursued by the parties in furthering their mutual relations. It can encompass both direct and indirect
strategies and does not inhibit interpretations which might be associated
with the theoretical movements mentioned. The most important consideration in choosing this model is that it offers the opportunity to use analysis
to clarify the ambiguous issue of MNCs described in the introduction. This
analysis concerns the MNC whose local personnel management 'runs up
against' a diversity of national traditions in the field of industrial relations,
and the MNC as a strategic actor in an internationally organized system
which is still in the process of development.

5 The system model of national industrial relations

As mentioned previously, Dunlop (1958) provided an important impetus
toward using a specific analytical framework in the study of industrial
relations by applying system-theoretical insights. The core of this framework consists of the idea that industrial relations can be viewed as a system
or subsystem of society, just as we speak of political or economic
subsystems. For a proper understanding of this approach, we must
emphasize that it is an analytical and, hence, an abstract presentation of
issues. To talk in terms of a system of industrial relations is not intended
'simply to describe in factual terms the real world of time and space'
(Dunlop, 1958: 16). In Dunlop's view, this type of system of industrial
relations consists of four basic components:

1 *actors* or *parties*;
2 the *rules*;
3 an *ideology*;
4 an *environmental context*.

The actors are employees and their organizations, employers and their
organizations, and the government. These three actors maintain relations
with one another within an environment made up of three tightly
interwoven contexts, respectively the technological features of the work
situation (the technological context), the market opportunities or limitations (the economic context), and the relative distribution of power
between the actors (the political context). These contexts should be
understood as dynamic forces which bring about constant change in the
relationships and the results of the interactions between the actors. The
most important objects of study in industrial relations are the rules, which
are in effect the product of mutual cooperation and opposition between the
actors. These rules are both substantive and procedural in nature.
Substantive rules are the requirements and conditions for the application
of labour, whereas procedural rules involve the way in which the parties
actually arrive at and formulate these rules. Finally, the system is
complemented by an ideology which binds the separate actors to one

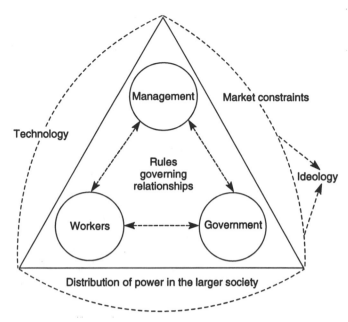

Figure 13.1   *The system of industrial relations according to Dunlop (Bomers, 1976: 5)*

another. This is 'a set of ideas and beliefs commonly held by the actors that helps to bind or integrate the system together as an entity' (Dunlop, 1958: 16). Each of the actors may have its own ideology, but if no form of consensus exists between them, there cannot be a stable system of industrial relations. Dunlop's analytical framework is illustrated in Figure 13.1.

Bomers used Dunlop's model to construct a supplementary analytical framework for studies into industrial relations at an international level. Although Dunlop distinguishes between various levels of industrial relations, he did not by any means design this conceptual framework for the issue of the multinational or of international industrial relations. In Dunlop's view, the most general level of the system of industrial relations extends no further than the national borders of a specific country. That is why, in actual practice, his frame of reference is applied in particular to classify and describe *national* systems of industrial relations. This leaves no room for the possibility that one of the actors might operate above or beyond the borders of the national system, or that there might even be a network of relations at the supranational level. As a result of the enormous growth in the number of MNCs and the development of the EU, an analytical framework which focuses purely on the national level is no longer enough. In Dunlop's model, the sources of power and rules are situated within strictly national frameworks. What makes a multinational so unusual from the industrial relations perspective is that this type of enterprise has a decision-making system which is no longer tied to the borders of the national system. In this respect, the definition of the MNC which Piehl (1974) gives is still the most appealing. Piehl mentions three criteria as decisive when identifying a multinational. In addition to the very obvious fact that such an organization trades products, capital and labour across national borders and that physical production, trade and services are spread across various different countries, Piehl identifies the presence of a concern centre as the most essential feature. This is where the most important strategic decisions are taken and where an international strategy is developed which will be applied in various countries. It may well be, as most MNCs in fact claim, that the various national subsidiaries are legally and organizationally autonomous: the essential point is, however, that a multinational policy centre controls the decisions which are taken in these national subsidiaries and considers these a part of its international strategy. This means that although top management or headquarters of an international company may be located in a particular country in a physical sense, the decision-making system takes no account of the borders of this same country. An MNC operates as an actor in various different systems of industrial relations, and this very fact means that it will be viewed as a potentially destabilizing (or, in milder terms, asymmetrical) force within a national system of industrial relations. Bomers illustrated this as shown in Figure 13.2.

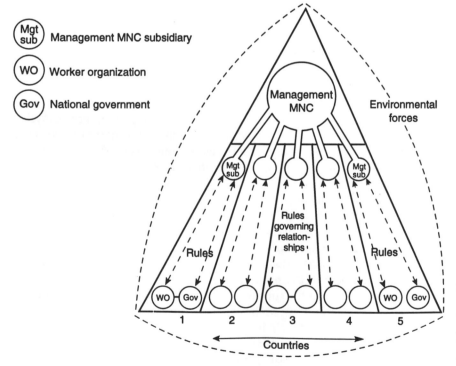

Figure 13.2 *Multinational enterprises and national systems of industrial relations (Bomers, 1976: 15)*

This model is a good illustration of the core of the issue related to the functioning of a multinational corporation within national systems of industrial relations. First of all, the management of a local subsidiary does not function as a completely autonomous actor within a national system. Certainly in the case of essential issues, local management must coordinate its policy with the MNC's headquarters. Secondly, the model also provides a fetching illustration of the fact that in developing its strategy, management at headquarters moves above and beyond the borders of national systems, situating itself largely out of reach of the national parties. Litvak and Maule (1972: 62) once described the MNC aptly as a corporation 'octopus'. Governments and trade unions in the various countries only deal with the tentacles of this corporation. The head or nerve centre lies outside the sphere of influence of these parties. This tentacle structure makes it possible for the MNC to develop an international strategy in a largely unilateral fashion. Governments and trade unions do scarcely have any influence on this strategy, even though it may have a definite impact on the vital interests of employees, trade unions and governments in those countries where the MNC has set up subsidiaries.

To finish this section, we will provide a summary of the most important problems which MNCs may create for parties which are themselves forced to function within the frameworks of national systems of industrial relations. We will concentrate in particular on those aspects which might lead to a disruption of the precariously balanced negotiating relationship between national employee representatives and the management at one of a multinational's national subsidiaries.

One of the most fundamental problems is that national governments, trade unions and even works councils may *not know about or understand the decision-making process* within the MNC. Although MNCs as a group display a wide range of differences with respect to the degree of centralization of decision-making, in actual practice the competencies vested in the parent company and its subsidiaries are often strictly divided. Strategic decisions on investment, planning, research and development etc. are generally highly centralized, whereas local subsidiaries are allowed greater autonomy when it comes to sales, purchasing and personnel policy issues. Multinational corporations regularly claim that their national subsidiaries have adapted to local customs and rules in industrial relations. The immediate suggestion is frequently that local management is entirely autonomous in local industrial relations issues and that it complies strictly with the requirements and rules of the country in question. Any mention of the possibility that the negotiating relationship might be unequal is firmly denied in such circles.

Unions and works councils sometimes argue that the decision-making structure is often not nearly as clear and simple as the MNC claims. In fact, they complain that in actual practice, the division of authority is consciously obscured. A very important condition for effective negotiations or other forms of regulation is to be able to determine precisely how far the authority of the parties you are negotiating with extends. For example,

---

MNCs override local practices

MNCs often argue that they adapt to local customs when it comes to industrial relations. There are, however, examples of MNCs that try to impose their own practices in this area on the parties in other countries. US multinationals had a reputation for doing this in the past, but recently it has been Japanese corporations which have frequently had this accusation hurled at them. Buoyed by their reputation as the developers of the most effective management and organization principles, the Japanese often introduce their own specific practices in industrial relations at their foreign subsidiaries, including the 'enterprise union' as it is known. An example closer to home is DAF's takeover of British Leyland. During the takeover, which has since been dissolved, the number of individual trade unions in the British subsidiary was reduced drastically and a form of co-determination was introduced at the same time, which more or less resembled Dutch practice in this respect (see Haveman in Albeda et al., 1989: 45ff.).

---

national parties sometimes have trouble determining where precisely the power of decision lies in issues that play a role in the negotiating process. The unions have the impression that they are negotiating with a particular party (local management), but the true power to approve the result of the negotiations lies elsewhere, namely with headquarters. Moreover, a shadowy process may arise in which responsibilities are shoved on to another party. While the local management team might swear that they are doing nothing more than following the guidelines set by headquarters, headquarters in turn insists that the management at the subsidiary involved is entirely responsible for this type of issue. What little research has been conducted into this aspect has shown that the more everyday and operational aspects are handled autonomously by local management, but that as soon as less routine affairs such as collective bargaining are at issue (and certainly when an industrial conflict threatens to erupt), nothing happens without the concern's central management being consulted.

A second aspect which may have an equally negative impact on the equality of the parties in the local negotiating process is that the local parties *may not know about or adequately understand the overall international strategy* and the entire range of activities which the MNC carries out in various countries. An important factor impeding such understanding may be the obscure nature of financial reporting and clarification. There simply are no global standards governing such reports, and this means that the demands and requirements in the various countries where an MNC has established subsidiaries can be wildly divergent. In this connection the phenomenon of 'transfer pricing' should be mentioned, that is, a system of internal pricing between the various subsidiaries within an MNC. By maintaining different transfer prices, the MNC is able to manipulate the profit figures in its various subsidiaries without violating any legal requirements. The profits can accumulate at the location which is most favourable fiscally or in other senses, in this way misrepresenting the actual origins of the company's profits in their entirety.

A final threat to national negotiations is the power of an international company to *reorganize its production factors internationally*. Depending on the chosen strategy, this may mean that in one country subsidiaries are being reorganized, restructured or even closed down, while at the same time in another country new subsidiaries are being set up or mergers or joint ventures are being entered into. This type of contradictory outcome of investment decisions which are part of an international strategy naturally also ensures that it becomes difficult for employees and trade unions to implement an international counter-strategy. The employees in the various subsidiaries often have conflicting interests. Whereas employees in one country may be facing redundancies as a result of a decision taken at headquarters, in another country they will be heralding that same decision as a source of new employment. The power to reorganize production and services on an international scale naturally has a major impact on the negotiating process at national level. Multinationals can threaten to remove production units to another location or refrain from making necessary investments whenever they are confronted with demands and conditions which they find unacceptable. In this connection we should mention a related factor, namely that a multinational has the option of actually moving production temporarily to a production facility in another country in the event of strike action. In practice this kind of move can seriously undermine the negotiating position of the local trade unions, because it means that a strike will have very little effect on the total level of production or on the economic position of the company.

6   The system model and international industrial relations

In the previous section we used Dunlop's analytical model to sketch the problem of multinational corporations within national systems of industrial relations. Using examples, we showed that the MNC, with its supranational decision-making structure, can be seen as a potential threat to what is often a precarious internal balance and coherence within these systems. The question that automatically arises is how this balance can be recovered. Efforts to do so can be executed on various different levels, as Figure 13.3, taken from Bomers (1976), demonstrates.

It has been demonstrated that trade unions, employees and governments make attempts to achieve a balance of power at the various different levels simultaneously. Within MNCs, however, the centre of decision-making power lies beyond the reach of the national unions and governments, so that the most effective approach is to form international power blocs as a counterweight. The other actors can set as many rules, requirements etc. at national level as they want, but the fact remains that they are regulating

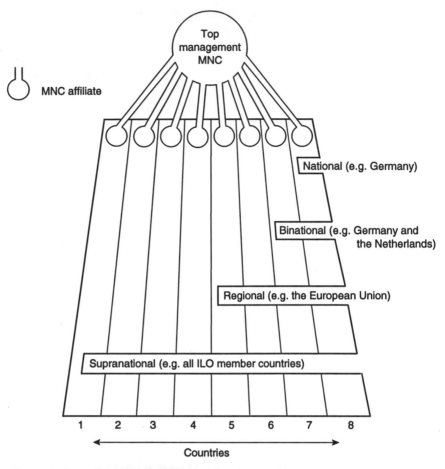

Figure 13.3 *The various different levels at which attempts can be made to recover the power balance between employees, governments and MNCs (Bomers, 1976: 24)*

only a tentacle of the MNC. It would be difficult, for example, to forbid an MNC at the national level to decrease or even suspend investment in its subsidiary in the relevant country. It is unrealistic to think that the balance can be restored effectively at the national level alone. That is why in the course of time attempts have been made in this direction at various international levels. The *binational level*, for example, is when employees from the MNC's subsidiaries in two different countries undertake joint action. The employees in one subsidiary can refuse to take over production of the other subsidiary in the case of a strike. Or coordinated action can be undertaken to reverse a corporate decision which has an impact on two or more subsidiaries. History presents us with many examples of similar types of action. The biggest problem is that the events are often of a temporary nature and do not lead to more permanent forms of regulation.

There is a greater chance of this happening if the action undertaken is transnational in nature. The best example at *regional level* is the European Union, which has already made a start at setting up a regulatory framework at the European level (see Chapter 16).

The ideal is, finally, to develop a *worldwide framework* which is valid in every country in which the MNC has established a subsidiary. Even if developments within the EU result in a legitimate and effective European system of industrial relations, the worldwide activities of the MNC still have not been covered. This is, by the way, the complaint heard from MNCs whose home base is in Europe and whose activities are concentrated in the Union. They argue that an increase in European regulations would hamper them in their competition with other multinationals. At the global level, nothing more has come about than the so-called codes of behaviour for MNCs set up by the United Nations, International Labour Organization and the International Chamber of Commerce. Since there are scarcely any sanctions attached to these codes, their significance is mainly moral. The preceding already more or less indicates that it is only at the regional level of the European Union that we can find evidence of the development of an international system of industrial relations as described by Dunlop. Bomers (1976) has used Dunlop's original diagram to visualize this type of international system (see Figure 13.4).

This model can be seen as an analytical illustration of a European system of industrial relations whose outlines have already become visible. It is only at European Union level that we recognize the minimum conditions required for a system of industrial relations at the international level. There actors, rules and institutions (for a detailed analysis, see Chapter 16) are in place, but they have not yet formed a real system of industrial relations at the European level. Indeed, the effort has just begun. It will be a long time before we reach the most legitimate and ultimate stage, with completely autonomous European trade unions negotiating directly with European employers and reaching European collective agreements backed up by European collective labour law, and with typical national differences in labour and corporate law being harmonized. Indeed, the question is whether this ultimate stage will ever be reached, given the enormous barriers that must be overcome by all of the parties involved in this process of development. Below we will discuss a number of important factors that can frustrate the development of an effective international system of industrial relations.

7   Barriers to effective international regulation

In this closing section we will discuss an important barrier to the creation of an effective regulatory framework for multinational corporations at an international level. It immediately becomes clear how much remains to be done if international industrial relations are to achieve full legitimacy.

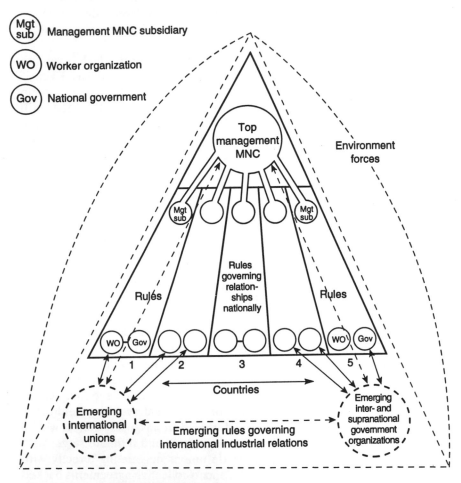

Figure 13.4 *Conceptual model for international industrial relations (Bomers, 1976: 30)*

The most important initial obstacle is formed by the actors themselves. The biggest problem standing in the way of the development of an effective counterweight against the multinational is the lack of autonomy and power accorded to the international representative organizations, both on the part of employees and governments. It is still the case that neither national trade unions nor national governments are making any concerted effort to transfer essential elements of their jurisdiction to international organizations. Even in the European Union, which has gone the furthest in creating a supranational political union, this is still the biggest obstacle to an integration which is successful in more than just an economic sense.

It is no wonder then that international trade unions are viewed as 'paper tigers'. In a formal sense they can count on a large following, making it possible for them to mobilize employees in the various countries. When it comes to developing an independent supranational strategy and under-taking international action, however, they are entirely dependent on the willingness of the national unions to relinquish some of their power. In reality this leads to dramatic strategic inequalities between MNCs and what should be their natural international opponents. The fact is that the international trade unions do not have a worldwide or regional decision-making system at their disposal which in any way is comparable with that of most MNCs. International trade unions are not capable of developing international strategies and activities in an integral fashion; neither are they able to direct their affairs from a powerful supranational policy centre. The few examples of international counter-moves *vis-à-vis* MNCs usually consist of temporary collaborations between national unions. It was only with difficulty that we were able identify a case in which an international trade union undertook action against an MNC on behalf of its affiliated unions, and even then this action was limited to what we might call logistical support. Until now, the role of international trade unions has been limited to representation in international organs associated with the UN and EU, and the majority of their time and energy goes into meetings and consultations.

Piehl (1974) compiled an almost exhaustive list of factors which still go a long way towards explaining the unwillingness of the national parties, in particular the trade unions, to delegate some of their authority to international collaborative organizations. We will limit ourselves to dis-cussing the three most fundamental of these factors:

1   *The national context of the parties.* Trade unions were created within a specific national system; furthermore, after more than a century, they have grown used to relying on the national government to help them achieve their objectives, often in close association with political parties. The emphasis within trade unions is still on national political interests and their first impulse is to seek solutions within the familiar national frameworks and procedures which they themselves may have fought long and hard to create.

This attitude, which is deeply anchored in union policy, has major repercussions for the structure and working methods of international trade unions. Even the ETUC, a unity organization of trade unions from Europe which at first glance appears to be a strong and coherent organization, suffers in reality from a lack of manpower at its headquarters in Brussels. The ETUC has received no mandate from its affiliates to develop and implement policy on its own power. The few administrators that there are within this organization are appointed by the national unions and are financially completely dependent on them.

2   *Major strategic, organizational and cultural differences between trade unions.* These differences naturally result from the national context mentioned above. For example, the way in which the German trade union movement is organized, lobbies and positions itself in politics and govern-ment, not to mention its financial resources, is entirely different from the approach taken by French or British unions. The problems this causes

when attempting to formulate a strategy that each party can accept must not be underestimated, especially not when a whole range of national and at times nationalistic elements start to play a role.

3   *The enormous national differences in the structure and culture of industrial relations.* These differences are often seen as one of the most important expressions of a particular nation's cultural heritage. This becomes especially pronounced if we look at national differences in the nature and intensity of legislation in the area of industrial relations, levels and approaches to negotiations, the degree of involvement of the various pressure groups in socio-economic policy etc. (see also Chapter 14). These differences are so deeply rooted in specific national customs and traditions that they represent one of the biggest roadblocks on the route to harmonization of legislation, rules and requirements in the field of industrial relations within the European Union. At times governments and member states even retain these differences as an argument against relinquishing any real autonomy to a type of European government.

In conclusion, we can state that as long as national parties are unwilling to delegate fundamental elements of their autonomy to supranational organizations, the prospects for the effective internationalization of industrial relations remain rather bleak. MNCs will undoubtedly fully exploit and even speed up economic integration within the European Union, and continue, for a long time, to reap the benefits of the faltering political and social integration in the field of industrial relations.

For personnel management within international companies, this will mean that the degree of adaptation to local customs in industrial relations in their various subsidiaries will, at least for now, remain on the strategic agenda. Furthermore, there is no expectation of developing an effective regulatory framework at international level for making cross-border policy decisions in the field of personnel management/industrial relations. It will be largely up to the MNCs to decide whether supranational frameworks for consultation and negotiation with European trade unions will be created to regulate personnel issues with an international scope. With respect to European co-determination, the most we can expect in the short term is some type of basic facility which will afford the MNCs a great deal of interpretive leverage given their strategic might. Co-determination will not bring about much deviation from the initiatives now being taken in some MNCs with regard to international consultations with their own personnel. In this way they are offering their employees the possibility of staying abreast of international corporate strategy and the associated personnel and organizational consequences thereof. These are strictly voluntary arrangements with no compliance obligation and in practice they go no further than the supply of information. They are more a part of the corporation's strategy to increase the loyalty and commitment of its own 'human resources' than a contribution to the development of international industrial relations between autonomous and representative interest organizations.

14 National variations in worker participation

Hans Slomp

1	Introduction	291
2	A short historical note	292
3	Works councils	293
	Composition and election	293
	Works council rights	296
	National differences	297
4	Trade union representation	300
	Differences in union networks	300
	Union delegates and works councils	301
5	The nature of worker participation	304
	Northern Europe	305
	France and Spain	305
	Variations in worker participation within countries:	
	the case of German Mitbestimmung	306
6	Differences in the nature of participation	307
	A few explanations	308
	Industry bargaining as an explanation	308
7	Works council differences in perspective	310
8	Worker participation in other European countries	311
	The Nordic countries	311
	Italy	312
	The United Kingdom	313
9	Worker participation in the United States and Japan	313
	The United States	314
	Japan	314
10	Towards 'training alliances'?	315
	The future of worker participation systems	315
	Is there any future at all?	316
11	Conclusion	316

1 Introduction

Worker participation in enterprise decision-making has been a popular topic in industrial relations literature since the late 1960s. Today, the German works councils in particular figure in every discussion of new trends in European collective bargaining. This chapter compares participation rules and participation practices in Europe, the United States and Japan, and their place in industrial relations. The main question addressed here is: what are the basic national variations in worker participation, and which form has the brightest future – or any future at all?

Because works councils are often seen as the 'real' worker participation institutions, after a short historical note the third section of this chapter will compare the rules and practices of works councils in those EU member states in which such councils have been active for some time (Belgium, Denmark, France, Germany, the Netherlands and Spain; Italy is excluded for its lack of continuity, but is referred to later). The focus on this group of countries is then extended to include the role of the trade unions in worker participation and the various industrial relations systems. The next step is to consider other European nations, as well as the United States and Japan. At the end of the chapter the focus is on the future as we attempt to answer the main question. The chapter therefore starts with a narrow, concrete focus, but its scope gradually widens and becomes more abstract. Our examination only covers general rules and the overall record of worker participation practice; we will not be concerned with specific fields like new technologies and shop-floor participation, even though some of the research on which we have based our discussion is based specifically on such issues.

2   A short historical note

Works councils date mainly from 1945. The major reason for their introduction was the need to generate a rapid economic recovery after the Second World War. This was seen as a collective effort, one not to be disrupted by employer–union conflicts. Moreover, in countries where many employers had supported the fascist cause, as in Germany and France, worker supervision of enterprise policy provided a second motive to set up some form of worker participation in enterprise decision-making. In Germany, works councils had sprung up spontaneously at the end of the First World War. They had been accorded official recognition, but were crushed under the Nazi dictatorship.

Worker participation did not play an important role in industrial relations in the 1950s and 1960s, due to the centralization of bargaining in most of Europe. It was not until the 1968 May revolt in Paris, under the banner of self-management (*autogestion*), that worker participation aroused much interest among workers or unions. A powerful and international 'participation offensive' ensued, which changed in the 1980s to 'defensive' action in response to the spread of new technologies and new forms of work organization (for example quality circles), and informal and management-inspired forms of worker participation. The latter will not be covered here, since they have been introduced as part of a one-sided managerial policy, the approach being to grant privileges rather than endow the enterprise workforce with enforceable rights.

In addition to the spread of new technologies, and related to it, a partial decentralization of collective bargaining in Europe from sector to enterprise formed a new impetus for developments in worker participation. Students of industrial relations, traditionally devoting most of their attention to the state and the national level, now turned to enterprise decision-making and to the local unions and works councils as the core of industrial relations (Hancké, 1991; Katz, 1993; Locke, 1990; Turner, 1991). Repeated EC efforts to implement guidelines for worker participation stimulated international comparisons of worker participation (Biagi, 1990; Däubler and Lecher, 1991; European Trade Union Institute, 1990b; Industrial Relations Services, 1990). Such comparisons reveal considerable national differences in legislation or formal regulations between the countries of Western Europe. However, only a few international comparisons also cover differences and similarities in worker participation *practice*: a recent project of the European Foundation for the Improvement of Living and Working Conditions (Cressey and Williams, 1990; Gill and Krieger, 1992) and the large IDE project, which was carried out in the 1970s (IDE, 1981).

3   Works councils

We will first look at a number of national differences between works council rules in the six member states of the European Union in which such councils have existed for some time (based on Koene and Slomp, 1991).

Composition and election

In each country, enterprises of a certain minimum size are required to set up a works council. This size ranges from six employees in Germany to 100 in Belgium (see Table 14.1). More common is a minimum of 35 (Denmark, the Netherlands) or 50 (France, Spain). This limit has been subject to two opposing trends. Initially, there were efforts to bring this minimum requirement more into line with existing practice, that is, to raise it, for instance, from 25 to 100 in the Netherlands and from 25 to 50 in Denmark. Later, under pressure to make provisions for greater worker participation, both of these countries lowered the minimum again, to the present size. In Denmark the change was effected by a national joint agreement. In contrast to the other countries, the Danish works councils have not been provided for by law, but by a 'cooperation agreement' which has been formulated in rather general terms.

Compliance with this obligation (a question hardly ever touched on in comparative surveys) varies with the size of the enterprise. National data show that Denmark has the best record, combining a low size requirement with a high rate of compliance (80 percent), and Belgium the worst, combining a high size requirement with a low compliance rate (60 percent). That even German law is not sacred can be seen in German enterprises

Table 14.1   Works councils: spread, size and election procedure

	Belgium	Denmark	France	Germany	Netherlands	Spain
Name	Ondernemingsraad (OR)/Comité d'entreprise (CE)	Samarbejdsudvalg (SU)	Comité d'entreprise (CE)	Betriebsrat (BR)	Ondernemingsraad (OR)	Comité de empresa (CE)
Legal base	Law 1948: National collective agreement no. 9, 1972	National cooperation agreement (Samarbejdsaftale) 1947/1964/1970/1986	Law 1946/1975/1982 (1982: lois Auroux)	Law (BetrVG) 1952/1972	Law (WOR) 1950/1971/1979/1981	Law (Estatuto de los trabajadores) 1980
Minimum size of enterprises for which obligation exists (no. of employees)	200 (1948) 150 (1956) 100 (1973)	25 (1947) 50 (1964) 35 (1986)	50	6	25 (1950) 100 (1971) 35 (1981)	50
Percentage of relevant enterprises with a works council	60%	80%	75%	Over 100: 80% 50–100: 60% 5–10: 10%	Over 100: 83% 35–100: 41%	n.a.
Concern-wide works councils	No	Yes	Comité central d'entreprise Comité de groupe Comité interentreprises	Gesamtbetriebsrat (GBR) (large enterprise or concern-division) Konzernbetriebsrat (KBR) (concern)	Centrale ondernemingsraad (COR) (concern) Groepsondernemings-raad (GOR) (concern-division)	

	6–25	4–12	3–15	1–31	3–25	5–75
Size and composition	Parity	Parity	Employer is president	Employees only	Employees only	Employees only
Elections: term of election	Nationwide ('social elections'): 4 years	Different times: 2 years	Nationwide: 2 years	Nationwide: 4 years	Different times: 3 years	Nationwide: 4 years
Right of nomination	Trade unions (*cadres*: employees)	Trade unions	First ballot: trade unions Second ballot: employees	Trade unions/3 or more employees	Trade unions/one-third of unorganized employees	Trade unions/employees
Electoral colleges	*Arbeiders/ouvriers* (manual) *Bedienden/employés* (clerical)	No provisions: in practice separate colleges manual–clerical	*Ouvriers* (manual) *Employés* (clerical) *Cadres*	*Arbeiter* (manual) *Angestellte* (clerical)	No (in practice separate colleges manual–clerical)	*Obreros* (manual) *Empleados* (clerical)
Minimum employment at firm for active/passive voting right	3 months/6 months	No provisions	6 months/12 months	None/6 months	6 months/12 months	1 month/6 months
Turnout at latest elections	72%	n.a.	70%	79%	74% (average)	n.a.
Unionization rate of members	Almost 100%	100%	Majority	75%	74%	90%

with less than ten employees, in which, not surprisingly, works councils are highly exceptional.

There are three variations in council composition. The first one is a parity (joint employee–management) council (Belgium, Denmark). This composition may lead to rather arbitrary management decisions on who is considered a managerial employee. In Belgium management sometimes promotes recalcitrant *cadre* members into this category in order to prevent their election on the employees' side. In practice, such upper echelon staff do not always take an active role, but leave council work on the employer's side to one or two managers. The council becomes a forum for employees and management. In Belgium and Denmark the director always chairs the meetings. The same goes for the second, French, type: although the French works councils consist of employees, the director acts as chairperson. The third type is a completely autonomous council, consisting only of employees. Germany has had such employee councils from the very start (1922; reintroduced in 1952); the Netherlands shifted from the second to the third type in 1979; and Spain imitated the German example in 1980.

Council elections, at least for the employee seats, are held every two to four years; the turnout is 70 percent or more, which is not much higher than in local or national elections. In countries characterized by union competition, like Belgium, France and Spain, elections are a real popularity contest between the unions; in Germany they constitute a popularity poll for the dominant DGB. In Denmark and the Netherlands elections are organized at random times and lack national significance. The Belgian and Danish unions enjoy a nomination monopoly; as a consequence, the works councils in these countries consist of organized workers. The only exception is the *cadre* electoral college in Belgium, in which non-union 'house lists' are allowed. In the other countries groups of (unorganized) workers have a right to nominate candidates – in France only in the second ballot – but the unions still occupy the majority of seats.

Works council rights

What about the councils' rights? Without exception the primary right of a works council is to receive information about the general condition and prospects of the enterprise (the right of information). This is most clearly demonstrated in the latest legal document establishing works councils, the Spanish *Estatuto de los trabajadores*, in which the list of competencies opens with: '*1.1. Recibir información . . .*'. The second is the right to offer advice in economic matters (the right of advice, or consultation), and the third consists of co-decision-making in social and personnel affairs. In a number of countries the latter right has been extended to include a veto or corresponding right, as the German term *Mitbestimmung* (co-determination) suggests (see Table 14.2).

A more detailed analysis of the first right reveals that all councils have the right to be informed about the company's social and economic state of affairs and prospects. This covers information which has to be supplied on an annual or quarterly basis, and information to be forwarded before a decision is taken in a specific field. The type of periodical report to be presented is prescribed in greater detail in France and Belgium than in the other countries. In France such reports include quarterly data on the volume of orders, production schedules, employment figures and likely changes in capital goods and production methods which may affect working conditions. In French enterprises of over 300 employees, management also has to provide the annual *Bilan Social*, which contains a range of information on social matters. Other countries focus less on information as a right in itself. German and Dutch law specifies the types of decisions about which the works councils have to be informed in advance; the kind of information to be provided is not listed in detail.

Council rights in economic affairs never go beyond information and consultation. Despite this limitation, the social effects of economic decisions – in particular the consequences for the level of employment – are a major, if not the main concern of works councils in any of these countries (Albertijn et al., 1990: 24; Henriet et al., 1987: 10).

In contrast, council rights regarding social and personnel issues generally do not stop at information and consultation, but may extend to a veto right, either formulated as such or set forth as an explicit obligation for management to obtain council consent before a decision is implemented. The list of subjects covered by such rights is longer in Germany and the Netherlands than in the other countries. It includes working time, rules pertaining to employment, career planning, dismissal of workers, health and safety, systems of payment, in-job training and staff assessment. On paper, this makes the Dutch and the German councils the most powerful of the countries under comparison. Their position is reinforced by the obligation imposed upon the employer to negotiate in good faith with the council on such subjects. A similar obligation exists in Denmark.

In most countries, the councils are not allowed to deal with subjects covered by collective agreements. This implies that works councils are not permitted to change such agreements. They may work out the details of such agreements, however, allowing them some freedom of interpretation. In Germany, where sector bargaining is a more sacred principle than in the other countries, this resulted in a *Betriebsvereinbarung*, a management–works council agreement.

National differences

The most explicit differences can be summarized as follows:

1 The Danish councils are covered by a national agreement which leaves open a number of points. The other countries possess extensive statutory regulations.
2 The minimum enterprise size varies from six employees in Germany to 100 in Belgium; the other countries set a limit at 35 or 50 employees.
3 The Belgian and Danish unions enjoy a monopoly in the nomination of candidates; in France the union monopoly is limited to the first ballot.

Table 14.2 Works councils: provisions and rights

	Belgium	Denmark	France	Germany	Netherlands	Spain
Minimum number of meetings each year	12	6	12	No regulations	6	6
Chairperson	Employer	Employer	Employer	Elected by works council	Elected by works council	Elected by works council
Important subcommittees (see also: other institutions of participation)	Committees for: social enterprise funds canteen staff transport	None	Economic committee (enterprises over 1,000) Committees for social activities	*Wirtschaftsausschuss* (economic affairs) Committees for social affairs	*Arbo-comité* (health and safety) Various committees for economic and social affairs	n.a.
Provisions and privileges for council members	Costs paid Time off Protection against dismissal	Costs paid Time off Protection against dismissal	Costs paid (0.2% off wages) Time off (max. 20 hours per month, plus 5 days of educational leave) Contribution in social activities Protection against dismissal	Costs paid Time off Protection against dismissal	Costs paid Time off (max. 60 hours, plus 5 days educational leave) Protection against dismissal	Costs paid Time off (max. 15–40 hours per month) Protection against dismissal
Information rights	Distinction in four categories: basic info. (each 4 years) annual info. (econ. and social) quarterly info. (econ. and social) incidental info. (in case of important events)	No detailed prescriptions; depends upon issues at hand	Distinction in four categories: basic info. (each 4 years) annual info. (econ. and social, incl. *Bilan Social* in enterprises over 300 empl.) quarterly info. (econ. position and employment) incidental (in case of important events)	No general prescriptions: depends on issues at hand	No general specifications; depends upon issues at hand Twice a year general info.	No general specifications; depends upon issues at hand

Rights in economic matters	Information	Consultation	Consultation in case of important decisions on a number of points	Enterprises of 20 empl.: consultation in number of important decisions, incl. collective redundancies. Council must be enabled to influence the decision (*Interessenausgleich*)	Consultation in number of economic decisions. Council must be enabled to influence the decision (consultation restricted in enterprises under 100 empl.)	Information and consultation
Rights in social affairs	Consultation on number of points. Co-determination on a few points (notably rules of employment and dismissal, administration of social funds). In most sectors, obligation of unanimity, which induces council to comply	Consultation. Bargaining joint agreements, in particular about general rules of personnel policy	Consultation on general rules of social policy. Veto-right in flexitime. Organization of extensive social services and meetings (canteen, Christmas festivities, library, holiday resorts)	Information and consultation on a large number of points. Co-determination on some points, notably rules of employment and dismissal. Negotiate enterprise agreements on these points (*Betriebs-vereinbarung*)	Co-determination of general rules about large number of points (*instemmingsrecht*)	Information and consultation on number of points. Negotiate collective agreements
Main activities	Receiving information	Consultation. Bargaining	Receiving information. Organizing social activities	Consultation. Bargaining	Consultation. Bargaining	n.a.
Conflict-solving institutions	Appeal to Labour Court	Arbitration by the national and parity cooperation committee (*samarbejdsnaevnet*)	Appeal to Labour Court	Arbitration by (permanent or ad hoc) parity committees (*Einigungsstelle*)	Appeal to Court of Justice, in most cases preceded by mediation by a sectoral and parity committee (*bedrijfscommissie*)	Appeal to Labour Court

4   The Belgian and Danish councils are joint councils. Their Dutch, German and Spanish counterparts consist of employees only. The French position is in between.
5   The Belgian and French councils enjoy extensive information rights. In contrast, the Danish, Dutch and German council rights are formulated more explicitly as co-determination or bargaining rights.

The lines of division in 3 and 4 overlap. A union monopoly in nomination and a parity or joint council go hand in hand. This point requires a closer look at trade union representation within the enterprise (see Table 14.3).

4   Trade union representation

The trade unions are often represented in the firm by trade union representatives or union delegates who may have some freedom of action. (The British term 'shop steward' suggests too much freedom and will not be used here.) This kind of union representation within the enterprise is covered by law in France and Spain. In the other countries it is the subject of national (that is, all-industry) or industry agreements. As a result there are broad variations in size, nomination procedures and competencies within each country. Despite the lack of national uniformity, some general lines can be drawn with respect to the delegates' activities and functions. In this case a division into three groups seems feasible, with rather sharp demarcation lines. Belgium and Denmark constitute one category, Germany and the Netherlands belong to a second, and France and Spain to a third.

Differences in union networks

The two major Belgian union federations – the Catholic ACV/CSC and the socialist ABVV/FGTB – as well as the Danish LO possess extended networks of union delegates in most industries and even in relatively small enterprises. The networks were established before the Second World War and have been firmly entrenched ever since. In Belgium their position has been recognized in a number of national and 'interprofessional' agreements. In Denmark they are covered by the same agreement as the works councils.

Germany and the Netherlands lack such dense networks of union delegates. In fact, it was not until the wave of militancy in the late 1960s and early 1970s that the largest German and Dutch unions, IG Metall and the Industriebond respectively, became interested in developing such grassroots activities. Until the late 1960s Dutch trade unions explicitly refrained from establishing trade union representatives within enterprises. Their policy originated in the 'post-war settlement', a 'Great Exchange' in which they traded representation within the enterprise for a strong union role in the national Social and Economic Council (Nobelen, 1991). Like their Dutch colleagues, the German *Vertrauensleute* are mainly confined to larger enterprises in metallurgy and engineering.

Trade unions in France and Spain are not well represented within the enterprise either. The French *délégués syndicaux* and the *sections syndicales* were finally accorded official status in 1968, after a long period in which any kind of trade union activity within French enterprises was suppressed – a tradition that did not altogether come to an end in 1968. Trade union rights were extended by the socialist government in the early 1980s, as part of the *lois Auroux*. The Spanish *secciones sindicales* have their roots in extra-legal institutions originating under Franco. They were legalized after the Franco period.

The existence of networks of union delegates is one reason for the high union density (60 percent or more) in Belgium and Denmark, and for its stability in the 1980s. Stability, in turn, is a good basis for setting up such networks. There are union delegations in most Belgian enterprises of over 50 employees. As in Denmark, they are active in social matters, and in large enterprises the chief delegate meets regularly, as often as once a week, with management to discuss social problems. They also constitute the core of the works councils.

Union delegates and works councils

This division suggests a link between the trade union monopoly in the nomination of works council candidates and the parity (joint employer–employee) composition of such councils. In the case of a union monopoly and high union density, as in Belgium and Denmark, a council consisting only of employees would be a duplicate of the trade union delegation. Under that condition, the councils' primary task is not so much to represent the workforce (which is the task of the union delegates) as to serve as a forum in which the union delegates, as workforce representatives, meet with the employer. The council is not really necessary for this contact, however; witness the frequent absence of works councils in Belgian enterprises. Moreover, it is not uncommon for delegates in Denmark and Belgium to meet with the employer, take a short break, and meet again, this time as the official works council (sometimes they even skip the second part altogether). Hence, the works council is second in line, behind the delegates.

Germany and the Netherlands have much lower union densities than Belgium and Denmark, at about 40 percent and 26 percent respectively. Although the union delegates tend to dominate the works councils, a neat distinction is generally made between union work and works council activities, if only because the works councils represent many non-union members, in the Netherlands even more than in Germany. According to opinion surveys in both countries, works council members (both union and non-union) regard the union delegates as a service institution benefiting

Table 14.3   Trade union representation and other forms of worker participation

	Belgium	Denmark	France	Germany	Netherlands	Spain
Trade union representation						
Name	Vakbondsafvaardiging/ délégation syndicale	Tillidsmaend	Section syndicale Délégués syndicaux	Vertrauensleute(körper)	Kaderleden	Sección sindical de empresa Delegados sindicales
(Legal) base	National agreement 1947 National collective agreement no. 5, 1971	Sector agreements	Law 1968 Law 1982 (lois Auroux)	Sector agreements	Sector agreements	Law 1980 (Estatuto de los trabajadores)
Spread	Very extended	Very extended	Extended	Limited	Limited	n.a.
Minimum size of enterprise	20–50 (average)	n.a.	50	Large enterprise only	Large enterprise only	250
Size of representation	ca. 1–10	n.a.	1–5	n.a.	n.a.	1–4
General rights	Bargaining social affairs within framework of collective agreement	Bargaining social affairs within framework of collective agreement	Bargaining social affairs and labour conditions	Mainly complaint handling	Mainly complaint handling	Bargaining social affairs and labour conditions

Health and safety committee	Parity committee, composed like works councils	Parity committee, composed like works council	Committee of employees, employer is chairperson	Subcommittee of works council	Subcommittee of works council
Representation on management board/supervisory board	No	One-third of supervisory board (min. of two representatives) in enterprises of 35 employees	One member on management board or supervisory board, but without right to vote	At least one-third of supervisory board in companies over 500 employees, up to one-half in large mining and steel companies. One direcor on management board of large companies	No representation. Consultation right in nomination of board members. Right of objection against nomination of members of supervisory board
Other institutions of worker participation	No	No	*Délégués du personnel* for complaint handling. *Groupes d'expression* for discussion of labour complaints	Committee of higher echelon staff members. Enterprise meeting twice a year in enterprises of 10–35 employees	*Delegados de personal* for complaint handling

the works council, and they see the works council as rather autonomous *vis-à-vis* the trade unions – comparable to the councils' independence from the employer (Borgmann, 1986; Looise, 1989). The link with the unions is much closer in the larger German enterprises, in particular in the IG Metall's domain, which has been the main subject of research on Germany (Streeck, 1984, 1992; Turner, 1991). There are hardly any Dutch companies in which the union–council relationship approaches the one found in the German car industry, and as a rule the works council independence *vis-à-vis* the unions is greater in the Netherlands than in Germany. The existence of two independent and competing journals for works council members, which both publish council news and the activities of a number of independent training institutes for council members, confirms this independence. (The German magazine *Mitbestimmung* is published by the DGB, Deutscher Gewerkschaft Bund.)

The Dutch and German 'dual system', in which trade unions operate at the branch level and industry wide, while works councils function in the enterprise, suits conditions different from those in Belgium and Denmark – a lower union density and a weaker union presence within the firm. Since the task of representation cannot be claimed by the trade union delegation, as in Belgium and Denmark, the council is primarily a representative institution. The comparison reveals the link between nomination procedures and council composition in the four countries. When workforce representation is a trade union affair, the councils function as an intermediary between management and trade unions. In countries where the unions are not able to forward such a claim, the works council performs that task.

The same reasoning holds to some extent for France and Spain. Their union density is the lowest in Europe (about 15 percent) and the Spanish councils are independent, both formally and informally. The French councils are not, but even in France unions and employers draw a sharp line of distinction between the councils and trade union activities. However, the French and the Spanish situations require a discussion of the nature of worker participation.

5 The nature of worker participation

Of course, there are wide variations in activities and in the influence exercised by works councils and trade union delegations, as well as in their relationship with the enterprise management. The differences are not only cross-national, but also regional and sectoral within each country, and are in particular related to industrial branch (active councils in the metallurgy and engineering industries, passive ones in the construction industry) and even more to enterprise size. Despite this variation, it is possible to make a few general comments based on national research findings and comparative research. This makes a more profound division into two groups possible, which can provide an explanation for some of the differences and similarities in worker participation (Slomp, 1990).

Northern Europe

For four of the countries surveyed – Belgium, Denmark, Germany and the Netherlands – the national as well as the comparative literature almost without exception point to the same kind of worker participation with certain distinct features (Gevers, 1989; Looise, 1989; Martens, 1989; Michels, 1989).

First, there is some form of integration within managerial decision-making. Although many council members and trade unionists complain about the late stage at which they are informed and their lack of influence – and probably rightly so – they are nevertheless involved in major enterprise decisions, exercising more influence in social and personnel matters than in economic and financial questions. Comparative research confirms this position. The four countries score high in worker involvement in technology decisions (Cressey and Williams, 1990; Gill and Krieger, 1992) and in social and personnel matters. On economic issues, however, most councils in these countries are rather passive (Hoffmann and Neumann, 1987: 308; Looise and De Lange, 1987: 25–31).

Secondly, the relationship between management and the works council and/or the union representation can only rarely be described as a sustained cold war and hardly ever results in an open labour conflict. Cooperation prevails and in the smaller countries the relationship is often characterized as one of harmony. In Belgium, Germany and the Netherlands this obligation to cooperate is laid down in the law. The German law speaks of *vertrauensvolle Zusammenarbeit* (cooperation based upon mutual trust) and explicitly forbids the works council to call strikes. But the law is actually less significant than the third feature which these countries have in common: if a case of sustained non-cooperation or latent conflict arises, the unions, and sometimes employers' organizations as well, use their power to encourage the parties to undertake mutual steps towards cooperation and integration. If an open breach occurs, the organizations assume responsibility for resolving the conflict. The Germans have their joint *Einigungsstelle*, but this body is set up on a case-by-case basis, and union representatives and management reach agreement before the (neutral) chairman has to cast a vote. The Danish have a permanent and national cooperation committee (*Samarbejdsnaevnet*) for this purpose. In Belgium and the Netherlands union–employer mediation also precedes and often preempts legal action by any of the parties. The three features – integration, cooperation and union coordination or even discipline – amount to a form of 'disciplined integration' between the works council and union representation in managerial decision-making (cf. Turner 1991).

France and Spain

In contrast, in France and Spain this cooperative integration is a far less common phenomenon. The relationship between works councils and/or union sections is characterized as much by conflict as by cooperation or mutual adaptation – indeed, sometimes even more so. In France the strained relations can lead to the marginalization of the works council, not only by management but also by the unions. Many French works councils concentrate on a number of social services, notably the company cafeteria and the library, and a number of social events, like Christmas parties, rather than on enterprise policies (Henriet et al., 1987: 87–88; Dufour and Mouriaux, 1986). In Spain, a country with one of the highest strike rates in Europe, almost half of the strikes are started by the *secciones sindicales*. In both countries, unions and employers stay at arm's length, and they explicitly do not adhere to cooperative integration. The strained relationship results in a lower rate of participation (Alós-Moner and Lope, 1991; Bilbao, 1991: 261; Kaiero, 1988). France scores very low in recent comparative research (Cressey and Williams, 1990; Gill and Krieger, 1992).

It is not the existence of a dual system, but rather the distinction between disciplined integration in the smaller countries and Germany as opposed to contentious, aloof relations or marginalization in France and Spain that forms the major dividing line in worker participation.

Variations in worker participation within countries: the case of German Mitbestimmung

This distinction does not mean that there are no differences within the northern European 'group' or even within countries of the northern European 'group'. The scope of the subjects covered and the influence exercised varies mostly in Germany. The IG Metall-steered 'co-determination complex' in the large German firms, and especially in the German car industry, probably represents the most powerful form of worker participation anywhere (Streeck, 1984; Cressey and Williams, 1990; Gill and Krieger, 1992). In the smaller German enterprises, most councils are just as passive or weak as in small enterprises elsewhere (Hoffmann and Neumann, 1987). This co-determination complex includes three elements.

First, in most larger enterprises some or all of the works council members are exempted from work for council activities. This gives them more time to reduce the information gap with management, and to become actively involved in the company's social and personnel policy. In the other countries (with Belgium as a possible exception), most of the members are exempted only part of the time (and in France mainly for the council's social and cultural activities).

Secondly, and far more important, is that the workers in larger German companies are also represented on the supervisory board (*Aufsichtsrat*). The term *Mitbestimmung* (co-determination) often refers to this specific type of participation. There are three variations:

- one-third of the supervisory board in companies over 500 employees;

- half of the board (but with a deciding vote for the board's president, elected by the shareholders) in companies with a workforce of over 2000;
- half of the board in large steel works and coal mines.

In the latter two forms, union officials may also be elected to the board (the IG Metall chairman is a board member at Mercedes Benz and other companies). In those companies the appointment of the P&O (or personnel) manager is also subject to union consent. This combination of participation arrangements means that the works council is often informed beforehand on important decisions – and it is the timing of the information which is often the decisive factor, since early notice allows the council to draft alternative plans (Bamberg et al., 1987). Moreover, the approval procedure for the personnel manager permits the union to influence the personnel department and thus provides an easy opportunity to recruit new union members among newly hired employees. Worker representation on the board also exists in a few other countries, but in much weaker forms. In France, for example, the prevailing management–union antagonism prevents it from increasing the influence of the works council.

A third point, stressed by the leading German scholar Wolfgang Streeck, and a major issue in recent industrial relations literature, is the participation of German unions and works councils in vocational training and retraining within the enterprise (Mahnkopf, 1992; Streeck, 1992; Thelen, 1992). The works council's involvement increases its integration in the company's social policies, but it also makes itself an invaluable partner in training activities for management. This form of 'productivity alliance' between the unions or works councils and company management allows the works council to demand employment guarantees for the company workforce (the 'internal' labour market) in exchange for worker mobility. Redundancies do not lead to dismissal, but to mobility within the company. In the other countries union involvement in training programmes is less well developed and 'productivity alliances' are based on wage restraint, more overtime work, or other measures.

These features mainly apply to the larger German enterprises – of which the larger car manufacturers have been a popular subject of research. Works councils and unions in smaller German firms treat each other with great reserve, as noted before. In Belgium, Denmark and the Netherlands the nature of participation resembles that in Germany, without Germany's more powerful forms of participation.

6 Differences in the nature of participation

What accounts for the north–south division? The literature offers various explanations for national differences, and these explanations might also apply to differences between north and south (summarized in Cressey and Williams, 1990; Gill and Krieger, 1992; Turner, 1991).

A few explanations

The first explanation is related to the nature of the workforce, involving factors such as skill levels and the proportion of skilled workers in industry. This might explain, for instance, differences in participation between companies with a large manual workforce and firms mainly employing clerical workers, who tend to be more career-oriented and less unionized. The point also refers to national differences in skills and in worker autonomy and responsibility within the manual workforce, German workers enjoying broader training and more job autonomy than their French, British or US counterparts. All of the countries mentioned here are high-skill economies, however, with a large clerical workforce. As a consequence, this particular explanation has lost some of its salience.

Other explanations refer to the company structure and to management characteristics. An example is the reference to the traditional antagonism in French management–workforce relations. Of course this tradition is a powerful force, but German employers have never welcomed unions either, certainly not to the extent that employers in the smaller countries do.

A third type of explanation points to a cohesive and strong union movement. Despite its relatively low union density compared to Belgium and Denmark (and other Nordic countries), the German union movement is considered strong in organizational terms. On the other hand, the density of Dutch unions has for a number of years dropped below that of the French, and Belgian and Dutch unions are at least as fragmented as the Spanish: the Belgians have a similar 'duopoly' of two large union federations, while the Dutch almost approach the French fragmentation.

A fourth explanation focuses on legal provisions and legal backing of participation. Indeed, Germany has extensive participation legislation, with a number of laws governing the works councils and worker representation on the supervisory board. Denmark hardly has any legal rules at all, however; by contrast, French worker participation remains weakly developed, despite some fine pieces of legislation, including the Auroux measures of the early 1980s. This shows the need to differentiate between legislation which more or less follows existing practices (as is the rule in northern Europe) and laws which aim at introducing radical change, as in France. Such differentiation brings us to discussion of the system of industrial relations.

Industry bargaining as an explanation

Indeed, it is the system of industrial relations, and more specifically the degree of industry (or all-industry) bargaining, which seems to offer an explanation for the north–south division (Slomp, 1990). This kind of bargaining requires at least some union power and cohesion, of course, but depends more on how this power and cohesion are used, rather than on their existence alone. In the smaller countries and Germany, the industry sector is still the primary meeting place between unions and employers. Sector bargaining shifts the point of gravity in industrial relations from the enterprise and the shop floor to broader levels. This has not (yet) been undone by recent decentralization trends. Company bargaining was common enough in smaller nations (unlike in Germany, where Volkswagen is one of the few concerns to negotiate its own agreements). Most enterprise agreements, however, still tend to follow sector agreements – or at least policy guidelines and trade union demands – established previously at sector level. Moreover, they are negotiated by union officials from outside the enterprise, with the union delegation in a secondary position.

Collective bargaining at sector and national levels has resulted in a 'neutralization' or 'pacification' of the enterprise and the shop floor. Like the trade unions themselves, trade union representatives are under a distinct obligation to maintain labour peace during the term of the collective contract. In this form of *Tarifpartnerschaft*, as it is called in Germany, the organizations not only assume the obligation to refrain from conflicts, they also take on the commitment to hold their members to the peace obligation. For the unions this amounts to a pledge to prevent autonomous action by the enterprise workforce. By creating a sheltered niche for worker participation, the pacification of the enterprise allows the emergence and the recognition of works councils and union representatives as institutions of cooperation rather than conflict or confrontation.

In contrast, French and Spanish industrial relations are to a much lesser extent characterized by a shift of labour conflict to the industry level (Lope et al., 1989; Ruesga and Santos, 1991). Collective bargaining in the strict sense, as practised in northern Europe, is certainly not exceptional, but neither is it common. Peace clauses exist, but the unions are unwilling (and unable) to enforce compliance. The recent low tide in the French strike rate does not imply a major deviation from that tradition, since the socialist governments of the 1980s have encouraged enterprise bargaining, rather than conflict-solving institutions. In combination with the very loose and decentralized structure of the French unions, and with the recently acquired enterprise bargaining rights, this leaves the union delegates ample room for manoeuvre, at least as far as union control is concerned. It is management, not the interplay of unions and management, which limits worker participation, as is the case in the other countries. Although French private sector industrial relations are increasingly characterized by union–management accommodation, the unions and the employers are still far from a new 'consensus' society (Wilson, 1991), witness the term *coopération conflictuelle*, coined by the CFDT. The employers primarily seek such mutual understanding with the relatively weak councils, in this way bypassing the unions – and marginalizing the councils as a result.

What is at stake here is a separation between subjects that are negotiated at industry level and subjects dealt with in the process of worker participation. The separation is not necessarily one of distributive versus other matters, since employment issues are also distributive and are often handled within the firm. In general, wages and the number of working hours are sector matters, covered by formal agreements, while wage structure and working time specifications may be dealt with at enterprise level. It is not the exact line of division between the subjects that counts, however, but rather that they are in fact divided and that major terms and conditions of employment, including basic wage rates, are negotiated at industry level. Even the German car works (covered by the regional metallurgy agreements) adhere to the distinction, despite the works councils' relatively large bargaining scope (the results of which are laid down in the *Betriebsvereinbarungen*).

The legal extension of employment terms does not constitute a functional equivalent for this type of formal bargaining. It is practised more in northern Europe than in France, where it covers rather marginal minimum conditions, without much practical meaning. Moreover, the use of this instrument only shows that the organizations by themselves do not have the capacity to negotiate at the sector (or national) level, and to impose the results on sector employers (and employees).

Using this separation as a basic explanation, other references have additional value. Although the existence of a legal framework does not seem a valid explanation in and of itself, it could explain differences between the more powerful German *Mitbestimmung* and worker participation in Belgium or the Netherlands. Union cohesion could also explain in some part the differences within this group: unions in Denmark and Germany are more cohesive than in Belgium and the Netherlands – and they score higher in worker influence (Cressey and Williams, 1990; Gill and Krieger, 1992). This difference may also be due to worker representation on the board in the former two countries.

7   Works council differences in perspective

Our analysis, in which we have considered the works council and union representation in combination, has shown that the basic line of division lies between France and Spain on the one hand and the other four countries studied on the other. In the latter category, worker participation is embedded in a union–employer relationship of collective bargaining – *Tarifpartnerschaft*, to use the German term, or *overleg*, the Dutch term, which suggests even more cooperation and harmony. Not only the employers, but also the unions limit the workers' participatory activities, in this way preventing any threat to either collective bargaining or the pacification of the enterprise level. In France and Spain the union role in limiting the function of worker participation is much more weakly developed, leaving ample room for enterprise union–employer conflict, in which the union section is a major actor.

What, then, is the relevance of the five distinctions made in Section 3? Let us look at each in turn.

The first one, between Denmark's rather open joint agreements and the other countries' elaborate legal provisions, is of great interest to labour law students, but its relevance for the nature of industrial relations is limited. In both Denmark and Belgium, union representation is more important for worker participation than the works council and is ruled by joint agreement. Moreover, since 1962 a number of joint agreements have covered aspects of the Belgian works councils; examples are the 'interprofessional' collective agreement no. 9 signed in 1972 and the technology agreement concluded in 1983. The two countries resemble each other not only in worker participation, but also in their respective industrial relations systems, in particular in the way the summit organizations closely monitor industrial relations, and in the importance of national agreements. The point is that legal backing as such is in fact not crucial, as France's Auroux legislation also makes clear.

Minimum enterprise size requiring a works council (point 2) is not important either. Germany has the lowest limit, but there are nevertheless no works councils in small enterprises. Belgium has the highest, but union representation fills the gap in enterprises with 50 employees or even fewer. In more general terms, in Western Europe worker participation starts in effect with 35–50 employees.

We have already mentioned a link between the nomination rules for works council members and works council composition (points 3 and 4). In Belgium and Denmark, worker representation is a trade union affair and the works council a joint employer–union committee. In Germany and the Netherlands, the council serves as an intermediary between management and the trade unions. The distinction is of importance for its relation to union density and trade union organization, and not for the nature of worker participation.

The legal focus on information rights (point 5) reveals the influence of the French legal tradition in Belgium. Its practical meaning is limited, however. The overall record of Belgian worker participation is similar to that in Germany, the Netherlands and, above all, Denmark. As in item (1) above this point is of greater relevance for comparative labour law than for industrial relations. Even more than the distinction mentioned in (1), it demonstrates how similar formal rules can camouflage completely different practices, and *vice versa*. We will now shift our attention to the rest of Europe and investigate whether this same distinction holds.

8   Worker participation in other European countries

The Nordic countries

Even within the group of Nordic nations the common nature of worker participation is hidden behind a variety of rules – based either on the law or joint agreements. In these countries union representation enjoys priority over works councils. Sweden has been the most radical (or logical) in this respect. Since the extension of bargaining rights to all social and personnel issues in the path-breaking 1976 Co-determination Act (*Medbestemmande-lagen*), Swedish unions have neglected the works councils, leading to their disappearance. Trade union representation has become the only institution of worker participation. In fact this was hardly a break with the past, since councils had already been monopolized by trade union delegates, as in Denmark and Norway. It was rather an attempt to de-institutionalize the point of contact between local union and management and bring it in line with prevailing practices between employers and unions and with Sweden's high union density (over 80 percent). However, the nature of union participation is similar to that in the German or Dutch 'dual system'. Its influence is probably greater, due to the numerical strength of the unions, their firm hold over most of the workforce, and the backing of powerful legislation (Levie and Sandberg, 1991: 254; Pontussen, 1990: 327). Worker participation in Austria, which has more or less imitated the German 'dual' system, is also of a comparable nature (Diefenbacher and Nutzinger, 1992). Hence, the various systems of worker participation in northern Europe are similar in nature, with scarcely any disparity between 'dual' systems and a union monopoly of worker participation. In other words: worker participation functions well without works councils. What appears to be crucial for its functioning is not institutionalization in councils, but the separation between (mainly distributive) issues handled at industry level, and (working environment) issues taken up, under the unions' watchful eye, by institutions of worker participation and coordination.

Italy

Italy has a long history of changes in participation institutions, from the age-old *commissione interna* to recent informal and autonomous worker committees (*cobas*), a number of which have sprung up outside the reach of the unions. Works councils have been prominent at times but totally neglected at others, by the unions as well as by spontaneous worker committees. The Italian industrial relations system has traditionally shown similarities with the French one (especially in its degree of politicization), but more than in France, it has always been a patchwork of local and regional variations – without a framework of national rules. It is this variation which seems to be the very essence of the Italian system. It is no coincidence that a leading student of Italian industrial relations (Locke, 1990) has noted the resurgence of the local union. This pluriformity or – depending upon one's appraisal – fragmentation illustrates a major feature of the system: the great freedom of action enjoyed by local unions and the relative lack of coordination by industry unions. Although collective bargaining at sector level and even at the national level (on issues like the *scala mobile*, for example) is a central element in Italian industrial relations, local unions enjoy great autonomy in a number of fields, including working time, bonuses and profit-sharing, new technologies, redundancies and even wages, with local agreements preceding national ones (Locke, 1990: 368). This leads to a wide variety of participation practices and to union influence on managerial decision-making. The recent trend towards formalization is mainly affecting the enterprise level, and not the pluriformity within and among industries (Ferner and Hyman, 1992b: 554). Cooperative and integrative forms exist alongside more conflictual ones. The two forms also alternate with each other or with an almost complete union absence.

The United Kingdom

Pluriformity and fragmentation are typical of the UK as well. Indeed, the core feature of British industrial relations is perhaps the central role played by workplace union activities, seen most clearly in the autonomy of the shop stewards. Since the 1960s, shop stewards have almost supplanted union leaders as the main actors in bargaining. The reforms put through by recent Conservative governments have reinforced that trend, inspiring unilateral management decision-making without collective bargaining, and leaving the shop stewards as the last champions of union influence in managerial decision-making. Although employers in enterprises with union recognition agreements have not tried to withhold such recognition, the unions' role in decisions on terms and conditions of employment has been reduced. This has been a process of marginalization rather than 'derecognition', although the latter has received wide publicity, such as attended the move by major national newspapers to the 'non-union' London Docklands (Edwards et al., 1990: 22–24; Pontussen, 1990; Smith and Morton, 1993: 102–104). While Italian pluriformity has a mixed record, with both union failures and successes, the British cannot claim any union successes at all.

There are several patterns of worker participation in Western Europe, then. In northern European countries the unions enforce both worker participation (against employers) and its aspect of cooperation and integration (against more radical workers). In France and Spain, worker participation is more conflictual, a feature which is also enforced by the unions to some extent. In the United Kingdom and Italy, local unions dominate the scene, leading to even greater variety at regional and enterprise levels.

9   Worker participation in the United States and Japan

These two countries seem to occupy positions at the opposite ends of the European spectrum.

The United States

American industrial relations have invariably been described as adversarial, as a relationship of confrontation leaving hardly any place for worker participation or for union activities within the firm – other than grievance procedures. Expectations of more cooperation have not materialized (Kochan et al., 1986; Turner, 1991). According to a recent poll, American managers still see scarcely any room for union or worker participation. Of a long list of issues, only seniority provisions were generally considered to be appropriate for joint management–union decision-making (Perline and Poynter, 1991: 185). Non-union firms are still preferred by most managers. The unions' struggle has been to gain union recognition at the company or plant level, and union recognition has been understood by both parties to mean collective bargaining about wage issues. While unions were mainly preoccupied with gaining recognition of their own organization as a bargaining partner, management used informal participation schemes as a weapon to break the unions (Taplin, 1990). The country has been a leading exporter – even to Japan – of management-inspired and non-union worker participation or 'managerialism' (Hekscher, 1988). As a consequence, formal participation devices are underdeveloped but still more contested than any in Europe. The co-management experiment conducted at GM's Saturn plant, in which union leaders act as co-managers and the local union is heavily involved in day-to-day operations, remains an isolated attempt at radical change (Rubinstein et al., 1993).

Japan

The Japanese system has combined 'spring offensives', in which radical demands were articulated, with enterprise unionism, almost exclusively devoted to productivity growth. The radicalism of the spring offensive was lost or became a mere symbol in the 1970s, due to the combined efforts of a number of enterprise unions in automobile and steel companies. Since that time the enterprise unions have played a dominant role in national industrial relations, shifting the union focus to wage restraint in exchange for lifetime welfare provisions. The union role in the larger companies has increasingly become integrative and cooperative, following the example of the union at Toyota. The collapse of the more oppositional union at Nissan heralded the victory of this type of cooperative enterprise unionism – an element in the management-inspired forms of worker integration and worker participation known as 'toyotism' (Hiwatari, 1993: 18–23, 28). The degree of union integration in the company is shown by the fact that shop-floor supervisors and foremen, who are part of the official company chain of command, also act as shop union leaders. As in the United States, works councils are exceptional. However, a number of Japanese companies have instituted 'joint consultation systems' with union or elected worker representatives. Joint consultation decisions need not be limited to social and personnel issues, but may also cover economic questions, such as major investments (Chalmers, 1989: 202–207; Hiwatari, 1993: 3; Koike, 1988: 252–255; Woodiwiss, 1992: 132–133). Both the overlap of union and company representation on the shop floor, and the fact that enterprise unions rather than industry unions are the core of the union movement, make the Japanese form of participation totally different from anything seen in Europe. In the latter the unions are autonomous organizations which operate independently of the company and which may challenge company management in its support of worker participation. The effect is that Japanese 'productivity alliances' between management and unions are concerned not with training, as in Germany, but with imposing strict employment conditions. They resemble German alliances in promoting workforce mobility within the firm, although in Japan mobility is also possible between the firm and its subsidiaries.

To summarize, two types of worker participation predominate in the industrial world: one in which the unions force their members to maintain the peace so that they do not interfere with industry bargaining, and a second in which local unions have a (somewhat) free hand. The former, to be found in northern Europe, leads to cooperative and relatively powerful worker participation. The latter may lead to conflictual enterprise relations (France, Spain) or to a patchwork of cooperative and conflictual forms, in general without much power (United States, United Kingdom, Spain). Japan is an exceptional case in the 'cooperative' category, since it is the enterprise management rather than the unions which imposes cooperation.

10   Towards 'training alliances'?

The future of worker participation systems

Recent economic and social changes, like 'lean production', 'just-in-time production', the break-up of large companies into relatively autonomous firms, human resource management and management-inspired forms of participation in shop-floor decisions and quality control, are currently stimulating the discussion on worker participation (in the new terminology: employee participation). Authors who are sympathetic with worker participation are almost threatening to 'write off' the United States and United Kingdom if they do not adjust their industrial relations systems to more cooperative ones (Berg, 1993). Non-union firms, the distant relationship between unions and management, and the union preoccupation with 'conservative' issues like wages do not create favourable conditions for greater union involvement or worker participation in the near future. Japan offers at best a frightening prospect (Roth, 1992), with companies seemingly sovereign and unions dependent on them. Italy provides a few examples of recommendable union–management cooperation, but the real model is Germany, and in particular the 'co-determination complex' of the German automobile works. Among its assets are the degree of cohesion within the union movement, in particular the unions' (or IG Metall's) combination of centralized strength and shop-floor decentralization, strict legislation on worker participation, and, perhaps most important, union involvement in training programmes, both inside and outside the enterprise.

Is there any future at all?

Some authors even believe that the economic prospects of a nation will to some extent depend on their systems of worker participation (Sabel, 1991, 1993; cf. Thelen, 1992). As a consequence, pessimism prevails concerning the economic prospects of the United States and the United Kingdom. Both their response and that of the Japanese to the current pace of technological change and international competition seem to be based on cost reduction strategies. This response consists of a monopoly of management-imposed forms of worker participation, a (further) decline in union influence, wage restraint, and, ultimately, either serious wage cuts or, as the only other alternative, mass redundancies due to disinvestment and an exodus to low-cost countries. In contrast, Germany may have a better future. The German management strategy is not one of wage restraint, but of training and retraining, in order to retain a highly skilled labour force and a leading position in high-technology production. The low-cost strategy applied in the former countries either leads to clashes with the unions (US and UK) or takes the form of 'productivity alliances' such as the enterprise unions in Japan. German unions are heavily involved in the reskilling strategy, but in contrast to the Japanese model, this strategy is coupled with the continuous improvement of employment conditions and job protection. (The increase in unemployment in Germany is seen as a disturbing factor, due mainly to German reunification.) This conclusion would seem to apply to the smaller nations in the northern European group as well, provided that the unions there are able to become more actively involved in employee (re)training programmes within the enterprise. The right management–union relationship is already in place. What is required is a shift in union focus towards enterprise-based training, even in Sweden, where the unions have focused on retraining unemployed workers (Thelen, 1992).

The conclusion of this (somewhat speculative) reasoning is that only those unions that succeed in combining cooperation with management and a concentration on training services have a future. Only under these circumstances will worker participation prosper and function as an incentive to join a union. Whatever its merits, this kind of reasoning leads to one conclusion at the very least: worker participation will occupy a far more central place in industrial relations than ever before.

11   Conclusion

In countries where works councils operate, they cannot be considered in isolation from trade union representation in the enterprise. The two are twin institutions, acting almost as communicating vessels. When we consider them in combination, we see that the nature and extent of worker participation is determined not by the existence of a 'dual system', but by the level at which the major terms and conditions are negotiated. Where formal sector agreements predominate, both the employers and the unions create a sheltered niche for worker participation, while at the same time limiting its scope and forcing it into a role of cooperation. In the second group enterprise-level regulation of the terms and conditions of employment predominates. Both trade union representatives and works councils may be agents of conflict (and bargaining) with management. This means that the main line of division in worker participation is determined by the national system of industrial relations, rather than by legal rules or union strength in itself.

15 Multinational corporations and industrial relations: policy and practice

Ulke Veersma

1 Introduction   318

2 Multinationals and systems of industrial relations   319
Limitations to the ethnocentric approach   319
Level of decision-making   320
*Industrial relations policy in MNCs and national regulatory
frameworks*   323

3 Internationalization as the rationalization of production through
the reallocation of employment   327
The new international division of labour   328
Social dumping   331
Social dumping in the European Union   333

4 Conclusions   336

1 Introduction

In this chapter we will discuss in greater detail the role and strategy of multinational corporations (MNCs) in shaping industrial relations. The internationalization of trade and industry and the dominant role of MNCs in this process have put pressure on systems of industrial relations.

Section 2 will investigate the tension between MNCs and national regulatory frameworks for labour: what is the position occupied by industrial relations policy in the overall policy of an MNC, and what sort of friction can arise between an MNC's policy and national systems of industrial relations? We will first focus on the level of decision-making associated with this policy domain within MNCs. National systems of industrial relations are being put under more pressure as the decision-making power with respect to personnel issues is centralized at the concern level. That is why we will take a closer look at the relationship between the parent company and subsidiaries in host countries, and the problems that can arise in this relationship.

Section 3 will discuss phenomena such as *social dumping* as an expression of the new global division of labour. In certain cases, MNCs exploit differences between countries with respect to industrial relations systems and terms and conditions of employment. Production costs can be lowered by relocating labour-intensive segments of production to countries that offer employees a lower level of social protection. The relocation of production and employment is often concurrent with reorganizations, redundancies and wage cuts in those countries where the MNC originally carried out its production activities or at least that part of them. Changes in the global division of labour and the problems that this creates for existing systems of industrial relations will form the main concern of the third section of this chapter.

2   Multinationals and systems of industrial relations

This section will focus on the field of tension between the activities carried out by MNCs and national systems of industrial relations. In this context, such systems are mainly seen as regulatory frameworks; in other words, as a source of rules which shape the relationship between employers and employees. The tension between an MNC's policy and a national framework may be expressed in the form of confrontations between a subsidiary's management, which is attempting to implement policy plans decided on at headquarters, and local (or national) interest groups, which advocate existing traditions and regulatory structures for labour. The subsidiary's management is sometimes faced with the difficult choice between loyalty in following the central policy line to the letter and trying to institute effective management within a given power structure. MNCs are searching for ways to mitigate such strained relations. Such solutions might include devolving the responsibility for industrial relations policy to the subsidiaries, or developing a strategic industrial relations policy at MNC level. In the latter case, industrial relations within the subsidiaries may itself become the object of strategic policy interventions. In this section we will focus on the way in which industrial relations policy is created within MNCs and the level at which this occurs.

Limitations to the ethnocentric approach

MNCs and systems of industrial relations in host countries can interfere with each other in various different ways and to various different extents. The most extreme example is when headquarters imposes patterns of industrial relations on its subsidiaries in host countries. This is the approach taken by the ethnocentric MNC, in Perlmutter's taxonomy (1969). Placed within the analytical framework provided in Chapter 13, this approach allows very little variety between the various subsidiaries, while decisions on social policy issues and industrial relations will be taken at the top of the pyramid. The literature provides ample examples of North American MNCs that attempted to make their foreign subsidiaries union-free. Other examples include Japanese MNCs setting up enterprise unions at foreign subsidiaries. Such practices follow traditional Japanese industrial relations, but are not at all according to West European traditions, where employee interests generally find representation in broadly organized, independent trade unions.

An ethnocentric approach to industrial relations policy, in which a subsidiary's policy is dictated directly by the parent company, is subject to limitations and restrictions, however. First of all, institutional and cultural variety make it highly unlikely that an MNC will be able to maintain a centralized industrial relations policy in all of the various countries where it has subsidiaries without encountering difficulties or having to make modifications. As the case study below indicates, when viewed from various cultural settings, the policy goals, models and concepts will be subject to a wide variety of interpretations.

> *A study conducted in an American MNC showed that opinions held on employee participation in the parent company may deviate sharply from the opinions held in the host countries. For example, the management of a subsidiary in the Netherlands will have a different view of participation than corporate management. The former considers employee participation as an expression of social values such as democracy, as an instrument for improving mutual relations and the quality of labour, and not as a way of stimulating better performance (McFarlin et al., 1992: 376–377). The MNC's 'corporate culture', on the other hand, considers such participation above all às a competitive weapon, something particularly obvious in the initiatives taken to increase productivity (McFarlin et al., 1992: 376). The authors of this study advised American MNCs to formulate their objectives for employee participation programmes in accordance with the host country, and to allow participation models to vary according to local circumstances. Implementation should take local sensitivities into account (1992: 378).*

Secondly, it is questionable whether a centralized approach to industrial relations policy actually produces the best results. After all, from the 1980s on, there has been a tendency to decentralize industrial relations, so that closer coordination can be achieved between the factor labour and the production strategies applied within a company. Local management, furthermore, is better able to respond to local circumstances, such as changes in industrial relations and fluctuations in the local labour market. The extent to which a (rapid) response to local changes can be formulated depends on the degree of policy decentralization within the MNC and the degree of autonomy accorded to the subsidiaries. That is why, in actual practice, MNCs show gradations in the degree of policy centralization/ decentralization when it comes to industrial relations. Depending on a number of factors, which we will discuss below, the emphasis in one case will be on autonomy for subsidiary management, while in another case central coordination of policy is emphasized.

Level of decision-making

Hamill (1984) investigated to what extent MNCs steered their industrial relations policy towards centralization or decentralization. He also

Table 15.1 *The locus of decision-making (number of firms)*

	Decided mainly by parent/reg. HQ	Approved by parent/reg. HQ	Consult with or seek advice of parent/reg. HQ	Decided mainly by the UK subsidiary
Operating budget	15	10	1	4
Capital investment	15	9	2	4
Union recognition	4	3	4	19
Employer association membership	5	2	3	20
Negotiations/collective bargaining[1]	—	2	1	18
Structure of collective bargaining[1]	5	1	1	14
Wage increases	—	17	6	7
Wage payment systems	10	1	1	18
Pensions	6	9	7	8
Fringe benefits	6	5	6	13
Settlement of strikes[1]	—	—	6	15
Numbers employed	12	6	4	8
Recruitment of managerial staff	—	6	—	24

[1] Unionized firms only. Twenty-one of the 30 firms studied were unionized. Fourteen of these were unionized for both manual and white-collar workers with 7 recognizing manual worker trade unions only.

Source: Hamill, 1984: 31

attempted to clarify why MNCs differed in the degree of centralization/decentralization of industrial relations and personnel policy. He collected his data in interviews conducted at the British subsidiaries of 30 foreign MNCs. These subsidiaries were active in three different sectors: chemicals, electro-technical industry and mechanical engineering. The study revealed that certain subjects tended to be dealt with centrally and others decentrally (see Table 15.1). Not surprisingly, decisions related to investment and the size of the budget were almost always taken by the head office, or were at least subject to head office approval. Immediately following these decisions, and in fact related to them, were decisions related to employment. Because employment determines a significant portion of the production costs, any decisions on this point were generally also taken centrally, at the parent company. Other subjects, such as trade union recognition, collective bargaining, strikes and compensation systems, were decided at the subsidiaries (Hamill, 1984: 32).

The striking thing about Table 15.1 is that there are tremendous differences in the degree to which corporate management at the 30 companies studied is involved in industrial relations policy at the various British subsidiaries. The MNCs can be divided into three different groups, ranging from one extreme, in which industrial relations and social policy are highly centralized, to the other extreme, in which such policies are highly decentralized. Between these two extremes is a category of MNC where top management is indeed involved in decision-making on issues related to wage costs, such as the number of workers and wage rises, but where an equal number of other issues are decided decentrally.

As an explanation for the differences between MNCs with respect to industrial relations policy, Hamill mentions five important structural factors (Hamill, 1984: 33).

First, the *degree of integration of production activities*. According to Hamill this factor is of crucial importance. A large degree of integration of production activities will be accompanied by centralized decision-making on industrial relations policy. Integration is first of all related to the mutual interdependence of production activities in geographically separated subsidiaries and the consequent interdependencies in integrated production networks. But integration might also pertain to a highly dependent relationship between the corporation and various subsidiaries, and to the evolution of international labour markets as a consequence of the coordination of activities within the firm. The strict relationship between integration of geographically separated production processes and a centralized industrial relations policy can be explained best by looking at the sensitivity of production networks to disruptions. A halt in production in one subsidiary, due to strike action for example, has immediate and sometimes far-reaching consequences for other nodes of the integrated network. Corporate management will have to be more closely and actively involved in industrial relations policy in the various subsidiaries in order to prevent such disruptions and to secure the continuity of the activities. Marginson (1992: 534) also pointed out the importance of the degree of integration. In sectors where subsidiaries are mere components in a worldwide production chain (for example in the car industry), and in sectors characterized by a large degree of horizontal integration (for example retail trade chains and financial institutions), there is a tendency to standardize rules and procedures. Standardization and centralization of decision-making are mutually conducive. As a result, the autonomy of divisions and operating companies may be severely restricted.

The second factor is the *home country of the parent company*. In ethnocentric MNCs, there is a tendency to let the practices and traditions of the home country make inroads into the policy of the subsidiaries in other countries. Ethnocentricity reinforces a centralized industrial relations policy. An ethnocentric orientation is more in vogue among North American and Japanese MNCs than European ones (Hamill, 1984: 34).

The third factor identified by Hamill is the *form of establishment of the subsidiary*. The chance that corporate management will actively interfere with industrial relations and personnel policy in a particular subsidiary will increase if the subsidiary was started up by the parent company (so-called 'greenfield subsidiaries') (Hamill, 1984: 34; Marginson, 1992: 537). The process of internationalization within MNCs may take a different route, for example through takeovers or mergers with existing companies. In that case certain practices and traditions may have already established themselves. It then becomes more obvious that local management should be allowed to retain a significant measure of autonomy.

Fourthly, the *profitability of the subsidiary* must be considered. A subsidiary which is successful will not have to fear much interference from the upper echelons. Subsidiaries that perform weakly, however, or that run the risk of becoming the scene of social unrest, can expect a restriction of local autonomy and interference from the parent company.

The *interests of the parent company as a source of investment in the subsidiary* are the fifth and final factor. The greater the subsidiary's dependence on the parent company for investment and financing, the more it will have to deal with centralization and interference from the top (Hamill, 1984: 34).

Industrial relations policy in MNCs and national regulatory frameworks

In the previous section we focused on the level of decision-making for industrial relations in MNCs because this level has important consequences for the stability of national regulatory frameworks. A centralized approach toward industrial relations and personnel policy precludes flexibility in responding to local and national traditions, practices and circumstances. If the choice is for an unabashed centralized approach, the existing regulatory frameworks may be put under great pressure. It is highly likely that such an approach will elicit a grassroots response. For example, depending on the balance of power, the subsidiary may become the scene of tension and conflicts, which will eventually impede the implementation of any central policy plans. A certain degree of autonomy for the subsidiary's management is therefore generally desirable. It makes it possible to achieve the objectives which have been set within the existing system of relationships, traditions, practices and circumstances.

This is not to deny that MNCs can have an active hand in shaping industrial relations within their subsidiaries, even more so than companies that do not operate internationally. They have a number of instruments at their disposal which they can use to put interest groups under pressure; they can for example threaten to transfer production activities to more 'business-friendly' countries or regions. They might make new investments contingent upon changes to existing practices in personnel and industrial relations. Such modifications sometimes have serious consequences for the existing regulatory frameworks, as the following case examples illustrate.

Until now it has been uncommon in the Netherlands for company management and company unions to conclude agreements at the company level. MNC subsidiaries frequently adopt local practices when arranging terms and conditions of employment in collective bargaining agreements. Such agreements are reached after negotiations at the sector level between employers' associations and industry-level unions affiliated with the 'recognized' trade union federations (FNV, CNV or MHP). But exceptions to this rule are made by Dutch MNCs such as Philips, which conclude their own enterprise agreements.

In 1992, the Swedish furniture corporation Ikea caused a stir when it attempted to organize its employees into a company union. Together with the works council, this union was to conclude an agreement with the corporation. FNV and CNV protested violently and demanded that the agreement for the furniture sector should apply to Ikea's employees as well. Ikea's strategy was so contrary to tradition in Dutch industrial relations that it led to a national conflict between employers and trade unions. When the affair was discussed in the Stichting van de Arbeid (Labour Foundation), the national bipartite consultative body for employers' associations and trade unions, the employers' representatives expressed the opinion that the fundamental right to conduct free wage bargaining made it possible for Ikea to conclude an agreement with its personnel on its own. The trade unions, on the other hand, argued that Ikea's action was threatening the tradition of sector-level bargaining. In their view, a company agreement for Ikea personnel was unfair competition.

Ikea finally won the conflict with the help of the national employers' associations. The company is not obliged to retain the provisions of the collective agreement for the furniture industry, and if the recognized trade union federations want to take part in the negotiations, they must associate themselves with the other parties.

The example of Ikea given above indicates that a specific industrial relations policy within a specific MNC can act as an important catalyst in stimulating certain developments which had lain dormant until then. More specifically, it can reinforce existing tendencies in the industrial relations systems in most European countries, such as decentralization of industrial relations, differentiation of terms and conditions of employment, and flexibility (Baglioni and Crouch, 1990). The advantages of a corporatist structure of industrial relations – that it controls fluctuations and battles unfair competition within sectors and curbs inflation as a consequence of sharp pay rises – are apparently considered of lesser importance than they used to be. That is why institutions which until now guaranteed a certain socio-economic order and the regulation of labour are frequently considered superfluous (Purcell, 1993). Institutionalized industrial relations, in which it is precisely the specific national characteristics which are expressed and which determine a national economy's power to respond to changing competitive relations and labour market fluctuations, are even considered as an obstacle to change in some countries. This question was particularly crucial in the United Kingdom in the 1980s, but now the majority of European countries question whether socio-economic institutions are capable of adapting to worldwide developments (Ferner and Hyman, 1992a).

Another example of the way in which an MNC's policy can put pressure on a national regulatory framework is the study conducted by Mueller and

Purcell (1992) into negotiations on working time arrangements in the European automobile industry. This study involved nine subsidiaries belonging to four different corporations in various European countries. The researchers believe they have uncovered a remarkable degree of convergence in the employment and industrial relations policy of these automobile companies. A number of factors play an important role. The first is the globalization of product markets and the increasing degree of integration of production activities, a process which is being stimulated because parts and semi-manufactures can be traded easily across national borders. In addition, Mueller and Purcell point out that competition has become sharper (for example, Japanese automobile manufacturers) and that overcapacity is keeping costs low. Finally, fierce competition is leading to a general trend toward constant product improvement and an extreme concern for quality. All of the various subsidiaries are subject to the same productivity and quality norms, making it possible to compare performance down to the smallest detail. This in turn leads to convergence in employment and organization policy, and, as we will see, in industrial relations policy. For example, Mueller and Purcell have determined that policy in the subsidiaries was focused on extending operating hours, so that they might make the best possible use of capital-intensive machinery. Operating hours were extended by introducing a system of shifts or other flexible working time arrangements. Negotiations concerning the introduction of working time systems tailored specifically to automobile production generally took place at the plant or subsidiary level.

The way such negotiations proceeded reflected the traditions and practices in the various different countries. The results of these negotiations, however, were highly similar; on top of that, negotiations always took place decentrally, even in countries such as Germany which have a tradition of sector bargaining. In each case, local negotiators were threatened with disinvestment if the negotiations did not lead to the desired result. There was positive pressure as well, for example the promise on the part of the employer to modernize and invest in the most competitive technology, provided that favourable bargaining outcomes could be reached. Mueller and Purcell reached the following conclusion:

> The trend towards two-tier bargaining, with framework agreements at national or company level and detailed negotiations on plant level was found in all countries. It allows management to link the negotiations of issues such as work organization or matching running time to reward-and-punish tactics in investment decisions. Continuous productivity and quality comparisons become used as an additional factor to spur cross-border imitation of apparently successful approaches to the achievement of productivity. (1992: 30)

These conclusions tend to mitigate our previous remarks on the importance of institutional diversity between countries for the degree to which an MNC will centralize its industrial relations policy. Under specific circumstances, it seems possible to implement central policy agendas at the local level.

> Our study of a capital-intensive sector in an industry where integrated markets have emerged in the last decade . . . leads us to suggest that in those industries faced with similar pressures, and where there is a dominance of multinational companies, it is likely that the pressure for common standards of productivity and performance will mount, irrespective of national systems of industrial relations. (Mueller and Purcell, 1992: 31)

It is also possible that in certain sectors, the industrial relations and personnel policy of MNCs will reduce the differences between industrial relations and terms and conditions of employment in the various countries. Taken to its extreme, this trend will lead to the development of sectoral regulatory frameworks at the European (or international) level and to increasing differences between regulatory frameworks within countries, as a consequence of the differences between sectors. It is not clear whether we would still be dealing with a dominant national regulatory framework or national practices and traditions in such an event. We can only speculate about this, as Mueller and Purcell have already observed:

> The unresolved question is how national industrial relations systems which seem to serve the small and medium-sized domestic producers well will find means of surviving once the bigger players have withdrawn. Does multi-employer bargaining make sense if the bigger employers are no longer bound by agreements? It may be that two 'systems' of industrial relations emerge in Europe: one for large integrated companies where the focus is on plant activity and active works councils; another serving the smaller domestic producers and those firms in sheltered markets based on the varied traditions and practices of national industrial relations arrangements. (1992: 31)

There is another point which Mueller and Purcell do not discuss: whether a system of multinational industrial relations will develop within MNCs. They seem to suggest that industrial relations within MNCs will become crystallized at the plant level, and that it will not be the trade union representative but the works council that will play a decisive role in this process.

Others disagree, pointing out that trade unions may be able to adopt a stronger position in MNCs with tightly integrated but geographically spread-out production networks. Marginson (1992), for example, claims that there are opportunities to develop transnational bargaining structures in MNCs with highly integrated production networks which are sensitive to disruption, and in MNCs where the same type of activity is spread out over different locations in various different countries. The uniformity of working conditions, the required know-how and skills etc. will prompt the trade unions to compare employment terms and working conditions between countries, allowing them to develop cross-border activities (Marginson, 1992: 538). Enderwick (1982) also emphasizes that highly integrated worldwide production chains are sensitive to disruption. In his view, the relative bargaining power of the trade unions increases in MNCs, along with the degree of integration of the production activities (Enderwick, 1982: 37). Many products result from the assembly of parts and semi-manufactures produced in different countries. For example, less than half the goods currently imported into the United States consist of finished products such as cars, VCRs and other consumer products. In 1990, more than half of the total value of imports and exports consisted of *intra*-firm trade and transport of parts and semi-manufactures and associated services (Reich, 1991: 114). MNCs operate in 'global webs' consisting of a network of relations between suppliers and end-producers. The image that emerges is of an MNC which not only operates on a global scale, but is also highly dependent on its own internal trade in end-products, semi-manufactures and intangibles such as know-how (Enderwick, 1982: 37). For many MNCs, the price tag attached to having a worldwide division of labour is an acute sensitivity to any disruption in the production and supply flows. According to Enderwick, their attempts to avoid or prevent such disruptions, for example as a result of strikes, may lead them to pay higher wages and to use financial incentives as a way of regulating industrial relations (Enderwick, 1982: 37).

3   Internationalization as the rationalization of production through the reallocation of employment

In the previous section we discussed how policy on industrial relations is formulated within MNCs and the possible consequences for national regulatory frameworks. Because MNCs operate across national borders, they can set up production wherever the most favourable conditions present themselves. In this section we will describe whether, and to what extent, the differences between the labour markets in various countries are important and can be exploited. Opportunities to produce at different locations have increased, in particular as a result of advances in information and communications technology and the increasing liberalization of world trade. These factors have led to an accelerated geographical relocation of production. Furthermore, there are indications that the current worldwide trend toward restructuring should be seen in the light of far-reaching rationalization processes and that the replacement of an expensive workforce by the cheap labour available in countries with lower levels of social protection constitutes an attractive alternative for the substitute of labour by capital (Enderwick, 1982: 36).

The international relocation of employment and the phenomenon known as 'social dumping' which accompanies this trend have not gone unnoticed by the public and policy-makers. Social dumping occurs when companies transfer their production activities and employment in order to exploit lower wages and inferior working conditions in peripheral countries, thereby putting wages and working conditions in the original production countries under pressure. Employees in countries that offer a greater measure of social protection often have no other choice than to agree to the plans for reorganization put forward and to accept the downward adjustment of their employment terms and conditions. When a decrease in the level of protection is negotiated with the trade unions, this is known as *concession bargaining* (Sengenberger, 1992: 146–147). In the case of social dumping, competition focuses on differences in terms and conditions of employment and working conditions. By relocating production activities, companies hope to achieve a sharp reduction in expenditure, including the cost of labour. We should mention here that it is not only MNCs that apply this type of cost-reducing strategy. The increasing liberalization of world trade makes it possible for every business to decide to produce in countries where circumstances are most favourable from the perspective of production.

In this section we will provide several examples of the rationalization processes which lie at the root of international investment and employment flows. At the same time we will attempt to clarify the position of the trade unions in the face of these processes. Social dumping is by no means limited to the relocation of production from north to south, from industrialized to developing countries. The phenomenon can also be observed regularly within industrialized regions, as we can see from the *social dimension* debate within the European Union. That is why we will also discuss in this section examples of the relocation of employment within Europe.

The new international division of labour

MNCs operate across borders, setting up joint ventures intended to broaden their basis for R&D investment. The global shifts in production which occur as a result, and the ensuing global distribution of employment, are designated in the literature as the international division of labour (Schoenberger, 1989; see also Chapter 1). The underlying assumption is that it is possible to split up and redistribute tasks within the production process. In general tasks are divided into three types:

1 those related to the preparation, organization and management of production processes;
2 those that require a certain level of skill;
3 operational tasks which do not require special training.

In companies, production tasks are split up and distributed over various jobs which differ in value; in the same way, production processes can be split up into individual, unequal segments which may or may not require skilled labour. Such segments can then be distributed geographically. Subsidiaries responsible for particular segments are located where the circumstances are most favourable, one of the factors in this decision being the state of affairs on the local labour market (wages, availability of suitable workforce etc.).

In the old international distribution of labour, segments of the process consisting of routine operational tasks performed by unskilled workers were relocated to countries with (extremely) low wages (known as peripheral or developing countries). Examples of sectors which took advantage of this international division of labour are the textile industry and the electronics sector. Both transferred the better part of their activities to Asia and Latin America in the late 1960s and early 1970s. Given the sometimes awkward working conditions, the approval or protection of dictatorial regimes was often required. As a reaction to these typical 'runaway' industries, Western countries found themselves driven to taking protectionist measures (Lipietz, 1986: 32).

The most important difference between the old and new international division of labour is that, now, process segments requiring skilled labour are also being relocated on a global scale, indeed increasingly to the periphery. In the old international division of labour, most of the products and parts manufactured in developing countries were exported to the core countries: production in the periphery, consumption in the prosperous core. In the new division of labour, supply and demand, production and consumption follow much more complex patterns. Flows of goods and capital are not determined by consumer demand in the core countries alone, nor solely by the attempt to reduce costs as a competitive tactic, but also by the increasing demand from a growing urban middle class and a more highly skilled working class in the (former) peripheral countries. An important development in this trend has been the rise of the NICs (newly industrialized countries), formerly peripheral countries which have captured a solid position within current global competition and have achieved a remarkable level of economic growth. In essence the new division of labour is a variation on Fordist production applied worldwide. Fordism is the name given to an intensive cumulative regime based on serial mass production and on the growth of markets for standardized mass products. Lipietz calls the new phenomenon *peripheral Fordism* and he suggests that there is a combination of rising consumer needs in NICs and cheap re-exports to core countries. The automobile industry is a typical example. When plants were initially established in peripheral countries (for example Spain, Mexico and Brazil), it was a case of penetrating markets that were closed to foreign companies. Local subsidiaries were opened only to serve the local market. The next stage was the large-scale re-export to North-western Europe and the United States (Lipietz, 1986: 32–33).

The differences between the old and the new international division of labour indicate the relative changes that can arise in countries in a comparatively short period of time. According to Lipietz, Korea is no longer a typical workshop country, with a great deal of labour performed in the home and cottage industries where product parts are made in inferior conditions and under poor employment terms. Since the 1970s, this country has experienced balanced growth in its domestic demand and a steady rise in wages, although the latter has not entirely kept pace with productivity (Lipietz, 1986: 33). The new international division of labour is the result of technical advances and the liberalization of world trade, both of which continue to boost this trend. Modern information and communications technology has made it possible to split up activities and distribute them geographically. On the other hand, the availability of labour and qualified workers and their relative costs in various countries also has an impact on the division of products into components and, as a consequence, on the design of such products. In this way, internationalization contributes to a specific type of technological development, resulting in the disintegration of the production process. This is in turn a precondition for further internationalization, so that a self-activating process has been initiated (Ietto-Gillies, 1992: 16).

The international division of labour is also based on the attempt to exploit opportunities to standardize products or parts, production processes or process segments, in so far as companies relocate their activities in order to utilize cheap, low-skill labour. Standardization is an important condition for utilizing unskilled labour, while *deskilling* is in turn a condition for lowering labour costs by paying lower wages. Both propositions – standardization and deskilling – can be considered suspect. First of all, it is questionable whether standardization should be the ultimate goal within industry. The automobile industry, for example, which used to be the archetype of standardized mass production, is now increasingly turning to diversified quality production. That means offering a wider assortment of more or less tailor-made quality products. This leads to a growing need for flexible, motivated, highly skilled workers who are able to operate more or less independently in the production process. Increasingly, technology is making it possible rapidly to modify production processes in order to produce different products and product specifications. This may prompt some industries, such as the electronics sector, to locate what used to be routine, deskilled activities in core countries (Schoenberger, 1989: 95–97).

The second proposition – deskilling – has by now been subject to enough criticism in the literature. In certain cases, companies gain no more by lowering wages through deskilling than they would from the added value contributed by skilled, productive, flexible and committed employees. According to Schoenberger, the benefits gained by restructuring and relocating activities depend not only on technical opportunities and geographically determined supply factors, but also on competitive strategies (Schoenberger, 1989: 97ff.). For example, product development may require a close connection between R&D, marketing and production. Interplay is particularly important in rapidly changing markets, where companies must respond quickly and flexibly to fluctuations in demand and to their competitors' product strategies. From a strategic point of view, it may be important to have a significant share of an upper market segment. Furthermore, some companies have made major investments in training and employee careers, so that it would be uninteresting for them to take too much advantage of short-term profits as a consequence of national differences in wages.

This should serve as a warning to us not to jump to the most obvious conclusions. The effort made by companies to minimize costs by standardization and deskilling is not the only motor driving the international displacement of production and employment. Neither is locating as many segments of production as possible to countries with a lower level of social protection the only competitive strategy. Indeed, it is perhaps not even the best strategy. Nevertheless, the theory of the new international division of labour discussed above provides a good framework for understanding the relocation of employment and the role of MNCs in this.

Social dumping

The case studies in this section are an illustration not only of the trends described above, but also of the concrete consequences of the new international division of labour for employment, employment conditions and industrial relations. We commented previously that the geographical distribution of production leads to reorganizations and shut-downs in core countries. Such steps no longer exclusively involve activities for which only unskilled or low-skilled labour is required.

> *The North American firm Quarterdeck Office Systems relocated part of its activities to Ireland. Calls concerning the operation of a computer program are immediately transferred to Dublin, where an employee provides the necessary advice for a third of the hourly wage paid to an American employee at that level. Other firms have transferred activities requiring skilled labour from the United States to Ireland; examples are the processing of life insurance policies and checks on insurance taken out in the United States. ABB is a Swedish–Swiss transnational which produces high-tech products such as robots. This firm has been exploring opportunities in the former Eastern Bloc since the fall of the Berlin Wall. Thirty companies belonging to the concern are located there, employing 25,000 people. After two years, the majority of these companies have become profitable. The biggest expansion in personnel took place in the Czech Republic and Romania (6,000 and 1,600 employees respectively). In the Czech Republic, ABB has established a joint venture for the manufacturing of industrial turbines, ovens and power plants. The concern as a whole is undergoing a reorganization, however, which will involve 1,000 redundancies a month, starting in August 1993 for a period of 18 months. Investment in Western Europe has declined as a result of a dip in demand. ABB views Eastern Europe and the Far East as strategic growth areas. (NRC Handelsblad, 20 August 1993)*

For many companies international competition, stimulated by the economic crisis of the 1990s, has forced them to lower production costs. Despite the large measure of capital intensity of many advanced companies, cost-cutting measures usually involve wages in the first instance. This is generally accompanied not only by cuts in personnel in the core countries, but also by a downward adjustment of the terms and conditions of employment for existing personnel, sometimes in consultation with the trade unions in which case the term concession bargaining has been used (Sengenberger, 1992: 147).

KLM Dutch Royal Airlines employs the strategy of lowering wage costs by forcing personnel to make concessions such as wage freezes and jumps in productivity on the one hand, and by shifting activities to low-wage countries on the other. This has been accompanied by the establishment of cooperative ventures intended to lead to a merger with Swissair, SAS and Austrian Airlines. By November 1993 negotiations were stopped for several reasons. Nonetheless, KLM is looking for other partners and has common interests with North-West Airlines in the United States. KLM is investigating the possibility of transferring its Income and Transport Information division, involving 400 employees. The Computer division is also being considered. Employees in India with academic credentials work for much lower wages (8,000 rupees per month). Other airlines, such as Swissair, have gone even further in this regard. Eighteen months ago freight administration was transferred to India, and plans have been made to relocate transit administration as well (NRC Handelsblad, 27 July 1993). The rationalization process includes contracting out services and concentrating on core activities. Further cuts among KLM's personnel will be made possible by the concentration of activities in the new cooperative venture between the airlines mentioned above. On 12 July 1993, the managing boards of the four airlines notified the relevant trade unions and works councils that as a result of this cooperation, 6,000 jobs would disappear within the next four years. Some 10,000 out of the total of 76,000 employees would have to be made redundant in the same period. In accordance with the statutory obligation to apply for advice, KLM passed this information on to the works council in August, before negotiations with the merger partners began.

The role of the trade unions is frequently limited to concluding a social plan which governs redundancies and attempts to prevent forced redundancies and to ensure voluntary redundancies through normal employee turnover. Before a social plan can be negotiated, the MNC is obliged to indicate clearly what the competitive and financial position of the company is, and, subsequently, why structural conditions have made redundancies unavoidable. Relatively new in the present vogue for rationalization is that far-reaching sacrifices are being made by personnel without their receiving 'hard and fast' employment guarantees in return. The international situation in the airline industry has forced the trade unions to make concessions concerning wage freezes. The poor financial position of the Belgian airline, Sabena, led to economy measures in which wage reductions for pilots and flight engineers were considered. After the unions refused to agree to these plans, Sabena threatened with redundancies, putting pressure on the unions. In August the unions were ultimately forced to accept the proposals.

As is the case with other car manufacturers, Volkswagen is also in the throes of a reorganization. This is taking place with the approval of the trade unions and works councils, who have agreed to a considerable cut in personnel. After sustaining losses of 1,600 million D-marks over the first half of 1993, an agreement was made to accelerate the reduction in personnel from 112,924 to 100,000 in the course of 1993 and 1994. 'Normal turnover' has been applied as the most important means of achieving this goal, in addition to early retirement. Another section of the accompanying social plan states that as of the end of 1994, early retirement will be possible for employees who have reached the age of 55 (*NRC Handelsblad*, 20 August 1993). By late October 1993 it was apparent the initial redundancy plan was no longer enough. Volkswagen now fears that it will ultimately have to let a third of its personnel go, but as an alternative to overt dismissals the company has proposed cutting the working week to four days, with the accompanying loss of wages. The trade unions have accepted the proposal, as the alternative was less attractive. The example of Volkswagen illustrates that even at the company level, pathbreaking initiatives can be taken and that dismissal is not the only way to decrease labour costs.

Social dumping in the European Union

Social dumping practices are also a factor within trading blocs such as the European Union. There are, in any event, numerous examples which seem to indicate that employment shifts within the EU have been inspired by differences in terms and conditions of employment and industrial relations between the various member states. As early as the 1980s, pessimists pointed out that the integration of the European market could pose a danger to the higher standard of living and better social protection provided in certain member states, while less prosperous member states would never be able to raise their living standards because companies there competed on the basis of lower prices and wages (Wise and Gibb, 1993: 153). An uneven distribution of employment and prosperity within Europe was expected not only as a result of the 'different speeds' at which northern and southern European countries were developing, but also as a consequence of the United Kingdom's refusal in 1989 to sign the EC's Social Charter (see also Chapter 16). According to Prime Minister Thatcher, this would have led to socialist, bureaucratic practices being let in through 'the back door' by Brussels (Wise and Gibb, 1993: 163). In 1991, The UK refused to sign the Social Chapter of the Maastricht Treaty. In the ongoing debate on Europe's 'social dimension', the UK's rejection has gained a prominent place on the agenda. At issue is not only the distribution of employment within the EU, however, but also investment from outside the EU. In 1987, the largest portion of Japanese investment in the EC went to the United Kingdom (second and third place were held by Luxemburg and the Netherlands respectively). Although the UK has had to relinquish its first place since then, Japanese direct investment in that country nevertheless increased from US$ 2,010 million in 1980 to US$ 6,598 million in 1987 (Wise and Gibb, 1993: 261).

The first reason given by Wise and Gibb for this trend is the wage costs. These lie approximately 20 percent below those in other important EU economies. Another reason is the high level of unemployment, which has increased employee willingness to accept no-strike agreements or representation through enterprise unions. The first explicitly bans labour unrest, while the second certainly implies such a ban. Still other reasons are the favourable attitude of the British government toward foreign investors and Japanese familiarity with the language – additional, but certainly not unimportant factors (Wise and Gibb, 1993: 261–262). The government's helpful attitude is expressed in its direct financial support of investment by Japanese MNCs. Pared back employment terms and the possibility of initiating far-reaching reforms in industrial relations are the British government's trump cards in attracting investment at the cost of socio-economic developments in other EU member states.

The fear of social dumping practices in the EU which we mentioned previously is by no means unfounded, as can be seen in the example given below.

> *The most striking example is the Hoover affair. In January 1993, Hoover, a manufacturer of vacuum cleaners, announced that it was closing a subsidiary in Dijon, France. Of the 700 jobs there, 600 would be lost. Hoover, owned by the US company Maytag, decided to transfer operations to another subsidiary located near Glasgow in Scotland. The necessary investment capital was acquired by making use of the company's pension funds and by tapping EC funding. In Scotland Maytag reached an agreement with the AEEU, MSF and APEX trade unions to freeze wages for a period from February to December 1993. At that point wage levels would be reconsidered. The agreement, the precise wording of which was kept secret by both management and unions, also contained provisions governing flexibility and efficiency increases, as well as measures which would bring the terms and conditions of employment in line with Hoover's subsidiary in South Wales. The reasons given included the world recession and a fall in demand for household appliances. In addition, a no-strike provision went into effect for the duration of the agreement. Agreement was also made that the company would only negotiate with the unions as a group. Given the extremely high level of unemployment in the region, the Scottish unions clearly signed the agreement under duress. Two clauses in the agreement would have been unimaginable in France: the 'peace' clause and the exclusion of pension rights for new employees for a period of two years (see* European Industrial Relations, *March 1993). The relocation of production and employment out of France brought loud cries of protest from the French socialist government and the unions there. The general secretary of the communist-oriented CGT union, Louis Viannet, called the agreement 'frightening'. The government responded by asking the European Commission whether, in the first place, the support extended by the state was in keeping with EC legislation and, secondly, whether the Directive governing the protection of workers' rights was at issue, since investment money*

had been extracted from the pension fund. Prime Minister Bérégovoy also levelled the accusation of social dumping.

Prime Minister Major's standpoint was diametrically opposed to this and is a good illustration of how far the two governments are removed from each other in terms of political ideology. On 2 February he responded to questions put to him by Parliament by saying that industry would set up where it had the most chance of being efficient and competitive. Reacting to a statement made by M. Delors, President of the European Commission, that Great Britain had turned itself into a paradise for foreign investment by refusing to sign the social protocol, Major said that the protocol would lead to higher costs for business, which would destroy jobs and mean a loss of competitive strength. More in general, the British government supports the idea that there should be little interference on the part of the state in regulating working schedules and patterns of working time, so that wage costs can be kept lower than on the Continent. Compared with other EC countries, the United Kingdom has the largest percentage of employees who work irregular hours. In 1990, for example, 16 percent of all employees worked more than 48 hours per week, as opposed to an average of 5 percent for the EC as a whole. The dismissal procedure in the UK is the most flexible of the EC as well, together with that of Denmark (The Economist, *24 July 1993).*

Countries like the United Kingdom seem to compete on the basis of inferior terms and conditions of employment and more flexible industrial relations, which indicates a short-term strategy aimed at cost-cutting. In actual practice, however, concessions on the part of the employees and their unions usually do not lead to a rapid and lasting recovery of the competition position (Sengenberger, 1992: 147). Sengenberger compares strategies aimed at cost reductions with strategies aimed at innovation in production. In innovation strategies, the emphasis has shifted from cost-cutting to supplying a wide assortment of customer-oriented high-quality goods. In switching to an innovation strategy, a company can call upon the support of the unions in carrying through a reorganization. The success of the innovative approach agreed upon in negotiations depends to a large extent on the willingness of the unions to hive off unprofitable activities and support new competitive ones instead (Sengenberger, 1992: 149). In another variation on innovation strategy, the company increases the involvement of its employees without union intervention by pursuing a human resource policy. Although one often encounters a mixture of the two strategies mentioned, and the two do not rule one another out, our description is at any rate an indication of the choices which exist at the moment.

An innovation strategy requires highly qualified employees and a large measure of commitment and involvement. That is why, in addition to social dumping, many sectors have alternatively focused on human resource management as well.

In the global competitive battle, however, innovation strategies also have their limitations. A high added value and a highly skilled workforce are no hard-and-fast guarantees for a better position on the world market. After all, even in the new high-tech growth sectors, European industry is losing ground to competitors from the Pacific region. Toshiba sells more semi-conductors than Philips, SGS-Thomson and Siemens put together, for example (Versteeg, 1993).

4 Conclusions

The new international division of labour and the ferocious level of competition seem to reinforce one another. It is not yet obvious where the limits are on the relocation of activities from former core countries to the (former) periphery. We must not forget the situation of the countries of the former Eastern Bloc in this regard. Since the economies there have been reorganized along free-market principles, fierce competition has erupted in for example, the metal industry and other traditional industrial sectors, in which the willingness of low-wage countries to work under inferior conditions plays an important role.

The present relocation of employment involves not only low-skill activities, as was the case in the old international division of labour, but also jobs that require a higher level of qualification. Low-wage countries, in particular the NICs, increasingly seem able to compete with rich Western countries when it comes to quality of goods and services. An innovation strategy which aims to achieve a high added value will not guarantee European trade and industry a solid position on the world market. A strategy of cost reduction, on the other hand, offers little prospect of lasting success; there will always be a country which can pay lower wages somewhere in the world. Neither is it unthinkable that the standard of living in the West will drop to the level of developing nations. An innovation strategy based on diversified, high-quality production seems, after all, to offer the best chances. It also makes better coordination possible between labour market characteristics, such as a highly skilled workforce with traditions of employee participation, and company strategies that offer a valid response to the changing tenor of international competition. This is a challenge which should be met not only at the national level, but increasingly at the European level as well.

16   European social policy and European industrial relations

Ad Nagelkerke

1	Introduction	337
2	European social regulations	340
	Policy-making	340
	Political bodies and their authority	340
	Sources of social policy	341
	Legislation from Brussels	343
	Problems associated with European policy-making	345
	The role of labour and management	346
	Interest organizations and their authority	346
	Cooperative and advisory bodies in Brussels	348
	The social parties in Brussels	349
	Transnational arrangements	350
	Problems associated with collective consultations at European level	352
3	Possible consequences of the European integration process for existing industrial relations practice	353
	Four scenarios for a European system of industrial relations	354
	Scenario I: segmented transaction model	355
	Scenario II: regime competition model	356
	Scenario III: accommodation model	357
	Scenario IV: mosaic model	357
	The position of MNCs in the four scenarios	358
4	Summary and conclusions	360

1   Introduction

In Chapters 13 and 15, we indicated that the traditional national regulatory frameworks are becoming less and less effective. At the root of this problem is the process of internationalization, in which technological, economic and political factors exert a reciprocal influence on one another. For example, in an effort to escape being crushed between the North American and South-East Asian trading blocs, the European Community in the early 1980s began to map out its programme of internal market expansion, increased competitiveness and technological cooperation. 'Europe 1992' was an energetic response to long-term processes of internationalization, but the project itself has in turn generated greater economic vitality. The disadvantages of market fragmentation, limited monetary discretion – the currency crises of 1992 and 1993 made painfully obvious how powerless the individual central banks are in the face of the international capital market – and institutional pluralism have inspired economic, monetary and political initiatives in Brussels such as have never been witnessed before.

In the social arena, the dwindling authority of the national frameworks is becoming more obvious all the time. Unfortunately, European initiatives in this area face more difficulties than those in other fields. In the short term this could lead to a policy vacuum which would allow companies that operate internationally more strategic scope to shape their own social policy. It is not yet clear whether the Maastricht Treaty, which came into force on 1 November 1993, will actually provide a powerful stimulus for the development of a European social policy. The Social Protocol annexed to the Treaty has provided certain levers by introducing more flexible decision-making procedures and greater involvement by labour and management. This Treaty also changed the name of the European Community to the *European Union*. The EU not only has jurisdiction over socio-economic affairs (as did the EC); its powers extend to matters of security and foreign policy, and to judicial and police policy. As from 1 November 1993, European institutions are no longer referred to as EC institutions, but as EU institutions.

To understand the process of European integration since 1985, it may help to consider a few of the different policy dilemmas which the Union has faced. The first is the contrast between 'coercive constructivity' and the impossibility of predicting and taking into account the many different developments. After the Maastricht Treaty, the contours of what was considered a desirable economic model – even those of a political organization – became less blurred, although strong counteractive forces rose in opposition. European integration should be viewed as an ideal, an expression of constructivism (cf. Dahrendorf, 1992). The apparent lack of vision with respect to certain internal dynamic forces and environmental factors, such as the processes shaping the former Eastern Bloc, is, however, a structural defect in the architecture. A related dilemma associated with European integration concerns the economic motive itself, in fact the logic of integration. The projected scenarios do not contain a blueprint for a socio-economic order. Initially the idea prevailed that economic integration, if successful, would be followed by social integration. The documents intended to support and design integration, the Single European Act (SEA) and the White Paper 'Completing the Internal Market', devoted little space to promoting social cohesion, however. The measures set forth in these documents were predominantly directed at economic objectives. Economic Europe was expected to come into being as much as possible within the context of European social pluralism. The emergence of the European Social Charter and its associated action programme signalled a departure from this idea in its purest form.

Related to the above is the third contrast, concerning the best coordination mechanism for socio-economic development: the market or a set of regulations (and the various forms thereof). On the one hand, this is a question of weighing up the debits and credits of various institutional combinations. On the other hand, it is a question of legitimacy: why is it necessary to pursue a (government) social policy? Social policy is viewed as the development of norms, rules, structures and instruments related to work, income and the health of workers. It includes both labour law in the broadest sense and policy on the labour market, employment and schooling, income and social security, and working conditions.

For some, social policy is a necessary condition for economic and political integration. They want Brussels to devote its attention to the social dimension in order to prevent 'social dumping', that is, the use of relatively poor social provisions and regulations as a way of gaining competitive advantages (see Chapter 15). According to this view, social dumping will lead to social conflict. Others advocate the 'economist' line of thought discussed earlier. They fear that economic progress will be blocked by social rules and regulations, whether European or national. For example, the European Monetary Union (EMU) criteria of the Maastricht Treaty, which include strict cuts in government spending along with deregulation in other areas, ignore the social consequences to which the application of such standards might lead (if applied too rapidly). The Protocol annexed to the Treaty does not link monetary (and political) union to social consequences. This brings us to the fourth contrast. The first group advocates powerful European structures, umbrella provisions at the European level and a supranational social policy, that is, the expansion of a Union '*espace social*'. Should this prove too difficult, then the best national arrangements should be preserved. Their opponents, on the other hand, opt for national and local arrangements, but only if subject to the pressures of the market. This is in line with the principle of subsidiarity, which locates decision-making at the most effective lowest level and which is closely linked to the issue of national autonomy (unanimity versus qualified majority voting) on the one hand and to the idea of a 'social partnership' between organizations of employers and employees on the other.

In the following section we will focus on European regulations. The distinction made above, between European governmental arrangements and the agreements made between labour and management, will be elaborated further on. First we will look at the political and institutional framework within which 'social policy' can be created. Next we will discuss sources and examples of social policy, and then move on to explore the meaning of collective consultations at the European level, as well as a number of voluntary initiatives at the company level. We will also discuss the specific problems associated with implementing social policy at the European level. Section 3 offers several scenarios for European industrial relations and social policy based on different assumptions. The question as to what the contents of a European social policy will be has not yet been answered. Should it provide a minimum level of basic rights, or should it be a coherent policy encompassing work, income and health that will leave the door wide open for a European set of rules? Or should it be a policy package that lies somewhere in between these two extremes? We will return to this topic at the end of the chapter.

2   European social regulations

When we refer to European social regulations, we usually mean the agreements concluded in Brussels between the various national governments, cast in the form of laws, guidelines, decisions and recommendations (see below). Other consultations that take place in Brussels are those between European organizations of employers and employees, possibly in conjunction with representatives of the European Commission. Agreements reached between these parties are laid down in proposals, recommendations, covenants and collective agreements. In order to allow both circuits to function, a whole variety of bodies have been created to support and execute these agreements. What we call the European level is not synonymous with 'Brussels', even though most organizations have offices there and most advisory and consultative bodies meet there.

An important aspect of the study of industrial relations is constantly to probe where the various parties stand. This applies equally when the object of study is the European level. For example, the history of national industrial relations has taught us that the power of employers to act autonomously has been diminishing for a long time in favour of employees on the one hand (democratization, trade unions) and society on the other (social embeddedness, legislation). Recently, however, this trend has reached a turning point. Shifting coalitions of interest organizations and governments have been engaged in an ongoing battle to create order in the area of employer autonomy. A similar change can be seen in the relatively new trend toward a 'social Europe'. A battle is also being waged between various parties on this level – between individual countries and the EU, between governments on the one hand and labour and management on the other, between European organizations and their affiliates, and, of course, between employer and employee representatives at the supranational level – each hoping to gain independence from the other.

Policy-making

Political bodies and their authority

The principal political institution of the European Union is the Council of Ministers, and in particular the summit meetings of government leaders. The Council consists of the ministers from each member state, with different ministers attending different meetings according to the policy agenda (for example, social matters are discussed by the 12 ministers for Social Affairs and Employment). Although the Council as a body does not maintain direct contacts with employer and employee organizations, the national governments do within their own borders. An important point of contact between the Union and representatives of employees and employers is the European Commission. The Commission can draft European legislation and policy proposals and has the machinery to effect implementation. There is also a European Parliament, which since 1979 has been elected directly by the citizens of Europe; however, its limited powers allow it very little political clout. Another important body within the Union is the Court of Justice, which rules on conflicts between the member states, between national governments and organizations, between different organizations and between organizations and private individuals. In the 35-year history of the EC, most of the regulations on social issues have been the work of the Commission and the Council of Ministers. Various rules may have been prompted by proposals submitted by labour or management (for example the advisory committees) or may have led to joint declarations following consultations.

Various instruments have been devised to implement and legitimize European social policy. The most important are the structural Funds, of which there are three: the European Social Fund (ESF), the European Fund for Regional Development (EFRD) and the European Agricultural Guidance and Guarantee Fund, Guidance Section (EAGGF).

Sources of social policy

Five important sources can be identified which have formed the basis for social policy; the most remarkable thing about them is that most of the developments in this area have been quite recent. Considered over time, two trends can be distinguished: first, decision-making procedures have become more flexible and the authority exercised by Brussels is increasing; secondly, the part played by labour and management in policy-making is expanding slowly. These trends are clearly related to the autonomy issue discussed earlier.

The first source of social policy is the *Treaty of Rome* itself. There are a number of compulsory articles with general application (for example Art. 48 and 49 on the freedom of movement of workers, and Art. 51 on social security for migrating workers) and a few non-compulsory ones related to employment terms (such as Art. 120 on paid holidays) (Venturini, 1988: 14). Secondly, there is the 1987 amendment to the Treaty of Rome, the *Single European Act* (SEA). Art. 100a (coordination of provisions concerning public health, safety, environmental protection and consumer protection), 118a (improvement of the working environment) and 130a–130e (economic and social coordination) are compulsory. A new, non-compulsory social provision is indicated in Art. 118b: to promote contacts between labour and management leading to contractual relations at the European level, should they so desire. Another important change introduced by the Single European Act is that for the first time, decision-making on social issues became possible on the basis of qualified majority voting, although this pertains specifically to issues of safety and health at work. The SEA also got the 'social dialogue' going again at the European level (Art. 118b). Prior to 1985, consultations between the Commission, trade union representatives and employers' associations were frequently ad hoc and produced only minimal results. The Val Duchesse discussions which began in 1985 have provided more structure for the consultations and have occasionally led to joint proposals (Nagelkerke and Veersma, 1992: 238–239; see p. 348 below).

A third source of social regulations and policy is the *Union Charter of the Fundamental Social Rights of Workers* (known as the '*Social Charter*'), which was adopted by 11 of the 12 member states in late 1989, the United Kingdom being the only member state not to sign. Many of the Charter's provisions reaffirm earlier policy positions. Unlike the two previous sources discussed, however, the Charter is only a declaration of intention from which no rights may be derived. The Charter focuses on the right to freedom of movement, work and equitable pay, the improvement of living conditions and employment terms, the right to social protection, the freedom of association and collective bargaining, vocational training, the right of men and women to equal treatment, the right to information, consultation and worker participation, health and safety in the working environment, the protection of children and adolescents, old-age pensions and, finally, the need for specific measures in the workplace for the disabled. The steps considered necessary by the signatory states may be taken by various different parties: by labour and management, by the member states themselves or by EU institutions. Subsidiarity is a guiding principle in these matters (Stichting van de Arbeid, 1991: 21).

A fourth important source is the *Social Protocol* annexed to the Maastricht Treaty, whose contents had already been agreed in principle by labour and management (in this case ETUC, UNICE and CEEP; see p. 349 below) shortly before the Treaty was signed. The United Kingdom's unwillingness to accept the 'Social Chapter' of the draft Treaty resulted in a protocol/agreement signed by the 11 other member states setting forth the Treaty's social policy. The Protocol is important for two reasons. First, it extends the social issues to be decided on the basis of a qualified majority vote to include the right of workers to information and consultation. Secondly, Art. 4 of the Protocol reaffirms that discussions between management and labour may lead to Union-wide agreements. If such agreements involve the issues referred to in Art. 1 of the Protocol, they will be implemented by a Council decision on a proposal submitted by the Commission. The Protocol provides for the necessary procedures in such a case.

Art. 1 of the Social Protocol summarizes the multifaceted social integration problem in a few sentences as shown opposite.

Finally, the jurisprudence of the *European Court of Justice* is the fifth source of social policy. This is evident in the regulations on the emancipation of women with respect to work (cf. Hoskyns, 1991: 29). In a more general sense, the significance of the Court is related to a growing awareness among the citizens of the various member states that the Union should support political and social rights. They use the Court as 'a comprehensive judicial arm to EC social policy', with the inevitable result that the position of the Union in this area is becoming stronger at the

> ## Article 1 of the Social Protocol annexed to the Maastricht Treaty
>
> The Union and the Member States shall have as their objectives the promotion of employment, improved living and working conditions, proper social protection, dialogue between management and labour, the development of human resources with a view to lasting high employment and the combating of exclusion. To this end the Union and Member States shall implement measures which take account of the diverse forms of national practices, in particular in the field of contractual relations, and the need to maintain the competitiveness of the Union economy.

expense of the member states (Teague and McClelland, 1991: 15). On this point, a shift in autonomy is evident.

Legislation from Brussels

Rules are closely tied to values and norms. Norms are values and opinions grounded in everyday social practice. Like regulations, which are consciously produced, norms are often inextricably tied up with their cultural context, although a number of them (for example the work ethic) can be found almost everywhere. 'Common European' norms do not yet exist as such. This might be a profound reason for the flawed institutional structure of the European Union.

With respect to European legal instruments, we can distinguish the following:

1 'Regulations' are applicable to all member states and binding on the citizens of each member state.
2 'Directives' target specific objectives and are usually indirect in nature, meaning that they must first be transposed into national legislation.
3 'Decisions' are binding only on individual persons, firms or member states.
4 'Recommendations' and 'opinions' have no legal force.

Two important goals which the Union tries to achieve by means of compulsory legislation in the form of regulations and directives are coordination and harmonization. Coordination means that various different national provisions are synthesized without the provisions themselves being altered. Harmonization, on the other hand, means that different laws are brought into line with one another with respect to their contents and/or level. Coordination, for instance, is used in the case of the freedom of movement of workers, whereas harmonization is applied to working conditions and cross-border employee participation (see Ministry of Social Affairs and Employment, 1991: 4). In cases where compulsory provisions are inopportune, recommendations can be used to prevent laws from deviating too much from one another.

Regulations and directives on social issues have the most significance in the area of labour law. After 35 years, however, the European Union has only a meagre harvest to show for all its efforts, particularly in substantive terms. Discussions on a number of proposals have been long, sometimes interminable, because the Council seems unable to reach a decision. Some proposals never make it past the drawing board and any discussion is tabled. In other cases, proposals which have gained the approval of the Council have yet to be incorporated into national legislation. As we noted above, decisions handed down by the European Court of Justice have stimulated progress in legislation and changes in existing legislation. The ratification of the Social Charter also speeded things up. Nevertheless, even now numerous proposals are languishing away due to a stalemate.

Important examples of European social law

- Directives on equal treatment for men and women, in particular regarding equal pay for men and women (75/117), access to employment, vocational training and promotion (76/207); a draft directive was submitted on 6 November 1987 on the principle of equal treatment for men and women in matters of social security.
- Three draft directives concerning atypical employment contracts (as of 29 June 1990, focusing on part-time work, employment contracts for a fixed period of time and temporary employment):
    a directive which is to prevent unfair competition by means of atypical employment relationships;
    a directive on establishing the same working conditions and employment terms for all employees with atypical employment contracts;
    a directive governing specific aspects of safety and hygiene for employees on contracts for a fixed period of time and for temporary employees (adopted by the Council on 25 June 1991; 91/383).
- Draft directive related to specific aspects of working time (from 3 August 1990; minimum rest periods, minimum conditions for shift work, night work, protective measures related to work pace; draft amended as of 23 April 1991).
- Proposal on the Articles of Association governing a European Company in which a particular form of worker participation is provided for at management level (new proposal as of 25 August 1989).
- Draft directive on the founding of a European works council in companies or concerns that have a Union dimension (as of 12 December 1990; amended as of 20 September 1991; see Van Ruysseveldt, 1993: 79).

European social policy is shaped by means of programmes and implemented with the help of the various structural Funds. The main objective of the Funds is to reinforce economic and social coordination within the Union. Although all the structural Funds have a social dimension, it is the

European Social Fund (ESF) that is particularly occupied with this issue. Its special goal is to combat long-term unemployment and stimulate the employment of young people (Commission of the European Communities, 1991: 24).

Problems associated with European policy-making

There is no doubt that the creation of a new supranational regulatory framework is undermining the authority of existing institutional patterns. In order to acquire new authority, the old autonomy must be dismantled. This mechanism is of course also evident in the political-institutional processes in Brussels. The price of integration can be expressed in terms of the loss of sovereignty suffered by the member states. Supporting and opposing forces are part of this process.

One of the fundamental areas of tension in the European context is the controversy between the national governments and the supranational institutes. The latter are, specifically, the Commission, its administrative backup, the European Parliament and a few important advisory bodies. The Council of Ministers or its representatives usually support national arrangements unconditionally. And if it should happen that the member states are forced to comply with agreements made at the European level, then the national interest is still highly significant in determining the ultimate result. At issue is not only European versus national law, but the question as to who gets to decide as well. There is power at stake. It might be said that down through the years, the various Councils of Ministers have opposed or weakened many of the initiatives submitted. Despite various modifications leading to qualified majority voting, the social agenda is still determined by unanimity to a large extent. Many of the Commission's proposals are never considered seriously by the Council of Ministers, if at all.

But rumblings have been heard in recent years, and the Maastricht project has made national political egoism more difficult. Moreover, the existing European circuit might create its own integrative dynamism, a kind of functional spill-over effect. For example, despite significant opposition, the Commission was able to get the social dimension on the agenda and has shown itself capable of using its initiatives to draw attention to social policy and keep it there, although this requires the Commission to coordinate its efforts with the issues under discussion at the various national levels.

A second and related problem is the enormous variety of socio-institutional patterns, covering the type of arrangements and their contents, and the degree of involvement required of the various parties. For example, there are tremendous legal and practical differences in the field of collective bargaining, worker participation, conflict management etc. Each country has its own model of industrial relations, as it were, and each model is the result of a years-long search for effective and legitimate institutions. The various models of industrial relations are closely tied to the specific national culture, to which great value is attached. That is why it is so difficult to design provisions that do not appear contrary to familiar patterns and lead to rejection. By now the principle of subsidiarity has been generally accepted, meaning that social arrangements must be provided for decentrally as much as possible (national, regional and local levels). From this perspective, diversity in social patterns is considered highly desirable.

Thirdly, it will come as no surprise that employer and employee representatives have not yet developed a coherent European structure of industrial relations (see discussion of the social parties in Brussels below). If they had, and if transnational bargaining were able to take place, for example, then the EU could obviously have a much greater say on social issues. Technological and economic developments have not yet progressed to such an extent that we have been forced to seek out broad, cross-border systems of consultations. Nevertheless, if we take the automobile industry as an example, the rising level of competition could inspire European companies not only to introduce painful production and organizational changes affecting various countries, but also to initiate strategic economic cooperation. This would make coordination with the trade unions from the various countries concerned highly desirable, which in turn would make cross-border frameworks a real possibility.

Given the resistance offered by various institutions, Brussels will have to choose between two classic approaches and one relatively new one when it comes to European social policy: (1) remove obstacles to the labour market by encouraging international educational and training projects, cultural exchanges, data comparison, mobility subsidies etc.; (2) provide platforms for consultation at the Union level, whether general, sectoral or 'transcorporate'; and (3) respond to new political, technological and economic changes which require orchestration, but for which national structures do not (yet) exist.

The role of labour and management

Interest organizations and their authority

Employers and employees have their own organizations in Brussels, both confederal and at sector level (see Nagelkerke and De Nijs, 1991; Commission of the European Communities, 1992; Visser and Ebbinghaus, 1992). There are several bipartite forms of consultation between the interest groups at various levels.

International sector-level trade unions are often referred to as International Trade Secretariats (ITS). These are independent organizations in particular branches, such as the International Metalworkers' Federation (IMF) and the International Transport Workers' Federation (ITF). Their most important tasks are to gather information for the various national organizations and distribute it among them, and provide support in the event of conflicts. The ITSs have set up special cooperative associations related to multinationals, known as world concern councils. They also

European confederal organizations of employers and employees

An umbrella organization is the European Trade Union Confederation (ETUC), founded in 1973. By 1992 the ETUC had 45 affiliated trade union federations from 22 different European countries, both within and outside the EU, representing some 45 million employees. This means that approximately 95 percent of the organized working population in Western Europe is represented, equal to about 40 percent of the total number of European employees (ETUI, 1990a: 11–12). The goal of the ETUC is to promote the interests of employees at the European level and to safeguard democracy throughout Europe.

The most important European employers' association is the Union of Industrial and Employers' Confederations of Europe (UNICE), founded in 1958. In 1992 it represented 17 central employers' associations within the EU and 15 outside the EU from a total of 22 different countries. UNICE's objective is to inform, coordinate, support and represent its members at the European level, and to achieve as large a measure of entrepreneurial freedom as possible.

A number of public employers are represented in the European Centre of Public Enterprises (usually referred to by its French acronym, CEEP). Representation was concentrated in 1992; for example, a Benelux organization represents 17 Belgian, two Luxembourg and two Dutch public companies. The 'Geschäftsführer der deutschen Sektion der CEEP' has 37 affiliates, and the Greek KEDEO, 53 public company members.

founded the European trade union committees, which are formally independent of the ITS and ETUC, but which maintain regular contact with these organizations and work with them in putting pressure on the decision-making bodies of the EU. Their aim is to consult with employers' associations on a broad range of different topics in joint consultative bodies organized by industrial sector at the EU level, reaching decisions wherever possible. An important goal of the committees is to develop cross-border collective bargaining structures with multinational companies.

Employers too have a large number of different European sector organizations with further internal subdivisions. Their principal endeavours are to coordinate activities, provide information to their members and lobby. Because they lack a bargaining framework in which they can meet the trade unions, the sector organizations concentrate on the European institutions. The organizations at the European level have an extremely restricted mandate from their national affiliates. Like ETUC and UNICE, the sector organizations focus predominantly on the national level. They are often no more than discussion groups whose members follow events in Brussels closely and report on important developments.

Cooperative and advisory bodies in Brussels

There are various advisory and consultative bodies in the European Union through which the representative organizations can become involved in decision-making. They meet regularly with the Commission in informal, frequently ad hoc advisory and consultative bodies. In certain instances, the national trade unions have their own representatives on European councils and committees. We will briefly outline the most important consultative bodies of the European Union (Nagelkerke and De Nijs, 1991: 208ff.; Venturini, 1988: 22–23).

The *Economic and Social Committee* (ECOSOC) is a general advisory body which both the Commission and Council must consult when considering various policy proposals pertaining to agriculture, transport, harmonization, social policy etc. The Committee may also offer unsolicited advice. At present there are 189 members from various social and economic sectors: national organizations of employers and employees, interest groups in agriculture, small and medium-sized enterprises, consumers, trade, transport and the professions. Its wide-ranging membership, the non-compulsory nature of its recommendations and the fact that it lacks a statute mean that the ECOSOC has very little power. It did, however, play an important role in setting up the Social Charter.

There are also a number of special advisory committees composed of representatives from various social and economic organizations, which the Commission must consult when considering specific topics such as vocational training or the freedom of movement of workers.

The *Standing Committee on Employment* is a joint committee consisting of the Commission on the one hand and national representatives of employers, employees and governments on the other. Its purpose is to coordinate national labour market policy and Union objectives. This body meets two to three times annually to discuss a wide range of specific and often current labour market problems. Despite its difficulty reaching consensus, the committee was instrumental in introducing various directives (on collective dismissal and on the right of men and women to equal treatment) and recommendations. It has also offered advice on technological development and the use of ESF funding.

By 'social dialogue' we mean the consultations conducted between representatives of the Commission, ETUC, UNICE and CEEP, often called the *Val Duchesse discussions*, referring to the castle in Brussels (Hertoginnendal) where the meetings were once held. The Single European Act explicitly stated that the social dialogue was to be revitalized after several relatively non-committal, irregularly scheduled meetings. The great 'Europe 1992' integration project should and would include a social dimension. The negotiating rounds began in 1985 with great enthusiasm, with two working committees being set up. The results were minor, however. The most important was a 1987 joint declaration emphasizing the link between new technologies and schooling, continuing education and training. Commission president Delors provided new inspiration in 1989 at the Egmont consultations by focusing the discussion on how to achieve greater coordination between the working committees, which had been reorganized in the mean time. Progress remained slow, but a joint declaration released on 31 October 1991 was significant in clearing the way for agreements at the European level (see the following section).

Finally, there are *joint labour–management committees*, which offer recommendations, either at the request of the Commission or on their own initiative, on issues for which the Commission must formulate a 'structural policy'. There are various committees for the agrarian sector, the iron and steel industry, coal, road transport, inland shipping, marine transport, fishing and the railways. Certain other sectors have informal consultative bodies.

The social parties in Brussels

In view of the remarks made in the previous section, it will come as no surprise that labour and management have provided little in the way of regulatory provisions themselves. Indeed, their role may almost be neglected. Consultations at the European level have never progressed past the stage of non-committal discussions. Even under the auspices of the Commission, the two sides have gone no further than to draft a few joint declarations. The 'social dialogue' has only gained feeble support from the national organizations; on top of that, there has been no supporting framework within which employers and employees could negotiate over employment terms. The advisory committees and other consultative bodies at the Union or European sector level often lack the instruments and authority to push items on their social agenda beyond the traditional national context. Bipartite European consultative bodies have scarcely managed to produce recommendations or incentives for discussions within the individual countries or sectors. No single arrangement on employment terms within multinationals has seen the light of day. Neither has there ever been a joint employment plan or project to combat unemployment. In short, the social side of European integration has been tackled almost exclusively from within the central political and administrative framework.

Nevertheless, given the current socio-economic balance within Europe, a social policy, whether far-reaching or narrow in scope, cannot come about without the cooperation of labour and management. This is certainly the case if the plans are to be implemented by individual countries, regions, sectors and companies. There has been some progress on this point in recent years. For example, in late 1991 the European confederations presented a few of their own procedural initiatives which, as mentioned above, were annexed to the Maastricht Treaty in the form of a protocol. These initiatives have cleared the way for social accords which could in turn affect collective bargaining agreements in individual countries. UNICE in particular backed down; prior to this it had considered the consultations merely a forum for discussion and nothing more. Another development was the extended form of consultation. For example, a start-up European dialogue within the public utilities sector led to a joint declaration concerning continuing education for employees, while in the retail trade agreements were reached on vocational training. Yet another development is best illustrated by the founding of a pan-European organization of aeroplane pilots, called 'Cockpit'. This cross-border grouping of interests was prompted on the one hand by the common problems afflicting the various European airlines and on the other by the introduction of new international air traffic regulations.

Transnational arrangements

Other significant agreements are those reached between multinational employers and European trade unions as well as a number of other voluntary cross-border settlements, although they can in no way be seen as a category of collective bargaining. There have also been a few sector agreements between international organizations of employers and employees. A final important development is that employees at different subsidiaries of European multinationals are beginning to consult one another more frequently.

On 7 October 1985, the European Metalworkers' Federation and Thomson Grand Public (later Thomson Consumer Electronics) reached two protocol accords concerning the establishment of a double information and advisory structure, one between management and the unions and the other between management and the employee representatives appointed by the unions (European Trade Union Institute, 1991: 13; Gold and Hall, 1992: 15). Recently this double structure was replaced by a single body on which both employees and (European) trade union representatives have seats (Carley, 1993: 14). Other European concerns followed the example set by this French multinational. Various survey studies have revealed a number of characteristics typifying these joint committees (cf. Gold and Hall, 1992, 1993; Carley, 1993).

Sector-level agreements are uncommon, although this is changing (as indicated in the previous section). Joint committees (and informal working committees) in industrial sectors discuss sector problems and opportunities for development, sometimes offering recommendations. The Commission originally hoped that these joint committees would make collective bargaining possible in a wider context, but that has not been the case.

Finally, in recent years there has been an increase in the number of contacts between employees working at the various subsidiaries of multinationals in different countries. Such initiatives have generally been introduced and supported by the trade unions, the International Trade Secretariats or the European trade union committees. One of the implicit goals is to gain the recognition of management. Carley (1993) gives the following examples.

- The International Federation of Commercial, Clerical and Technical Employees (FIET) and its European subsidiary Euro-FIET have called meetings for employees at Rank Xerox, Ikea and, together with the

Aspects of cross-border agreements governing information and consultation within 'European' companies

- A wide range of approaches has been taken with respect to formalizing such initiatives. Agreements reached by Bull, Thomson, Elf Aquitaine, Europipe (1991), Bayer (1991), Continental (1991), Hoechst (1991) and, from 1992 on, AGF, St Gobain, Volkswagen, Eurocopter, Airbus Industries (Staff Council) and Continental Can Europe were set down in writing. BSN-Gervais Danone, Nestlé and Péchiney base their agreements on 'agreed practice'. There are informal agreements initiated by management at Rhône-Poulenc, GEC-Alsthom and Asea Brown Boveri (and St Gobain until May 1992) and by the employees at Allianz and Mercedes–Benz (and at Volkswagen until February 1992). Significant for the EU are certain accords reached in Scandinavia, for example at the Scansped Group AB, SAS, Statoil, etc. (see Agotnes, 1993: 22–23). Finally, we should report that agreements are presently being negotiated in various other companies such as Crédit Lyonnais and Accor.

- There are also differences in the degree to which trade unions are involved in both the formal and the informal arrangements. Some have been set up with the direct participation of the employees, whereas others have involved the trade unions. Trade union representatives are usually chosen from among the company's employees. At BSN, Nestlé and Thomson, trade union participation has been set forth in explicit agreements, whereas in other companies the unions are free to appoint their own representatives.

- Remarkably, until 1991/92, most of the written agreements governing information and consultation at the European level were of French origin. This was closely related to French legislation from 1982 on group works councils. Recently a rising number of German companies have followed the French example.

- The bodies have little authority beyond their right to receive and discuss information. According to Gold and Hall, 'social dialogue' or 'exchange of views' is often intended to mean consultation, but it is not consultation such as is provided for in some national legislation, with established procedures and the opportunity to influence other parties (Gold and Hall, 1993: 10). In this respect, the BSN agreements are more substantial, but the most far-reaching is the agreement concluded at Volkswagen in 1992, which introduced, for the very first time, a formal consultation procedure (Carley, 1993: 14). Europipe, a French–German joint venture, has provided for employee representation on the supervisory management board. The representatives are recruited from the companies in both countries. Discussions are usually restricted to specific divisional or group concerns.

- Despite the limited number of companies involved, the influence of joint information and consultative committees on policy-making within the European Union has turned out to be quite substantial. This can be inferred from the degree of similarity between such committees and the Commission's proposals for a European works council. Gold and Hall (1992: 64) see the unanimity rule and the attitude of the United Kingdom as significant obstacles to rapid acceptance of the directive, however.

EMF, Digital. The latter eventually grew into a 'European works council', although without management recognition.

- The International Metalworkers Federation (IMF) and the European Metalworkers' Federation (EMF) are in the process of investigating European works councils and testing management on this topic at Siemens, General Motors, Philips, Electrolux and Whirlpool.
- The European Committee of Food, Catering and Allied Workers within IUF (ECF–IUF) regularly organizes meetings with employee representatives from Coca-Cola.

Problems associated with collective consultations at European level

Why is it so difficult to create a more significant industrial relations structure at the supranational level? There are a number of reasons, fundamentally related to changes in the autonomous positions of the various actors. There is, first of all, the fact that the majority of interest organizations resist having to relinquish authority to organizations at the European level. This attitude is in turn a consequence of the wide range of cultural styles and structures (cf. Van Ruysseveldt, 1993: 88) and of the fact that most of the income is still distributed at the national and regional levels. Despite their fundamentally different attitudes toward the market versus regulation dilemma, there are remarkably few differences between employers and employees in this respect. When trade unions insist on provisions at the European level on certain topics, there are usually powerful national reasons for doing so.

In a deeper sense, the problem is also related to the practical impossibility of aggregating employee interests. Unlike the impersonal and cosmopolitan interests of capital, labour and wages are often tied to local conditions. Reorganizations and employment relocations such as those undertaken by multinationals make employees at one location grateful while those at another mourn. No wonder it is so difficult to coordinate employee action. Even so, if free capital movements affect employment seriously enough, a crisis point may be reached at which it becomes clear just how necessary and urgent it is for workers to join forces across national borders and develop common organizations. But will it ever come to this crisis point? It depends on the types of jobs being affected and the categories of workers involved: are they well represented within organizations? The removal of high-skill positions to South East Asia or the former Eastern Bloc, a trend becoming evident in the industrial sectors (*NRC Handelsblad*, 22 September 1993), will no doubt bring the crisis closer, politically and otherwise.

A third reason is that Brussels has yet to develop a powerful institutional framework. On the contrary, the recent trend toward intergovernmental action reveals that national political representatives do after all have the reins firmly in hand when it comes to coordination. Of further importance is that within the present Union system, interest organizations only consult indirectly with the actual decision-makers, that is, the Council of Ministers.

On the other hand, we should remember, as we mentioned before, that politicians have had little incentive to look beyond their own national interests, precisely because the social interest organizations are unable to create powerful European rules and structures. There is a circular link between these two factors.

A fourth factor is the fact that, in the past ten years, a process of decentralization has become apparent in industrial relations systems all across Europe. The emphasis on micro-economic efficiency, the growing importance of company-specific relations and the rising tide of individualism have pushed governments to deregulate and privatize, and labour and management to make work and working hours more flexible and employment terms more differentiated. There is no room in this picture to expand the scope of bargaining to the European level, nor is a special form of European 'pattern bargaining' plausible. In this case a turning point might once again be possible. After all, if the various national frameworks lose power, cross-border developments may make (new) European rules necessary.

A fifth factor is that along with decentralization, the power of the trade union movement has been undermined in most European countries through a combination of deregulation, individualization and loss of membership. Along with large differences in union density between countries, this could slow down progress in introducing European regulatory provisions and possibly lead to a triple fragmentation of the trade union movement. The first group would be composed of strong national unions for specific target groups in high-skill occupations, who would coordinate successfully at the European level. The recent synchronization of trade union demands within multinationals has been a forerunner of this trend (Teague, 1993: 360). A second group would consist of a few powerful European unions for specific cross-border employees, while the third group would be made up of a whole range of weak employee associations. This will be the final blow to the 'old' trade union movement as the catalyst of social change. Whether this will actually come to pass is not yet certain, however. Too many changes are taking place simultaneously and important future developments cannot be assessed properly as yet.

3   Possible consequences of the European integration process for existing industrial relations practice

It is difficult to calculate the precise significance that European developments will have for national industrial relations systems and for the social policy pursued by companies, including multinational ones. A lot depends on how the integration process proceeds further. We can, however, try to gain greater understanding by considering a few models in which we have worked out a number of variables. We can call these models 'scenarios', and use them to estimate the effect that integration will have on both industrial relations systems and on the scope given to MNCs.

Four scenarios for a European system of industrial relations

International trends in economy and technology constitute the central factor in the process of European integration (cf. Schmitter and Streeck, 1991). Economic change both accelerates and decelerates the (political) integration process. On the other hand, the responses to economic trends can be wide-ranging. Policy-making not only shapes economic developments, it also gives these developments a certain dynamic. An interesting approach is to link two associated trends to the process of economic and political integration, that is, labour mobility in Europe and the nature of policy considerations on European integration. Other factors are naturally considered constant, which detracts from the credibility of the scenario, but this is a well-known problem in analytical constructions.

Labour mobility is certainly a crucial factor. We can assume that the idea behind the first basic right mentioned in the Social Charter – the freedom of movement of workers – was to use the increased mobility of workers to stimulate integration, economic or otherwise. If worker mobility increases sharply in the next few years, many adjustments will have to be introduced. A large measure of unhampered mobility will level out prices and costs and lead to institutional and policy adjustments with respect to labour markets and social security. An increase in worker mobility may lead to the formation of European labour markets, making supranational regulations unavoidable. A low level of mobility will scarcely require any adjustments or will only have an impact in the long run. The level of mobility is therefore an important factor in constructing the four scenarios. Another significant aspect is the level of capital mobility. Even if worker mobility remains weak, unobstructed capital movements will still have certain specific effects on the labour market, such as a narrowing of wage gaps. Nevertheless, in my opinion, real European integration will have taken place only after large-scale European labour markets have been established. On the other hand, large-scale capital movements could upset certain predictions. That is why we will not discuss them here, again in view of the analytical construct.

The second factor is whether European integration is being stimulated with certain market considerations in mind (the economist model) or whether economic integration is being explicitly linked to a social policy, either by Brussels or by the member states themselves. The economist or reductionist model would consider many national social arrangements as unfair competition and demand deregulation and institutional adjustments. If the market is to be the coordinating factor in a whole range of different areas, then downward pressure will be the result. Brussels would only produce a minimum number of regulations related to a restricted number of aspects. A philosophy linking integration to social policy, on the

		Mobility	
		High	Low
Economism	High (economist policy orientation)	Scenario I Segmented transaction model	Scenario II Regime competition model
	Low (social policy orientation)	Scenario III Accommodation model	Scenario IV Mosaic model

Figure 16.1 Scenarios for the development of European industrial relations

other hand, would lead to further institutional grounding and to rules and regulations exceeding the minimum, giving Brussels a greater role. The question as to whether the policy pursued can be identified as purely economist or not is therefore an important one for the scenarios.

The developments mentioned above allow us to assume that (1) there will be an increasing level of international competition and interdependence of economic activity, and (2) there will be progress in actually working out the Maastricht agreements. The level of labour mobility and the nature of the prevailing ideology can act either as mutual reinforcements or as mutual constraints. Positioning the two variables in a matrix gives us Figure 16.1.

In the scenario, we in fact implicitly assume that individual systems of industrial relations are identical. That is of course not so; different countries start from very different positions. Each system has its own historically determined institutional balance between economic efficiency and social justice, a balance which determines the internal dynamics of the system and its ability to respond to outside factors. The consequences of the changes predicted for the European scene will differ from country to country. We will, however, not discuss their impact on the industrial relations systems of the individual countries further.

Scenario I: segmented transaction model

For many countries, a situation in which there is a high degree of labour mobility and a policy aimed at reducing the number of social arrangements (dominance of economist policy) may lead to a relatively explosive and segmented transaction model of industrial relations. Market and policy are working toward the same goals: the lowest possible prices, costs and, as a consequence, incomes. In countries which have enjoyed a large degree of social protection and extensive social provisions – often those countries with relatively peaceful industrial relations – there will be stout resistance to any attempt to subvert such social gains. The rise of specialist, well-equipped trade unions for specific groups of workers or within specific companies is very likely. The fear expressed by some observers that a new 'underclass' might develop, composed of the unemployed and those with absolutely no prospects, might well become reality in this scenario. Even in those countries with a relatively low level of social protection, the departure of important sections of the workforce and a harsher social policy may initially lead to widespread social unrest. Nevertheless, for these countries the mobility of companies and of new investment may have a positive effect on employment in the long term. Capital mobility, on the other hand, is caused by more than low wages and low levels of worker protection.

Existing institutional frameworks will be in a state of uproar. Brussels may become extremely important as a political centre, but it is also possible that European integration will stumble to a halt or indeed that 'Europe' will disintegrate. The trade union movement, so fragmented at present, will no longer be able to avoid stepping in at the European level, however. In general, in this scenario the existing balance between social justice and economic efficiency is completely upset.

Scenario II: regime competition model

A low level of labour mobility and a policy based on the economist philosophy suggest a policy competition model, especially if accompanied by a large degree of capital mobility as well. The institutional deregulation will be less serious than in the first scenario. To some extent the situation will resemble that which prevailed in Europe for a long time. Although progress was slow, economic integration was possible and relatively unhampered by the wide variety of industrial relations systems. Proponents of the economist approach busied themselves with setting up the economic Union while ignoring the institutional framework of the individual countries. Indeed, the majority of countries set about constructing a relatively generous welfare state. By the 1980s, however, market-oriented thinking had begun to exercise a powerful appeal in most of the countries of Europe. Social institutions were deregulated and modified, and the launch of 'Europe 1992' stimulated gigantic flows of capital throughout the Union. If we project this scenario further, we can see that the increasingly interdependent economic conditions of the 1990s allow countries to take advantage of the various industrial relations systems as an 'asset'. The quality of tripartite or bipartite consultations may after all influence the competitive position of various countries. Corporatist systems of industrial relations can exploit their relatively peaceful co-existence, while other countries will be able to use their high level of labour market flexibility to their advantage. Both situations call on the various industrial sectors in different ways, depending on factors such as the capital intensity of production, the level of production integration, the required labour qualifications, the distribution and the diversity of production, the prevailing management philosophy, the competitive regime etc. In this context, any regulations proceeding from Brussels would be absolutely inappropriate.

Scenario III: accommodation model

A high level of worker mobility and a social policy orientation may lead to an accommodation model. Processes of change will be manipulated in such a fashion that a large degree of social protection can be retained. The levelling effect of the market can no longer be corrected by the national authorities alone. Brussels can assume an important role in creating a social market economy and in maintaining reasonable levels of prosperity. Open borders and the threat of social dumping will make a type of supranational social policy unavoidable. The principle of subsidiarity will be restricted by the high level of worker mobility. The powerful attraction that wealthier regions will exercise will make transfers of capital and investment flows to poor regions necessary. Migration from outside the EU will furthermore also lead to common arrangements. One might even label this 'Euroformity'. National systems of industrial relations will be injected, slowly but surely, with Union elements. An increasingly important institutional and legislative framework will be erected in Brussels. Encouraged by the high level of labour mobility and by the philosophy of social policy, 'new-style' industrial relations will be subject to simultaneous tests of economic efficiency and social justice. This may perhaps lead to new regime competition, this time at EU level – a tripartite model of competition as opposed to the Japanese bipartite model, with its profound interdependencies between government and business on the one hand and the American monistic market model on the other.

Scenario IV: mosaic model

Finally, a low degree of worker mobility and an emphasis on social policy could mean that the present, pluralist mosaic model will be retained. Europe lacks its own powerful internal dynamics; 'external forces' meet the traditional resistance and are accounted for in national formulas only after a long period of time. There may be a certain degree of conservatism which is expressed in an emphasis on specific national features and accomplishments, and Brussels will only be allowed to bring less advantaged countries – generally those that offer workers a low degree of social protection – in line with the rest to a certain extent. In the case of highly mobile capital, protectionism becomes a realistic option, even on the part of Brussels itself. If, on the other hand, it is the Union rather than the individual countries which gets the upper hand in designing social policy, then a more balanced model based on global competitive relations may be possible. In that case, European pluralism in industrial relations and regional economic positions could be turned into an advantage. Still, the chance of this happening is thought to be small. Instead, a low level of worker mobility in relation to fierce international competition makes it easier for a country to look for its own national solutions, possibly in cooperation with countries that have similar institutional patterns. A Europe that progresses at different speeds is the obvious result.

We may conclude that the first scenario will bring about severe institutional deregulation followed by European institutionalization. In the second scenario we may expect a lean institutional profile at the national levels, while the third scenario makes European institutionalization unavoidable. The fourth scenario, finally, assumes relatively few modifications to the current institutional pluralism.

The position of MNCs in the four scenarios

Each of the four scenarios has different consequences for multinationals and their social policy, quite apart from the degree to which they as a group exercise or are able to exercise an influence on these processes. A sharp rise in labour mobility means that any advantages that MNCs gain by exploiting wage differences will disappear rapidly. There will be labour market adjustments for a whole range of occupational groups leading toward comparable wage levels in different countries and regions. The introduction of a single currency will stimulate this process, making wage comparisons an easy matter no longer obscured by the 'money illusion' phenomenon. A high level of mobility will help achieve a particular supply of labour. A low level of mobility will make it possible for MNCs to exploit wage differences for a longer period of time. If policy is squarely in the economist camp (market-oriented integration), then MNCs, even more than other types of companies, will have the opportunity to develop their own forms of consultation and social policy. This would be much less the case if the emphasis were on social policy. What would, however, be of particular importance is whether the rules and regulations adopted were handed down by Brussels or by the member countries, since in the latter case MNCs would be able to play off one country against another.

To simplify our discussion, we will divide MNCs into two categories: those that compete on the basis of price and those that compete on the basis of quality. This distinction is important because the two options, certainly in their purest forms, can have different consequences for a company's social policy. In the first case, labour is viewed as a cost factor which is to be minimized as much as possible, whereas in the second, labour is seen as a source of increased added value. The dichotomy, in other words, is between wages as an expression of productivity (neoclassical theory), versus productivity as an expression of wages (efficiency wage theory). In the latter case, falling under the jurisdiction of internal company policy, a rising level of motivation is expected to yield important productivity gains. The competitive regime is of course also related to other factors, including the type of product. Price competition is frequently associated with products as product–market combinations, whereas quality competition often focuses on broader product concepts, product–technology–market combinations. The relative vulnerability of production networks is also significant, of course. A final important consideration is the relationship between the parent company and its subsidiaries, encompassing such factors as the nature of industrial relations in the home country (see Chapter 15). It is a difficult task to include all these factors in our simple scenarios, however, so we will content ourselves with a more general outline.

Scenario I is the most liberal scenario for MNCs. As a group, very little would hinder them from developing a 'corporate economy' by means of mergers and alliances. Companies will cream off the top of the labour market in order to obtain the best employees for the best price. It may be expected that MNCs competing on the basis of price will transfer a large number of activities to low-wage countries, and that MNCs competing on the basis of quality will locate themselves in areas with relatively high wages. Both will introduce sharper divisions in HRM policy for different types of employees, however. Employees with company-specific qualifications or strategic know-how will be treated differently from employees who are more easily replaced. MNCs competing on quality will have a larger core of privileged employees, however, than the other type of MNC. The trade union movement, sharply fragmented by internal divisions, will increasingly be passed by in favour of enterprise or 'yellow' unions, which will take over the trade union role.

In scenario II, MNCs will be able to play off international unions and governments against each other in the economic arena. They can profit from the fact that countries and regions are competing to attract investment (cf. Gretschmann and Sleijpen, 1993). 'Divide and conquer' strategies will have room to proliferate, since the role of both government and labour and management will be undercut less sharply than in scenario I. In this situation, price-competitive MNCs will have the opportunity to engage in 'concession bargaining', with employees relinquishing part of their wages in exchange for job security. Nevertheless, various relatively expensive activities will be hived off or transferred to low-wage countries. Companies emphasizing quality production will pay much better wages; union density will drop and existing consultative bodies within the company itself may become more important. Many MNCs will gear their HRM policy toward binding large sectors of their workforce to the company. The position of the national trade unions will be ambiguous. Martin and Ross believe that 'regime competition' will lead to a weakening of trade union power because participation privileges and income standards will plummet in the interests of competition (Martin and Ross, 1992: 49). This prediction is plausible, certainly when price-competitive, cost-minimizing MNCs are dominant. On the other hand, participation in tripartite national circuits aimed at protecting the national competitive position may, following West European tradition, furnish the trade unions with considerable power.

Important in scenario III is the level where social policy is hammered out: in Brussels or in the member states. In the latter case, MNCs will become mobile. Neither price-competitive MNCs nor those competing on the basis of quality will have any interest in locating activities in a socially progressive country. The latter type of company can, after all, gain a top-quality workforce by taking advantage of mobility within relatively low-wage countries. It is true that the levelling effect on wages will taper off after a period of time, but this will only be at the expense of major shifts in employment. It is therefore clear that this scenario is only relevant at the Union level, where price and quality competition might gain a more concentrated and concerted level of support. It is also conceivable that we will see the creation of Euro-MNCs: internationally active companies that are obliged to take Euro-legislation into account and which emphasize specific HRM features in their company policy.

Finally, scenario IV places the most restrictions on MNCs. If Brussels puts no limits on capital mobility, there is a strong possibility that MNCs will transfer a considerable number of jobs out of Europe and concentrate some of their activities, those which are immune to conflict, in the poorer regions of the Union. High-quality employment may continue to exist, but the economic burden for MNCs could grow quite heavy due to the possible high premiums for large-scale unemployment. This scenario resembles the situation as it was in the early 1980s.

Finally, we should emphasize once again that the scenarios are merely concepts based on two factors which vary almost digitally. Reality is much more complex and requires us to develop variations on these scenarios based on more precise data. On top of this, new, frequently unexpected developments succeed one another continuously. Very often, although not always, undesirable developments can be counteracted. The events that shook Eastern Europe are a good example of such unexpected developments. Few observers could have accurately predicted the fall of Communism and the subsequent political and military consequences. The same type of phenomenon also affects European integration. Perhaps the concept 'Europe' has to be reconceived entirely (Alting von Geusau, 1993). The tension in Europe between arranging and contriving on the one hand and voluntary action and market mechanisms on the other is always present – and that is a logical fact, given that the economy is embedded in a socio-political context, both at the national and at the international level.

4   Summary and conclusions

In general, if we once again consider the situation as it is today, we may conclude that a *political-administrative structure* has been developed at the European level, which has intensified the focus on national interests. This has impeded the development of supranational socio-economic policy and a supranational industrial relations structure. There is, on the other hand, a network of European interest organizations, ad hoc committees and consultative bodies, but their significance and decisiveness remain restricted. The lack of direct links between labour and management on the one hand and the Council of Ministers on the other, the fact that the national interest organizations have not yet given the European organizations in Brussels conclusive and authoritative mandates, and the wide variety of national institutions and legal frameworks, are the most important obstacles. The new political-economic objectives set out by Delors in 1985 have done little to change the situation so far: the Council of Ministers continues to be divided over the course to be taken (economism versus social policy). At the same time, various political and socio-economic policy circles still attach too much importance to national or regional prerogatives.

Any sudden acceleration in the integration process such as set forth in the Maastricht Treaty is viewed with caution at the national level. The debate on Maastricht made clear that the pressure to create an intergovernmental Union is increasing: that is to say, a Union managed by the various member states and not by a supranational body which supersedes them. Closely related to this is the growing support for the principle of subsidiarity. Official documents often include something to the effect that details must be worked out in accordance with the arrangements and traditions as they exist in the individual countries.

There are, however, other forces at work which may turn out to be stronger than the political-institutional factors mentioned above aimed at consolidation. The friction is similar to that found in institutional thinking (cf. Nagelkerke, 1992): technological and economic change and modest attempts at institutional renewal are countered by the vested institutions, that is, the existing national and supranational order and the positions of power associated with this order. Political and social dynamism is the result.

The constant state of friction between efforts at renewal and consolidated counteraction makes it difficult to take legislative steps at the Union level. Aggravating factors, certainly when it comes to *social issues*, are the restricted authority of the European Parliament, the weak position of the Economic and Social Committee and the unanimity rule, which often spells doom for Commission proposals. A policy discouraging social dumping only stands a chance of surviving if it is based on a restricted number of minimum rules (cf. Spyropoulos and Fragnière, 1991: 33). On the other hand, the adoption of the Social Charter and the Social Protocol annexed to the Maastricht Treaty has led to an increase in the number of Commission proposals. Both the scope for action and the flexibility of the decision-making procedures have clearly increased.

In order to reach a coherent and effective system of industrial relations, a number of structural changes will have to be effected. An important underlying condition is the creation of *cross-border labour markets*. Only in such a context can forms of collective bargaining be developed and serve to bolster the international units affiliated with the national organizations.

Until now, EU regulations and directives have only had a very restricted impact on *company* personnel policy, particularly in *multinationals*. There are very few regulations, and many of those which have been adopted were based on existing national legislation to a certain extent. Directives can be moulded at the national level to fit in with the customs of the country in question. Moreover, they often constitute the backlash of developments which have already affected actual practice to some degree. In addition, directives such as those on equal treatment and equal pay for women and men, or safety at work, will probably be implemented in smaller companies, which often do not have transfrontier activities, rather than in MNCs, which often have already applied them. Finally, EU regulations and directives cannot alter management prerogatives. Draft proposals concerning a European works council and a European company have been dragging on for years, while other proposals are simply shoved into the bottom drawer and left there indefinitely.

A good example can be found in the directives on atypical employment relationships. These are types of employment aimed at greater external flexibility, that is, the power to recruit and dismiss personnel easily. The aim of the three directives is to ensure that employees working in atypical employment relationships have the same legal rights in all of the various countries, since national differences might disturb the competitive balance or the functioning of the internal market. An equitable legal position in this case means equality in social security, annual holidays, extension of temporary contracts, training opportunities, representation on works councils, financial and social benefits etc. If these directives are adopted, they will have an impact on the personnel policy of certain companies in particular countries: it will become more difficult to skim off labour markets by offering jobs under specific conditions. The directives certainly do not stand in the way of flexible employment relationships, but they do create a 'floor' below which the employment terms cannot drop. Decision-making on these directives has been put off time and again, although one of them, on safety and hygiene for temporary employees, has been adopted.

The lack, at least for the time being, of a set of European regulations that have a significant impact on industrial relations touches on a final point of principle: 'For the moment there is not a single civil right which is defended by the European Union' (Dahrendorf, 1992: 85). In truth, the Union has not introduced any *social civil right*. For example, the terms used are 'working conditions' or 'freedom of movement of workers', not 'disablement' or 'the rights of the unemployed'. For the average citizen, Europe is still a long way off. Solace and security must still be sought within the national context.

References

Acuff, F., 1984, *International and Domestic Human Resources Functions: Innovations in International Compensation*. New York: Organization Resources Counselors, pp. 3–5.

Adler, N.J., 1983, 'Cross-cultural management: issues to be faced', *International Studies of Management and Organization*, 13 (1–2), pp. 7–45.

Adler, N.J., 1984a, 'Expecting international success: female managers overseas', *Columbia Journal of World Business*, 19 (3), pp. 79–85.

Adler, N.J., 1984b, 'Women in international management: where are they?', *California Management Review*, 26 (4), pp. 78–89.

Adler, N.J., 1986, *International Dimensions of Organizational Behaviour*. Boston, MA: Kent Publishing.

Adler, N.J., 1986/87, 'Women in management world-wide', *International Studies of Management and Organization*, 16, Fall–Winter, pp. 3–32.

Adler, N.J., 1987, 'Pacific Basin managers: a gaijin, not a woman', *Human Resource Management*, 26 (2), pp. 169–192.

Adler, N.J., 1991, *International Dimensions of Organizational Behaviour*. 2nd edn. Boston, MA: Kent Publishing.

Adler, N.J., 1993, 'Competitive frontiers: women managers in the triad', *International Studies of Management and Organization*, 23 (2), pp. 3–23.

Adler, N.J. and Bartholomew, S., 1992, 'Managing globally competent people', *Academy of Management Executive*, 6 (3), pp. 52–65.

Adler, N.J. and Ghadar, F., 1990, 'Strategic human resource management: a global perspective', in: Pieper, R. (ed.), *Human Resource Management: An International Comparison*. Berlin: De Gruyter, pp. 235–260.

Agotnes, H., 1993, 'Developments in the Nordic Countries', *P+ European Participation Monitor*, 6 (2), pp. 22–24.

Ajiferuke, M. and Boddewyn, J., 1970, 'Culture and other explanatory variables in comparative management studies', *Academy of Management Journal*, 35, pp. 153–164.

Albeda, W. et al., 1989, *Naar Medezeggenschap op Europees Niveau?* The Hague: SMO.

Albertijn, M., Hancké, B. and Wijgaerts, D., 1990, 'Technology agreements and industrial relations in Belgium', *New Technology, Work and Employment*, 5 (1), pp. 18–30.

Alós-Moner, R. and Lope, A., 1991, 'Los sindicatos en los centros de trabajo', in: Miguélez, F. and Prieto, C. (eds.), *Las relaciones laborales en Espana*. Madrid: Siglo XXI, pp. 233–250.

Alting von Geusau, F., 1993, Contribution to the congress 'Europe Revisited', Tilburg, 4 June 1993.

Baan, E. van der, 1992, *Inventarisatie Voorbereidingscursussen*. Utrecht: University of Utrecht, Centre for Policy and Management.

Baglioni, G. and Crouch, C. (eds.), 1990, *European Industrial Relations: The Challenge of Flexibility*. London: Sage.

Baker, J.C. and Ivancevich, J.M., 1971, 'The assignment of American executives abroad: systematic, haphazard, or chaotic?', *California Management Review*, 13, pp. 39–44.

Bamberg, U. et al., 1987, *Aber ob die Karten voll ausgereizt sind . . . 10 Jahre Mitbestimmungsgesetz in der Bilanz*. Cologne: Bund Verlag.

Bandura, A., 1977, *Social Learning Theory*. Englewood Cliffs, NJ: Prentice-Hall.

Barham, K. and Devine, M., 1990, *The Quest for the International Manager: A Survey of Global Human Resource Strategies*. London: Ashridge Management Guide/Economist Intelligence Unit.

Barham, K. and Devine, M., 1991, *The Quest for the International Manager: A Survey of Global Human Resource Strategies*. London: Ashridge Management Guide/Economist Intelligence Unit.

Bartlett, C.A., 1986, 'Building and managing the transnational: the new organizational challenge', in: Porter, M.E. (ed.), *Competition in Global Industries*. Boston, MA: Harvard Business School Press, pp. 367–401.

Bartlett, C.A. and Ghoshal, S., 1987a, 'Managing across borders: new strategic requirements', *Sloan Management Review*, 28, Summer, pp. 7–17.

Bartlett, C.A. and Ghoshal, S., 1987b, 'Managing across borders: new organizational responses', *Sloan Management Review*, 28, Fall, pp. 43–53.

Bartlett, C.A. and Ghoshal, S., 1989, *Managing Across Borders. The Transnational Solution*. Boston, MA: Harvard Business School Press.

Bartlett, C.A. and Ghoshal, S., 1990, 'Matrix management: not a structure, a frame of mind', *Harvard Business Review*, 68 (4), pp. 138–145.

Bartlett, C.A. and Ghoshal, S., 1992a, 'What is a global manager?', *Harvard Business Review*, September/October, pp. 124–132.

Bartlett, C.A. and Ghoshal, S., 1992b, *Transnational Management: Text, Cases and Readings in Cross-Border Management*. Homewood, IL: Irwin.

Bates, M. and Kiersey, D.W., 1984, *Please Understand Me*. California: Prometheus Nemesis.

Baumgarten, K.E.E., 1992a, 'Expatriate failure and success: a search for potential predictors'. Thesis, Faculty of Applied Educational Science, University of Twente, Enschede, The Netherlands.

Baumgarten, K.E.E., 1992b, 'A profile for international managers and its implications for selection and training'. Thesis, Faculty of Applied Educational Science, University of Twente, Enschede, The Netherlands.

Beer, M. et al., 1984, *Managing Human Assets*. New York: Free Press.

Berg, P.B., 1993, 'Training institutions and industrial relations in Germany and the United States: the importance of inter-institutional linkages for understanding labor adjustment'. Paper, University of Notre Dame, Paris.

Biagi, M., 1990, 'Forms of employee representation at the workplace,' in: Blanpain, R. (ed.), *Comparative Labour Law and Industrial Relations in Industrialised Market Economies*. Deventer: Kluwer.

Bilbao, A., 1991, 'Trabajadores, gestión económica y crisis sindical', in: Miguélez, F. and Prieto, C. (eds.), *Las relaciones laborales en Espana*. Madrid: Siglo XXI, pp. 251–267.

Birtwhistle, A., 1990, 'The Funding Study Research Programme: some early research findings (GB)', in: Mulder, M., Romiszowski, A.J. and van der Sijde, P.C. (eds.), *Strategic Human Resource Development*. Amsterdam/Rockland: Swets and Zeitlinger, pp. 87–102.

Black, J.S., 1988, 'Work role transitions: a study of American expatriate managers in Japan', *Journal of International Business Studies*, 19, pp. 277–294.

Black, J.S. and Gregersen, H.B., 1992, 'Serving two masters: managing the dual allegiance of expatriate employees', *Sloan Management Review*, Summer, pp. 61–71.

Black, J.S. and Mendenhall, M., 1990, 'Cross-cultural training effectiveness: a review and a theoretical framework', *Academy of Management Review*, 15(1), pp. 113–136.

Black, J.S. and Mendenhall, M., 1991, 'A practical but theory-based framework for selecting cross-cultural training methods', in: Mendenhall, M. and Oddou, G. (eds.), *Readings and Cases in International Human Resource Management*. Boston, MA: PWS-Kent.

Bolweg, J.F., 1989, 'Stroombeleid: een nieuwe wijze van kijken', in: Kluytmans, F. (ed.), *Human Resource Management: Verzakelijking of Vernieuwing*. Deventer/Heerlen: Kluwer/ Open University.

Bolwijn, P.T. and Kumpe, T., 1990, 'Manufacturing in the 1990s – productivity, flexibility and innovation', *Long Range Planning*, 23 (4), pp. 44–57.

Bomers, G.B.J., 1976, *Multinational Corporations and Industrial Relations: A Comparative Study of West Germany and the Netherlands*. Assen/Amsterdam: Van Gorcum.

Borg, M., 1982, 'Repatriation of executives'. Paper presented at the 1982 EIBA Conference, INSEAD, Fontainebleau.

Borg, M., 1988, *International Transfer of Managers in Multinational Corporations*. Stockholm: Almqvist and Wiksell International.

Borgmann, W., 1986, *Reformgesetz in der Bewährung: Theorie und Praxis des Betriebsverfassungsgesetzes von 1972*. Opladen: Westdeutscher Verlag.

Brewster, C., 1988, *The Management of Expatriates*, Human Resource Centre Monograph 2. Cranfield: Cranfield Institute of Technology.

Brewster, C., 1991, *The Management of Expatriates*. London: Kogan Page.

Brislin, R.W., Cushner, K., Cherrie, C. and Yong, M., 1986, *Intercultural Interactions: A Practical Guide*. Beverly Hills, CA: Sage.

Broderick, R. and Milkovich, C., 1991, *Breaking the Glass Ceiling*. Ithaca, NY: ILR School, Cornell University.

Burack, E.H. and Smith, R.D., 1982, *Personnel Management: A Human Resource System Approach*. New York: John Wiley.

Byrne, J.A., 1992, 'Management's new gurus: business is hungry for fresh approaches to the global market place', *Business Week*, 31 August, pp. 42–50.

Carley, M., 1993, 'Voluntary initiatives – an update', *P+ European Participation Monitor*, 6 (2), pp. 14–22.

Carnevale, A.P., Gainer, L.J. and Villet, J., 1990, *Training in America: The Organization and Strategic Role of Training*. San Francisco: Jossey-Bass.

Carrol, S.J., Pains, F.T. and Ivancevich, J.J., 1972, 'The relative effectiveness of training methods – expert opinion and research', *Personnel Psychology*, 25, pp. 495–509.

Cedefop, 1990, *Vocational Training Scenarios for Some Member States of the European Community. A Synthesis Report for France, Greece, Italy, Portugal, Spain and the United Kingdom*. Berlin: Cedefop.

Chalmers, N., 1989, *Industrial Relations in Japan: The Peripheral Workforce*. London: Routledge.

Chalofsky, N.E. and Reinhart, C., 1988, *Effective Human Resource Development*. San Francisco: Jossey-Bass.

Chandler, A.D., 1962, *Strategy and Structure: Chapters in the History of the Industrial Enterprise*. Cambridge, MA: MIT Press.

Child, J., 1972, 'Organizational structure, environment and performance: the role of strategic choice', *Sociology*, 6, pp. 1–22.

Child, J., 1981, 'Culture, contingency and capitalism in the cross-national study of organizations', in: Cummings, L.L. and Staw, B.M. (eds.), *Research in Organizational Behaviour*, vol. 3. Greenwich: JAI press.

Child, J. and Tayeb, M.H., 1983, 'Theoretical perspectives in cross-national organizational research', *International Studies of Management and Organization*, 12, pp. 23–70.

Christis, J., Dols, H., Doorewaard, H., Fruytier, B. and Martens, W., 1981, *Techniek, organisatie, arbeidsmarkt*. The Hague: Staatsuitgeverij.

Coase, R.H., 1937, 'The nature of the firm', *Economica*, November, pp. 386–405.

Collis, D.J., 1991, 'A resource-based analysis of global competition: the case of the bearings industry', *Strategic Management Journal*, 12, pp. 49–68.

Commission of the European Communities, 1991, *Social Europe: The European Social Fund*. 2/91 (CEG SE). Brussels: CEC.

Commission of the European Communities, 1992, *Directory of Professional Organisations in the European Community*. Brussels: CEC.

Conrad, P. and Pieper, R., 1990, 'Human resource management in the Federal Republic of Germany', in: Pieper, R. (ed.), *Human Resource Management: An International Comparison*. Berlin/New York: De Gruyter.

Cressey, P. and Williams, R., 1990, *Participation in Change: New Technology and the Role of Employee Involvement*. Dublin: European Foundation for the Improvement of Living and Working Conditions.

Crozier, M. and Friedberg, E., 1977, *L'acteur et le système*. Paris: Editions du Seuil.

Dahrendorf, R., 1992, 'The New Europe', *Journal of European Social Policy*, 2 (2), pp. 79–86.

Dalin, P., 1989, *Organisatie-ontwikkeling in school en onderwijs*. Alphen on the Rhine: Samsom.

Daniels, J.D. Pitts, R.A. and Tretter, M.J., 1984, 'Strategy and structure of US multi-nationals', *Academy of Management Journal*, 27 (2), pp. 292–307.

Daniels, J.D., Pitts, R.A. and Tretter, M.J., 1985, 'Organizing for dual strategies of product diversity and international expansion', *Strategic Management Journal*, 6 (3), pp. 223–237.

Däubler, W. and Lecher, W. (eds.), 1991, *Die Gewerkschaften in den 12 EG-Ländern: Europäische Integration und Gewerkschaftsbewegung*. Cologne: Bund Verlag.

Davidson, M. and Cooper, G., 1987, 'Female managers in Britain – a comparative perspective', *Human Resource Management*, 26 (2), pp. 217–242.

Devanna, M., 1987, 'Women in management: progress and promise', *Human Resource Management*, 26 (4), pp. 469–481.

Devanna, M., 1988, *Male/Female Careers – The First Decade: A Study of MBAs*. Management Institute Research Report, Columbia University Graduate School of Business.

Diefenbacher, H. and Nutzinger, H.G. (eds.), 1992, *Mitbestimmung in Europa; Erfahrungen und Perspektiven in Deutschland, der Schweiz und Österreich. Konzepte und Formen der Arbeitnehmerpartizipation*. Heidelberg: FEST.

Dijck, J.J.J. van, 1991, 'Internationalization: strategy, structure and process', in: Dijck, J.J.J. van and Wentink, A.A. (eds.), *Transnational Business in Europe: Economic and Social Perspectives*. Tilburg: Tilburg Academic Press, pp. 151–161.

Dobbins, G. and Platz, S., 1986, 'Sex differences in leadership: how real are they?', *Academy of Management Review*, 11, pp. 118–127.

Dore, R., 1973, *British Factory – Japanese Factory: The Origins of National Diversity in Industrial Relations*. London: Allen and Unwin.

Dore, R.P. and Sako, M., 1989, *How the Japanese Learn to Work*. London: Routledge.

Dowling, P.J. and Schuler, R.S., 1990, *International Dimensions of Human Resource Management*. Boston, MA: PWS-Kent.

Doz, Y., 1986, *Strategic Management in Multinational Companies*. Oxford: Pergamon Press.

Doz, Y. and Prahalad, C.K., 1981, 'Headquarters' influence and strategic control in MNCs', *Sloan Management Review*, 23, Fall, pp. 15–29.

Doz, Y. and Prahalad, C.K., 1991, 'Managing DMNCs: a search for a new paradigm', *Strategic Management Journal*, 12, pp. 145–164.

Drucker, P.F., 1992, *Managing for the Future*. Oxford: Butterworth-Heinemann.

Dufour, C. and Mouriaux, M.-F., 1986, *Comités d'entreprise: Quarante ans après*. Paris: IRES.

Dülfer, E., 1990, 'Human resource management in multinational and internationally operating companies', in: Pieper, R. (ed.), *Human Resource Management: An International Comparison*. Berlin: De Gruyter, pp. 261–283.

Dunbar, E. and Ehrlich, M., 1986, *International Human Resource Practices: Selecting, Training, and Managing the International Staff: A Survey Report*. New York: Columbia University-Teachers College, The Project of International Human Resources.

Dunlop, J., 1958, *Industrial Relations Systems*. Carbondale, IL: Southern Illinois University Press.

Edström, A. and Galbraith, J., 1977, 'Transfer of managers as a coordination and control strategy in multinational organizations', *Administrative Science Quarterly*, 22 (2), pp. 248–263.

Edström, A. and Lorange, P., 1984, 'Matching strategy and human resources in multinational corporations', *Journal of International Business Studies*, 15, Fall, pp. 125–137.

Edwards, P. et al., 1990, 'Great Britain: still muddling through', in: European Trade Union Institute, *Workers' Representation and Rights in the Workplace in Western Europe*. Brussels: ETUI.

Egelhoff, W.G., 1988, 'Strategy and structure in multinational corporations: a revision of the Stopford and Wells model', *Strategic Management Journal*, 9, pp. 1–14.

Enderwick, P., 1982, 'Labour and the theory of the multinational corporation', *Industrial Relations Journal*, 13 (2), pp. 32–43.

European Industrial Relations, 1993, 'The Hoover affair and social dumping', *European Industrial Relations*, 230 (March), pp. 14–20.

European Trade Union Institute, 1990a, *The European Trade Union Confederation (ETUC): Its History Structure and Policy*. Brussels: ETUI.

European Trade Union Institute, 1990b, *Workers' Representation and Rights in the Workplace in Western Europe*. Brussels: ETUI.

European Trade Union Institute, 1991, *The Social Dimension of the Internal Market: Part IV European Works Councils*. Brussels: ETUI.

Evans, P., Lank, E. and Farquhar, A., 1989, 'Managing human resources in the international firm: lessons from practice', in: Evans, P., Doz Y. and Laurent, A. (eds.), *Human Resource Management in International Firms: Change, Globalization, Innovation*. London: Macmillan, pp. 113–143.

Evans, P. and Lorange, P., 1989, 'The two logics behind human resource management', in: Evans, P., Doz, Y. and Laurent, A. (eds.), *Human Resource Management in International Firms: Change, Globalization, Innovation*. London: Macmillan, pp. 144–161.

Eyraud, F., D. Marsden and Silvestre, J.J., 1990, 'Occupational and internal labour markets in Britain and France', *International Labour Review*, 129 (4), pp. 501–517.

Farmer, R.N. and Richman, B.M., 1965, *Comparative Management and Economic Progress*. Homewood, IL: Irwin.

Feijen, C.J., 1993, 'Scholing van werkenden in de voedings- en genotmiddelenindustrie'. Paper for the Educational Research Days in Maastricht. Nijmegen: Institute of Applied Social Science.

Ferner, A. and Hyman, R., 1992a, 'Introduction', in: Ferner, A. and Hyman, R. (eds.), *Industrial Relations in the New Europe*. Oxford: Blackwell.

Ferner, A. and Hyman, R., 1992b, 'Italy: Between political exchange and micro-corporatism', in: Ferner, A. and Hyman, R. (eds.), *Industrial Relations in the New Europe*. Oxford: Blackwell, pp. 524–600.

Force, 1992, *Synoptic Tables: Information Available in the Twelve Member States on Continuing Vocational Training*. Brussels: Commission of the European Communities.

Freedman, S. and Phillips, J., 1988, 'The changing nature of research on women at work', *Journal of Management*, 14 (2), pp. 231–251.

Frietman, J. and de Vries, B., 1987, *Docenten op stage*. Nijmegen: Institute of Applied Social Science.

Galbraith, J.R. and Kazanjian, R.K., 1986, 'Organizing to implement strategies of diversity and globalisation: the role of matrix designs', *Human Resource Management*, 25 (1),pp. 37–54.

Geertz, C., 1973, *The Interpretation of Cultures*. New York: Basic Books.

Gevers, P., 1989, 'Vertegenwoordigend overleg en medezeggenschap in de onderneming', in: *Belgian Society for Industrial Relations, 50 Jaar arbeidsverhoudingen*. Bruges: die Keure, pp. 255–276.

Ghoshal, S., 1987, 'Global strategy: an organizing framework', *Strategic Management Journal*, 8, pp. 425–440.

Ghoshal, S. and Nohria, N., 1989, 'Internal differentiation within multinational corporations', *Strategic Management Journal*, 10, pp. 323–337.

Ghoshal, S. and Nohria, N., 1993, 'Horses for courses: organizational forms for multinational corporations', *Sloan Management Review*, Winter, pp. 23–35.

Giddens, Anthony, 1986, *The Constitution of Society*. Berkeley and Los Angeles: University of California Press.

Gill, C. and Krieger, H., 1992, 'The diffusion of participation in new information technology in Europe: survey results', *Economic and Industrial Democracy*, 13, pp. 331–358.

Glynn, S. and Gospel, H., 1993, 'Britain's low skill equilibrium: a problem of demand?', *Industrial Relations Journal*, 24 (2), pp. 112–125.

Gold, M. and Hall, M., 1992, *Report on European-level Information and Consultation in Multinational Companies – An Evaluation of Practice*. Luxemburg: European Foundation for the Improvement of Living and Working Conditions.

Gold, M. and Hall, M., 1993, 'Experience with voluntary initiatives', *P+ European Participation Monitor*, 6 (2), pp. 9–14.

Golden, K.A. and Ramanujam, V., 1985, 'Between a dream and a nightmare: on the integration of human resource management and strategic business planning process', *Human Resource Management*, 24, Winter, pp. 429–452.

Goldstein, I.L., 1986, *Training in Organizations: Needs Assessment, Development, and Evaluation*. Monterey, CA: Brooks/Cole.

Gouldner, Alvin W., 1976, *The Dialectic of Ideology and Technology: The Origins, Grammar and Future of Ideology*. Basingstoke: Macmillan.

Gretschmann, K. and Sleijpen, O.C.H.M., 1993, 'Europa als dekmantel', *Economisch Statistische Berichten*, 31 March, pp. 288–291.

Gronhaug, K. and Nordhaug, O., 1992, 'International human resource management: an environmental perspective', *International Journal of Human Resource Management*, 3 (1), pp. 1–14.

Grootings, P. and Hövels, B., 1981, *Sociale ongelijkheid in het arbeidsbestel*. Nijmegen: Institute of Applied Social Science.

Guest, D.E., 1987, 'Human resource management and industrial relations', *Journal of Management Studies*, 24, pp. 503–521.

Guest, D.E., 1989, 'Human resource management: its implications for industrial relations and trade unions', in: Storey, J. (ed.), *New Perspectives on Human Resource Management*. London: Routledge.

Hamill, J., 1984, 'Labour relations decision-making within multinational corporations', *Industrial Relations Journal*, 15 (2), pp. 30–34.

Hancké, B., 1991, 'The crisis of national unions: Belgian labour in decline', *Politics and Society*, 19 (4), pp. 463–487.

Harris, P.R. and Moran, R.T., 1991, *Managing Cultural Differences*. Houston, TX: Gulf Publishing.

Harvey, M., 1985, 'The expatriate family: an overlooked variable in international assignments', *Columbia Journal of World Business*, Spring, pp. 84–92.

Hay Management Consultants, 1992, *Inkomens en pakketvergelijking 1992*. Utrecht: Hay Management Consultants.

Hays, R.D., 1971, 'Ascribed behavioural determinants of success–failure among US expatriate managers', *Journal of International Business Studies*, 5, pp. 25–37.

Hedlund, G., 1986, 'The hypermodern MNC – a heterarchy?', *Human Resource Management*, 25 (1), pp. 9–35.

Heilman, M., 1979, 'High school students' occupational interest as a function of projected sex ratios in male-dominated occupations', *Journal of Applied Psychology*, 64, pp. 275–279.

Heilman, M. and Guzzo, R., 1978, 'The perceived cause of work success as a mediator of sex discrimination in organizations', *Organizational Behaviour and Human Performance*, 21 (3), pp. 346–357.

Heilman, M. and Saruwatari, L., 1979, 'When beauty is beastly: the effects of appearance and sex on evaluations of job applicants for managerial jobs', *Organizational Behaviour and Human Performance*, 23, pp. 360–372.

Hekscher, C.C., 1988, *The New Unionism: Employee Involvement in the Changing Corporation*. New York: Basic Books.

Heller, J., 1980, 'Criteria for selecting an international manager', *Personnel*, 57, May–June.

Henriet, B., Harff, Y. and Bourdonnais, J., 1987, *Les comités d'entreprise: Moyens d'action et interventions économiques*. Paris: CRESST.

Hiwatari, N., 1993, 'Towards the highest stage of enterprise unionism?: Union reorganization amidst flexible restructuring and aging society in Japan'. Paper, Institute of Social Science, Tokyo.

Hoffmann, L. and Neumann, U., 1987, 'Interessenvertretung im Klein- und Mittelbetrieb'. Unpublished dissertation, Göttingen.

Hofstede, G.H., 1980a, 'Motivation, leadership and organization: do American theories apply abroad?', *Organizational Dynamics*, Summer, pp. 42–63.

Hofstede, G.H., 1980b, *Culture's Consequences: International Differences in Work-Related Values*. Beverly Hills, CA: Sage.

Hofstede, G.H., 1991, *Cultures and Organizations: Software of the Mind*. London: McGraw-Hill.

Hofstede, G.H. and Bond, M.H., 1988, 'The Confucius connection: from cultural roots to economic growth', *Organizational Dynamics*, 16 (4), pp. 4–21.

Hogan, G.W. and Goodson, J.R., 1990, 'The key to expatriate success', *Training and Development Journal*, 8, pp. 50–52.

Hoof, J.J.M. van, 1986, 'Interfaces en tussenschakels', *Tijdschrift voor arbeidsvraagstukken*, 7 (2), 15–28.

Hoof, J.J.M. van, 1987, *De arbeidsmarkt als arena*. Amsterdam: SUA.

Horner, M., 1972, 'Toward an understanding of achievement-related conflicts in women', *Journal of Social Issues*, 28, pp. 157–175.

Hoskyns, C., 1991, 'Working women and women's rights: the development and implications of EC policy', in: Milner, S. and Hantrais, L. (eds.), *Workers' Rights in Europe*. Birmingham: Cross-National Research Papers, pp. 23–33.

Hossain, S. and Davis, H.J., 1989, 'Some thoughts on international personnel management as an emerging field', in: *Research in Personnel and Human Resource Management*, Supplement 1, pp. 121–136.

Hövels, B., 1987, *Naar een versterking van het leerlingwezen*. The Hague: Ministry of Social Affairs and Employment.

Hövels, B. and Peschar, J., 1985, *Tussen wal en schip: een onderzoeksprogramma op het terrein van onderwijs en arbeidssituaties*. Nijmegen: Institute of Applied Social Science.

Huiskamp, M.J., 1992, 'Arbeidsverhoudingen en sociotechniek: een nieuwe benadering', *M&O: Tijdschrift voor organisatiekunde en sociaal beleid*, 46 (Nov./Dec.), pp. 491–506.

IDE International Research Group, 1981, *Industrial Democracy in Europe*. Oxford: Clarendon Press.

Iersel, J. van, 1985, 'Arbeidsmarkt en arbeidsproces: beroepsgerichte volwasseneneducatie in het spanningsveld tussen de vraag en het aanbod van kwalificaties', in: Kraayvanger, G. and van Onna, B. (eds.), *Arbeid en leren. Bijdragen tot de volwasseneneducatie*. Baarn: Nelissen, pp. 119–132.

Ietto-Gillies, G., 1992, *International Production: Trends, Theories, Effects*. Cambridge: Polity Press.

Industrial Relations Services, 1990, *Employee Participation in Europe*. London: IRS.

Inkeles, A. and Levinson, D.J., 1969, 'National character: the study of modal personality and sociocultural systems', in: Lindzey, G. and Aronson, E. (eds.), *The Handbook of Social Psychology*, vol. 4. Reading, MA: Addison Wesley.

Jong, J.A. de, 1991, 'The multiple forms of on-site training', *Human Resource Development*, 2 (4), pp. 307–317.

Kaiero, A., 1988, 'Participación de los trabajadores en la empresa: relaciones laborales y contexto social en Europa y en España', *Estudios de Deusto*, 36, pp. 391–435.

Kanter, R., 1977, *Men and Women of the Corporation*. New York: Basic Books.

Katz, H.C., 1993, 'The decentralization of collective bargaining: a literature review and comparative analysis'. Paper, New York State School of International Labour Relations, Ithaca, NY.

Kayzel, R., 1985, *Opleidingsbeleid in de grafische industrie*. The Hague: Staatsuitgeverij.

Kemenade, J. van, 1981, 'Het onderwijsbestel in hoofdlijnen', in: Kemenade, J.A. (ed.), *Onderwijs: Bestel en beleid*. Groningen: Wolters-Noordhoff, pp. 34–94.

Kern, H. and Schumann, M., 1984, *Das Ende der Arbeitsteilung?* Munich: C.H. Beck.

Kessels, J. and Smit, C., 1991, 'Opleiden en leiding geven zijn niet te scheiden', in: Kessels, J., Smit, C. and Kruijd, D. (eds.), *Opleiden op de werkplek*. Deventer: Kluwer, pp. 97–104.

Klink, M.R. van der, 1989, *Werkend leren voor volwassenen*. Nijmegen: Catholic University of Nijmegen, Institute for Social Pedagogy and Adult Education.

Kluckhohn, F.R. and Strodtbeck, F.L., 1961, *Variations in Value Orientations*. Westport, CT: Greenwood Press.

Kluytmans, F. and Paauwe, J., 1991, 'HRM-denkbeelden: de balans opgemaakt: een aanzet voor een onderzoeksagenda', *M&O: Tijdschrift voor organisatiekunde en sociaal beleid*, 45 (4), pp. 279–303.

Kochan, T.A., Katz, H.C. and McKersie, R.B., 1986, *The Transformation of American Industrial Relations*. New York: Basic Books.

Koene, A.M. and Slomp, H., 1991, *Medezeggenschap van werknemers op ondernemings-niveau: een onderzoek naar de regels en hun toepassing in zes Europese landen*. The Hague: VUGA.

Koike, K., 1988, *Understanding Industrial Relations in Modern Japan*. New York: St Martin's Press.

Kraayvanger, G. and Onna, B. van, 1987, *Intermediaire voorzieningen*. The Hague: Organisation for Strategic Labour Market Research.

Lammers, C.J., 1987, *Organisaties vergelijkenderwijs*. Utrecht: Het Spectrum.

Lammers, C.J. and Hickson, D.J., 1979, *Organizations Alike and Unlike: International and Interinstitutional Studies in the Sociology of Organizations*. London: Routledge and Kegan Paul.

Lane, C., 1989, *Management and Labour in Europe: The Industrial Enterprise in Germany, Britain and France*. Aldershot: Gower.

Lanier, A., 1979, 'Selecting and preparing personnel for overseas transfer', *Personnel Journal*, 58 (3), pp. 160–163.

Lauglo, J. and Lillis, K., 1989, *Vocationalizing Education: An International Perspective*. Oxford: Pergamon Press.

Laurent, A., 1983, 'The cultural diversity of Western conceptions of management', *International Studies of Management and Organization*, 1/2, pp. 75–96.

Legge, K., 1989, 'Human resource management: a critical analysis', in: Storey, J. (ed.), *New Perspectives on Human Resource Management*. London: Routledge.

Levie, H. and Sandberg, A., 1991, 'Trade unions and workplace technical change in Europe', *Economic and Industrial Democracy*, 12, pp. 231–258.

Lincoln, J. and Kalleberg, A., 1990, *Culture Control and Commitment: A Study of Work Organization and Work Attitudes in the United States and Japan*. Cambridge: Cambridge University Press.

Lindblom, C.E., 1987, 'The science of muddling through', in: Pugh, D.S. (ed.), *Organization Theory: Selected Readings*. Harmondsworth: Penguin Books, pp. 238–255.

Lindert, P.H., 1986, *International Economics*. Homewood, IL: Irwin.

Lipietz, A., 1986, 'New tendencies in the international division of labor: regimes of accumulation and modes of regulation', in: Scott, A. and Storper M. (eds.), *Production, Work, Territory*. Boston: Allen and Unwin.

Litvak, I. and Maule, C., 1972, 'The union response to international relations', *Industrial Relations*, pp. 62–71.

Locke, R.M., 1990, 'The resurgence of the local union: industrial restructuring and industrial relations in Italy', *Politics and Society*, 18 (3), pp. 347–379.

Logger, E. and Vinke, R., 1989, *Effectieve beloningspakketten*, Themacahier IV Human Resource Management. Deventer: Kluwer.

Looise, J.C., 1989, *Werknemersvertegenwoordiging op de tweesprong: vakbeweging en vertegenwoordigend overleg in veranderende arbeidsverhoudingen*. Alphen on the Rhine: Samsom.

Looise, J.C. and De Lange, F.G.M., 1987, *Ondernemingsraden, bestuurders en besluit-vorming*. Nijmegen: Institute of Applied Social Science.

Lope, A., Jordana, J. and Carrasquer, P., 1989, 'La nova etapa de l'acción sindical a España: transformaciones laborales y canvis estratégicas', *Revista de Sociología*, 32, pp. 89–114.

Mahnkopf, B., 1992, 'The "skill-oriented" strategies of German trade unions: their impact on efficiency and equality objectives', *British Journal of Industrial Relations*, (30) 1, pp. 61–81.

Marginson, P., 1992, 'European integration and transnational management–union relations in the enterprise', *British Journal of Industrial Relations*, 30 (4) pp. 529–545.

Marshall, J., 1984, *Women Managers: Travellers in a Male World*. London: Wiley.

Martens, H., 1989, 'Ansaztzpunkte und Grenzen unternehmens-übergreifender gewerk-schaftlicher Mitbestimmungspolitik unter den Bedingungen des Mitbestimmungsgesetzes '76', in: Diefenbacher, H. and Nutzinger, H.-G. (eds.), *Mitbestimmung in Betrieb und Verwaltung, Konzepte und Formen der Arbeitnehmerpartizipation*. Heidelberg: FEST, pp. 89–109.

Martin, A. and Ross, G., 1992, 'The changing place in European political economies and cultures: the end of labour's century', in: European Centre for Work and Society, *New Patterns of Industrial Relations in Europe*. Brussels: ECWS.

Maslow, A.H., 1970, *Motivation and Personality*. New York: Harper and Row.

Maurice, M., Eyraud, F., d'Iribarne, A. and Rychener, F., 1986, 'Des entreprises en mutation dans la crise: apprentissage des technologies flexibles et émergence de nouveaux acteurs'. Research Report, Laboratoire d'économie et de sociologie du travail, Aix-en-Provence.

Maurice, M., Mannari, H., Takeo, Y. and Inoki, T., 1988, 'Des entreprises françaises et japonaises face à la mécatronique. Acteurs et organisation de la dynamique industrielle'. Research Report, Laboratoire d'économie et de sociologie du travail, Aix-en-Provence.

Maurice, M., Sellier, F. and Silvestre, J.-J., 1977, 'La production de la hiérarchie dans l'entreprise: recherche d'un effet sociétal'. Research Report, Laboratoire d'économie et de sociologie du travail, Aix-en-Provence.

Maurice, M., Sellier, F. and Silvestre, J.-J., 1982, *Politique d'éducation et organisation industrielle en France et en Allemagne: essai d'analyse sociétale*. Paris: Presses Universitaires de France.

Maurice, M., Sorge, A. and Warner, M., 1980, 'Societal differences in organizing manufacturing units: a comparison of France, West-Germany and Great Britain', *Organization Studies*, 1, pp. 59–86.

McEnery, J.G. and DesHarnais, G., 1990, 'Culture shock', *Training and Development Journal*, 44 (4), pp. 43–47.

McFarlin, D., Sweeney, P. and Cotton, J., 1992, 'Attitudes toward employee participation in decision making: a comparison of European and American managers in a United States multinational company', *Human Resource Management*, 31 (4) pp. 363–383.

Méhaut, P., 1990, 'French corporate training: historical considerations and new prospects', in: Mulder, M., Romiszowski, A.J. and van der Sijde, P.C., *Strategic Human Resource Development*. Amsterdam/Rockland: Swets and Zeitlinger, pp. 119–130.

Mendenhall, M., Dunbar, E. and Oddou, G., 1987, 'Expatriate selection, training and career-pathing: a review and critique', *Human Resource Management*, 26, pp. 331–345.

Mendenhall, M. and Oddou, G., 1985, 'The dimensions of expatriate acculturation: a review', *Academy of Management Review*, 10 (1) pp. 39–47.

Michels, A.M.B., 1989, 'Medezeggenschap in Deense ondernemingen is een toonbeeld voor Nederland,' *NAMENS*, 3 (4) pp. 39–44.

Miles, R.E. and Snow, C.C., 1986, 'Organizations: new concepts for new forms', *California Management Review*, 28 (3) pp. 59–70.

Miller, E., 1972, 'The selection decision for an international assignment: a study of the decision-makers' behaviour', *Journal of International Business Studies*, 3, pp. 49–65.

Milner, S., 1991, 'Worker's rights in Europe: implications of 1992 for social policy and the "social actors" ', in: Milner, S. and Hantrais, L. (eds.), *Workers' Rights in Europe*. Birmingham: Cross-National Research Papers.

Ministry of Social Affairs and Employment, 1991, *De sociale dimensie en het voorzitterschap*. The Hague: Ministry of Social Affairs and Employment.

Mintzberg, H., 1983, *Structures in Fives: Designing Effective Organizations*. Englewood Cliffs, NJ: Prentice-Hall.

Mintzberg, H., 1988a, 'Opening up the definition of strategy', in: Quinn, J.B., Mintzberg, H. and James, R.M. (eds.), *The Strategy Process*. Englewood Cliffs, NJ: Prentice-Hall, pp. 13–20.

Mintzberg, H., 1988b, 'Strategy-making in three modes', in: Quinn, J.B., Mintzberg, H. and James, R.M. (eds.), *The Strategy Process*, Englewood Cliffs, NJ: Prentice-Hall, pp. 82–88.

Mitrani, A., Dalziel, M. and Fitt, D., 1992, *Competency Based Human Resource Management*. London: Kogan Page.

Momsen, J., 1991, *Women and Development in the Third World*. London: Routledge.

Moran, R., 1985, 'Cross-cultural contact – are women the answer to problems of culture clash?', *International Management*, 40 (5), p. 118..

Morgan, G., 1986, *Images of Organization*. Beverly Hills, CA: Sage.

Morgan, P.V., 1986, 'International human resource management: fact or fiction?', *Personnel Administrator*, 31 (9), pp. 43–47.

Mueller, F. and Purcell, J., 1992, 'The Europeanization of manufacturing and the decentralization of bargaining: multinational management strategies in the European automobile industry', *International Journal of Human Resource Management*, 3 (1) pp. 15–34.

Mulder, M., 1993, 'Training, determinants of successful programs', in: Husèn, T. and Postlethwaite, T.N. (eds.), *The International Encyclopedia of Education*, 3rd edn. Oxford: Pergamon Press.

Mulder, M., 1994, 'Vocational training and human resource development in an international perspective', in: Mulder, M. (ed.), *Studies on Continuing Vocational Training*. Lisse: Swets and Zeitlinger.

Mulder, M., Akkerman, J.S. and Bentvelsen, N., 1989, *Bedrijfsopleidingen in Nederland*. The Hague: Institute for Research Education.

Mulder, M. and Luijendijk, R.A.A.J., 1990, 'Training and development in the Netherlands', in: Mulder, M., Romiszowski, A.J. and Sijde, P.C. van der (eds.), *Strategic Human Resource Development*. Amsterdam/Rockland: Swets and Zeitlinger, pp. 103–118.

Münch, J., 1990, 'Lernen am Arbeitsplatz: Bedeutung innerhalb der betrieblichen Weiterbildung', in: Schlaffke, W. and Weiss, R. (eds.), *Tendenzen betrieblichen Weiterbildung: Aufgaben für Forschung und Praxis*. Cologne: Deutscher Institutsverlag, pp. 141–176.

Murray, F.T. and Murray, A.H., 1986, 'SMR Forum: global managers for global businesses', *Sloan Management Review*, 27 (4), pp. 75–80.

Nadler, L., 1980, *Corporate Human Resources Development: A Management Tool*. New York: Van Nostrand Reinhold.

Nagelkerke, A.G., 1992, *Instituties en economisch handelen: een onderzoek naar de wetenschappelijke betekenis van de institutioneel-economische benadering*. Tilburg: Tilburg Academic Press.

Nagelkerke, A.G. and de Nijs, W.F., 1991, *Regels rond arbeid Arbeidsverhoudingen in Nederland en op het niveau van de Europese Gemeenschap*. Leiden/Antwerp: Stenfert Kroese.

Nagelkerke, A.G. and Veersma, U., 1992, 'Industrial relations in Brussels: social dialogue and working conditions', in: Dijck, J.J.J. van and Wentink, A.A. (eds.), *Transnational Business in Europe: Economic and Social Perspectives*. Tilburg: Tilburg Academic Press, pp. 233–248.

Naisbitt, J. and Aburdene, P., 1985, *Re-inventing the Corporation*. New York: Warner Books.

Negandhi, A.R., 1987, *International Management*. Newton, MA: Allyn and Bacon.

Nijs, W.F. de, 1989, 'Profielen van Personeelsmanagement in Europa', *Bedrijfskunde*, 61 (2), pp. 115–123.

Nijs, W.F. de, 1992a, 'Patterns of industrial relations and personnel management in three European countries', in: Dijck, J.J.J. van and Wentink, A.A. (eds.), *Transnational Business in Europe: Economic and Social Perspectives*. Tilburg: Tilburg Academic Press, pp. 248–258.

Nijs, W.F. de, 1992b, 'Human resource management en arbeidsverhoudingen', in: Kluytmans, F. and Vander Meeren, W. (eds.), *Management van Human Resources*. Deventer: Kluwer, pp. 120–140.

Nobelen, P.W.M., 1991, *Facetten van medezeggenschap*. Assen: Van Gorcum.

OECD, 1985, *The Integration of Women into the Economy*, Special Report. Paris: Organization for Economic Co-operation and Development.

OECD, 1990, *Labour Market Policies for the 1990s*. Paris: Organization for Economic Co-operation and Development.

OECD, 1993, *The OECD Employment Outlook*. Paris: Organization for Economic Co-operation and Development.

Oechslin, J.-J., 1987, 'Training and the business world: the French experience', *International Labour Review*, 126 (6), pp. 653–667.

Ohmae, K.O., 1985, *Triad Power: The Coming Shape of Global Competition*. New York: Free Press.

Oliver-Taylor, E.S., 1993, *Compatibility of Vocational Qualifications in the European*

Community and Vocational Training in the United Kingdom, Germany, Belgium, France, Italy and Spain. Beckenham: Stem Systems.

Ondrack, D.A., 1985, 'International transfers of managers in North American and European MNC's', *Journal of International Business Studies*, 16, Fall, pp. 1–20.

Onstenk, J., forthcoming, *Leren en opleiden op de werkplek: een verkenning in zes landen.* Bunnik: A&O Beleidsstudies.

Paauwe, J., 1986, 'De personeelsfunctie: kenmerken, dilemma's en uitdagingen, PZ in 1990: Professional of neventaak?', *Intermediair*, 20.

Paauwe, J., 1991, 'Limitations to freedom: is there a choice for human resource management?', *British Journal of Management*, 2, pp. 103–119.

Perline, M.M. and Poynter, D.J., 1991, 'Union and management perception of managerial prerogatives: some insight into the future of co-operative bargaining in the USA', *British Journal of Industrial Relations*, 28 (2), pp. 179–196.

Perlmutter, H.V., 1969, 'The tortuous evolution of the multinational corporation', *Columbia Journal of World Business*, 4 (1), pp. 9–18.

Peters, T.J. and Waterman, R.H., 1982, *In Search of Excellence: Lessons from America's Best-Run Companies.* New York: Harper and Row.

Phatak, A.V., 1989, *International Management.* Boston, MA: PWS-Kent.

Piehl, E., 1974, *Multinationale Konzerne und Internationale Gewerkschaftsbewegung.* Frankfurt am Main: Europäische Verlaganstalt.

Pontussen, J., 1990, 'The politics of new technology and job redesign: a comparison of Volvo and British Leyland', *Economic and Industrial Democracy*, 11, pp. 311–336.

Porter, M.E., 1980, *Competitive Strategy.* New York: Free Press.

Porter, M.E., 1986a, 'Changing patterns of international competition', *California Management Review*, 27, Winter, pp. 9–40.

Porter, M.E., 1986b, 'Competition in global industries: a conceptual framework', in: Porter, M.E., *Competition in Global Industries.* Boston, MA: Harvard Business School Press, pp. 15–56.

Porter, M.E., 1990, *The Competitive Advantage of Nations.* Basingstoke: Macmillan.

Powell, G., 1988, *Women and Men in Management.* Beverly Hills, CA: Sage.

Powell, G., Posner, B.Z and Schmidt, W.H., 1984, 'Sex effects on managerial value systems', *Human Relations*, 37 (11), pp. 909–921.

Prahalad, C.K. and Doz, Y.L., 1987, *The Multinational Mission.* New York: Free Press.

Prahalad, C.K. and Hamel, G., 1990, 'The core competence of the corporation', *Harvard Business Review*, May–June, pp. 70–91.

Prasad, S.B. and Shetty, Y.K., 1976, 'An approach to strategic control in MNCs', *Sloan Management Review*, 23, pp. 5–13.

Price Waterhouse, 1991, *Price Waterhouse Cranfield Project on International Strategic Human Resource Management.* Report.

Pringle, R., 1989, *Secretaries Talk.* London: Verso.

Pucik, V., 1984, 'The international management of human resources', in: Fombrun, C.J., Tichy, N.M. and Devana, M.A. (eds.), *Strategic HRM.* New York: Wiley, pp. 403–419.

Pugh, D.S., Hickson, D.J., Hinings, C.R. and Turner, C., 1968, 'Dimensions of organization structure', *Administrative Science Quarterly*, 13, pp. 65–105.

Punnett, B.J., Crocker, O. and Stevens, M., 1992, 'The challenge for women expatriates and spouses: some empirical evidence', *International Journal of Human Resource Management*, 3 (3), pp. 585–592.

Purcell, J., 1993, 'The end of institutional industrial relations', *Political Quarterly*, 64 (1), pp. 6–23.

Quinn, J.B., 1988, 'Strategic change: "Logical incrementalism" ', in: Quinn, J.B., Mintzberg, H. and James, R.M. (eds.), *The Strategy Process*, Englewood Cliffs, NJ: Prentice-Hall, pp. 94–103.

Ragins, B. and Sundstrom, E., 1989, 'Gender and power in organizations', *Psychological Bulletin*, 105 (1), pp. 51–88.

Ramsey, H., Pollert, A. and Rainbird, H., 1992, 'A decade of transformation? Labour market flexibility and work organisation in the United Kingdom', in: OECD, *New*

Directions in Work Organisation: The Industrial Relations Response. Paris: Organization for Economic Co-operation and Development, pp. 169–196.

Rapoport, R. and Rapoport, R.N., 1976, *Dual Career Families Re-examined.* London: Robertson.

Regini, M. (ed.), 1992, *The Future of Labour Movements.* London: International Sociological Association.

Reich, R.B., 1991, *The Work of Nations: Preparing Ourselves for 21st-Century Capitalism.* New York: Alfred A. Knopf.

Reynolds, C. and Bennett, R., 1991, 'The career couple challenge', *Personnel Journal,* March, pp. 46–48.

Robock, S.H. and Simmonds, K., 1983, *International Business and Multinational Enterprise.* Homewood, IL: Irwin.

Rojot, J., 1990, 'Human resource management in France', in: Pieper, R. (ed.), *Human Resource Management: An International Comparison.* Berlin/New York: De Gruyter.

Romiszowski, A.J., 1981, *Designing Instructional Systems: Decision Making in Course Planning and Curriculum Design.* New York: Nichols Publishing.

Römkens, L. and Vries, B. de, 1986, *Arbeidsorganisaties en hun stagebeleid.* Nijmegen: Institute of Applied Social Science.

Ronen, S., 1989, 'Training the international assignee', in: Goldstein, I.L. (ed.), *Training and Development in Organizations.* San Francisco: Jossey-Bass.

Rose, Michael, 1985, 'Universalism, culturalism and the Aix Group', *European Sociological Review,* 1, pp. 65–83.

Rosener, J., 1990, 'Ways women lead', *Harvard Business Review,* 68 (6), pp. 119–125.

Roth, S., 1992, 'Japanisation, or going our own way: new 'lean production' concepts in the German automobile industry'. Paper, IG Metall, Frankfurt am Main.

Rothwell, S., 1991, 'Women and employment in Europe', *European Business Review,* 91 (1), pp. 22–28.

Rubinstein, S., Bennett, M. and Kochan, T., 1993, 'The Saturn Partnership: co-management and the reinvention of the local union', in: Kaufman, B. and Kleiner, M. (eds.), *Employee Representation: Alternatives and Future Directions.* Madison, WI: IRRA.

Ruesga, B. and Santos, M., 1991, 'La negociación colectiva', in: Miguélez, F. and Prieto, C. (eds.), *Las relaciones laborales en España.* Madrid: Siglo XXI, pp. 379–402.

Rugman, A.M., 1987, *International Business: Firm and Environment.* New York: McGraw-Hill.

Rugman, A.M. and Verbeke, A., 1992, 'A note on the transnational solution and the transaction cost theory of multinational strategic management', *Journal of International Business Studies,* 23 (4), pp. 761–771.

Sabel, C.F., 1991, 'Moebius-strip organizations and open labor markets: some consequences of the reintegration of conception and execution in a volatile economy', in: Bourdieu, P. and Coleman, J.S. (eds.), *Social Theory for a Changing Society.* Boulder, CO: Westview Press, pp. 23–61.

Sabel, C.F., 1993, 'Can the end of the social democratic trade unions be the beginning of a new kind of social democratic politics?' Paper, Massachusetts Institute of Technology.

Savage, C.M., 1990, *5th Generation Management.* Bedford, MA: BARD Productions, Digital Press.

Schmitter, P.C. and Streeck, W., 1991, 'From national corporatism to transnational pluralism: organized interests in the Single European Market', *Politics and Society,* 19, pp. 133–165.

Schneider, S.C., 1988, 'National vs corporate culture: implications for human resource management', *Human Resource Management,* 27 (2), pp. 231–246.

Schneider, S.C. and De Meyer, A., 1991, 'Interpreting and responding to strategic issues: the impact of national culture', *Strategic Management Journal,* 12, pp. 307–320.

Schoenberger, E., 1989, 'Multinational corporations and the new international division of labour', in: Wood, S. (ed.), *The Transformation of Work?* London: Unwin Hyman, pp. 91–101.

Schuler, R.S., 1987, *Personnel and Human Resource Management.* St Paul: West Publishing Company.

Schuler, R.S. and Jackson, S.E., 1987, 'Linking competitive strategies with human resource management practices', *The Academy of Management Executive*, 1 (3), pp. 207–219.

Scott, W.R., 1981, *Organizations: Rational, Natural and Open Systems*. Englewood Cliffs, NJ: Prentice-Hall.

Scullion, H., 1992, 'Recruiting and developing international managers', *Multinational Employer*, April, pp. 14–18.

Sekaran, U., 1986, *Dual-Career Families: Contemporary Organizational and Counselling Issues*. San Francisco: Jossey-Bass.

Sengenberger, W., 1992, 'Intensified competition, industrial restructuring and industrial relations', *International Labour Review*, 131 (2), pp. 139–154.

Sharma, S., 1990, 'Psychology of women in management: a distinct feminine leadership', *Equal Opportunities International*, 9 (2), pp. 13–18.

Siveking, N., Anchor, K. and Marston, R.C., 1981, 'Selecting and preparing expatriate employees', *Personnel Journal*, 3, pp. 197–202.

Slomp, H., 1990, *Labor Relations in Europe: A History of Issues and Developments*. Westport, CT: Greenwood Press.

Smith, A., 1776, *An Inquiry into the Nature and Causes of the Wealth of Nations*. New York: Modern Library Edition, 1937.

Smith, P. and Misumi, J., 1989, 'Japanese management: a sun rising in the West?', in: Cooper, C.L. and Robertson, I.T. (eds.), *International Review of Industrial and Organizational Psychology 1989*. Chichester: John Wiley.

Smith, P. and Morton, G., 1993, 'Union exclusion and the decollectivization of industrial relations in contemporary Britain', *British Journal of Industrial Relations*, 31 (1), pp. 97–114.

Solomon, C., 1990, 'Careers under glass', *Personnel Journal*, April, pp. 96–105.

Sorge, A. and Warner, M., 1986, *Comparative Factory Organisation: An Anglo-German Comparison of Management and Manpower in Manufacturing*. Aldershot: Gower.

Spyropoulos, G. and Fragnière, G. (eds.), 1991, *Work and Social Policies in the New Europe*. Brussels/Maastricht: European Center for Work and Society.

Staehle, W., 1986, 'Industrial relations and Europe's multinationals', in: Macharzina, K. and Staehle, W. (eds.), *European Approaches to International Management*. Berlin/New York: De Gruyter.

Stichting van de Arbeid, 1991, *Enkele aspecten van de sociale dimensie van Europa 1992*. The Hague: SvdA.

Stopford, J.M. and Wells, L.T., 1972, *Managing the Multinational Enterprise*, New York: Basic Books.

Streeck, W., 1984, *Industrial Relations in West Germany: A Case Study of the Car Industry*. London: Heinemann.

Streeck, W., 1992, *Social Institutions and Economic Performance: Studies of Industrial Relations in Advanced Capitalist Economics*. London: Sage.

Sullivan, J.F., 1972, 'Indirect compensation: the years ahead', *California Management Review*, 15 (2).

Sundaram, A.K. and Black, J.S., 1992, 'The environment and internal organization of multinational enterprises', *Academy of Management Review*, 17 (4), pp. 729–757.

Taplin, I.M., 1990, 'The contradiction of business unionism and the decline of organized labour', *Economic and Industrial Democracy*, 11, pp. 249–278.

Teague, P., 1993, 'Towards social Europe? Industrial relations after 1992', *International Journal of Human Resource Management*, 4 (2), pp. 349–376.

Teague, P. and McClelland, D., 1991, 'Towards "social Europe"? Industrial relations after 1992', in: Milner, S. and Hantrais, L. (eds.), *Workers' Rights in Europe*. Birmingham: Cross-National Research Papers, pp. 8–23.

Thelen, K., 1991, *Union of Parts: Labor Politics in Postwar Germany*. Ithaca, NY: Cornell University Press.

Thelen, K., 1992, 'The changing character of industrial relations in contemporary Europe'. Paper, Princeton University.

Thierry, H.K., Koopman-Iwema, A.M. and Vinke, R.H.W., 1988, *Toekomst voor prestatie-beloning?* The Hague: SMO.

Tillaart, H. van den, 1993, *Scholing van werkenden in de detailhandel*. Paper for the Educational Research Days in Maastricht. Nijmegen: Institute of Applied Social Science.

Toffler, A., 1984, *Previews and Premises*. London: Pan Books.

Torbiörn, I., 1976, *Att leva utomlands: en studie av utlandssvenskars anpassning, trivsel och levnadsvanor* (Living Abroad: A Study of the Adjustments of Swedish Overseas Personnel). Uddevalla: SNS.

Torbiörn, I., 1982, *Living Abroad: Personal Adjustment and Personal Policy in the Overseas Settings*. New York: John Wiley.

Touraine, A., 1955, *L'évolution du travail ouvrier aux usines Renault*. Paris: Centre National de la Recherche Scientifique.

Townsend, A.M., Scott, K.D. and Markham, S.E., 1990, 'An examination of country and culture-based differences in compensation practices', *Journal of International Business Studies*, 4, pp. 667–678.

Triandris, H.C. (ed.), 1972, *The Analysis of Subjective Culture*. New York: John Wiley.

Tung, R.L., 1979, 'US multinationals: a study of their selection and training procedures for overseas assignments', *Academy of Management Proceedings*, 39, pp. 298–301.

Tung, R.L., 1981, 'Selecting and training of personnel for overseas assignments', *Columbia Journal of World Business*, 16 (1), pp. 68–78.

Tung, R.L., 1982, 'Selection and training procedures of US, European and Japanese multinationals', *California Management Review*, 25 (1), pp. 57–71.

Tung, R.L., 1988, *The New Expatriates: Managing Human Resources Abroad*. Cambridge, Mass.: Ballinger.

Turner, L., 1991, *Democracy at Work: Changing World Markets and the Future of Labor Unions*. Ithaca, NY: Cornell University Press.

UNCTAD, 1993, *World Investment Report 1993: Transnational Corporations and Integrated International Production*. New York: United Nations.

Valkenburg, F. and Hulskes, A., 1983, *Kwalificatie-ontwikkeling tijdens de beroepsloopbaan*. Tilburg: Institute for Labour Research.

Van Ruysseveldt, J., 1991, 'Arbeidsverhoudingen, arbeidsruilrelaties en technologische innovatie: gezichtspunten vanuit cross-nationale en inter-sectorale vergelijkingen', in: *Informatietechnologie en arbeidsorganisatie in de dienstensector*. SISWO International Research Seminar on Work no. 3, October 1991. Amsterdam: SISWO, pp. 71–104.

Van Ruysseveldt, J., 1993, 'Ontwerpen van Europese medezeggenschap', *Tijdschrift voor Arbeidsvraagstukken*, 9 (1), pp. 78–90.

Vander Meeren, W. and Kluytmans, F., 1992, 'Management van personeelsstromen', in: Kluytmans, F. and Vander Meeren, W. (eds.), *Management van human resources: Stromen, stimuleren, structureren*. Heerlen/Deventer: Open University/Kluwer, pp. 51–72.

Venturini P., 1988, *Een Europese sociale ruimte voor 1992*. Brussels: Commission of the European Communities.

Verhoeven, N.G., 1991, *Continuing Training in Firms and Trainer Development in the Netherlands*. Berlin: Cedefop.

Vernon, R.G., 1966, 'International investment and international trade in the product cycle', *Quarterly Journal of Economics*, May, pp. 190–207.

Versteeg, F., 1993, 'Rijke wereld vreest voor vertrek van banen', *NRC Handelsblad*, 19 June.

Vinke, R.H.W., 1993, *Handboek belonen*. Deventer: Kluwer.

Vinke, R.H.W. and Thierry, H., 1985, *Flexibel belonen: van cafetariaplan naar praktijk*. Deventer: Kluwer.

Vinnicombe, S., 1987, 'What exactly are the differences in male and female working styles?', *Women in Management Review*, 3 (1).

Visser, J. and Ebbinghaus, B., 1992, 'Making the most of diversity: European integration and transnational organisation of labour', in: Greenwood, J., Grote, J.R. and Ronit, K. (eds)., *Organized Interests and the European Community*. London: Sage, pp. 206–238.

Warmerdam, J. and Berg, J. van den, 1992, *Scholing van werknemers in veranderende organisaties*. The Hague: Ministry of Social Affairs and Employment.

Warner, M. and Turner, L., 1973, 'Trade unions and the multinational firm', in: Tudyka, K.P. (ed.), *Multinational Corporations and Labour Unions*. Nijmegen: Socialistische Uitgeverij Nijmegen, pp. 169–189.

Watson, T.J., 1977, *The Personnel Managers: A Study in the Sociology of Work and Employment*. London: Routledge and Kegan Paul.

Weick, K.E., 1979, *The Social Psychology of Organizing*. Reading, MA: Addison Wesley.

Wentling, R.M., 1992, 'Women in middle management: their career development and aspirations', *Business Horizons*, 35 (1), pp. 47–54.

Williamson, O.E., 1975, *Markets and Hierarchies: Analysis and Antitrust Implications*. New York: Free Press.

Wilson, F., 1991, 'Democracy in the workplace: the French experience', *Politics and Society*, 19, pp. 439–462.

Wise, M. and Gibb, R., 1993, *Single Market to Social Europe*. Harlow: Longman.

Woodiwiss, A., 1992, *Law, Labour and Society in Japan: From Repression to Reluctant Recognition*. London: Routledge.

Index

Tables and figures in italic; HRM = human resource management; MNC = multinational corporation.

ABB (Asea Brown Boveri), 17, 331
accommodation model, industrial relations, 357
accounting, functional strategies, 44–5
actors, aiding managers, *190, 192*
actors and systems, 100, 103, 105, *106*, 110–11, 115
Acuff, F., 78, 79
'adhocracy', 57
Adler, N.J., 26, 79, 205, 206, 224–5, 231–3, 240–3, 245–6, 249–50
Adler, N.J. and Bartholomew, S., 82
Adler, N.J. and Ghadar, F., 85–9, 91, 183, 220, 264
administrative heritage in companies, 36, 65–7
administrative mechanisms, 68
administrative structures, *100*
advisory bodies, Brussels, 348–9
Ajiferuke, M. and Boddewyn, J., 127
appraisal of international staff, x, 144–55, 261–3; criteria, 262–3; variation between countries, 151–2
apprenticeships, 116–17; France, 169; Germany, 121, 166; United Kingdom, 165
Asia, women's employment, 235–6; *see also* Japan
attitude change, 72–3
Aufsichtsrat, 306
Austria, worker participation, 312
authority: comparisons, France/Germany/UK, 100; survey of relationship to, 135–8
authority systems, organizations as, *132*
autogestion, 292
automobile industry, 324–5, 329

balance sheet, compensation, 257–9
Bandura, A., 217
Barnevik, P., 17
Bartlett, C.A. and Ghoshal, S., 30, 36–8, 40, 41, 47, 52, 56, 58, 61, 63–5, 69, 71, 72, 76, 95–6
Bates, M. and Kiersey, D.W., 240–1
Baumgarten, K.E.E., 81
Beer, M., 95, 157
behaviour in organizations, 102–7
Belgium: trade unions, 300, 301, 308; worker participation, 305; works councils, 294–5, 298–9, 302–3, 311
Betriebsvereinbarungen, 297, 310
Black, J.S. and Gregersen, H.B., 197
Black, J.S. and Mendenhall, M., 217
Bolweg, J.F., 157
Bolwijn, P.T. and Kumpe, T., 32–3
Bomers, G.B.J., 281, 285–6
Borg, M., *190*, 193–4, 197
Brewster, C., 189
budget system, compensation, 256–7
business management, 64
Byrne, J.A., 54

CAD/CAM technologies, 32
career planning, 225
cash, compensation, 265, 267
cash flow, international, 7–8
CCA International/Europanel, survey, 152

centralized hub, 60, 61
centralized sourcing, 45
centres of excellence, within MNCs, 22
CFDT, 309
Chalofsky, N.E. and Reinhart, C., 76
Chandler, A.D., 54
change: manager's ability to effect, 263; need for, in organizations, 53–4; process, 72–3; resistance to, 36
Christian World Confederation of Labour (CWCL), 274
CNV, 323–4
coaching, in training, 214, 216
Cockpit, 350
co-determination complex, Germany, 315
collective consultations, Europe, 352–3
collectivism versus individualism, survey, 135–7, *136*
Collis, D.J., 35
co-management, USA, 314
commitment: in top international managers, 202–3; women's careers, 238–40
communications, 31, 69
company culture, 36
company training: France/Netherlands, 170–1; structures, 175–8; UK/Germany, 165–6
comparative advantage, 4–5, 11–12
compensation, international staff, x, 82–3, 144–55, 252–69, *267*; components, *146*; differences, 147–52, 260–1; European, 264–9; forms, 83, 146–7; functions, 145; international policy, 264–6; methods, 256–61; objectives, 145, 255–6; trends, 155
competitive advantage, 11–14, 22–4
competitive strategies, 36–43
complementarity, 116
complementary contribution model, women's role, 232
complexity: HRM, 92–3; structures and environment, 69–70
computerization, effect, 19, 78
computer-numerically controlled (CNC) machines, 119, 120
concession bargaining, 328
conflict resolution mechanisms, 68
Confucian dynamism, 135
Conrad, P. and Pieper, P., 164
consumer electronics, 34, 37–8, 39
consumer power and preferences, 31, 77, 124
convergence hypothesis, 125, 126
coopération conflictuelle, 309
cooperative bodies, Brussels, 348–9
coordinated federation, 59–60, *61*
core competence, 35
core employees, 172
cosmopolitan managers abroad, 195, 196–7, 200
cosmopolitanism, 20
cost advantages, 4–6, 11
cost-efficiency strategy, 39
cost-leadership strategy, 39
Council of Ministers, EU, 340, 345, 352, 361
country-specific advantages (CSAs), 4, 41, 42

cross-border agreements, Europe, 351
cross-cultural interaction, *87*
cross-cultural training, 206–9, 209–18; goals, 213;
    methods, 213–18; need to include partner,
    221–2
cross-national differences: analysis, 107–12;
    personnel and organization, 99–123
cross-national organizational research, 125–7
cross-referencing, 103, 107
Crozier, M. and Friedberg, E., 112
cultural approach to organization and
    management, 125–6
cultural differences, 124–5; and HRM, 138–42
cultural diversity: of Western conceptions of
    management, 131–5; and work organization,
    130–5
cultural sensitivity, needed in international
    managers, 212
cultural transformation, 68–9
culturalism, in HRM, x, 110, 127
culture: defined, 127–30; factor in personnel and
    organization policies, 124–43; influence on
    product life cycle, 85–6; survey of national,
    135–8
culture shock, 223, *224*

Daniels, J.D., 55, 56
data management mechanisms, 68
Davidson, M. and Cooper, G., 242
decentralization, European industrial relations,
    353
decentralized federation, 59, *61*
decision-making: MNCs and industrial relations,
    x, 320–3, *321*; and national cultural differences,
    140–1
deferred income, compensation, 265, 267
délégués syndicaux, 301
Delors, J., 335, 348–9, 361
Denmark: basic pay negotiations, *150*;
    organizations, nature, *132–4*; pay systems, *147*;
    trade unions, 301, 308; worker participation,
    305; works councils, 294–5, 298–9, 302–3, 311
deployment cycle, *227*
deregulation, European, 356, 358
design parameters, second-generation models, 67
deskilling, 330
detergents industry, 33, 37, 39
Devanna, M., 238–9, 244
developing countries, women's employment,
    236–7
development, *see* human resource development;
    training and development
dialectical theory, 104–5
differentiation strategy, 39, 85
Dijck, J.J.J. van, 52n, 53–4
distributed sourcing, 45
diversified multinational corporations (DMNCs),
    67n, 68
division of labour, 4; France/Netherlands, 172–3;
    HRD and staff flow policy, 162–3;
    intensification, 122; international, 328–31;
    Taylorist, 163, 164; trends, 16–22, 77; UK/
    Germany, 167–8
Dobbins, G. and Platz, S., 241
domestic phase, product life cycle, 85; and HRM,
    88
domestic responsibilities, and women's
    employment, 236
Dore, R., 101
Doz, Y. and Prahalad, C.K., 63–4, 67n, 68
Drucker, P., 51–2
dual careers, and international management,
    246–9
dual training, Germany, 164
Dülfer, E., 94
Dunlop, J., 279, 280, 281

Dunning's eclectic theory of international
    production, 9–11, 40, 41

East Germany: pay conditions, *147*;
    redundancies, 164–5
Eastern Europe: consumers, 21; expatriates' need
    of training, 207; labour availability, 17; trade,
    336, 338
eclectic theory, *see* Dunning
Economic and Social Committee (ECOSOC),
    348, 361
economic factors, and international HRM, 79
economies of scale, 4, 6–7; and MNCs, 23
economies of scope, MNCs, 23–4
ECU points, 266–9
Edström, A. and Galbraith, J., 181, 244
Edström, A. and Lorange, P., 49
education: companies' influence on, 162; France/
    Germany, 116–18; needed in the West, 17
educational system, 159; and labour system, *158*,
    160–2
efficiency, demand for, 32–3
Egelhoff, W.G., 55
Einigungsstelle, 305
employers, European organizations of, 347
employment conditions, international, *265*
encastrement, 115
Enderwick, P., 326–7
environmental factors, in organizations, 53–4, 70,
    94
equity model, of woman's role, 232
ethnocentrism, 43, 44, 45, 48, 130, 322; and
    industrial relations, 319–20; and
    internationalization, 84; and staff transfers,
    184; and staffing, 80, 82
Eurocompensation, 264–9
'Euroformity', 357
Euro-multinational companies, 360
Europe: competition with Japan and USA, 21–2;
    expatriate training, 207; possible integration,
    122; life styles, 152; MNCs' use of expatriates,
    49; women's employment, 235
European Agricultural Guidance and Guarantee
    Fund (EAGGF), 341
European Centre of Public Enterprises (CEEP),
    347
European Commission, 340, 341, 345
European Community, 275–6, 293, 337; *see also*
    European Union
European Court of Justice, 341, 342
European Fund for Regional Development
    (EFRD), 341
European Metalworkers' Federation, 350
European Monetary Union (EMU), 339
European Parliament, 341, 361
European Professional Qualifications Council, 162
European Social Fund (ESF), 341, 344–5, 348
European Trade Union Confederation (ETUC),
    276, 289, 347
European Union (EU), xii, 340; companies and
    education, 162; cooperation and advisory
    bodies, 343, 348–9; industrial relations, 274,
    287, 288, 290; and research, 21; social
    dimension debate, 328; and social dumping,
    333–6; and women's employment, 235
'Europhoria', 277
Evans, P. et al., 174–5
Evans, P. and Lorange, P., 89–90, 91
expatriates, xi, 254–5; acculturation, 188–9, 190;
    allegiance, *197*; assignment period, 190–2;
    communication with, 224; failure, 79, 206; not
    employed as managers, 184; MNCs' use of, 49,
    185, 190–2; repatriation, 192–4; training and
    development, 209–18; variety, *255*; women
    managers, 243, 245–6
expenses, professional, 265, 267

external analysis, strategic planning, 30–4
external labour market, 160

family structure organizations, 142
Far East, MNCs' use of expatriates, 49
femininity versus masculinity, survey of culture, 135–8, *136*, *139*
finance and accounting, functional strategies, 44–5
firm-specific advantages (FSAs), 40–1, 42
firm strategy and structure, 14
firms, ideal types, *32*
flexibility: in companies, 32–3, 35, 52, 57; in managers, 263
flexible manufacturing, 32
flexible plant production, 46
flow, society effect approach, 113, 114
fordism, peripheral, 329
foreign direct investment (FDI), 2, *3*, 8
France: basic pay negotiation, *150*; company training, 170, 175; division of labour, 172–3; education, 117–18; machine tool industry, 120–1; management/workforce relations, 308; and management by objectives, 152; organizational structures, 100–2; organizations, nature, *132-4*; pay systems, *147*; personnel and organization, 100–22; staff flow policy, 171–2; trade unions, 301, 304, 308; vocational training, 169–70; worker participation, 305–6; works councils, 294–5, 298–9, 302–3
Freedman, S. and Phillips, J., 239
functional differentiation, France/Germany/UK, 100
functional flexibilization in jobs, 162
functional management, 64, 96–7
functional policies, integration, 48–9
functional strategies, 43–6

Galbraith, J.R. and Kazanjian, R.K., 52, 57
Geertz, C., 128
Gell, R., 18
gender, *see* women
gender-related behaviour, 238
geocentrism, 43, 44, 45, 48; and internationalization, 84; and staff transfers, 184; and staffing, 80
geographic dispersion in corporations, 26–8, 79
geographic management, 64
geographic subsidiary management, 97
Germany: co-determination, *see* Mitbestimmung; company training, 165–6, 175–6; compensation, comparison with Netherlands, *154*; division of labour, 167–8; education, 116–18; machine tool industry, 120–1; and management by objectives, 152; organizational structures, 100–2; organizations, nature, *132-4*; personnel and organization, 100–22; qualifications, comparison with UK, 19; staff flow policy, 166–7; trade unions, 300, 301, 304, 308; unemployment, 316; vocational training, 164–5; work discipline, 117; worker participation, 305, 306–7; works councils, 291–2, *294-5*, *298-9*, *302-3*
Ghoshal, S., 22, 23
Ghoshal, S. and Nohria, N., 52, 67, 69–70
Giddens, A., 103, 112
glass ceiling, 237, 243
global business management, 96
global companies: competitive strategies, 42; and expatriates, 49
global cost leadership, 40
global differentiation, 40
global environment, and MNCs, 30–2
global industries, strategic planning, 33–4
global organizational model, transnationals, 60–1
global phase, product life cycle, 86; and HRM, *88*

global strategy, MNCs, 37–8
globalism, key to future, 20
Glynn, S. and Gospel, H., 163
Gouldner, Alvin W., 108
government: influence on international HRM, 79; intervention, 20
grandes écoles, 174
Gronhaug, K. and Nordhaug, P., 94

Hamill, J., 320–3
hardship allowances, 259
harmonization, European Union, 343
Harris, P.R. and Moran, R., 221
headquarters, attitudes to subsidiaries, 43, *44*
Hecksher–Ohlin (H–O) theorem on international trade, 5–6, *7*
Hedlund, G., 63
Heilmann, M., 238, 241–2
Heller, J., 187
heroes, cultural, 129
heterarchical MNCs, 63
hierarchical relationship systems, organizations as, *134*; France/Germany/UK, 101
Hofstede, G.H., 110–11, 128, 129, 135–8, 140
Hofstede, G.H. and Bond, M.H., 135
home-net system, compensation, 257–9
Hoover, 334
horizontal integration in MNCs, xi
Horner, M., 238–9
Hossain, S. and Davies, J., 82, 90–1, 94
host country, barriers to women managers, 244–5
host-country nationals (HCNs), xi, 81, 185, *186*, *187*; and cross-cultural training, 222–3; lack of research on, 49
human resource development (HRD), 113; Europe, 156–78; Japan, 15; for managers, 174–5; staff flow policy and division of labour, 162–3, 168–9
human resource management (HRM): activity patterns, and organizational configurations, 78–9, 83–90; complexity on international front, 92–3; developments in, 76–9; domestic and international, 91–2; functional strategies, 43; and industrial relations, 271–90; and international manager shortage, 161; and macro-environmental influences, *94*; overview of international, 79–83, 94–5; phases, and internationalization, 86–9, *88*; policy, in MNCs, x, 49; practices, and cultural differences, 138–42; theories and models, in MNCs, 75–98

IBM: global differentiation, 40; management development, 184; survey of culture, 135
ICFTU (International Confederation of Free Trade Unions), 274
ideational perspective, on cross-national variation, 127
IG Metall, 300, 306–7
Ikea, 324
income levels, international comparisons, *149*
individualism, and economic future, 20
individualism versus collectivism, survey of culture, 135–8, *136*
industrial and sectoral structures, 113–14
industrial democracy, international, xi–xii
industrial relations, xi, 271–2, 277–80; consequences of European integration, 353–60; decentralization, Europe, 353; ethnocentric approach, limitations, 319–20; and international HRM, 272–7; in MNCs, 318–36; national, system model, 280–5; policy in MNCs, and national regulatory frameworks, 323–7; regulation, international, 287–90; scenarios, 354–8; and social policy, 337–62; system model, international, 285–7

Industriebond, 300
industry bargaining, and worker participation, 308–10
industry-level strategic planning, 33–4
Inkeles, A. and Levinson, D.J., 135
innovation strategy, 39
innovativeness, demand for, 32–3
input and output markets, 22–3
INSEAD, 131
insurance, in compensation, 265, 267
integrated network model, 63
integration; of functional policies, 48–9; of jobs, 162
integration and differentiation needs, 47, 70
integration-responsiveness framework, 47, 70
interest organizations, and European social policy, xi, 346–53
internal analysis, strategic planning, 34–6
internal business factors, compensation differences, 147–8
internal labour market, 160
international competitive advantage, transaction cost model, 42
international competitive strategies, 36–43
international division of labour, 1–24, 328–31
international era, strategic planning, 31, 34
international managers, see managers, international
international organizational model, 59–60
international phase, product life cycle, 86; and HRM, 88
international staff/staffing: analysis, 201–2; assignments, 253–5; compensation and appraisal, 252–69; creation, 179–204; design, 203; implementation, 203–4; policy (re)design, 201–4; profiles sought, 211–12; re-entry into home culture, 223–6; states of mind, 43; training and development, 205–28; variables influencing training needs, 211
international strategy, MNCs, 38
international trade: determinants of, 4–7; statistics, 2–3
international trade secretariats (ITS), 346–7
international trade unions, 274–5
international transfers of staff: analysis, 181–5; archetypes, 194–200; cycle, 185–94; functions of managers, 198–200; policies, 183–4; reasons, 181–3
internationalization: effects, 122–3; history, within organization, 66; and international division of labour, 1–24; paradoxes, ix–x; reallocation of employment, 327–36; stages, 55; theory of, x
intra-industry trade, international, 6
investment, by companies, 7–8; inward and outward, 3
Italy: basic pay negotiations, 150; organizations, nature, 132–4; pay systems, 147; worker participation, 312–13

Japan: company training, 176; distribution system, 41; electrical engineering, comparison with UK, 101; expatriate training, 207; human resources, 15; imports, 6; interest in, 125–6; machine tool industry, 120–1; MNC strategies, 37, 66; MNCs' use of expatriates, 48, 49, 185; organizational programmes, 111–12; Porter's analysis of national competitive advantage, 14–16; price and quality specialities, 33; senior managers' origins, 187; training appreciated, 208; US investment in, 8; view of work, 117; worker participation, 314–15
Japanese companies: global organizational model, 60; process of organizational change, 72–3
job rotation, 69; in training, 214, 216
joint consultation systems, Japan, 314
joint labour–management committees, 349

Kanter, R., 230, 242
KLM, 18, 332
Kluckhohn, F.R. and Strodtbeck, F.L., 128
knowledge transfer, 34
Korea, 329

labour: availability, 8–9; intelligence needed, 77; and management, social policy, 346–53; mobility, European, 354, 358
labour market, 113, 114, 159–60; coordination with education, 160–2; segments, 159
labour system, and educational system, 158
Lammers, C.J. and Hickson, D.J., 142
Lane, C., 15
Latin America, use of expatriates in MNCs, 49
Laurent, A., 131, 141–4
leadership: of companies, inherited, 36; needed in managers, 212; national cultural differences, 140–1; and women, 240–1
legislation, European, on social policy, 343–4
licensing of products, 10
Lincoln, J. and Kalleberg, A., 112, 117
Lipietz, A., 329
Litvak, I. and Maule, C., 283
local going-rate system, compensation, 259–60
locally oriented, managers abroad, 195–6, 199
location advantages, see country-specific advantages
longitudinal analysis, 63–70
low unit cost plant production, 46

Maastricht Treaty, 333, 338, 349
machine structure organizations, 142
machine-tool makers, comparisons, 120–1
McKinsey, staff transfers, 184
macro-environmental influences, 94
male–female differences, in motivation, 238–9
management: changing role, 230–1; cultural diversity of Western conceptions, 131–5; forms, 64; and labour, social policy, 346–53; recruitment, 80; 'soft skills', 230, 244
management by objectives (MBO), 140, 152
management development, 69, 182
managerial behaviour: and cultural differences, 138–41; and women, 240–1
'managerialism', 314
managers, international: acculturation, 188–9, 190–1; advice for, 204; assessment, xi; assignments, 82–3, 253–4; conceptions of management, survey, 131–5; development, 95–8; functions, 198–200; HRD for, 174–5; income levels, 149; motives, 191, 193, 194; organizational factors, 243; profiles, 194–200; qualities, 187–9, 263; role in transnational companies, 95–8; senior managers' origins, 187; shortfall in, 160–1; technical experts, comparison with, 119; training, 190; transnational, development, 95–8; ultimate destinations, 195; women, see next entry; see also middle managers
managers, international, women: advantages, 249; barriers in host country, 244–6; change, avenues for, 250; dual careers, 246–9; male resistance, 244; organizational factors, 243; role, 243–50; socio-cultural factors, 244–9; see also women managers
managers' management systems, 68
manual workers, basic pay negotiations, 150
Marginson, P., 322, 326
market requirements 1960–2000, 32
marketing, functional strategies, 45
Marshall, J., 240, 242
Martin, A. and Ross, G., 359
Marx, K., 274
masculinity versus femininity, survey of culture, 135–8, 136, 139

Maslow, A.H., 138
matrix structures, 54, 60
Maurice, M. et al., 113
Maytag, 334
'mechatronic age', 120–2
Medbestemmandelagen, 312
Meisterbrief, 166
Mendenhall, M. and Oddou, G., 188
mental programmes, 110–11
Mexico, relations with USA, 21
middle managers: changing role, 54; income
  levels, *149*; international, 80, *149*
Miles, R.E. and Snow, C.C., 52
Miller, E., 189
Mintzberg, H., 57, 90
Mitbestimmung (co-determination), 296, 304,
  306–7, 310
mobility, *see* staff flow
Momsen, J., 236
Moran, R., 246
Morgan, P.V., 79
mosaic model, European industrial relations,
  357–8
motivation: in international managers, 212; and
  national cultural differences, 138–40; women's
  careers, 238–50
Mueller, F. and Purcell, J., 324–6
multiculturalism, and corporations, 26–8, 79
multidimensionality, of MNCs, 63
multidomestic companies: competitive strategies,
  41–2; and expatriates, 49; progress to
  transnational, 58–9; strategy, 23
multidomestic era, strategic planning, 31, 33
multidomestic strategy of MNCs, 37
multinational corporations (MNCs): analysis of,
  63–70; competitive advantage, 22–4;
  competitive strategies, 37–9; complexity of
  structures, 69–70; and domestic corporations,
  26–8; in European industrial relations, 358–60;
  and European Union regulations, 361–2; and
  industrial relations, 280–5, 318–36;
  internationalization stages, 54–5; investment
  by, 2–3; and local practices, 284; organizational
  structure, 51–74; reasons for, 7–11; strategic
  planning, 25–50; strategic planning process,
  28–30; strategies, comparison, 39–40; and
  subsidiaries, 43–4; and trade unions, 275–85
multinational phase: and HRM, 88; product life
  cycle, 86
Myers–Briggs type indicator (MBTI), 240

Naisbitt, J. and Aburdene, P., 76
national competitive advantage: criteria for a
  theory, 11–12; determinants, 12–14; Japan as
  an example, 14–16
national culture, 135–8; differences, and HRM,
  138–42; practices, and internationalism, ix–x
nationalism: and economic future, 20; inter-war,
  31
natural systems, organizational behaviour, 102
'naturalized' managers abroad, 194–5, 198–9
needs, hierarchy of, 138
Netherlands: basic pay negotiations, *150*;
  company training, 170–1, 176–7; compensation,
  comparison with Germany, *154*; division of
  labour, 172–3; expatriate training, 207;
  organizations, nature, *132–4*; pay systems, *147*;
  staff flow policy, 171–2; trade unions, 300, 301,
  304, 308; vocational training, 169; worker
  participation, 305; works councils, 294–5,
  298–9, 302–3
networks, 54, 69
new technology, influence, 162–3
new world order (Reich), 17–21
newly industrialized countries (NICs), 329
nomothetic theory, 104–5, 117

non-identical reproduction, in organizational
  behaviour, 107, 116–18
Nordic countries, worker participation, 305,
  311–12

OECD, and women's employment, 234
Ohmae, K.O., 21
Ondrack, D.A., 182–3
open systems, organizational behaviour, 102
organization of work, 113
organizational anatomy, 71
organizational behaviour, 102–7
organizational capability, 35–6
organizational configurations, 58–63, *61*, *67*, 93
organizational design, and national cultural
  differences, 141–2
organizational development, and staff transfers,
  182–3
organizational life, actor/system configurations,
  106
organizational outcomes, modes of generation,
  108–9
organizational psychology, 71, 72
organizational research, cross-national, 125–7
organizational structure, in MNCs, x, 51–74; first
  generation, 54–6; second generation, 56–8;
  relating to strategic demands, *59*; France/
  Germany/UK, 100–2
organizations: as authority systems, *132*; as
  hierarchical relationship systems, *134*; as
  political systems, *132*; as role formalization
  systems, *133*; restructuring, 53–4
output markets, MNCs' care for, 22–3
'outsourcing' (cheap labour), 18
overleg, 310
ownership advantages, for MNCs, 9–10

parent-country nationals (PCNs), xi, 81, 185, *186*,
  187
Parsons, T., 115
partners of international managers: fitting in, 188,
  209, 243, 247; male problems, 248; need for
  training, 221–2
pay, *see* compensation; income; wages
performance appraisal, *see* appraisal
performance criteria, *32*
performance indicators, 69–70
performance-related pay, 146–7, 151
Perlmutter, H.V., 43–4, 48, 66, 90; analysis of
  attitudes, 80, 84–5
personnel administration, in MNCs, xi
personnel management: and industrial relations,
  271–2; international view, 272–3; route to
  HRM, 77–9; *see also* human resource
  management
personnel practices, and cultural differences,
  138–42
Peters, T., 240
Peters, T.J and Waterman, R.H., 57, 143
Philips, 17, 324
Piehl, E., 274, 282, 289
policy-making, social regulations, 340–6
political systems, organizations as, *132*
polycentrism, 43, 44, 45, 48; and
  internationalization, 84, 90; staff transfers, 184;
  and staffing, 80
Porter, M.E., 40, 42; analysis of national
  competitive advantage, 4, 11–14, 22, 62;
  'Porter's diamond', 12, *13*
positive economic nationalism (Reich), 20
Powell, G., 238, 241
power distance, survey of culture, 135–7, *136*
pragmatic reconciliation, 109
Prahalad, C.K. and Doz, Y.L., 46
Prahalad, C.K. and Hamel, G., 35
Prasad, S.B. and Shetty, Y.K., 76

primary segment, labour market, 159–60
primary terms of employment, 146
process and structure, 58
process design criteria, 67
product innovation, France/Netherlands, 173
product life cycle (PLC) theory, 8–9, 11, 85
product/market combinations, *see* strategic
  business units
product–market logic, 89
product/market/technology (P/M/T) dimension,
  and HRM, 91–2, *92*, 93
production: activities, integration, 322;
  comparison with maintenance, 119; facilities
  overseas, versus exports, 8; functional
  strategies, 45–6
productivity alliances, 307; Japan, 315, 316
professionalization, 118–19
protectionism, 20, 329; tariffs, 31
Pucik, V., 81
Punnett, B.J., 248–9
pyramid organizations, 142

quality, demanded, 32–3
quality strategy, 39

Ragins, B. and Sundstrom, E., 237, 239, 242
Ramsey, H., 167
rational systems, organizational behaviour, 102
reciprocal interdependence, 115–16
reconciliation, ideological and pragmatic, 108–9
recruitment and selection of international
  managers, 187–90; typical MNC procedure, 189
reflexivity, 108
regime competition model, European industrial
  relations, 356–7
regulatory frameworks, national, and MNCs,
  323–7
Reich, R.B., 17–21
repatriation of international managers, 192–4;
  problems of re-entry, 223–6
research: differentiation and integration, 69; dual-
  career couples, 248–9; electronics industry,
  France/Germany/Japan, 121–2; on HRM
  strategies, 43; international management,
  ethnocentric, 49; internationalization, 55–6;
  Japan, 15; subsidies needed, 20–1
rewards, *see* compensation
Reynolds, C. and Bennett, R., 247–8
Ricardo, D., 4–5, 12
rituals of culture, 129
Robock, S.H. and Simmonds, K., 255
robots, 6, 32
Rojot, J., 172, 173
role formalization systems, organizations as, *133*
Rose, M., 113
Rosener, J., 230, 240
Rothwell, S., 233, 240
Rugman, A.M., 9
Rugman, A.M. and Verbeke, A., 40–1, 42

Sabena, 332
Samarbejdsnaevnet, 305
Savage, C.M., 76
Schuler, R.S. and Jackson, C.E., 40
Scott, W.R., 102, 103
seasonal plant production, 46
secciones sindicales, 301, *306*
secondary segment, labour market, 160
secondary terms of employment, 146
segmented transaction model, European
  industrial relations, 355–6
self, conception of, survey, 135–8
self-referencing, 106, 108
Sengenberger, W., 335
service sector, growth, 77
service staff, in new world order, 18–19

sex role identity, 238
sex roles, management, 238–41
sexual harassment, 236
share option plans, 151
Sharma, S., 230, 240
Shell, 81, 82, 184
Single European Act (SEA), 338, 341
Siveking, N., 221
Smith, Adam, 4
Social Chapter, 333, 342, 348, 354, 361
social civil rights, and EU, 362
social/cultural/legal (S/C/L) dimension, and
  HRM, 92, 93, 94
social–cultural logic, 89–90
social dialogue, 348
social dumping: in European Union, 333–6, 339;
  by MNCs, xii, 318–19, 327, 331–3
social factors, and wages, 148, 150–2
social inequality, 129
social law, European, 343–5
social learning theory, 217–18
social parties, Brussels, 349–50
social policy, European: and industrial relations,
  337–62; legislation from EU, 343; problems,
  345–6; sources of, 341–3
social protocol, 338, 339, 342, 343, 361
social regulations, European, 340–53; policy-
  making, 340–6
socialization, 128, 249; and personal
  development, 107
societal effect approach to cross-national
  differences, 113–23; central tenets, 114–18; and
  HRM, x, 15, 127; illustrations, 118–22
Solomon, C., 237
Spain: basic pay negotiations, 150; trade unions,
  301, 304; worker participation, 305–6; works
  councils, *294–5, 298–9*
span of control, France/Germany/UK, 100
spending power, differences, 148, *149*
'spring offensives', 314
staff flow policy, x, 156–78; Europe, defined, 57;
  France/Netherlands, 171–2; HRD and division
  of labour, 162–3; and managers, 174–5; UK/
  Germany, 166–7
staffing, 80–1, 157
Standing Committee on Employment, 348
stockpile plant production, 46
Stopford, J.M. and Wells, L.T., 54–5, 63
strategic business units (SBUs), 28, 36
strategic decision-making, *see* decision-making
strategic demands, and organizational structures,
  59
strategic planning, in MNCs, 25–50; external
  analysis, 30–4; internal analysis, 34–6; process,
  28–30; process integrated, 46–9
strategy–structure investigations, 54–6, 70; to
  process, 56–8
Streeck, W., 307
structural and formal coordination mechanisms,
  68
structural change, 72–3
structural fit of organizations, 52
structuralist approach to cross-national
  differences, 112, 127
structuration theory, 112
structure, society effect approach, 113, 114
structure/process framework, 63–70, *65*
subsidiaries: creation, 31; form of establishment,
  322–3; headquarters' attitudes to, *44*;
  profitability level, 323; and success, 83
subsidiarity, 346
substantive pluralism, organizational behaviour,
  103, 104–6
Sweden: basic pay negotiations, 150;
  organizations, nature, *132–4*
Swissair, 18

Switzerland, organizations, nature, *132–4*
symbols of culture, 129
synergy effects, *see* economies of scope
systems and tools, administrative mechanisms, 68

T-groups, 214, 215
tariff barriers, 31
Tarifpartnerschaft, 309, 310
task forces, 69
Taylorism, 163–4
Technical and Vocational Education Initiative
    (TVEI), 165
technical dimension, societal approach, 114
technical experts, comparison with managers, 119
technological changes, 77–8
telecommunications switching, 34, 38, 39
terminology, confusion in, 30
terrorism, risks, 79
Texas Instruments, 18
Thatcher, M., 333
third-country nationals (TCNs), xi, 185, *186*, *187*;
    lack of research on, 49
Third World: exports, 6; labour supply, 17–18
Thomson Consumer Electrics, 350
Tillaart, H. van den, 172
time-related pay, 146–7
tokenism, women's employment, 242
top management, 97–8; attitudes, 66, 84–5, 90–1,
    93; recruitment, 80
Torbiörn, I., 217
total remuneration, 153–5
Touraine, A., 78
'toyotism', 314
trade unions: derecognition, 313; European, and
    US subsidiaries, 275–6; international groups,
    274–5; and MNCs, 275–80; power reduced,
    353; representation in MNCs, 300–4
training, x, 119; company, *see* company training;
    cycle, *209*; of expatriates, 209–18; international
    HRM, 81–2; of international staff, 219–33; on
    the job, 165–6; need for, 21–2
'training allowances', 315–16
training and development, x, 81–2; integration in
    HRM, 220–1; international staff, 205–28; as
    process, 219–20
training methods, 215–16; choice, 216–18; cross-
    cultural, 213–18; rigour, *218*
training needs: analysis, 210–11; search for
    profiles, 211–12
transaction cost model, for international
    competitive advantage, 10, 42
transaction cost theory, international production,
    9–11, 40
transformation, *see* change
transformation processes, flows and structures,
    114
transistors, development, 37–8
transition process, first to second generation, 70–3
transnational arrangements, European social
    policy, 350–2
transnational companies, 58–63; and centres of
    excellence, 22; competitive strategies, 42–3;
    ideal, 61–3
transnational era, strategic planning, 32, 34
transnational managers, development, 95–8
transnational organizations, 34, 60–3
transnational strategy, MNCs, 38–9
transnational structures, 54
transport costs, and MNCs, 8, 31
Treaty of Rome, 341
'Triad', x, 21–2, 81; *see mainly under* Europe,
    Japan, United States
Triandis, H.C., 129
Tung, R.L., 48–9, 81, 187–8, 207, 208, 217, 221

uncertainty avoidance, survey of culture, 135–7,
    136
unemployment, Europe, 316, 360
Unilever, 64; integration and differentiation
    needs, *47*; managers for China, 161; staff
    transfer, 184; training, 81
union delegates, works councils, 301–4
Union of Industrial and Employers'
    Confederations of Europe (UNICE), 347, 349
United Kingdom: basic pay negotiations, *150*;
    company training, 166, 177; division of labour,
    167–8; organizational structures, 100–2;
    organizations, nature, *132–4*; pay systems, *147*;
    personnel and organization, 100–22; versus
    Social Chapter, 333; staff flow policy, 166–7;
    vocational training, 164–5; women managers,
    243; worker participation, 313
United States: company training, 177–8;
    expatriate training, 207; imports, 327;
    international organizational model, 59–60;
    investment in Japan, 8; and Mexico, 21;
    product life cycle theory, 8–9; senior managers'
    origins, *187*; and training, 81, 208; women
    managers, 234–5, 243; worker participation,
    314
universalism, 125
unsettled, management abroad, 195, 196, 199–200
unskilled workers, redundancy in Western world,
    17, 19

Val Duchesse discussions, 342, 348
value changes, 111
values, cultural, 130
Vernon's product life cycle (PLC) theory, 8–9, 85
vertical integration, in MNCs, xi
Vertrauensleute, 301
Vertrauensvolle Zusammenarbeit, 305
Viannet, L., 334
village market organization structure, 142
Vinnicombe, S., 240–1
vocational training: France, 169–70; Netherlands,
    169; UK/Germany, 154–5
Volkswagen, 309, 332–4

wages: international comparisons, 144–5; manual
    workers' basic pay, *150*; *see also* compensation
Warmerdam, J. and Van den Berg, J., 171, 172
Wentling, R.M., 230
WFTU (World Federation of Trade Unions), 274
Wise, M. and Gibb, R., 333–4
women in employment: acceptance, 244–6; Asia,
    235–6; developing countries, 236–7; Europe,
    235; global, 233–4; perception of, 241–2; USA,
    234–5
women managers, xi, 229–51; advantages, 249;
    barriers, 237–42; career path factors, 238–42;
    dual careers, 246–9; global perspective, 231–3;
    international management, 243–50; in
    management, 231–7; skills brought, 230–1;
    views of, *232*; *see also* managers, international,
    women
worker participation, 291–317; differences in
    nature, 307–10; differences of views, in MNCs,
    320; future, 315–16; nature, 304–7
works councils, 291–2, 293–300; composition and
    election, 293–6; Italy, 312–13; national
    differences, 297–300, *298–9*, *310–11*; Nordic
    countries, 311–12; rights, 296–7; union
    delegates, 301, 304; United Kingdom, 313

youth training schemes (YTS), 165

zero-sum nationalism (Reich), 20

9447